CW00502196

COMING TO

FIFTEEN WALKS AROUND THE CITY

With best wishes

Sue Davies

BY SUE DAVIES

ISBN: 978-1-9996438-0-5
First Edition 2018

Published and Distributed by
Paolo Scremin
21 Westlands Avenue, Shinfield,
Reading, RG2 8EN, Great Britain

Distribution: paolo@paolophotography.co.uk

Printed and bound by
CPI Antony Rowe, Chippenham, England

For Harry
who came to love Florence with me

and for Amélie
for reasons that she knows of

The Duomo as seen from Via de' Servi

Preface and acknowledgements

The idea for this book was conceived over a convivial meal with friends. We were talking of Florence, which I had visited several times, when one of the party observed that, as I knew 'so much' about the place, I would make an excellent guide, and suggested that I write a book. The conversation moved on, but the idea stuck somewhere in the back of my mind. I began to acquire more books on the art and history of the city, and rapidly discovered that the 'so much' was actually 'very little'. My research, if that is not too grand a word, rapidly became a kind of obsession. I began visiting Florence more regularly and for longer, often for weeks at a time, and I must here thank all the lovely staff at the Hotel Loggiato dei Serviti, who made me (and continue to make me) feel so much at home. Whenever and wherever I came across a bookshop, new or second-hand, its art and history sections were ransacked and piles of books followed me home. Once read, the bibliographies of these were then scoured, and the book search department at Heffers in Cambridge put through its paces. My thanks go to the staff there, and in particular to Hilary and David for their patience and fortitude in the face of my numerous queries and requests. File upon file of notes began to accumulate, until, at last, I realized that, if I were to produce a book, I would have to start writing. Research is like a black hole – it can go on and on. There comes a moment when you have to draw a line under it and make a finished product out of what you have got. I began to bring the work into order. Draft typescripts appeared, several of them. My thanks go to my husband, Michael, and my friend, Prof. Harry Smith, who both read all these typescripts, criticizing, commenting and correcting. They also checked and timed the walks on the ground. Prof. Richard Goldthwaite, a distinguished economic historian of Renaissance Florence, kindly read the penultimate draft, gave me great encouragement, and made valuable suggestions as to other material that might be included, which I have incorporated. I cannot thank him enough for his time, interest and support.

There are many other people who must be mentioned here, and to whom I extend my heartfelt thanks. Prof. Herwig Maehler kindly helped me with the translation of the memorial to Carlo Capello's horse, and spotted the allusion to Virgil (see Walk 9). Dr. Elizabeth Bettles produced all the maps and plans, along with the Medici family trees, displaying exemplary patience on occasions in the face of much indecision on my part. Paolo Scremin took nearly all of the photographs used as plates in this book, and likewise showed much patience and good humour throughout the exercise. He also set the text up for printing. Without his input, the project would never have come to fruition. Finally, I would like to thank the staff at CPI Antony Rowe,

Chippenham, and especially Mark Radley, the Self Publishing Advisor, and Dave Biggs, the Technical Manager, for their help, efficiency and unfailing courtesy throughout the process of getting this book into print.

I have learnt so much in the course of my researches, and writing this little book has proved to be a real joy. I am still reading and learning, finding out things that I wish I'd found out earlier and included. My aim has been to try to bring the world of Renaissance Florence to life, and to help you, the reader, to people the streets of the city in your imagination. If just a few of you feel, after reading this, that you want to rush out to the nearest bookshop and, like me, ransack its shelves for more books on the subject, I shall have succeeded.

Statue in the Boboli Gardens

List of Contents

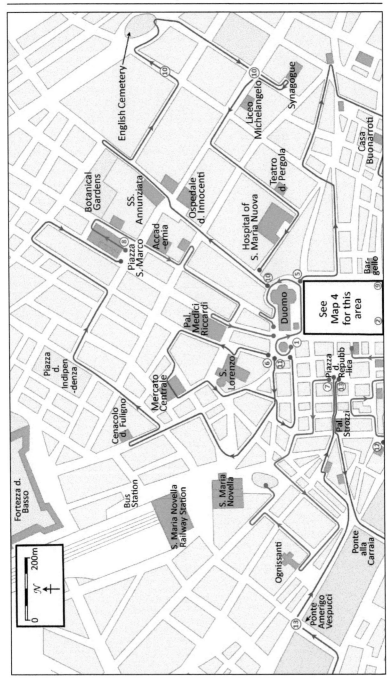

English Cemetery

Botanical Gardens

SS. Annunziata

Ospedale d. Innocenti

Liceo Michelangelo

Synagogue

Casa Buonarroti

Teatro d. Pergola

Piazza S. Marco

Accad-emia

Hospital of S. Maria Nuova

Bar-gello

Pal. Medici Riccardi

Duomo

See Map 4 for this area

Piazza d. Indipen-denza

Mercato Centrale

S. Lorenzo

Piazza d. Repubb-lica

Cenacolo d. Fuligno

Pal. Strozzi

Fortezza d. Basso

Bus Station

S. Maria Novella Railway Station

S. Maria Novella

Ognissanti

Ponte alla Carraia

Ponte Amerigo Vespucci

200m

N

0

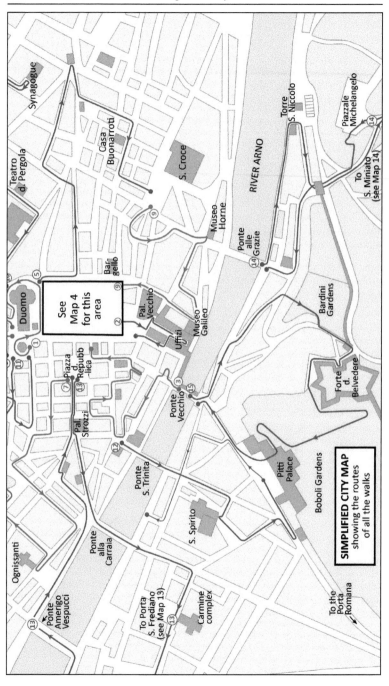

SIMPLIFIED CITY MAP
showing the routes
of all the walks

Introduction

How to use this book

This book consists of fifteen walks around Florence, which, between them, take in all the major museums and churches in the central city. You can follow each itinerary rigidly if you so wish, but you can also pick and mix as you feel inclined. For example, Walks 1-2, 4, 6, 10 and 13-15 are circular, and Walks 3, 8-9 and 11 almost circular. If your hotel lies at the far end of a walk, it makes little sense for you to plod to the designated starting point, do the entire circuit, and then walk home again, when you could pick the itinerary up part-way round. Likewise, you may find that only a certain part of a walk appeals, in which case do the bit that you want to do and then peel off on to another itinerary if you so choose. Some people may prefer to read the anecdotal material (shown indented in the list of contents and against a coloured background in the text) separately, either prior to or after the walk in question, rather than to try and do this en route. Others may want to follow the walks with no stops, returning later to visit any museums of their choosing. Early risers and late bedders in particular may find this a time effective method, especially in summer, with longer daylight hours. The early morning is my favourite time of the day, when you have the streets practically to yourself.

The walks are prefaced by a historical summary and an overview of fifty Florentine artists, and a few more historical interludes are set within the itineraries. You are not obliged to read any of these, though the better informed you are regarding the city's history, the more you will understand what you are looking at. Some people, I know, find long chunks of history unpalatable, so I have tried to pare these sections down to a minimum. I have, deliberately, not delved into the relationships that Florence had with her neighbours. A map of the Italian peninsula during the 12th-17th centuries consists of a patchwork of independent city states, and the political intrigues and machinations that went on were so complex, that any discussion of foreign relations would, inevitably, have resulted in a lot more verbiage.

On arrival in Florence, one thing you **must** do is to visit a Tourist Information Office and obtain a free updated list of the opening hours of the city's museums, galleries and major churches. This list is indispensable, and much valuable time can be wasted by not having the information that it provides. At the time of writing there were Tourist Information Offices at Amerigo Vespucci airport (at Terminal 1 arrivals), at 4 Piazza Stazione (near the railway station of S. Maria Novella and the neighbouring bus station), at 29 Borgo S. Croce, at 16 Via Manzoni, at 1 Via Cavour (near Piazza del Duomo), and in the Bigallo building near the base of Giotto's Campanile (which we pass near the beginning of Walk 1). For further information see www.firenzeturismo.it, a wide-ranging website which also offers details of accommodation, events, exhibitions and general advice for visitors.

Note on the captions and maps

Where a photograph illustrates something referred to in the accompanying text, the relevant section of text is highlighted in red. Captions are given only where there is no specific textual reference or when additional information is deemed desirable. Each walk is given its own dedicated map, and there is also a city map (pages 14-15) showing all the routes. Larger maps showing the city in greater detail are issued free at the Tourist Information Offices.

If time presses

Florence contains over one hundred museums and churches in the central city alone, and you cannot hope to see and do everything. If this is your first visit and you have only a few days at your disposal, I recommend that you concentrate on Walks 1-2, the shorter versions of Walks 5 and 6, and Walk 8. Take in the Ponte Vecchio at the beginning and the Mercato Nuovo and Orsanmichele at the end of Walk 3, omitting the rest of the itinerary. Don't miss the S. Maria Novella complex (Walk 7), the Bargello (Walk 9) and Piazza SS. Annunziata (Walk 10), but otherwise omit these walks, along with nos. 4 and 11. Over on the Oltrarno, I would concentrate on Walks 12 and 14. If you can squeeze in a visit to the Boboli Gardens at the end of Walk 12, you could omit Walk 15. The Brancacci Chapel should, ideally, be on your short-list, for which you need do only the shorter version of Walk 13.

The Boboli Gardens - the Island Pond

Entry to museums, galleries and churches

The updated list of opening hours of the city's museums, galleries and major churches, obtainable from the Tourist Information Offices, has already been referred to above. This list also gives details of entrance fees, combined, reduced and *gratis* tickets, and which venues can be visited using a museum card (www.firenzecard.it). It gives addresses and, in cases where advance booking is necessary/desirable, telephone numbers (for online bookings and further information see www.firenzemusei.it). The museum cards, called Firenze Cards (FC), have a set time limit and are not cheap. Before purchasing one, you would be well advised to work out how many venues you are likely to visit within the time limit, and to do a rough calculation of the costs involved.

To have given full descriptions of museums and galleries would have resulted in a tome too cumbersome to carry about. Furthermore, full descriptions have a limited lifespan, for collections can be rearranged, expanded, or even reduced. Within the walks I give a brief overview of each museum/gallery passed en route, to enable you to decide if it is for you or not (a quick-reference index to these brief descriptions is given on page 338). Nearly all the principal venues issue an information leaflet/plan with the ticket, as well as selling more detailed guide books and/or offering audio guides. With very few exceptions, Florentine museums have excellent information boards and labelling in English. You should have no problems navigating the buildings and their collections. One word of warning – many venues have exceptionally efficient air-conditioning systems, so do make sure that you always have a light-weight cardigan or similar garment with you.

The major church complexes - the Duomo, the Baptistery, Orsanmichele, S. Croce, S. Lorenzo, S. Maria Novella, S. Trinità, S. Spirito and S. Miniato – are described fully under their respective walks (again see the quick-reference index on page 338), but you will pass smaller churches that receive more cursory treatment, and some that, because of pressure of space, I do not draw attention to at all. While the major churches are open standard hours, many of the smaller ones have more restricted access. Nearly all have something in them worth seeing, so be opportunistic and take a look inside any that happen to be open. Try not to offend religious sensibilities by entering wearing inappropriate clothing, and remember that, like museums with their efficient air-conditioning, church interiors can be very chilly.

Tips on avoiding the crowds

Tourists flock to Florence like moths to a flame. The winter months are quieter, so if your sole object in visiting the city is to see the Duomo complex (Walk 1), the Uffizi Gallery (Walk 2) and the Accademia (Walk 8), then a winter trip may serve you well – and, of course, you'll miss the mosquitoes!

The disadvantages of winter are the greater risk of inclement weather and the shorter daylight hours. There are ways of avoiding the worst of the crowds, should you prefer a summer sojourn. If possible, avoid visiting the Ponte Vecchio and the hot-spots mentioned earlier in this paragraph on weekends. Pre-booking tickets where possible is advisable, or you can rise with the lark and get in the queue well before opening time, though for the Uffizi and the Accademia this will mean being there at least one hour in advance, and preferably more. Depending on the season, many venues are open from 8am and until well into the evening. Beating the arrival of the coachloads of tourists who are brought in from outside town, or waiting until they have departed, may be an option. By becoming a Friend of the Uffizi, you can skip the queue, visit as many times as you like, and benefit the Gallery financially. If you intend multiple visits, this idea may well appeal.

Getting about – transport in the city

In my view there is only one way to see the historic centre of Florence, and that is on foot. Fortunately, the historic centre is compact and, with very few exceptions, flat. The exceptions are the hill of S. Miniato al Monte (Walk 14), the Bardini Villa and Gardens, the Belvedere and the Boboli Gardens (all Walk 15). Less fortunate is the fact that pavements are normally either non-existent, or extremely narrow and obstructed at intervals by 'inginocchiate' ('kneeling') windows, the sills of which rest on protruding consoles at roughly head height.

Access to much of the centre is restricted to official vehicles, delivery vans and taxis. The drivers of such vehicles are, almost without exception, models of patience. Only rarely will they hoot you. Locals on bicycles and mopeds also display considerable patience, swerving to and fro to avoid pedestrians in their path. If you see one bearing down on you, probably the safest thing to do is to stand still.

The Bardini Villa and Gardens as seen from the Uffizi

You cannot hail a taxi on the streets, but have to ring for one or go to a taxi rank. There are main ranks in Piazza Stazione at the S. Maria Novella railway station, in Piazza del Duomo near the E end of the cathedral, just off Piazza S. Giovanni near the corner of Via de' Pecori with Via Roma, in Piazza S. Marco and, over on the Oltrarno, at Piazzale di Porta Romana.

A Hop On/Hop Off tourist bus goes round the ring-road and up as far as Piazzale Michelangelo (Walk 14). Up-to-date brochures giving the latest routes, stops and prices can be obtained from your hotel or from the Tourist Information Offices. You'll get good views of the ring-road, but you'll see nothing of the historic centre, as the buses are not allowed in. You have to walk from the various peripheral stops to your chosen venue(s). Walking directly across town is probably just as quick, if not quicker, and if you are heading for S. Miniato al Monte (Walk 14), then it's still a long pull uphill past Piazzale Michelangelo. Then there's the price. When I enquired as to the cost of a day ticket, I practically had to be picked up off the pavement. There is, however, a glimmer of silver lining here, in that a two-day ticket was only marginally more expensive than a day one. As one of the bus routes takes you right out to Fiesole, I advise you, if this system still applies, to opt for a two-day ticket and go out to Fiesole on one of the days.

Hotels, restaurants and shops

In his early 20th century guide *A Wanderer in Florence*, E. V. Lucas observes that compilers of guide books too soon make the discovery that either the time is always ripe for a new edition, or never. I favour the latter option, and, for this reason, have included hardly any mention of places to stay, eat and shop. Hotels can be chosen easily enough via the Internet. Restaurants come, go and change hands, as do shops. Hundreds of eateries are peppered all over the city, and menus and prices are displayed outside. You will be spoilt for choice. Up-to-date local knowledge of the best places to shop can be obtained from the Tourist Information Offices or from your hotel staff. Keep your eyes open as you follow the walks, and don't rush into purchasing too much of a tourist nature until you've had a wander around the Mercato Nuovo (Walk 3) and the area of the Mercato Centrale (Walk 6).

The dual street numbers, the Dante plaques and the palace courtyards

As you wander around, you will notice that a dual system of street numbering is in operation, with red numbers indicating business premises and blue numbers private residences. Where there is no ambiguity, I do not always bother to specify which series of numbers I am referring to.

Many of the walks include references to buildings with plaques on their façades bearing quotations from Dante's *Divine Comedy*. These plaques were put up at the beginning of the 20th century. There were originally thirty-four of them, but some have disappeared. It is possible that more may have vanished by the time you come to do the walks, so do not be too puzzled if you cannot always find them.

As you meander through the streets, you will catch tantalizing glimpses of beautiful courtyards and gardens through palace arches. Each year, usually on weekends towards the end of May, many of these are opened up, free of charge, to the public. Dates and full details of the participating palaces can be obtained from the Associazione Dimore Storiche Italiane (ADSI), Piazza S. Firenze 2; tel. 055-212452; e-mail toscana@adsi.it; www.adsi.it.

Useful things to have with you plus a few final tips

Florence can experience inclement weather all year round. Make sure that you are equipped with at least some light waterproofs and optional extra layers of clothing. You may also find insect repellent useful, for the river Arno flows through Florence, and water means mosquitoes. Other useful items to have at hand are light-weight binoculars (for viewing frescoes), a corkscrew (screw top wine bottles haven't caught on in Italy yet), a torch to facilitate reading in dim surroundings, some small change for the few remaining coin-operated light machines and for entry to some public toilets, and a basic Italian phrasebook. Just about everybody connected with the tourist trade speaks English, but most Italians will warm to you if you try to speak their language. You'll find that a little will go a long way. Take a plentiful supply of cash with you too, for although there are numerous change bureaus, you'll get a poor rate of exchange compared to that which you can get at home.

I have not included a night-time walk in this book, but Florence is magical at night, with many of the public buildings beautifully floodlit. Try to make time for walks after dark at least around the Duomo and Campanile, through the Piazza della Signoria and along the banks of the Arno.

The Palazzo Vecchio by night

One final tip. The taps in the bathroom will probably be marked C and F. C does not stand for cold but for 'caldo', which is Italian for hot. F stands for 'freddo', which is Italian for cold. I imagine that many a tourist, looking forward to a cool shower at the end of a long, hot day, has leapt gleefully into the cubicle and turned the C tap on full, only to be scalded.

Sources used and suggestions for further reading

As stated in the Preface, my aim in writing this book has been to try to bring the world of Renaissance Florence to life, and to help you to people the streets of the city in your imagination. To this end I have drawn frequently on contemporary sources. Fortunately, the Florentines were great writers, penning not only substantial historical tomes, chronicles, biographies and autobiographies, but also less substantial works, diaries, memoirs, letters, record books, account books and ledgers etc. I have restricted myself in the main to sources available in English, so those of you who do not read Italian can delve further if you wish to. Giorgio Vasari's *The Lives of the Painters, Sculptors and Architects* is available in several modern editions, as is Giovanni Boccaccio's *The Decameron*, Benvenuto Cellini's *Autobiography* and Dante Alighieri's *The Divine Comedy*. The translations of Dante given in this book are my own. For a translation of Giovanni Villani's *Chronicle*, see the Primary Source Edition reproduced by Nabu Public Domain Reprints, *Villani's Chronicle, being selections from the first nine books of the Croniche Fiorentine of Giovanni Villani*, translated by Rose E. Selfe and edited by Philip H. Wicksteed (Constable & Co. Ltd., London: 1906). For a translation of Luca Landucci's *Diary*, see *A Florentine Diary from 1450 to 1516 by Luca Landucci, continued by an anonymous writer till 1542, with notes by Iodoco del Badia*, translated by Alice de Rosen Jervis (J. M. Dent & Sons Ltd., London: 1927). Dino Compagni's *Chronicle of Florence* is available in translation in an edition by Daniel E. Bornstein (University of Pennsylvania Press, Philadelphia: 1986), while for the diaries of Pitti and Dati, see *Two Memoirs of Renaissance Florence. The Diaries of Buonaccorso Pitti & Gregorio Dati*, translated by Julia Martines and edited by Gene Brucker (Waveland Press Inc., Long Grove, Illinois: 1991).

The volume of literature available on Florence and the Renaissance is enormous. Were I to give a bibliography of the books that I have consulted, it would run to many pages. For those of you coming new to the subject, however, there are two 'golden oldies' which are, in my opinion, hard to beat, J. R. Hale's *Florence and the Medici. The Pattern of Control* (Thames and Hudson: 1977) and Gene A. Brucker's *Renaissance Florence* (John Wiley & Sons, Inc., New York: 1969). In lighter vein, you might also enjoy Francis King, *Florence. A Literary Companion* (John Murray (Publishers) Ltd., London: 1991), and Giuliana Artom Treves, *The Golden Ring. The Anglo-*

Florentines 1847-1862, translated by Sylvia Sprigge (Longmans, Green and Co., London: 1956). For more on the Pazzi conspiracy, see Lauro Martines, *April Blood. Florence and the Plot against the Medici* (Jonathan Cape, London: 2003). The information on Jacopo Peri given in Walk 7 is taken from Tim Carter and Richard A. Goldthwaite, *Orpheus in the Marketplace. Jacopo Peri & the Economy of Late Renaissance Florence* (Harvard University Press, Cambridge, Massachusetts: 2013). Two other tomes by Richard Goldthwaite also make fascinating reading, *The Building of Renaissance Florence. An Economic and Social History* (The Johns Hopkins University Press, Baltimore: 1980) and *The Economy of Renaissance Florence* (The Johns Hopkins University Press, Baltimore: 2009).

The Campanile by night

Historical summary

From the Roman period up to the end of the 12th century

The Roman colony of Florentia was founded in 59 BC at the limit of navigation on the Arno. The grid pattern of the original Roman layout can still be discerned in the plan of the central city. The Forum stood where Piazza della Repubblica now is, with the Calimala and Via Roma on the line of the N-S cardo, and Via degli Strozzi and Via del Corso on that of the E-W decumanus. The theatre was where Palazzo Vecchio now stands and the amphitheatre lay at the W end of Piazza S. Croce, where its outline can be traced round Via Torta, Via de' Bentaccordi and Piazza de' Peruzzi (Walk 9).

From the late 6th century AD the Lombards ruled Tuscany, until, in the late 8th century, they were replaced by the Franks. The Frankish margraves were vassals of the German Emperors, who now established the authority of the Holy Roman Empire. Florence, besides being a thriving political and commercial hub, became an important centre of Christianity. In 978, Willa, mother of Margrave Ugo, founded the abbey of the Badia (Walk 4), to which Ugo later made huge endowments. Not to be outdone, Hildebrand, the bishop, decided to found a monastery himself, and chose to do so at the shrine of S. Miniato (Walk 14). In 1069, Countess Matilda inherited the margravate and reigned until 1115. The city walls were rebuilt in 1078 as a defence against Emperor Henry IV, for Matilda had rebelled against him over the issue of his right to appoint the higher clergy, a right vehemently opposed by Pope Gregory VII.

Florence was by now the pre-eminent city of the region, having subjugated the surrounding territories. As a check on their power, the nobility from the subjugated territories were required to live for part of each year in Florence.

This policy turned out to be a mixed blessing, for feudalism was thus carried into the city itself. Powerful magnate families established themselves in fortified city strongholds with massive towers. By 1180 more than a hundred such towers punctuated the skyline. We shall see the remnants of many of these on several of the walks. On entering the city, many members of the nobility began to engage in commerce, while, aspiring to higher social status, rich and ambitious non-magnate merchants married themselves and/or their offspring into noble families.

Torre de' Marsili in Borgo S. Jacopo　Social mobility thus became an increasingly important factor.

The population of the city was increasing and a new, larger circle of walls was needed, this time including the Oltrarno. The city was divided into six 'sestieri', each with a militia responsible for guarding its particular section of walls. In 1207 a new government position was created, that of 'Podestà', the term of office being one year. This official had authority to administer civil justice, but, because finding a non-partisan candidate from the citizenry proved tricky, the Podestà had to be an impartial foreigner. So the 13th century began with Florence exhibiting a volatile mix of civic pride and unity combined with intense factionalism and personal rivalries.

The 13th century

During the first half of the 13th century, Frederick II, the Holy Roman Emperor, attempted to extend his political domination of the Italian peninsula. This didn't suit the papacy, who both urged the North Italian states to resist and encouraged Gallic ambitions on the peninsula, involving the French as Papal allies. So arose the two parties associated with this clash between pope and emperor – the Guelfs and the Ghibellines respectively. The political life of the 13th century was dominated by the continuous struggles between Guelfs and Ghibellines, the fortunes of each faction waxing and waning as battles were won and lost. In simplified terms, the Ghibellines were led by the landed nobility who saw advantages to themselves in the perpetuation of the feudal structure associated with the empire, while the Guelfs consisted of the minor nobility and the merchants whose commercial interests were best served by the French/Papal axis.

During the 1240s the Florentine Ghibellines managed to gain the upper hand, and eventually drove the Guelf leaders into exile. Giovanni Villani tells us that the violence lasted a long time, that there was fighting in the streets and from one tower to another, and that mangonels and other engines were employed day and night (*Chronicle* VI.33). A few years later, however, the Guelfs defeated the Ghibellines at the Battle of Figline, and in 1250 a government was formed which is referred to as the 'Primo Popolo' (the 'first government of the people'). One of the acts of this government was to command the reduction in height of all private towers to 50 braccia (*c.* 28m). The role of Podestà was redefined, becoming a judicial and administrative position, while a new post was created to oversee military and defence matters, that of the 'Capitano del Popolo'. Like the erstwhile Podestà, the Capitano had to be a neutral foreigner, for whom the Florentines built a new palace, now called the Bargello (Walk 9). Under this new regime Florence thrived, defeating her rivals, Pistoia, Pisa and Siena, and issuing her own coins – the gold florin, first issued in 1252, was destined to become an international currency and a European monetary standard.

For all its success, the Primo Popolo was short-lived. Frederick II had died, but, encouraged by Manfred, his son and heir, those Ghibellines who had remained in Florence revolted. Initially unsuccessful, they were driven from the city. Their properties were seized and/or destroyed, and the stones from the sacked buildings used to build the walls of S. Giorgio Oltrarno (Villani, *Chronicle* VI.65). The Ghibellines regrouped, however, and in 1260, with the aid of Manfred's German troops, defeated the Guelfs at the Battle of Montaperti. The Ghibelline leaders were all of a mind that Florence should be utterly destroyed and reduced to open villages, but this course of action was vehemently and eloquently opposed by Messer Farinata degli Uberti, so Florence was saved (Villani, *Chronicle* VI.81). The Ghibellines took some revenge, however. The Guelf leaders fled, their properties were sacked, and entire areas were reduced to ruins.

Ghibelline supremacy was also short-lived, for a few years later Charles of Anjou (brother of King Louis IX of France), urged on by the papacy and Guelf refugees, defeated Manfred and power passed back to the Guelfs, who now became dominant in Florence. Eventually, the 'Secondo Popolo' (the 'second government of the people') was established. The city was governed by a council of priors, chosen from candidates from the guilds and headed by a chief magistrate called the 'Gonfalonier of Justice'. The priors each served for two months, during which time they were housed and took meals together under one roof – we'll pass that roof on Walk 4. Draconian new laws, the famous 'Ordinances of Justice', were enacted in 1293, whereby members of the nobility were barred from government office, and, with so much of the city in ruins, many public works projects were put in train, in which the guilds played an important role. Yet another circle of walls was built, enclosing a much larger area than before, and with seventy-three towers and fifteen gates. These have nearly all disappeared, demolished in the 19th century to create a ring of Boulevards. The great projects for the new Cathedral of S. Maria del Fiore (Walk 1) and the Palazzo della Signoria (Walk 2) were begun, together with that for an enlarged church at S. Croce (Walk 5). All three are linked with the name of Arnolfo di Cambio. But things were not rosy with the Secondo Popolo, for factionalism again raised its ugly head. Two rival Guelf factions eventually emerged, the 'Whites' and the 'Blacks', led by the Cerchi and Donati families respectively. This complex period is dealt with more fully in the section entitled 'the big bad barons' at the end of Walk 4. Suffice it to say here that, in league with the French, the Blacks eventually gained the upper hand, and in 1302 six hundred Whites were sent into exile. Among them was Dante – he was never to return. The exiled Whites naturally went over to the Ghibelline cause and gave their support to the Emperor, Henry VII, who was beginning to reassert himself

S of the Alps. In 1312 he laid siege to Florence, but, fortunately for the Blacks, he withdrew after a short time and then obligingly died.

The 14th century

The government of the Secondo Popolo now decided to follow the example of the Primo Popolo and to entrust military and defence matters to a neutral foreigner. In 1313 Robert of Naples was chosen as 'signore' ('overlord') for five years. In the 1320s, threatened by the Lucchese tyrant Castruccio Castracani, the Florentine government invited Robert's son, Charles of Anjou, to take up the reins for ten years. Then, in 1342, Walter of Brienne, nominal Duke of Athens, who was related by marriage to the house of Anjou, was invited to manage affairs. We'll have more to say about him below.

The 1340s was a decade of cumulative disasters. In 1339 King Edward III of England, who had borrowed vast sums of money for his wars with France, defaulted on his debts. The Peruzzi and Bardi banks had overstretched themselves in support of him and their English branches went bankrupt. There was panic in Florence, which resulted in a run on the banks. In 1343 the Peruzzi and Bardi banks went down and, in a domino-like reaction, other banks began to fail. Simultaneously, there was trouble with Walter of Brienne, who, once installed as 'signore', began to run things very differently from the course envisaged by those who'd invited him. Perhaps in an attempt to broaden his power base, Walter began to grant more rights to the labouring classes, giving some of them guild status and thus making them eligible for public office. This, coupled with his introduction of new taxes, overbearing manner and blatant attempts to make himself dictator (see further Walk 2), proved too much for the majority of the citizens and in 1343 they rose up and drove him from the city.

With Walter of Brienne gone, a new regime was established with a broader power base than previously, the minor guilds now being brought more into government. The six 'sestieri' were replaced by four 'quartieri' (S. Giovanni, S. Maria Novella, S. Croce and S. Spirito), the priorate was reorganized, there was an overhaul of the tax system and of fiscal bureaucracy, and citizens now had the opportunity to become shareholders in the state finances. Two sectors of society, however, were not happy. The labouring classes, known as the 'Ciompi', were excluded from the above developments and all the rights granted to them by Walter of Brienne were revoked, thereby alienating them. The upper echelons of society, whose rights to power had been diluted ever since the 1293 Ordinances of Justice, were likewise disaffected. They coalesced within the so-called 'Guelf Party', which, henceforth, operated as a secondary 'behind the scenes' power base.

The banking crisis and the civic upheavals were compounded by crop failures in 1346 and 1347. There was unemployment and food shortage.

Giovanni Villani saw all this as retribution for the sins of avarice and usury. But the most horrific retribution was still to come, one that cost Villani his life, for in 1348 the Black Death reached the city, reducing her population by 50% at a stroke. A chastened but resilient Florence gradually put herself in order. Banking houses got back on their feet, and a number of new banks arose to replace defunct ones. Thus the Albizi, Alberti, Strozzi and Medici families came to prominence. One aftermath of the Black Death was that guilds and confraternities found themselves the beneficiaries of numerous wills. At Orsanmichele the Laudesi confraternity used their mountain of legacies to commission a tabernacle to house their new painting of the Madonna (Walk 3). Building was resumed by a new crew at the Campanile (Walk 1) and work started again at the Duomo.

Relations with Rome were in decline, the papacy now being viewed as a threat to the city's interests. Matters came to a head in 1375, when crops again failed and the papal governor of the Romagna blocked the export of grain to Florence. She promptly declared war on Pope Gregory XI and he countered with an interdict against the city. A committee was set up to run the war effort, its members being dubbed 'the eight saints'. The war lasted three years, and Florence found herself assuming the role of defender of regional liberty against both the papacy and the growing threat of Milan under Visconti rule.

In 1378, when 'the war of the eight saints' came to an end, the aristocrats within the Guelf Party attempted, unsuccessfully, to seize power. In the same year, the Ciompi, comprising in the main shirt-makers, dyers and wool-workers, decided to resurrect their claims and demanded again the right to form guilds. The famous 'Ciompi revolt' of 1378 was one of the most significant examples of urban social conflict in mediaeval Europe. The workers managed to achieve their objective, despite strong opposition from the major guilds. Their victory was short-lived, however, for in 1382 a group of wealthy merchants united with the aristocrats in the Guelf Party and succeeded in establishing an oligarchic government now known as the 'Popolo Grasso' (the 'prosperous Popolo'). The Ciompi were savagely suppressed, and the regime of the Popolo Grasso succeeded in holding power for more than forty years.

The first half of the 15th century

The early 15th century saw Florence pitted against powerful enemies, the most serious threat being posed by Filippo Maria Visconti of Milan, who waged active war during the 1420s. The financial strain of these wars was compounded by the fact that Florence had begun to face serious competition in the wool trade from the rest of Europe. A new tax, known as the 'catasto', was levied on property and income, and moves were made to diversify the textile industry. Silkworm culture was introduced to end dependence on oriental thread, and the technique of weaving silk with gold was developed. A decree of 1441 ordered farmers to plant a minimum of five mulberry trees on land that they worked, and in 1443 the exporting of raw silk from Florentine territory was forbidden. Luxurious brocades were exported both to Europe and the Near East, and the punishment for any manufacturer who took his skill elsewhere was death!

The grit and determination displayed by Florence in the face of her adversities was accompanied by a growth of pride and self-image. Oligarchic government notwithstanding, the city saw herself as the champion of republicanism and liberty against imperialism and tyranny, the heir of Periclean Athens and Republican Rome. This self-image helped to fuel an astonishing burst of intellectual and artistic creativity, which we now call the Florentine Renaissance. Scholars and intellectuals involved themselves in political life, and a series of brilliant humanist chancellors included Leonardo Bruni and Carlo Marsuppini, whose tombs we shall see at S. Croce (Walk 5). Orsanmichele (Walk 3) was embellished with statues, a new set of bronze doors for the Baptistery was commissioned from Ghiberti, work went forward on the Cathedral, and Brunelleschi was charged with constructing his famous dome (Walk 1).

Brunelleschi's dome at dawn

The tower of the Palazzo Vecchio

Although the mechanisms of republican government were maintained, they could be, and were, manipulated by powerful oligarchs. The leading oligarchs throughout the 1420s were Niccolò da Uzzano and Rinaldo degli Albizi, but the former died in 1431. Two years earlier, in 1429, a certain Giovanni d'Averardo de' Medici (known as Giovanni di Bicci) had also died, and his son, Cosimo de' Medici, had become head of the family. Cosimo espoused the cause of small-time business men and members of the lesser guilds who, since the establishment of the Popolo Grasso in 1382, had had only a minimal say in government. Rinaldo degli Albizi saw Cosimo as a serious threat to his power base and took steps to remove him, but his plan misfired badly. In autumn 1433, having obtained, through careful manipulation, a signorial council under his influence, Albizi accused Cosimo of aggrandizement and of planning to overthrow the regime, and got him arrested. Cosimo was consigned to a cell in the tower of the Palazzo della Signoria (later the Palazzo Vecchio), from which it was planned that he should never emerge. Failing to achieve Cosimo's murder, however, the Albizi camp had to content themselves with his banishment. Surprisingly, they then failed to rig the elections of subsequent signorial councils. As the rotational system of office began to work against him, Albizi was himself banished, along with many of his followers, and Cosimo was recalled to Florence in August 1434. He returned to a hero's welcome, and the rest, as they say, is history.

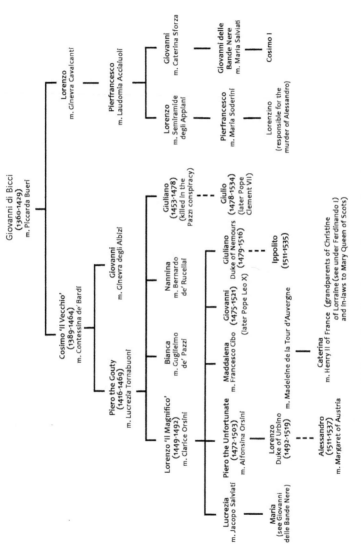

Medici family tree from Giovanni di Bicci to Alessandro

The second half of the 15th century

Cosimo, often called 'Il Vecchio' ('the elder') to distinguish him from later Grand Dukes with the same name, was a shrewd businessman, politician and statesman who was highly adept at PR. The organs of republican government were outwardly maintained, but manipulated as never before. Over the years Cosimo had carefully built up a large body of supporters, clients and dependants, and he now contrived that only these men held office. He managed in this way to exercise control for the next thirty years, during which time his popularity and public image soared. On the home front, Cosimo used his vast wealth to enhance Florence's reputation and his own public image. He played host to scores of visiting dignitaries, including emperors, princes and popes. Friendly relations were re-established with Rome. Pope Eugenius IV dedicated the new Duomo in 1436, and in 1439 was persuaded by Cosimo to transfer the ecumenical council discussing the union of the Eastern and Western Churches from Ferrara to Florence. This political coup brought to the city the Byzantine Emperor, the Patriarch of Constantinople, and a host of churchmen and scholars. The Patriarch died in Florence and we shall see his tomb in the church of S. Maria Novella (Walk 7). Cosimo's foreign policies were aimed at assuring peaceful and thriving conditions for commerce. In alliance with Venice, Florence defeated the Albizi exiles, who were in league with Milan, at the Battle of Anghiari in 1440. In 1447, however, on the death of Filippo Visconti, Cosimo shifted his support to Filippo's son-in-law and successor, Francesco Sforza, with whom he formed a close friendship, thereby removing the Milanese threat. An avid collector of art, antiquities, books and manuscripts, Cosimo gathered round him a circle of artists and learned men whom he encouraged and patronized. His two most important building projects in the city were the monastery of S. Marco and his own Palazzo Medici (both Walk 8), the latter of which became a benchmark for subsequent private palaces.

On Cosimo's death in 1464, the majority of the Medici clientele, mindful of their own interests, asked his son, Piero de' Medici (known as Piero the Gouty), to take up the reins. Plagued by ill health, Piero's time at the helm was short but not uneventful. The Medici had their supporters, but they also had their enemies. There were also those who, while they'd been content enough to play second fiddle to Cosimo, weren't going to take orders from Piero. The latter, headed by, amongst others, Luca Pitti, rebelled and the city was up in arms, but the plot was foiled. Luca Pitti promptly changed sides, was pardoned, and proceeded to build himself the Pitti Palace (Walk 12). The Medici position was strengthened still further. Piero the Gouty died in 1469 and his son Lorenzo picked up the reins in his turn. In 15th century Florence, 'Magnifico' was merely a common title of respect, but

Lorenzo Il Magnifico's ambit was nothing short of magnificent. Intelligent and charming, he had been trained in statesmanship and diplomacy, and was surrounded and nurtured by brilliant scholars.

During the 1470s relations with Pope Sixtus IV soured. The eventual result of this breakdown of relations was the famous Pazzi conspiracy of 1478, which is described more fully at the end of Walk 8. The events surrounding the conspiracy read rather like a thriller, with many a twist and turn of the plot. The conspirators aimed to murder both Lorenzo and his younger brother, Giuliano. Giuliano was killed, but Lorenzo survived. With his position and popularity much enhanced, he held on to power until his death in 1492, managing to steer a successful course through the turbulent political waters of the time and to maintain a fragile peace, so vital for Florentine trade and banking. To mend relations with Rome, he eventually negotiated the marriage of his daughter Maddalena to Francesco Cibo, illegitimate son of Pope Sixtus' successor, Innocent VIII. This family tie bore fruit a few years later when Innocent made Lorenzo's second son, Giovanni, a cardinal, an appointment that was to have a significant impact on the subsequent history of Florence.

On Lorenzo Il Magnifico's death in 1492 his eldest son, Piero, stepped into his father's shoes. Often referred to as Piero the Unfortunate, he lacked his father's charisma and experience, and forgot too that his position as leading citizen in Florence depended solely upon his popularity and the good-will of his supporters. He may, at another time, have managed to hang on to power, but, alas for Piero, a storm was about to be unleashed on the Italian peninsula in the person of King Charles VIII of France.

Back in 1490 Ludovico Sforza, who had ruled Milan for ten years in the name of his nephew Gian Galeazzo, refused to surrender power to the latter on his coming of age. Gian Galeazzo's wife appealed to her grandfather, King Ferrante of Naples, to intervene. Fearing Neopolitan involvement, Ludovico first encouraged King Charles to press home his historic Angevin claims to the crown of Naples, promising him Milanese support, and then went on to murder Gian Galeazzo. Coming down on the side of Naples, Piero was regarded as an enemy by Charles and thus found himself in a sticky position when, in the autumn of 1494, the French king crossed the Alps with his huge standing army and headed for Tuscany. Without Signorial authority, Piero rushed headlong to meet Charles and agreed to certain concessions, including the handing over of key fortresses and ports, Pisa among them. On his return to Florence, he was summoned by an angry Signoria to explain his conduct. Unwisely, he arrived at the Palazzo della Signoria accompanied by an armed guard. The great bell rang out, the citizens gathered and Piero fled, together with many members of his family and retinue. An official delegation was then sent to parley with King Charles. This whole episode is described more fully in the section entitled 'the French come to Florence' at the end of Walk 13. One of the ambassadors sent as part of the delegation was Fra Girolamo Savonarola.

Savonarola was a Dominican friar whom Lorenzo Il Magnifico had invited to Florence, and who had become prior at the monastery of S. Marco in 1491. A spiritual reformer, he had prophesied a cataclysm for Florence as punishment for her sinful lifestyle. That prophecy appeared to have been fulfilled in the person of King Charles. With the flight of the Medici, Savonarola now found himself catapulted to prominence. We'll learn more about him on Walk 8. Suffice it to say here that he became a rallying force and that his lead was initially followed enthusiastically by the majority of the citizens. The constitution was reformed along more republican lines to include a Great Council, and work was put in train at the Palazzo della Signoria to construct a hall large enough to accommodate this new organ of government. The result was the huge 'Sala del Maggior Consiglio' ('Room of the Great Council'; see further under Walk 2).

The situation in Florence remained volatile. Piero the Unfortunate tried repeatedly, though unsuccessfully, to re-establish himself by force of arms, while the Borgia Pope Alexander VI retaliated against voluble criticism from Savonarola by excommunicating him, promising to do likewise to anyone attending his sermons and threatening to confiscate all Florentine property in papal territories unless the city rid herself of this troublesome friar. There was no success in the war to regain Pisa, but there were recurrences of the plague and much agricultural disruption due to the movements of enemy troops. Savonarola's prophecies were turning sour and the mood swung violently against him. In April 1498 he and two colleagues were arrested, and six weeks later they were hanged and burned in the Piazza della Signoria.

The first half of the 16th century

In 1502 a change was made to the constitution whereby, instead of being a rotational office, the position of Gonfalonier of Justice was made a life appointment, just like the Venetian Doge. Piero di Messer Tommaso Soderini was elected and duly moved into the Palazzo della Signoria with his family. A contemporary diarist, Luca Landucci, whom we'll meet again on several of our walks, says that all Florence was in the Piazza to witness the event, as women inhabiting the Palazzo was something entirely new.

Soderini and his family didn't inhabit the Palazzo for long. Julius II was now pope and, in an effort to re-establish papal power, he decided to pit Spain against France in an attempt to drive the French from the Italian peninsula. Soderini favoured the French and Florence aligned herself with France, which proved to be a mistake. Spanish/papal forces came out on top and forced a settlement on the city which included among its terms the reinstatement of the Medici.

Following their expulsion from Florence in 1494, Cardinal Giovanni de' Medici and his brother Giuliano had divorced themselves from their eldest brother Piero, gone to Rome and ingratiated themselves with Pope Julius II. Both pope and Spain wanted to bring troublesome Florence to heel, and having Medici allies back in control there was a good way to do it. In 1512 Soderini stepped down as Gonfalonier and left Florence. Giovanni and Giuliano de' Medici re-entered the city under military escort along with their cousin Giulio and their nephew Lorenzo (son of Piero, who was dead by this time). Within six months of this triumphal entry Julius II died and Cardinal Giovanni de' Medici was elected pope, taking the name Leo X. He returned to Rome along with his brother Giuliano, who married the daughter of the Duke of Savoy and was given the title of Duke of Nemours before his premature death in 1516. Nephew Lorenzo was made 'Capitano' of Florence, while cousin Giulio, the illegitimate son of Lorenzo Il Magnifico's brother Giuliano, killed in the Pazzi conspiracy, was legitimized, made a cardinal and appointed as Archbishop of the city. The recipient of Niccolò Machiavelli's treatise *The Prince*, Lorenzo conquered Urbino in 1516 and thereby gained the title of Duke of Urbino. In 1518 he married Madeleine de la Tour d'Auvergne, a lady of French royal blood, and their daughter Caterina eventually became Queen of France and mother-in-law to Mary Queen of Scots. But Lorenzo too died prematurely, in 1519. It is his tomb and that of his uncle Giuliano, Duke of Nemours, that Michelangelo worked on in the New Sacristy at S. Lorenzo (Walk 6). There was another death in 1519 that was to have far-reaching consequences for Florence, that of the Holy Roman Emperor Maximilian. His grandson, King Charles V of Spain, succeeded him and thus became head of a veritable superpower.

Cardinal Giulio de' Medici, Archbishop of Florence, was left to govern the city, but only for a few years, because, following the deaths of Leo X in 1521 and his successor Adrian VI in 1523, Giulio became pope, taking the name Clement VII. Having run out of legitimate heirs, he produced two illegitimate ones to continue his family's dominance, Ippolito, bastard son of the Duke of Nemours, and Alessandro, supposedly the bastard son of the Duke of Urbino, but widely rumoured to be the son of Clement himself.

Clement VII, worried by the growing influence of superpower Charles, had formed an anti-Imperial/Spanish league (the League of Cognac). This was a big mistake. In 1527 Charles' troops marched S and sacked Rome. At this moment ambassadors arrived from England to discuss with the pope the divorce of Henry VIII from Catherine of Aragon. As Catherine was Charlie's aunt, it wasn't good timing! When news of the sack of Rome reached Florence, the city seized the moment, expelled the unpopular Ippolito and Alessandro, and re-established a republic in 1527. This republic was short-lived, for Clement made peace with Charles (he had little choice) and combined Spanish/papal forces again descended on Florence. The besieged city held out for nearly a year, thanks in part to sturdy defences hurriedly constructed by Michelangelo (Walks 14 and 15). It fell in August 1530 and the Medici were reinstated. Duke Alessandro had the great bell of the republic removed from the tower of the Palazzo della Signoria and symbolically smashed in the piazza. His government also decreed the construction of the huge Fortezza da Basso, which housed a garrison whose job it was to enforce Alessandro's rule whether the citizens wanted it or not.

Duke Alessandro married Margaret of Austria, daughter of Charles V, in 1536. The marriage was short-lived, for in 1537 Alessandro was murdered by his distant cousin Lorenzino. Members of the Medici clique were now worried that Charles might annexe the city and turn it into an Imperial viceroyalty, so they acted decisively and fast. News of Alessandro's assassination was kept secret and, just three days later, Cosimo de' Medici, another distant cousin, was nominated as his successor.

The second half of the 16th century

If the pro-Medicean power base thought that Cosimo was going to be a push-over, they couldn't have been more wrong. Determined, decisive and authoritative, he moved fast to dismantle any political opposition and ensure his own control. Die-hard republicans in exile were offered amnesty - those who rejected this offer were defeated at the Battle of Montemurlo in July 1537. With the victory of Montemurlo behind him, Cosimo turned his attention to gathering all power into his own hands. He gave support and huge sums of money to Charles V for his wars with France in exchange for the withdrawal of the Spanish garrison at the Fortezza da Basso, the cession of the port of Livorno and, later, dominion over Siena. He introduced new men into government and the constitution was gradually changed from a republican to an autocratic one. He became the supreme authority in the state and criticism of his regime was a capital offence. In 1539 he married Eleonora di Toledo, daughter of Charles V's Viceroy in Naples, and in 1540 he and his family moved from the Palazzo Medici into the Palazzo della Signoria, underlining the fact that Cosimo and the government were now one. So carefully and skilfully did he build up his autonomy that, eventually, he was able to maintain good relations with France and the papacy without offending Charles. In 1569, Pope Pius V created Cosimo Grand Duke of Tuscany, a title ratified by Philip II of Spain.

Cosimo I was succeeded by his son Francesco I, an inaccessible, reclusive character. On Francesco's death without legitimate male issue in 1587, his

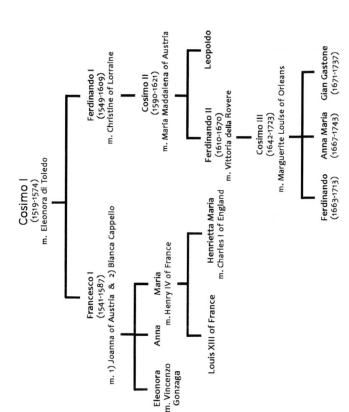

Medici family tree from Cosimo I to Gian Gastone

brother Ferdinando renounced his cardinal's hat and became Grand Duke. Ferdinando carried on where his father had left off. He completed the new free port at Livorno, built the Belvedere Fortress (Walk 15) and began the construction of the Chapel of the Princes (Walk 6). He strove to preserve and enhance the reputation of Tuscany both politically and artistically. He took a real interest in the University at Pisa and appointed Galileo to the chair of mathematics there. On the wider stage, he furthered his family's connections to European courts (especially that of France) and maintained good relations with the papacy, using the connections and influence built up during his years as a cardinal. He took advantage of Spain's weakness following the defeat of the Armada sent against England in 1588 to strengthen further Tuscan autonomy. He died in 1609 leaving Tuscany secure and independent.

The first half of the 17th century

Ferdinando I's successor, Cosimo II, was incapacitated by illness for much of his reign, dying of tuberculosis in 1621. His son, Ferdinando II, reigned for nearly fifty years, his rule coinciding, alas, with some economic downturns. The export branch of the wool industry declined rapidly, and the outbreak of the Thirty Years' War in 1618 led to the abandonment of Germany by silk merchants. With NW Europe embarking upon trans-Atlantic expansion, the Mediterranean was left as a secondary region, and Florence became increasingly isolated, with little potential for future growth. Ferdinando II was, however, an intelligent and cultured man. Under his auspices and those of his brother, Leopoldo, the 'Accademia del Cimento' ('Experimental Academy') was established in 1657. One of the purposes of this scientific society was to provide experimental proof of some of Galileo's theorems. Among its members was Galileo's pupil and disciple, Vincenzo Viviani (see further Walks 9 and 11). Ferdinando's own experiments included an attempt to isolate a poisonous substance in tobacco – what a prophet!

The second half of the 17th century through to the present day

Of Ferdinando II's son and grandson, Cosimo III and Gian Gastone, there is little to say. On the latter's death without issue in 1737, Tuscany was handed over by treaty to Duke Francis Stephen of Lorraine, who was betrothed to Maria Theresa, heiress to all the Hapsburg lands, and Austrian troops were moved in to support his rule. Gian Gastone's sister, Anna Maria, the last of the Medici, lived on at the Pitti Palace until 1743. She left the wonderful Medici collections, built up by her family over the centuries, to the new Grand Duke and his successors on the condition that they should remain intact on Tuscan territory, for, she said, not only were they an ornament and a benefit to the state and its people, but also 'an inducement to the curiosity of foreigners'. We owe her much.

With a brief interruption between 1809 and 1814, when the Grand

Duchy of Tuscany was conferred by Napoleon Bonaparte upon his sister, the Lorraine-Hapsburg dynasty ruled until 1859. In 1860 Tuscany became part of the unified state of Italy, and from 1865 to 1870 Florence was the capital of the new state. In a bid to live up to this new image, much restructuring of the city took place. Among other things, the city walls were demolished and replaced by boulevards, and the Old Market and surrounding mediaeval quarter were swept away and the Piazza della Repubblica created.

The 20th century dealt Florence some devastating blows. In 1944 the German army destroyed all the bridges except for the Ponte Vecchio. To make the latter impassable, they blew up the areas at each end of the bridge, causing terrible damage. The great flood of 1966 took its toll, and in 1993 a Mafia car-bomb exploded near the Uffizi, killing five people and damaging the Torre de' Pulci (Walk 2). As of old, however, Florence always bounces back. Conservation and restoration work are continuous, and the city is a monument to man's achievements in more ways than one.

Sunset over the Oltrarno

An overview of fifty Florentine artists

A catalogue of Florentine artists for the period from the end of the 13th to the end of the 16th century reads like a 'Who's Who' of art history. It is impracticable to give a full list, and you do not need to know the names of scores of artists in order to enjoy the art of Florence. A brief overview may, however, be useful and provide you with a few pegs to help you pin down some of the things that you are going to see. The following survey limits itself to fifty of the more famous artists and mentions just a few of their works.

We begin at the end of the 13th century with **Cimabue**, whose wonderful Crucifix, now in the S. Croce museum (Walk 5), was badly damaged in the 1966 floods. His Maestà, still rather Byzantine in feel, is housed in the Uffizi (Walk 2). At the end of the 13th century, the Florentines decided that they needed a bigger Cathedral, and in 1294 **Arnolfo di Cambio** was appointed as the 'capomaestro' ('head of works') for the Duomo (Walk 1). The Palazzo de' Priori (today's Palazzo Vecchio; Walk 2) was also entrusted to him.

Giotto, a pupil of Cimabue and a friend of Dante, created new forms in art which heralded Humanism and the Renaissance. His frescoes in the Bardi and Peruzzi Chapels at S. Croce survive (Walk 5), the altarpiece in the Baroncelli Chapel there is by him and his workshop, a magnificent Crucifix hangs in S. Maria Novella and another in Ognissanti (both Walk 7). There is a realism and intense humanity in his paintings that is absent from the works of earlier artists, as can be appreciated by comparing his Maestà, also in the Uffizi, with Cimabue's. After the death of Arnolfo di Cambio, Giotto eventually replaced him as capomaestro at the Duomo. He began work on the Campanile (Walk 1) in 1334, and by his death in 1337 the first storey was built. The reliefs which decorate the base of the Campanile were probably executed in part to his designs by **Andrea Pisano**, who also produced the first set of bronze doors for the Baptistery between 1330 and 1336.

The Giottesque school of painting continued to flourish throughout the 14th century and included **Taddeo Gaddi**, **Giovanni da Milano** and **Bernardo Daddi**. Taddeo decorated the Baroncelli Chapel, and Giovanni the Rinuccini Chapel, both at S. Croce (Walk 5). Bernardo's Madonna delle Grazie is in Orsanmichele (Walk 3). Other painters evolved a more solemn, didactic style. They included **Andrea Orcagna**, his brother **Nardo di Cione**, and **Andrea di Bonaiuto**. Orcagna was responsible for the stunning tabernacle which houses Bernardo Daddi's Madonna in Orsanmichele and for the altarpiece in the Strozzi Chapel at the end of the L transept in S. Maria Novella (Walk 7). The walls of this chapel were painted by his brother Nardo with scenes of the Last Judgement, Paradise and Hell, the last being a pictorial representation of Dante's *Inferno*. Andrea di Bonaiuto frescoed the Spanish Chapel at S. Maria Novella. Active towards the end of the 14th century was **Agnolo Gaddi**, son of Taddeo, who decorated the choir at S. Croce.

The so-called 'International Gothic Style' is represented by, among others, **Lorenzo Monaco**, **Gentile da Fabriano** and **Masolino**. S. Trinità (Walk 12) contains a chapel with frescoes and an altarpiece by Lorenzo, and Gentile's Adoration of the Magi was painted for the Strozzi Chapel of the same church (now the sacristy). This painting, often depicted on Christmas cards, is in the Uffizi, in company with paintings by Lorenzo Monaco. Masolino's best known contribution to Florentine art is to be found in the Brancacci Chapel in the church of S. Maria del Carmine (Walk 13). He worked on the frescoes here in company with **Masaccio**, who effected a revolution in the arts through his rigorous study and application of the new rules of perspective – see also his fresco of the Trinity at S. Maria Novella (Walk 7).

In 1401 the greatest artists of the time were invited to submit trial reliefs for a competition to choose who should be given the commission for a new set of bronze doors for the Baptistery. This competition is regarded as one of the watersheds which mark the change from Gothic to Renaissance art. The reliefs submitted by **Lorenzo Ghiberti** and **Filippo Brunelleschi** are in the Bargello (Walk 9). Ghiberti won, and in 1424 his new doors were installed (Walk 1). He subsequently went on to produce a further set, installed at the E entrance in 1452. In these final doors, his most celebrated work, he used perspective to such great effect that the scenes appear to extend far into the background. Michelangelo is said to have pronounced them as worthy of Paradise. The originals are in the Museo dell' Opera del Duomo. Ghiberti

Copies of two panels from Ghiberti's E doors showing the stories of Esau and Jacob, and Joseph and his brothers

and Brunelleschi were also rival contenders for the commission to construct the Cathedral cupola. They were initially appointed jointly, but Brunelleschi eventually took over full responsibility. Ghiberti was involved with his sets of Baptistery doors, not to mention commissions for bronze statues of S. Matthew and S. Stephen for Orsanmichele (Walk 3). His S. John the Baptist, completed a few years earlier for the same location, was the first life-size Renaissance statue to be cast in bronze. Brunelleschi's famous cupola, an astonishing feat of engineering, is one of the masterpieces of the Renaissance.

The period of Medici supremacy between 1434 and 1492 witnessed a blossoming of the arts. In the field of architecture, Brunelleschi, who had already designed the Ospedale degli Innocenti (Walk 10), was commissioned by Cosimo Il Vecchio to rebuild the church of S. Lorenzo (Walk 6). You could not get much further from Gothic architecture. The interior uses classical forms set off by the use of 'pietra serena' (a beautiful soft grey stone) against plain white surfaces, and the proportions and geometric perfection make a tremendous impact. Other buildings in the same style by Brunelleschi include the church of S. Spirito (Walk 12) and the Pazzi Chapel at S. Croce (Walk 5). The architect **Michelozzo** also undertook commissions for Cosimo, including the Medici Palace and the monastery of S. Marco (both Walk 8). The latter is famous for its frescoes and paintings by **Fra Angelico**.

Brunelleschi had studied the ruins of Ancient Rome in company with **Donatello**. Among the most famous works by Donatello are the statue of

Copy of Donatello's statue of Habakkuk on the Campanile

S. George (made for Orsanmichele) and the bronze of David. Both these statues are now in the Bargello (Walk 9). The relief panels of Donatello's bronze pulpits in S. Lorenzo (Walk 6) depict scenes full of dramatic intensity, and create amazing illusions of depth. In the Museo dell' Opera del Duomo (Walk 1) are his statues of Habakkuk and S. Mary Magdalene. Also here is his cantoria, made for the Duomo, along with the cantoria by **Luca della Robbia**, who, like Donatello, collaborated on the decoration of Brunelleschi's buildings. Luca created the medium of glazed terracotta, which became a family speciality. Stunning examples of his work can be seen at the Pazzi Chapel at S. Croce (Walk 5), in the Chapel of the Cardinal of Portugal at S. Miniato (Walk 14), and in S. Trinità (Walk 12), where his tomb for Benozzo Federighi is framed by an exquisite mosaic.

The delightful medallions showing babies in swaddling clothes on the façade of the Ospedale degli Innocenti (Walk 10) are perhaps the best-known work of Luca's nephew, **Andrea della Robbia** (see also page 248).

Donatello's work inspired a host of other artists, among them **Bernardo and Antonio Rossellino**, **Desiderio da Settignano**, **Mino da Fiesole** and **Benedetto da Maiano**. The tomb of the Cardinal of Portugal at S. Miniato (Walk 14) is by Antonio Rossellino, while that of Leonardo Bruni in S. Croce (Walk 5) is by Bernardo. Carlo Marsuppini's tomb, likewise in S. Croce, is by Desiderio, who was also responsible for a beautiful tabernacle in S. Lorenzo (Walk 6) and for a statue of S. Mary Magdalene in S. Trinità (Walk 12). The Rossellino workshop did the tomb of Giannozzo Pandolfini in the Badia (Walk 4), and Mino da Fiesole the tomb of Bernardo Giugni in the same church. Benedetto da Maiano's exquisite little pulpit graces one of the nave pillars at S. Croce. This was also the period which saw the revival of portraiture. Antonio Rossellino's bust of Francesco Sassetti (the manager of the Medici Bank) is in the Bargello (Walk 9), where can be seen also Benedetto's stunning rendering of Pietro Mellini as an old man, and Mino's busts of Cosimo's two sons, Piero the Gouty and Giovanni.

Mention has already been made of the Medici Palace (Walk 8). The walls of the private chapel there were decorated by **Benozzo Gozzoli**, a pupil of Fra Angelico, with frescoes showing the procession of the Magi. The altarpiece is a copy of a work by **Filippo Lippi**, whose exquisite painting of the Madonna and Child can also be seen at the palace. Filippo's son, **Filippino Lippi**, completed the fresco cycle in the Brancacci Chapel at the Carmine complex (Walk 13), left unfinished by Masolino and Masaccio, and executed the frescoes in the Strozzi Chapel to the R of the sanctuary in S. Maria Novella (Walk 7). The Badia (Walk 4) houses his painting of the Madonna appearing to S. Bernard. Filippo Lippi's most famous pupil was **Botticelli**, whose Primavera and Birth of Venus are in the Uffizi.

Experiments with perspective were carried to the extreme by **Paolo Uccello**, who painted a fresco cycle for the Green Cloister at S. Maria Novella (Walk 7). His three paintings of the Battle of S. Romano, now in the

National Gallery London, the Paris Louvre and the Uffizi, once decorated a room at the Medici Palace. His fresco of John Hawkwood can be seen in the Duomo (Walk 1), next to the fresco of Niccolò da Tolentino by **Andrea del Castagno**, a follower of Masaccio. Castagno too experimented with perspective, and you can play fascinating games standing in front of his fresco of the Last Supper at the Cenacolo di S. Apollonia (Walk 11).

Giovanni de' Rucellai, a wealthy businessman and respected intellectual, commissioned **Leon Battista Alberti** to complete the façade of the church of S. Maria Novella (Walk 7) and to design the Palazzo Rucellai and the Chapel of S. Sepolcro at S. Pancrazio (Walk 13). **Domenico Ghirlandaio** was responsible for the frescoes in the sanctuary at S. Maria Novella (Walk 7) and for those in the Sassetti Chapel at S. Trinità (Walk 12). He sets his stories against contemporary Florentine backgrounds and includes in his scenes portraits of real people. Other artists who should be mentioned are **Antonio and Piero del Pollaiuolo**, whose altarpiece once adorned the Chapel of the Cardinal of Portugal at S. Miniato (Walk 14; now replaced by a copy, the original being in the Uffizi), and **Verrocchio**, whose bronze statues of David and of the Incredulity of S. Thomas can be seen in the Bargello (Walk 9) and Orsanmichele (Walk 3) respectively. The Uffizi houses his painting of the Baptism of Christ. According to Vasari, the angel on the L in this picture was painted by Verrocchio's pupil, **Leonardo da Vinci**. Leonardo's painting of the Annunciation hangs nearby.

Perugino is represented by two wonderful frescoes, the Crucifixion (Walk 10) and the Last Supper (Walk 11), as well as by paintings in the Uffizi and the Palatine Gallery. He was the master of **Raphael**, again represented by paintings in these two great collections. **Michelangelo Buonarroti** began his career under the patronage of Lorenzo Il Magnifico. His most famous work is the David, housed in the Accademia (Walk 8), while his Pietà is in the Museo dell' Opera del Duomo (Walk 1). The Bargello (Walk 9) has his statue of Bacchus and bust of Brutus, and the Uffizi a tondo of the Holy Family. Examples of his genius can also be seen at the Casa Buonarroti (Walk 5) and at the New Sacristy at S. Lorenzo (Walk 6). Michelangelo represents the watershed between Early and High Renaissance. He created a new style that disrupted the balance of the earlier period and became a model for the Mannerist art of the 16th century.

During the first part of the 16th century, **Andrea del Sarto** created a school of painting at Florence and was dubbed 'the faultless painter' by Vasari. The Accademia, Uffizi and Palatine Gallery collections have examples of his work, and frescoes by him can be seen at SS. Annunziata (Walk 10). His pupils included **Pontormo**, an important early Mannerist, who is also represented at SS. Annunziata and at S. Felicità (Walk 15).

The succession of Cosimo I in 1537 brought to prominence two artists who, at the behest of the new ruler, changed the face of the city. **Vasari** constructed the Uffizi (Walk 2) and built the famous Corridor linking that building to the Pitti Palace (Walk 15). He also painted the cupola in the Duomo, and redecorated the interior of the Palazzo Vecchio. **Bartolommeo Ammannati** enlarged the Pitti Palace (Walks 12 and 15), which, after its purchase from the Pitti, became the home of the ducal family. Ammannati was also responsible for the bridge of S. Trinità (Walk 13) and for the fountain of Neptune in the Piazza della Signoria (Walk 2). **Cellini** and **Giambologna** graced the city with their sculptures (see Walk 2), as did **Bandinelli**, though some might say that 'grace' is the wrong word to use where Bandinelli is concerned. Certainly his statue of Hercules and Cacus outside the Palazzo Vecchio bears no comparison with the works of Michelangelo, Cellini and Giambologna. The Loggia de' Lanzi (Walk 2) houses Cellini's bronze statue of Perseus and Giambologna's statues of the Rape of the Sabine Woman and Hercules and the Centaur, and other examples of their work are in the Bargello (Walk 9). In the field of painting **Bronzino** came to the fore. His magnificent portrait of Eleonora di Toledo is in the Uffizi.

Giambologna's Rape of the Sabine Woman and (behind) Hercules and the Centaur

Walk 1

Begins in Piazza S. Giovanni and ends on the N side of the Duomo.

Takes in: the Baptistery, the Duomo and Campanile, the Bigallo and Misericordia Museums, and the Museo dell' Opera del Duomo.

Duration: 2 hours, excluding visits to the above. I have not ascended the Campanile, so cannot tell you how much time to allow for this. Likewise, I have not been up the cupola, for which there is invariably a long queue and which should be done as a separate enterprise. You should allow a minimum of *c.* 30-45 minutes each for the interiors of the Baptistery and the Duomo, though the timing for the latter is based on the fact that the E end is usually roped off. The Bigallo and Misericordia Museums are both very small – *c.* 20 minutes and 40 minutes respectively should suffice. The Museo dell' Opera del Duomo is magnificent, and you should allow a minimum of 2 hours.

Tips: Piazza S. Giovanni and Piazza del Duomo get incredibly crowded. My advice is to rise with the lark and do this walk before breakfast, when you can appreciate the exteriors of the Baptistery and the Duomo in peace. You can return to visit the interiors and the various museums later. If you do venture out early wrap up warm because, even in summer, the early morning breezes can be chill. The interiors of the Duomo, Baptistery and Museo dell' Opera del Duomo are described at the end of the walk, and, if this is your first visit to Florence and time presses, I advise you to concentrate on these, and to leave the Museums of the Bigallo and the Misericordia for a future trip. At the time of writing entry to the Duomo was free, but a ticket was required for the

Detail on the Baptistery

crypt, Campanile, cupola, Baptistery and Museo dell' Opera del Duomo. Tickets were available at the crypt and the Museum or from a ticket office at no. 7 Piazza S. Giovanni, opposite the N door of the Baptistery, and you had to purchase a single ticket (valid for 48 hours) covering these five venues, whether you wished to visit all of them or not. If ascending the Campanile and the cupola is beyond your capabilities, I do assure you that the crypt, Museo dell' Opera del Duomo and Baptistery will more than make up for the expense involved. The statuary and reliefs now on the Baptistery and the Campanile are copies; the originals are housed in the Museum. You may find that binoculars are useful on this walk.

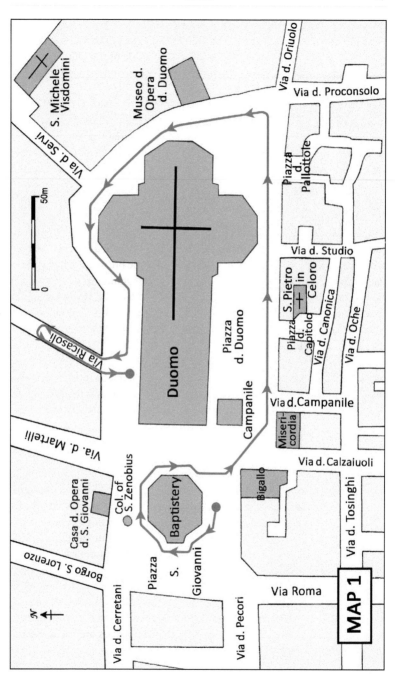

S. Michele Visdomini

Museo d. Opera d. Duomo

Via d. Servi

Via d. Oriuolo

Via d. Proconsolo

Piazza d. Pallottole

Via d. Studio

S. Pietro in Celoro

Piazza d. Capitolo

Via d. Canonica

Via d. Oche

50m

0

Via Ricasoli

Duomo

Piazza d. Duomo

Via d. Martelli

Campanile

Via d.Campanile

Misericordia

Via d. Calzaiuoli

Casa d. Opera d. S. Giovanni

Col. of S. Zenobius

Baptistery

Bigallo

Via d. Tosinghi

Borgo S. Lorenzo

Piazza S. Giovanni

Via d. Cerretani

Via d. Pecori

Via Roma

MAP 1

N

The Baptistery and the column of S. Zenobius

The octagonal Baptistery, founded sometime prior to 897, was built over the site of a Roman structure (tradition maintains that it was a temple to the god Mars, but in fact it was a house). The building as we see it today is almost certainly Matildan in origin (late 11th/early 12th century); the 14th century chronicler Giovanni Villani says that the lantern was completed in 1150. The walls are clad in green and white marble, the bichrome design reflecting the internal structural divisions. The corner piers were originally monochrome dark grey 'macigno' stone, but in 1293 the marble cladding was restored at the expense of the Calimala Guild (who by now held the patronage of the building) and the zebra stripes, designed by Arnolfo di Cambio, were added in emulation of contemporary structures at Pisa, Siena and Orvieto; perish the thought that Florence should be outdone by her rivals!

Walk to the S side of the Baptistery (as you face the building the Duomo will be on your R). At the S portal stand copies of Andrea Pisano's bronze doors (the originals are in the Museo dell' Opera del Duomo). Commissioned by the Calimala Guild, the doors were erected at the E portal in 1336 but moved to the S in 1424 to make way for new doors by Ghiberti. Andrea's name and the start date of 1330 run across the top of the doors. Below this are twenty-eight reliefs set in quatrefoil frames, twenty illustrating the life of John the Baptist and eight at the bottom showing the Theological and Cardinal Virtues. On mediaeval doors, the convention was for Old Testament scenes to be arranged from top to bottom, and, because he was a precursor of Christ, John's life is shown according to the Old Testament convention. The scenes, which read from L to R, first down the L leaf and then down the R one, are as follows: the Annunciation to Zechariah; Zechariah is struck dumb; the visit of the Virgin Mary to Elizabeth; the birth of John; Zechariah names his son John; John goes into the desert; John announces that he is not the Messiah; John announces the coming of Christ; John baptizes the crowds; John baptizes Jesus; Hope, Faith, Fortitude and Temperance; John reproaches Herod; John is taken to prison; John's disciples visit him; John's disciples go to Jesus; the dance of Salome; the beheading of John; John's head is presented to Herod; Salome presents John's head to Herodias; John's body is taken for burial; the burial of John; Charity, Humility, Justice and Prudence. Spare a moment to look at the superb original 15th century door-frame by Vittorio Ghiberti (son of Lorenzo), which is smothered with foliage, fruit and birds. I particularly like the owl near the top on the  R. Above the S portal are copies of bronzes of the Baptist, Salome and the executioner by Vincenzo Danti (1571). On the columns flanking the portal can be seen rectangles carved into the stone. The column on the R has a single rectangle, while the one on the L has, enigmatically, two, one inside the other. These are old units of measurement, the one on the R being the old Lombard foot.

Follow the wall of the Baptistery round clockwise along one side of the octagon to reach the S wall of the 'scarsella' (quadrangular apse). At the base of the wall at the L you'll see a re-used stone slab, originally part of a Roman frieze, showing the grape harvest and the transportation of wine amphorae.

Continue clockwise round the Baptistery to the N side of the building, where stands the column of S. Zenobius. Zenobius (337-417), the first bishop of Florence, later became a patron saint of the city. Originally buried at S. Lorenzo, his remains were later transferred to the Cathedral. Legend has it that, en route, his bier touched a dead elm tree, which immediately began to sprout. The present column commemorating the scene of this miracle was erected in the 14th century, the original one having been swept

away by floods in 1333. Near the column of S. Zenobius, at no. 7 Piazza S. Giovanni, is the attractive little Casa dell' Opera di S. Giovanni. The lunette over the door is flanked by the emblems of the Calimala Guild (the eagle clasping a bale of cloth) and contains a copy of a statuette of John the Baptist by Michelozzo (the original is in the Bargello; Walk 9). The Casa dell' Opera di S. Giovanni presently houses the ticket office for the Duomo complex (there are toilets here too). You should come here to purchase your ticket **before** queuing for entry to the Baptistery, Campanile or cupola.

Immediately opposite the little Casa dell' Opera di S. Giovanni lies the N entrance to the Baptistery. Lorenzo Ghiberti's first set of Baptistery doors was erected at the E portal in 1424, but moved to the N portal in 1452. The 1401 competition for the commission is seen as one of the watersheds between Gothic and Renaissance art. Several eminent artists tried their luck. The test was to design and execute a relief scene showing the sacrifice of Isaac set within a quatrefoil frame. The reliefs submitted by Brunelleschi and Ghiberti have survived and can be seen in the Bargello (Walk 9). One of the judges was Giovanni di Bicci, father of Cosimo de' Medici.

Like Andrea Pisano's doors, Ghiberti's have twenty-eight reliefs set in quatrefoil frames. Twenty of them illustrate the life of Christ, while the eight at the bottom show the Evangelists and Doctors of the Church. Being New Testament, the scenes of Christ's life are arranged from bottom to top, following mediaeval convention. The scenes, which read from L to R across both leaves, are as follows (beginning at bottom L): SS. Ambrose, Jerome, Gregory the Great and Augustine; the four Evangelists, SS. John, Matthew, Luke and Mark; the Annunciation to the Virgin Mary; the Nativity and the shepherds; the Adoration of the Magi; Christ among the elders; the Baptism of Christ; the Temptation of Christ; Christ drives the moneylenders from the temple; Christ walks on the waters; the Transfiguration; the resurrection of Lazarus; the entry into Jerusalem; the Last Supper; the Agony in the Garden; the betrayal by Judas; the Scourging of Christ; Christ before Pontius Pilate; the Way to Calvary; the Crucifixion; the Resurrection; Pentecost. The heads at the corners of each relief include a self-portrait of Ghiberti (LH leaf, central vertical band, 5th head down,

wearing an elaborate hat). Spare a moment to look at Ghiberti's lovely door-frame (original), again covered with flora and fauna; halfway up on the R you'll spot a stoat. Above the N portal are copies of statues of John the Baptist, a Levite and a Pharisee by Francesco Rustici, assisted, according to Vasari, by Leonardo da Vinci (Rustici and Leonardo both trained in Verrocchio's workshop).

Rustici and the 'Cauldron Club'

Vasari tells us that Francesco Rustici was a pleasant man who was very fond of animals. He tamed a porcupine that remained under his table, like a dog, and sometimes pricked guests' legs. He also had a tame raven that mimicked speech like a parrot. Rustici was a member of the so-called 'Cauldron Club'. Every so often he and his mates would meet up for a meal, with everybody bringing along something for the feast. On one occasion, Andrea del Sarto presented the assembled company with an octagonal church, like the Baptistery. The pavement, made to look like mosaic, was of jelly, and the columns were sausages, with bases and capitals made from parmesan cheese. The choir desk was made of cold veal, with a choir-book made of pastry, the letters and musical notes being formed with peppercorns. The singers were thrushes, larks and pigeons.

Continue clockwise round the Baptistery to reach the E portal. Halfway along the side of the octagon between the N and E portals there is a plaque set into the pavement with a quotation from Dante. We'll see many of these Dante plaques on our walks around the city. This one quotes *Inferno* XIX.17, where Dante refers to his beautiful S. Giovanni.

The porphyry columns on each side of the E entrance to the Baptistery were war booty, acquired in the early 12th century when Florence helped Pisa wrest Majorca from Muslim control. As soon as Ghiberti's first set of doors had been erected here in 1424, the Calimala Guild began planning a new set for the N portal. So impressed were the authorities with his work that there was no competition for the new commission, and the contract was signed in 1425. The doors were originally to have had smaller compartments, akin to the two earlier sets. However, the scheme was changed to ten larger panels, which gave Ghiberti more scope and enabled him to show two or three scenes simultaneously within the same frame, varying the height of the relief for individual episodes. This intermingling of high and shallow relief, coupled with the gilding and a breathtaking use of perspective, led to spectacular results, so much so that the Calimala Guild decided to instal the new doors at the E entrance and move Ghiberti's first set of doors to the N. The E portal of the Baptistery was called *Paradisium*, so when Michelangelo later declared Ghiberti's doors to be worthy of Paradise, he was, in fact, saying that they were a fitting adornment for this main entrance. Later generations have put a rather different connotation on his remarks and, indeed, he probably intended the ambiguity. In 1966 the floodwaters of the Arno ripped six of these panels from their frames! Just to remind you, the panels you see here now are copies, the originals being housed in the Museo dell' Opera del Duomo. The ten panels show stories from the Old Testament and follow the mediaeval convention of arranging these from top to bottom. Reading from L to R the stories are: Adam and Eve; Cain and Abel; Noah (with a wonderful pyramidal ark); Abraham and Isaac; Esau and Jacob (see page 41 for illustration); Joseph and his brothers (again see page 41); Moses receiving the Ten Commandments; Joshua and the fall of Jericho; David and Goliath;

the meeting between Solomon and the Queen of Sheba. It has been suggested that the inclusion of the last scene may be an allusion to the 1439 Council of Florence and the hoped-for reunion of the Eastern and Western Churches. Ghiberti framed the panels with statuettes of Old Testament characters in niches alternating with roundels containing heads. As on the N doors, there is a self-portrait (L leaf, 4th head down on the R). Immediately next to this, on the R leaf, is a portrait of Ghiberti's son Vittorio. As before, don't neglect the (original) outer frame, again decorated with flora and fauna; there's an owl on the top L of centre and a gorgeous squirrel halfway up on the R. Above the entrance are copies of the Baptist by Andrea Sansovino and Christ by Vincenzo Danti (the angel was added in the 18th century by Innocenzo Spinazzi). Before leaving the E portal, note the stone with part of a Latin inscription halfway down the RH side. Like the stone showing the grape harvest (see above), this has been re-used, and the inscription has nothing to do with the building.

Fickle summer weather

On our walks around Florence we shall frequently be referring to the *Diary* of an apothecary named Luca Landucci, who recorded all manner of things that went on in his native city from the mid-15th century through to 1515. One of the most important days in the year was the Feast of S. Giovanni in June, when there were celebrations throughout the town and when the Baptistery was hung with liturgical awnings attached to iron rings in its walls (if you stand on the steps fronting the Duomo, you can still see some of these rings at the base of the attic level on the E side). Despite the summer season, however, fickle weather often played havoc with arrangements. On 24th June 1488, for example, Luca records that a freak storm, with hail the like of which was never seen, ripped the awnings to shreds. A similar thing happened in 1503 and again in 1506. The awnings were clearly difficult enough to handle even without the added complication of freak weather conditions. On 22nd June 1501, while they were being erected, the ropes got entangled round the cross on the column of S. Zenobius and pulled it down, as well as bringing some tiles off a nearby roof, killing a man and breaking a boy's legs.

Halfway along the side of the octagon between the E and S portals there is another Dante plaque set into the pavement. Dante was exiled from Florence in 1302 (see historical summary) and never set foot in his native city again, so this quotation is very poignant and moving:
'If it should ever come to pass that the sacred poem to which heaven and earth have set their hands, so that it has made me thin for many years, should conquer the cruelty that has locked me out from the beautiful sheepfold where I slept as a lamb, an enemy to the wolves who make war on it, then with another voice and with another fleece I shall return as poet, and, at the font of my baptism, I will take up the crown' (*Paradiso* XXV.1-9).

The Cathedral façade

Opposite the E entrance to the Baptistery stands the Duomo. A façade was designed during the 1290s by Arnolfo di Cambio, the first 'capomaestro' ('head of works') for the new Cathedral, and construction was begun, but Arnolfo died at the beginning of the 14th century. Giotto was eventually appointed capomaestro in the early 1330s, but he devoted his attentions to the Campanile and himself died in 1337. The works were then supervised by Francesco Talenti and others, but the façade was by now low priority and was never finished. For the entry of Pope Leo X into Florence in November 1515 a fictive façade had hurriedly to be raised, which was apparently so splendid that Luca Landucci, in his *Diary*, says that everyone regretted seeing it taken down. By the end of the 16th century the old façade and its sculptures appeared old-fashioned, and in 1587 Grand Duke Francesco ordered its demolition. Some of the sculptures, along with a drawing made by Bernardino Poccetti, have survived and are now preserved in the

Museo dell' Opera del Duomo. The decision to demolish was not universally popular. One eye-witness recorded the event with much bitterness, calling it pitiable and referring to the ruination of the façade. A competition was held, but nothing came of this or of a later scheme in 1635. Models entered for these competitions are likewise preserved in the museum. Temporary decorations were applied for the marriage of Ferdinando I and Christine of Lorraine in 1589, and in 1688, when Ferdinando, son of Cosimo III, married Violante of Bavaria, the entire façade was again plastered and painted with fictive architecture. This survived into the latter part of the 19th century, when a design by Emilio de Fabris for a new façade was accepted.

The Bigallo, the Misericordia and the graveyard

Opposite the S entrance to the Baptistery (where we began our tour round the building), is a pretty Gothic building now housing a Tourist Information desk and the little Museo del Bigallo. Look at the frescoes on the wall facing the Baptistery. On the RH fresco you can still make out S. Peter Martyr preaching in 1245 in the Mercato Vecchio (the present-day Piazza della Repubblica). Over the heads of the assembled people can be seen a large black horse. This poor animal took fright and began to buck and rear before bolting off along today's Via degli Strozzi. It was clearly the devil in disguise, intent on causing havoc, but S. Peter Martyr was unperturbed. He made the sign of the cross, the horse stopped dead in its tracks and then disappeared into thin air. On Walk 13 we'll pass the spot where the horse supposedly vanished.

The little loggia on the Bigallo building was built for the Misericordia in the 14th century, but the Compagnia del Bigallo moved here in 1425 when the two confraternities merged. Members of the Misericordia wore distinctive black habits with hoods. They were especially active during plague years, giving medical help to the poor and burying the dead. Beneath the loggia, lost and abandoned children were exhibited for three days before being placed with foster-mothers. The charming little Bigallo Museum, which houses the archives of the company together with works of art commissioned by the confraternities, contains a fresco (1386) showing the Captains of the Misericordia entrusting children to foster-mothers outside the loggia, while a fresco of the Madonna of the Misericordia (1342) includes a view of Florence, with the Baptistery, Campanile and incomplete façade of the Duomo. In 1576 the Misericordia moved from the Bigallo, eventually ending up at the site just across the road, on the opposite corner of Via de' Calzaiuoli. It is still here, giving help to those in need and running an ambulance service. Its museum houses works of art commissioned by the confraternity, along with a miscellany of historical medical paraphernalia. On the façade of the Misericordia building can be seen a fresco by Pietro Annigoni (1970) showing a member of the confraternity bringing a body to be buried (the Annigoni Museum is housed in the Villa Bardini; Walk 15). Just in case you failed to read the Introduction to this book and haven't yet found a Tourist Information Office, let me stress here that you should now visit the desk in the Bigallo building and obtain the free updated list of the opening hours of the city's museums, galleries and major churches, which might save you much valuable time.

The ground that we are standing on was once occupied by a cemetery. Every respectable graveyard has a ghost, and the cemetery that lay between the Baptistery and the Duomo was no exception. According to legend, it was haunted by the ghost of the lovely Ginevra degli Almieri, who rose from her grave in 1396. Look under Walk 4 to find out what happened next.

The Campanile

The Campanile (see overleaf for illustration) was begun in 1334 and is still known as Giotto's tower, even though he died in 1337 and responsibility for the structure passed first to Andrea Pisano and then to Francesco Talenti. However, a drawing in the Museo dell' Opera at Siena supposedly shows a copy of Giotto's design for a Sienese campanile, and so similar is it to the Florentine tower that it's not hard to argue that Pisano and Talenti followed a basic design already projected by the great man. The design of the lowest storey, with its hexagons, can certainly be attributed to Giotto. Pisano added the storey with the lozenges and the one above that with niches for statues before leaving Florence in 1343. Talenti began work on the two 'bifore'

('two-arched') window stages, but in 1348 the plague wiped out his entire work crew. These stages were eventually finished in 1351 and the 'trifore' ('three-arched') window storey in 1359.

The designs of the reliefs in the hexagons and lozenges can be attributed to Andrea Pisano and his workshop. The programme of the reliefs as a whole is man's journey from creation to ultimate perfection and salvation, a subject taken from the tenets of Scholastic Philosophy, which divided human activity into three classes, *Necessitas* (mechanical and manual chores necessary for survival), *Virtus* (values forming the basis of social organization) and *Sapientia* (intellectual activities). The number seven symbolized perfection. There are seven lozenges on each side and there were originally seven hexagons on each side except the N. The opening up and enlargement of the door on the E side in the 1430s necessitated the transfer of two hexagons from here to the N. This left five blank spaces on the N, and in 1437 Luca della Robbia was given the commission for five additional hexagonal reliefs, installed in 1439. Ruskin, in his *Mornings in Florence*, maintained that a study of the Campanile reliefs would give you strength for life. I think that's going a bit far, but let's study them anyway. The programme begins with the creation of Adam on the W side. I should just remind you that all the reliefs and statues now on the Campanile are copies, the originals being in the Museo dell' Opera del Duomo, where they are beautifully displayed. The following description lists the works on each side from L to R.

W Side
Hexagons
Creation of Adam; Creation of Eve; Labours of Adam and Eve (note the
little bear cub climbing the tree on the R – we'll see him again later); Jabal,
inventor of animal husbandry; Jubal, inventor of music; Tubalcain, the first
blacksmith; Noah, the first man to plant a vineyard.

Lozenges (showing the planets according to the Ptolemaic system)
Saturn holding the wheel of time; Jupiter, shown as a monk, symbolizing
divine wisdom; Mars, shown as a mounted warrior; the Sun, shown as a
crowned Apollo; Venus holding two lovers; Mercury, shown with the sign
of Gemini; the Moon, shown seated on the waters and holding a fountain.

Statues

The statues on the W side, by Donatello and Nanni di Bartolo, were originally erected on the N side in the 1420s-30s, but were moved to the W in 1464. From L to R they are John the Baptist (by Nanni), Habakkuk (by Donatello; nicknamed 'Lo Zuccone' 'pumpkin-head' and said by Vasari to be a portrait of Giovanni di Barduccio Chiericini, an enemy of the Medici), Jeremiah (by Donatello; said to be a portrait of Francesco Soderini, also an enemy of the Medici), and Abdias (by Nanni). With the first twenty-two florins that Donatello received for the commission for Habakkuk, he paid off his tax arrears. He apparently used to swear by this statue and invite it to speak (see page 42 for an illustration of the copy of Habakkuk).

S side

Hexagons

Gionitus, inventor of astronomy; Building; Medicine, showing a seated physician with his patients; Hunting/Riding; Weaving; Legislation, showing Phoroneus, mythical king of Argos and inventor of laws; Daedalus, inventor of flight.

Lozenges (the Theological and Cardinal Virtues)

Faith, shown holding a cross and chalice; Charity, with a heart and cornucopia; Hope, shown with wings and praying; Prudence, shown with two heads, young and old, and holding a snake and a mirror; Justice, with scales and a sword; Temperance, shown pouring water into her wine; Fortitude, holding a club and a shield.

<u>Statues</u>
Four prophets (including Moses) by Andrea Pisano and collaborators.

<u>E side</u>
<u>Hexagons</u>
Navigation; Social Justice, showing Hercules and Cacus; Agriculture, showing Homogirus ploughing; Festivals, showing a four-wheeled theatre cart; Architecture, with Euclid drawing.

Lozenges (the Liberal Arts)

Astronomy, shown holding an astrolabe; Music, shown with a psaltery; Geometry, shown with a book and compasses; Grammar, shown teaching and holding a scourge; Rhetoric, shown with a sword and shield; Logic, shown holding shears; Arithmetic, shown counting.

Statues

Prophets and Patriarchs by Donatello and Nanni di Bartolo. The prophet on the far L (by Donatello) is traditionally supposed to be a portrait of Brunelleschi, while that on the far R (also by Donatello) is nicknamed 'Il Penserioso'. The identity of no. 2 (by Nanni) is uncertain, and no. 3 (a joint effort) shows Abraham and Isaac.

Don't miss the relief of the Annunciation on the flank of the Duomo to the R of the Campanile here. It probably dates to the early 1300s.

N Side
The reliefs and sculptures here are difficult to see owing to the railings.
Hexagons
Sculpture, showing Phidias at work (moved from the E side in the 1340s);

Painting, showing the Greek painter Apelles (likewise moved here in the 1340s); Grammar, showing a teacher with two boys; Logic/Dialectic, showing Plato and Aristotle in debate; Music, showing Orpheus charming the birds and animals; Geometry/Arithmetic, showing Euclid and Pythagorus in discussion; Astrology/Harmony, showing Pythagorus at an anvil.
Lozenges (the Sacraments)
Baptism; Confession/Penance; Matrimony; Holy Orders, showing a bishop (just the top of a lozenge, shaped to go over the Madonna and Child in the lunette over the old N door); Confirmation; Eucharist; Extreme Unction.
Statues
These statues by Andrea and Nino Pisano, alluding to prophecies of redemption, were erected on the W side in 1343, but moved to the N in 1464. From L to R they are the Tiburtine Sibyl, King David, King Solomon, and the Erythraean Sibyl.

You can ascend the 414 steps of the Campanile if you wish to, but don't join the queue until you've purchased your ticket from no. 7 Piazza S. Giovanni (see above). I will not accompany you, being scared of heights, but you will be in good company. George Eliot climbed to the top in the 1860s and described the experience as 'a very sublime getting-upstairs' – she did, however, add that her muscles were 'much astonished'.

The Duomo and its dome

Along the S side of Piazza del Duomo are several cafés and restaurants, and, if you're doing this as a post-breakfast walk, now may be the time for some refreshment while we consider the Duomo and its dome – which is just what Arnolfo di Cambio and Filippo Brunelleschi appear still to be doing in the statues by Luigi Pampaloni (1830) set against the façade of a building between Piazza del Capitolo and Via dello Studio.

By the end of the 13th century the Cathedral of S. Reparata didn't match up to the magnificence of the structures at Siena and Pisa, so something had to be done to save Florentine face. Furthermore, S. Reparata was too obscure a saint for the proud republic. A new Duomo dedicated to the Virgin was decided on, and given the title S. Maria del Fiore, i.e. S. Mary of Florence, Fiorenza being the mediaeval form of the city's name. The great Arnolfo di Cambio (who had a good international C.V.) was appointed as capomaestro. He was also called to work on the Palazzo della Signoria (Walk 2), S. Croce (Walk 5) and the Badia (Walk 4). So grateful were the authorities for his input that in 1300 they exempted him from paying taxes for the rest of his life. Present day governments might like to take note of this method of rewarding service to the state – given the choice between no taxes for life or an OBE which would you choose? Whether the Florentine authorities had an actuary on hand is unknown, but Arnolfo died soon afterwards, so he didn't, alas, reap that much benefit! Building began at the W end, and the old Cathedral of S. Reparata (which continued in use until 1375) was gradually encased within the new walls. As is often the case with lengthy projects, changes to the original specification were introduced as work proceeded. If you look at the S flank of the Duomo you'll see a pink marble architrave running horizontally just above the tops of the windows. This marks the original height of Arnolfo's aisles. However, once the building works had progressed as far as the first window beyond (E of) the door near the Campanile, a decision was taken to raise the height of the nave and the aisles. This is why the windows E of this point are larger and taller than those towards the

W end. Great decorative gables were added to the windows and door near the Campanile, in order to disguise as far as possible the discrepancies in height and scale.

Not only S. Reparata, but an entire area of the mediaeval city lay between the W and E ends of the new Duomo. In 1357 orders were given for the demolition of all the houses still standing within the projected walls of the new building. In 1366 no less than three committees were set up to advise on where and how to terminate the nave. There was even a public referendum. From this time dates Andrea di Bonaiuto's fresco in the Chapter House at S. Maria Novella (Walk 7), which shows a domed octagon at the crossing, but without a drum. Towards the end of the 1370s, when construction of the nave and aisles had reached the final bay before the crossing, the 'Porta de' Canonici' ('Door of the Canons') was built. The Madonna and Child with two angels in the tympanum is one of Niccolò di Pietro Lamberti's masterpieces. During the final decades of the 14th century and the first years of the 15th the three huge tribunes were constructed, and by 1418 the drum was almost finished. The challenge of the dome couldn't be put off any longer. Competitions were held and Vasari describes some of the proposals put forward. One involved filling the

drum with earth and adding more and more soil as the dome was raised. Removal of the spoil afterwards was to be facilitated by dint of burying gold florins in the earth as an incentive for everyone to cart barrowfuls away! Both Ghiberti and Brunelleschi put forward proposals. They were eventually appointed jointly, but Brunelleschi gradually took on sole responsibility. He'd been to Rome with Donatello to study classical domes, especially that at the Pantheon, and he insisted that the dome at Florence could be built without centring. He kept his ideas secret and, of course, everybody thought he was mad. One story goes that he challenged his competitors to stand an egg upright with no support. Everyone tried and failed. Brunelleschi then took the egg and cracked it down so hard on to the surface that the base broke and it stood upright in its own white. When the others claimed that they too could have done that, he agreed, but said that they hadn't thought of it, and if he told them his ideas they'd all use them.

Brunelleschi's method depended on a system of interlocking brickwork, the bricks being laid herringbone fashion. Each course, once completed, functioned like a compression ring, locking so as to be self-supporting. To lighten the structure Brunelleschi in fact built two domes, an inner and an outer one, with the space between housing more than 450 steps up to the lantern. If you decide to ascend the cupola, this is the way you'll go and,

as with the Campanile, I'll wait for you at the bottom! The ribs were designed to converge at the top on a final ring, above which the weight of the lantern would hold the entire structure under compression. Brunelleschi threw himself at his project with gusto, designing special suspended scaffolding and new devices for lifting. He carved turnips to show the masons how to shape crucial elements of stonework, and had canteens set up on the scaffolding to avoid men having to waste time going up and down for meals. I've found no reference to latrines being installed – perhaps it wasn't wise to stand beneath the scaffolding! Motive power for lifting building materials was provided by animals turning capstans in what is now the choir. There was a slight hiccough in 1434 when Brunelleschi was thrown into jail on the orders of the Construction Workers' Guild for not having paid his matriculation fee. The powerful Cathedral Works Committee retaliated by having one of the guild consuls likewise thrown into jail for his cheek! The cupola was completed by 1436 when Pope Eugenius IV consecrated the new Duomo.

Believe it or not, Brunelleschi had to compete again for the design of the lantern. He got the commission in 1436 (Cosimo Il Vecchio de' Medici was one of the judges), but construction only started in 1446, one month before Brunelleschi's death. It's sad to think that he never saw it. Completion took another twenty-five years and involved, among others, Michelozzo, Bernardo Rossellino and Giuliano da Maiano. Verrocchio's bronze ball and cross were installed at the beginning of the 1470s, and the archives of the Opera del Duomo record a payment made to the state trumpeters when they played on the lantern on this occasion (they must have been a bit out of breath!). Vasari noted that the entire structure challenged the heavens and that heaven seemed envious, for it was continually being struck by lightning. Luca Landucci records such a strike in his *Diary* on the night of 5th April 1492,  when the lantern was split almost in half. One of the marble brackets fell and struck the church roof, breaking the vaulting in five places and ending up stuck in the pavement. Much marble fell outside too, badly damaging some houses on the N side of the Duomo, though nobody was injured. This was, literally, a bolt from the blue, for Luca says that there were no clouds, and no storms, and the weather was calm. You can understand why people regarded this as a portent when, a few days later, Lorenzo Il Magnifico died. At the end of the *Diary*, entries in a different hand (perhaps that of Luca's son) record further strikes in 1542 on 6th August, 18th September, 14th October and 22nd December (clearly a bad year). At the start of the 17th century the ball and cross had to be replaced after being knocked down by a thunderbolt. The spot where they crashed to the ground is marked by a white marble disc set into the paving of the piazza SE of the Duomo (see further below). Grand Duke Ferdinando I had holy relics set within the cross before putting it back up as protection against further strikes. You'll perhaps be relieved to know that it is now protected by a lightning conductor.

The 'Sasso di Dante' and the 'crickets' cage'

On the façade of a building between Via dello Studio and Piazza delle Pallottole a plaque marks the spot where stood the famous 'Sasso di Dante' ('Stone of Dante'). Here, according to tradition, the great poet sat and contemplated, doubtless watching the works on the embryonic new Duomo before he was exiled in 1302. Charles Dickens refers to the stone in his novel *Little Dorrit*, and Wordsworth was moved to sit on it, which inspired him to write a sonnet. If you wish to emulate Wordsworth, you'll have to pop round the corner into Piazza delle Pallottole, where you'll find the stone on the R side, it having been moved here to avoid blocking the pavement.

Continue along to the top of Via del Proconsolo at the extreme SE corner of Piazza del Duomo. From here you get a splendid view of the E end of the Cathedral and, immediately beneath the tiles of the dome, of the only section of arcade and balustrade around the upper drum ever to have been erected. Brunelleschi intended such a feature, but his design is lost. In 1507

a competition was held, in which Michelangelo took part. The winners were 'Il Cronaca' (nicknamed thus because he was apparently a walking chronicle of classical monuments), Giuliano da Sangallo and Baccio d' Agnolo, who'd submitted a joint model. However, Il Cronaca died in 1508 and Giuliano then resigned, leaving Baccio to continue on his own. Inaugurated in 1515, the arcade/balustrade attracted unfavourable criticism and work was halted. Michelangelo famously called it 'a cage for crickets' (sour grapes?) and submitted another design in 1516, but the scheme was abandoned and the brick drum still lacks a marble casing. In the pavement of the piazza, more or less in line with the arcaded section of the drum and the corner of Via del Proconsolo, is the white marble disc marking the spot where the ball and cross hit the ground at the beginning of the 17th century (see above).

The area around the E end of the Duomo

Walking from the SE corner of Piazza del Duomo around the E end of the Cathedral you'll pass the Museo dell' Opera del Duomo on your R. This magnificent museum, referred to many times already, is described at the end of the walk. Not far beyond it, on the near corner of Via de' Servi, was the site of Donatello's studio. The building is marked by a bust and inscription,

and is now occupied by a restaurant that perpetuates the great man's name. This whole area was rebuilt in the late 1300s once the ground plan of the Duomo was finalized, with the buildings following the line of the Cathedral's E end. The 14th century character of the ground floor façades can still be made out, with large arches called 'Forni', because many of them housed public bakeries. Beyond Via de' Servi several houses are adorned with coats-of-arms, including that of the Wool Guild, who held the patronage of the Duomo.

The N flank of the Duomo

Keep going anticlockwise round the Cathedral and you'll eventually come to the 'Porta della Mandorla' ('Door of the Almond'), where, at the time of writing, you gain access to the dome – but don't join the queue before you've bought your ticket at no. 7 Piazza S. Giovanni. If you want a sneaky preview of what you'll see from the top, visit the Museo dell' Opera del Duomo and see the audio-visual presentation!

The importance of the Porta della Mandorla in the history of art cannot be overstated, for it illustrates perfectly the transition from Late Gothic to Renaissance style. The beautiful late 14th century door frame, carved in relief with foliage and representations of Hercules engaged in his various labours, was the creation of several artists, including Piero di Giovanni Tedesco and Niccolò di Pietro Lamberti. The tympanum originally contained a statue group of the Annunciation, but this was replaced at the end of the 15th century with a mosaic of the same subject by the Ghirlandaio workshop. In the gable is a relief of the Assumption of the Virgin by Nanni di Banco (*c.* 1418-20), with Mary shown enthroned in an almond-shaped aureole, from which the door takes its name. Note the little bear cub climbing the tree at bottom R, just as on the relief of the Labours of Adam and Eve on the Campanile. What he signifies is uncertain, but he may represent the desert/wilderness.

High up to the L of the Porta della Mandorla, just under the balustrade running beneath the shell-topped niches of the N tribune, is the head of a horned bovid. Perhaps simply an affectionate tribute to the animals who worked the capstans and dragged the loads, there is, of course, a story attached to it. Legend has it that the mason responsible was the lover of the baker's wife and set this symbol of a cuckold right opposite the baker's house.

Move along the flank of the Duomo until you reach Via Ricasoli running off to the R. Turn up here for a few yards and look on your L for no. 3 blue. Here is the Teatro Niccolini, formerly called 'Teatro del Cocomero', founded in the mid-17th century and built in the Italian style with a horseshoe arrangement of boxes rising through several levels – it has recently

been restored. At the centre of the façade is an unusual crest, believed by many to be a water melon ('cocomero'). It is, however, not a water melon, but a bomb, symbol of the 'Accademia degli Infuocati' ('Academy of the Fiery Ones'), a drama academy founded in 1648, which had its seat here.

Retrace your steps back to the Duomo. The door opposite the end of Via Ricasoli is the 'Porta de' Leoni' ('Door of the Lions'), framed by columns supported on recumbent lions (the RH lion has a little putto to help him). Its history parallels that of the door near the Campanile on the S flank of the Duomo, with the great triangular gable being added to adapt the appearance of the door to the new increased height of the nave and aisles (see above). Giovanni Cavalcanti tells us, in his 15th century *Istorie Fiorentine*, of an unfortunate citizen who resided in Via Ricasoli and who was plagued by a recurrent nightmare in which he was devoured by a lion. Attempts to cure him of his consequent terror of all felines were in vain. Eventually

it was suggested that he should try inserting his hand into the mouth of the RH lion on the Porta de' Leoni. This he agreed to do and, accompanied by a crowd of well-wishers, he bravely stuck his hand between the lion's jaws. Alas, a scorpion was nestling there. It stung him and he died. And on that tragic note we end our walk.

The interior of the Duomo

Some people experience a feeling of disappointment on entering the Duomo for the first time. Having been dazzled by the exterior, they expect the interior to be equally dazzling, and it isn't. Awe-inspiring might be a better word. This vast, cavernous space always puts me in mind of a gigantic limestone cave, where stalactites and stalagmites have merged to form the huge piers with foliate capitals. Your awe, however, might well be tempered by the fact that you'll find yourself shuffling round the aisles among hordes of other tourists, with large areas of the nave and the E end roped off. I give below a description of the main treasures, taking you around the interior in a clockwise direction beginning at the W end of the N aisle, where the tourist entrance was at the time of writing.

<u>The N aisle and the W wall</u>

The design of the circular stained glass window high over the door at the W end of the N aisle, showing S. Lorenzo with angels, is by Ghiberti (early 15th century). Before you reach the first pillar of the nave, note, on the wall to your L, 19th century busts of Emilio de Fabris (who designed the present façade) and Arnolfo di Cambio (original architect of the Cathedral). Between these busts is a statue of Joshua, worked on by Bernardo Ciuffagni, Nanni di Bartolo and Donatello (who probably modelled the head). The statue is supposedly a portrait of Cosimo Il Vecchio's friend Poggio Bracciolini. On the first pillar between the N aisle and the nave hangs a late 14th century painting by Giovanni del Biondo showing S. Zenobius (the frame is 19th century).

Turn round at this point to get a view of the counter-façade of the W wall. It is dominated by the monumental clock (mid-15th century), the face of which was frescoed by Paolo Uccello. In the four quadrants are painted the heads of the four Evangelists. The clockface has a single hand and is divided into twenty-four hours running anticlockwise. The clock uses the *hora italica* system of counting the hours, the last hour of the day (XXIIII) ending at sunset, a system used in Italy until the 18th century. The design of the circular stained glass window high above, showing Our Lady of the Assumption, is by Ghiberti (early 15th century). The mosaic in the lunette over the portal, showing the Coronation of the Virgin, is attributed to Gaddo Gaddi (early 14th century), with the flanking angel musicians by Santi di Tito (16th century). Mounted on the wall to the R of the main W door is the early 14th century tomb of Bishop Antonio d' Orso, by Tino di Camaino.

Continuing along the N aisle, you pass the Porta de' Leoni. Just beyond it is a bust of Antonio Squarcialupi, the Cathedral organist, from the workshop of Benedetto da Maiano (1490). The Latin epigraph beneath the bust, believed to have been written by Poliziano and/or Lorenzo Il Magnifico, tells how Squarcialupi unified inspiration and technique so that the Graces called upon Music as their fourth sister. Next to the bust is Andrea del Castagno's monumental fresco of Niccolò da Tolentino on horseback (1456). He was general of the Florentine army and, in 1432, beat the Sienese at the Battle of S. Romano. We come next to Uccello's monumental fresco of Sir John Hawkwood on horseback (1436). Hawkwood, an English condottiere, was a commander of the Florentine army until his death in 1394. Uccello's fresco, painted in monochrome *terra verde* to simulate a statue of bronze, has more than one vanishing point, with the knight and his horse shown on a plane parallel to the floor, and the sarcophagus and base depicted as receding upwards from below. E. V. Lucas relates an amusing anecdote about Sir John Hawkwood in his early 20th century guide entitled *A Wanderer in Florence*. On being beset by mendicant friars who prefaced their pleas with 'God give you peace', Hawkwood answered 'God take away your alms'. When the friars protested, Hawkwood told them that peace was the last thing he wanted, since, if it came, he would be out of a job and go hungry!

Just beyond the Hawkwood memorial is a statue of King David by Bernardo Ciuffagni (15th century), originally executed, like many of the other statues displayed in the aisles, for the old façade. The design of the stained glass window above, showing six saints, is by Agnolo Gaddi (late 14th century). Just prior to reaching the Porta della Mandorla at the end of the N aisle, another window designed by Gaddi (again with six saints) has beneath it a painting showing Dante holding open his *Divine Comedy*, with a wonderful view of Florence. The painting, by Domenico di Michelino, was commissioned in 1465 to commemorate the second centenary of Dante's birth. Hell (Inferno) is shown to the L and the Mount of Purgatory behind. Florence on the R represents Paradise, the new Jerusalem.

The E end
The N tribune (tribune of the Holy Cross)

The designs of the stained glass windows in the tribunes round the E end of the Duomo are by Ghiberti. On the floor of the N tribune is a calibrated meridian line installed by Leonardo Ximenes in 1754, which worked in conjunction with a small gnomonic opening (just 5cm in diameter) installed in 1475 by Brunelleschi's friend Paolo dal Pozzo Toscanelli in the lantern of the cupola. The gnomon pinpointed the exact moment of the summer solstice, when the sun's rays fell on a marble disc set into the pavement on the N side of the tribune. The later meridian line was used to measure variations in the curving of the ecliptic. The church had a vested interest in promoting such scientific enquiry, for meridians could be used to establish the dates of movable feasts such as Easter. Other highlights of the N tribune include altarpieces by Giotto and his workshop (*c.* 1305), Lorenzo di Credi and Bicci di Lorenzo (15th century). There is a marble altar (1447) by Andrea Cavalcanti (adopted son of Brunelleschi), and statues of S. Thomas (1580) and S. Andrew (1515) by Vincenzo de' Rossi and Andrea Ferrucci respectively, housed, like the other statues surrounding the crossing, in marble niches designed by Bartolommeo Ammannati in 1589 for the wedding of Grand Duke Ferdinando I and Christine of Lorraine.

The N sacristy and the E tribune (tribune of S. Zenobius)

The N sacristy lies between the N and E tribunes. It was here that Lorenzo Il Magnifico and his supporters retreated following the murder of his brother Giuliano during the Pazzi conspiracy of 1478 (see the section on the conspiracy at the end of Walk 8). The mid-15th century bronze doors are by Luca della Robbia and Michelozzo (Luca's only known work in bronze), and the glazed terracotta lunette depicting the Resurrection is also by Luca. His stunning 'cantoria' ('singing gallery'), which once surmounted the doors here, is now in the Museo dell' Opera del Duomo. To the L and R of the doors are inscriptions commemorating the consecration of the Cathedral in 1436 and the famous Council of Florence in 1439 respectively. The former relates how a magnificent raised wooden walkway was built from Santa Maria Novella (where Pope Eugenius IV was staying) to the Duomo to enable the pontiff and his train to pass through the crowds. If you are lucky enough to gain entry to the sacristy, with its magnificent 15th century intarsia woodwork by a variety of masters, you'll see works by, among others, Mino da Fiesole, Giuliano da Maiano and Andrea Cavalcanti.

The highlights of the E tribune include statues of S. Peter (1515-17) and S. John the Evangelist (1513-14) by Baccio Bandinelli and Benedetto da Rovezzano respectively, and the bronze casket of S. Zenobius by Ghiberti

(1442). The frontal relief on the sarcophagus shows the miracle of the boy brought back to life (see also Walk 5). The candleholders with angels in terracotta are by Luca della Robbia (1450).

The S sacristy and the S tribune (tribune of the Holy Conception)

The S sacristy lies between the E and S tribunes. The glazed terracotta lunette depicting the Ascension is by Luca della Robbia. Donatello's wonderful cantoria, which once surmounted the entrance, is now in the Museo dell' Opera del Duomo. To the L and R of the doors are inscriptions commemorating, respectively, the start of construction work on the Cathedral at the end of the 13th century and the relocation of the body of S. Zenobius to S. Reparata in the 5th century. The latter refers to the miracle of the dead elm (see Walk 1 above).

The highlights of the S tribune include statues of S. James the Younger (1576) and S. Philip (1577) by Giovanni Bandini, 15th century frescoes by Rossello di Jacopo Franchi, Bicci di Lorenzo and Lippo d' Andrea, and a Michelozzian altar containing relics of S. Reparata and other saints.

The central crossing

Beneath the crossing, the octagonal choir was adorned with eighty-eight bas-relief marble panels executed in the mid-16th century by Baccio Bandinelli. Twenty-four of these lovely reliefs, displaced by alterations to the structure in the mid-19th century, can now be seen in the Museo dell' Opera del Duomo. The wooden Crucifix by Benedetto da Maiano (late 15th century) was painted by Lorenzo di Credi in 1510. The area around the choir was paved with marble in the 1520s following a design created earlier by Il Cronaca. Above the choir, the great cupola is covered in frescoes by Giorgio Vasari and Federico Zuccari showing the Last Judgement and Final Triumph of the Church. Brunelleschi had wanted the inside of his cupola adorned with mosaics, mirroring the Baptistery, but this idea was never followed through. Vasari began work on the frescoes in 1572, but died in 1574. Zuccari took over in 1576 and completed the project in 1579.

The stained glass windows of the Duomo are among its chief glories, and the roundels in the drum beneath the cupola are, quite literally, the jewels in the crown. They are difficult to see and appreciate properly from ground level, but you will get a better view of them if you ascend the dome. For those of you who, like myself, have no intention of doing this, do not despair. The Museo dell' Opera del Duomo has an exceptionally good display showing the windows in projection. Uccello designed the Nativity, Resurrection and Annunciation (this last was destroyed during a storm in the 19th century), Ghiberti was responsible for the Presentation at the Temple, the Agony in the Garden and the Ascension, while the designs for the Deposition and the Coronation of the Virgin were done by Andrea del Castagno and Donatello.

If you stand with your back to the crossing, you will get a view along the nave, with its 16th century inlaid marble pavement designed by Baccio d' Agnolo, Giuliano Francesco da Sangallo and others. Against the piers at the E end of the nave are statues of S. James the Elder by Jacopo Sansovino (1511-17; N pier) and S. Matthew by Vincenzo de' Rossi (1580; S pier).

The S aisle

To the R (W of) the Porta de' Canonici is a bust of Marsilio Ficino by Andrea Ferrucci (1521). The stained glass window above, showing six saints, was designed by Agnolo Gaddi (1394). Another such window by Gaddi lies beyond this, above the statue of a prophet by Bernardo Ciuffagni. To the L of this statue is a funerary fresco commemorating Cardinal Pietro Corsini by Giovanni dal Ponte (1422). To the R of the statue is a similar fresco for Luigi Marsili by Bicci di Lorenzo and Neri di Bicci (1439). The W end of the aisle, beyond the door leading out to the Campanile, may well be roped off, in which case you will have to crane your neck. Here is a bust of Giotto by Benedetto da Maiano (1490) with an inscription beneath by Poliziano referring to Giotto bringing back to life the art of painting. Next to this is a statue of a prophet by Nanni di Banco (1408). Beyond this, the bust of Brunelleschi (1446) was modelled from the funeral mask by his adopted son, Andrea Cavalcanti. The inscription beneath, by Carlo Marsuppini, refers to the decision to honour Brunelleschi by allowing him burial within the Duomo (his tomb lies directly beneath, in the crypt). The circular stained glass window high over the door at the W end of the aisle was designed by Ghiberti (early 15th century). To the L of the main W door is a sarcophagus, but nobody is quite sure who lies buried within.

The crypt

The entrance to the crypt lies between the first and second pillars of the S aisle. Entry is not free, but tickets can be obtained here if you haven't already purchased them (see the tips at the beginning of Walk 1). In the crypt you'll see the remains of the ancient Cathedral of S. Reparata, including a very fine mosaic pavement. Here too is the tomb of Giovanni de' Medici (mid-14th century), along with his sword and spurs, many more tomb-slabs, and the tomb of Brunelleschi. Everything is beautifully laid out and well presented, with full and informative labelling in Italian and English.

Detail of the S flank of the Duomo

The interior of the Baptistery

If, on entering this stunning octagonal interior, you can bear to tear your eyes away from the mosaics in the dome, look first at the walls. The mainly bichrome confection of geometric designs and Romanesque motifs is particularly intricate in the gallery, with its graceful bifore arcading. The huge monolithic columns set around the lower walls come from a Roman structure. There is gold everywhere, on the Corinthian capitals that grace the columns and fluted pilasters, and behind the saints, patriarchs and prophets who gaze down from the friezes around the bases of the gallery and dome. More such figures decorate the arch of the apse and surround the 13th century mosaic of the *Agnus Dei* flanked by the Virgin and S. John the Baptist over the altar. The candelabrum to the R of the altar is 14th century.

To the L of the apse is a 17th century statue of S. John the Baptist by Giuseppe Piamontini, along with two Roman sarcophagi reused as tombs. One sarcophagus houses the remains of Guccio de' Medici (d. 1299), the other the remains of Bishop Giovanni da Velletri (d. 1230). To the R of the apse are two more tombs. The one nearest to the apse is that of Ranieri, Bishop of Florence from 1071-1113. The other, set cleverly between two of the Roman columns, is the tomb of Baldassare Cossa, who, in 1410, was elected pope by the Council of Pisa and took the name John XXIII. In 1413 Giovanni di Bicci (father of Cosimo Il Vecchio de' Medici) became the papal banker, which was good for business. He apparently received a precious mitre as a pawn for money loaned to Pope John, a pawn that was eventually redeemed by Pope Martin V in 1419. In 1415 John was deposed by the Council of Constance. He came to Florence, died in 1419, and was given a state funeral. In his will he left bequests to several of the city's charitable foundations and gave the right index finger of John the Baptist to the Baptistery. One of his executors was Giovanni, whose son Cosimo assumed responsibility for his aging father in negotiations for the construction of the tomb, designed and built during the 1420s by Donatello and Michelozzo. The coats-of-arms above the statues of the three theological virtues include those of the papacy, while the inscription on the sarcophagus refers to John XXIII *quodam papa* 'at one time pope'. The new pope, Martin V, was annoyed by this and asked for the inscription to be changed, a request that was politely ignored.

Now turn your attention to the magnificent 13th century mosaic pavement in *opus tessellatum*. With its fantastic geometric patterns, Romanesque motifs and signs of the Zodiac, it resembles a series of rich Eastern carpets laid side by side. The Zodiac originally lay just inside the N entrance and formed part of a solar clock, but it was moved nearer to the E entrance in the 13th century when the pavement was relaid. The sun at its centre is surrounded by a Latin palindrome which reads *en giro torte sol ciclos et rotor igne* 'I, the sun, turn the spheres and am encircled by fire'. There was originally a font, mentioned by Dante (*Inferno* XIX.16-20), in a large octagonal enclosure in the centre of the Baptistery, but it was removed in 1576 as part of an overhaul of the building for the baptism of Filippo de' Medici, first son of Grand Duke Francesco I and Joanna of Austria. Fragments from Dante's 'greater font' are preserved in the Museo dell' Opera del Duomo. The 'lesser font', installed *c.* 1370, can still be seen on the SE side of the building. Its beautiful marble reliefs are attributed to the school of Andrea Pisano.

Now look up to the dome, which has a span of *c.* 26m and a height of *c.* 34m, an impressive structure for its date. It is adorned with 13th century mosaics. At the very top, ornamental motifs and angels surround the base of the lantern. Below this, the section over the apse and the sections to each side of it are taken up with the Last Judgement. Christ is flanked by angels and saints, and beneath his feet the resurrected dead clamber out of their graves. Angels guide the blessed to Christ's R, while on the other side the damned are hustled to hell to be tormented by demons and devoured by the Devil. The remaining sections of the dome are divided into four continuous bands showing, from top to bottom, the stories of Genesis, Joseph, and the lives of Christ and John the Baptist. The sequences of events run clockwise.

Genesis scenes: the creation of heaven and earth, the creation of Adam and the creation of Eve; the temptation of Adam and Eve, Adam and Eve are reproached by God, the expulsion from Eden; the labours of Adam and Eve, Cain and Abel make sacrifices, God reproaches Cain for the murder of Abel; Lamech kills Cain, God orders Noah to build the ark, construction of the ark; the animals enter the ark, the flood.

Joseph scenes: Joseph's dream, Joseph tells his parents about his dream, Joseph joins his brothers; Joseph is sold by his brothers, they tell Jacob that Joseph is dead, Joseph is taken by the merchants to Egypt; Joseph is sold to Potiphar, Potiphar's wife accuses Joseph, Joseph in prison; Pharaoh's dream, Joseph interprets Pharaoh's dream, Joseph is appointed as vizier of Egypt; Joseph makes his brothers empty their sacks, Joseph makes himself known to his brothers, Joseph welcomes Jacob to Egypt.

Scenes from the life of Christ: the Annunciation, the Visitation, the Nativity; the Adoration of the Magi, the dream of the Magi, the Magi return home (don't miss the fish and the dinky little octopus here); the Presentation in the Temple, the dream of Joseph, the Flight into Egypt; the Massacre of the Innocents, the Last Supper, the Betrayal; the Crucifixion, the Deposition, the women at the tomb.

Scenes from the life of S. John: the Annunciation to Zechariah, the birth and naming of John, John retreats into the desert; John preaches to the crowds, John baptizes the crowds, John announces the coming of Christ; the Baptism of Christ, John reproaches Herod, John in prison; John sends his disciples to Christ, the disciples with Christ, the dance of Salome; the beheading of John, Salome presents the head of John, the burial of John. The designs of some of the John scenes have been attributed to Cimabue.

The Museo dell' Opera del Duomo

This stunning museum, which takes its name from a municipal institution founded at the end of the 13th century, contains material from, and relevant to, the Duomo, the Baptistery and the Campanile. There are architectural fragments, sculpted stones, reliefs and statuary, works that have, through the ages, graced these magnificent buildings, including pieces by Arnolfo di Cambio and his workshop, Tino di Camaino, Andrea Pisano, Talenti, Niccolò di Pietro Lamberti, Bernardo Ciuffagni, Nanni di Banco, Donatello and others. Here you will find all the original reliefs and statues that adorned the Campanile, along with sculptures from the original façade of the Duomo, of which there is an impressive mock-up. There are paintings by, among others, Bernardo Daddi, Giovanni del Biondo, Lorenzo di Bicci and Jacopo di Cione. There are crosses, reliquaries, vestments, missals, drawings, designs, plans, documentation for and models of the successive proposed façades and the cupola and its lantern. There are good audio-visual presentations explaining the construction of the cupola and showing the stained glass windows of the drum. The museum also has a collection of apparatus and implements used during construction works, including some of Brunelleschi's brick moulds. His funeral mask is here too. Here also are Luca della Robbia's and Donatello's exuberant cantorie, which once surmounted the sacristy doors in the Duomo. The museum houses many of Bandinelli's lovely marble bas-relief panels from the octagonal choir, along with Donatello's astonishing wooden statue of S. Mary Magdalene, Michelangelo's Pietà (intended for his own tomb), and the priceless silver-gilt altar frontal from the Baptistery (commissioned by the Calimala Guild in the mid-14th century and finished in the late 15th century with reliefs by Antonio del Pollaiuolo and Verrocchio). Last but not least, the museum has the three sets of bronze doors from the Baptistery. All of the above exhibits are beautifully displayed, making this museum a must-see. I advise you to purchase the highly informative and lavishly illustrated guide, which will help you to understand what you are looking at and set it in context.

Detail of the inlay on the Baptistery

Walk 2

Begins and ends at Piazza della Signoria.

Takes in: the Palazzo Vecchio, the Gucci Museum, the Loggia de' Lanzi and the Uffizi Gallery.

Duration: 2 hours, including the Loggia de' Lanzi but excluding visits to the Palazzo Vecchio, the Gucci Museum and the Uffizi Gallery. You should allow *c.* 2 hours for a visit to the Palazzo and *c.* 3 hours for the Uffizi Gallery (not including queuing time). The Gucci Museum can be done in 30 minutes.

Tips: Piazza della Signoria gets incredibly crowded, so my advice is the same as for Walk 1 – rise with the lark and do Walk 2 before breakfast. You can return to visit the Palazzo Vecchio and the Uffizi Gallery on another occasion (they are described at the end of the walk). Wrap up warm because, even in summer, early morning breezes can be chill. As this walk involves quite a bit of reading, rising early has the additional advantage that you can utilize the deserted chairs of the cafés in the piazza without having to pay through the nose for refreshments!

The building history of Piazza della Signoria and the Palazzo Vecchio

Towards the end of the 13th century, the Guelf government of the Secondo Popolo decided that its officials needed better, more imposing (and safer) accommodation than that offered by the Torre della Castagna (Walk 4), and work on the 'Palazzo de' Priori' ('Palace of the Priors'), as it was then

called, was put in train. The site chosen was highly symbolic. The century had been dominated by the bitter struggles between Guelfs and Ghibellines (see historical summary), and each faction, when in power, demolished the properties of its opponents. The Guelfs of the Primo Popolo had, in 1258, demolished the houses and towers belonging to the Uberti, a powerful Ghibelline clan, and had created a piazza on the site to ensure that they could never be rebuilt. Farinata degli Uberti had subsequently commanded the victorious Ghibelline forces at the battle of Montaperti in 1260, a victory which had toppled the Primo Popolo, so for the Secondo Popolo

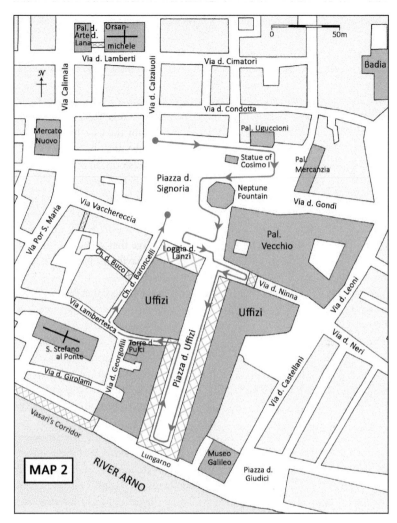

regide a double dose of opprobrium was attached to the family name. The
piazza occupying the site of the former Uberti houses was that portion of
Piazza della Signoria now behind (E of) the Neptune fountain and the
bronze equestrian statue of Cosimo I. For convenience, let us call this bit
'Uberti Square'. In 1294 the officials of the Secondo Popolo decided that
their new government palace should front this square, though they were
adamant that no part of the building should actually overlie former Uberti
land. We must remember, at this point, that the N façade of the palace was
originally the main one, not the W. Indeed, at this date, the W portion of

Piazza della Signoria didn't exist, the site still being occupied by houses and by the two churches of S. Romolo and S. Cecilia.

The design of the palace is traditionally attributed to Arnolfo di Cambio (also capomaestro at the Duomo), and, although the interior of the building subsequently underwent many changes, the external façades have remained virtually unchanged. The necessary land was purchased and building work began in 1299. The pre-existing Torre de' Foraboschi was incorporated into

the new palace, its base acting as the foundation for the great new bell-tower, the tallest in Florence (87m high). The presence of the pre-existing tower is disguised by the blind windows on the W façade. Above these, the building corbels out, and the W face of the tower is flush with the corbelled crenellations. The tower thus emphasizes its presence while at the same time denying its own mass. Near the top there are further corbels, and the tower is crowned by the belfry which housed the bell that summoned the citizens in times of crisis (smashed in 1532 by Duke Alessandro).

Cosimo Il Vecchio and Savonarola were both imprisoned in this tower.

Beneath the corbels on the W façade and extending round on to the N and S faces, can be seen a row of shields bearing emblems relating to the Republic. Nine emblems are depicted, with the series repeating itself. The gold *fleurs-de-lys* on a blue ground, which occur on the two shields on the N face, are probably a tribute to the French royal house of Anjou, allies of the Guelfs against the Ghibellines. On the extreme L of the W face is the flag of the people, a red cross on a white ground. Next comes a red lily on a white ground. The standard of the Republic originally bore a white lily on a red ground, but the Guelfs, when they wrested power back from the Ghibellines and established the Secondo Popolo, substituted a red lily for the white one. The half red/half white shield is the flag of the joint communes of Florence and Fiesole, and the crossed keys the flag of the church. The shield with a blue ground bearing the word 'libertas' is the flag of the priors, while the red eagle clutching a green dragon on a white ground is the emblem of the Guelf party. Next comes a white lily on a red ground, the original standard of the Republic (see above). At this point the series begins again (see page 100 for an illustration of seven of these emblems).

Pity poor Pitti

Like the cupola of the Duomo (Walk 1), the tower of the Palazzo Vecchio was often struck by lightning. Spare a thought at this point for Buonaccorso Pitti, who, on 11th November 1391, was at the palace when lightning struck the tower and grounded near him. He describes the incident in his *Diary*, saying that the fire touched the calves of his legs and that when he tried to stand up he collapsed. He was paralysed from the knees down and his legs felt as though they were on fire. His colleagues removed his stockings, which stank of sulphur, and it was discovered that all the flesh of his legs was covered with weals, the skin bleeding and the hairs singed. Even so, a mere half an hour later, he was able to move his legs, put on another pair of stockings and walk home. Just as well, for the poor chap was getting married the next day to the daughter of Luca di Piero degli Albizi.

As noted above, the N façade of the palace, overlooking 'Uberti Square', was the main one. The original façade here was that portion surmounted by the corbelled crenellations. The N portal, placed symmetrically in the centre of this façade, led directly into the 'Sala d' Armi', a vaulted hall giving access to a courtyard behind, from which stairs led up to the halls above. Nowadays, visitors do not enter via this door, but by one further to the E leading directly into the 'Dogana' ('Customs Hall'), off which lie the ticket office, information centre, cloakrooms, bookshop and café. This eastward extension of the palace was not begun until the 1340s, while the W portal, which leads directly into the courtyard behind the Sala d' Armi and thence through to the Dogana, was not opened up until 1380. Thereafter, the internal layout of the building underwent many alterations.

The Palazzo de' Priori was ready for occupation in just three years (the priors moved in in 1302), though work continued on the building until 1315. In 1304 and 1306 additional funds were allocated for paving the piazza, and in 1319 more properties to the W were acquired to allow expansion in this direction. In 1323 the 'ringhiera' was added, an L-shaped raised platform running round the exterior of the palace and used for civic ceremonies. The 1330s saw more repaving, but civic aspirations were almost thwarted in the early 1340s by the Duke of Athens, who had been invited to Florence to manage affairs, but who decided instead to make himself dictator. He seized the properties of citizens living around the piazza as lodgings for his troops, and planned to build a wall around the palace for his additional security. To this end, he had houses belonging to the church of S. Romolo (which still stood on the W side of 'Uberti Square') demolished, and he petitioned the pope for permission to demolish both this church and those of S. Cecilia (further W still) and S. Pier Scheraggio (immediately S of the palace). The pope refused permission, and, anyway, the hated Duke was ousted in 1343.

In the wake of all the high-handedness on the part of the Duke of Athens, it comes as no surprise that subsequent plans for the enlargement of the piazza were not popular with the citizens. Public feeling was running so high that the government eventually resorted to desperate measures. On the night of 20th November 1356, the church of S. Romolo and all its remaining properties were demolished without warning – and with no papal permission! 'Uberti Square' and the area to its W were now joined. The same priorate also approved the construction of the Loggia de' Priori, subsequently known as the Loggia della Signoria and Loggia de' Lanzi, though building didn't actually begin until the 1380s. We'll discuss the loggia further when we go over to look at the statues therein. In 1386 the oligarchic government of the Popolo Grasso emulated their 1356 forebears, and had houses and buildings associated with the church of S. Cecilia summarily demolished. Thus was the present piazza formed, and its nomenclature underwent transformation too - 'Priori' and 'Popolo' were now replaced by 'Signoria'. The piazza was repaved and Via de' Calzaiuoli was widened, its buildings aligned and their façades regulated to provide a suitably impressive civic thoroughfare linking Piazza della Signoria, Orsanmichele and the Duomo.

In 1494, following the expulsion of the Medici, a new legislative

body, the Great Council, was formed, and work was put in train at the Palazzo della Signoria to construct a hall large enough to accommodate this new organ of government. The result was Il Cronaca's vast 'Sala del Maggior Consiglio' ('Room of the Great Council'), now known as the 'Sala de' Cinquecento' ('Room of the 500'). So huge was the new hall that it had to be built in an annexe to the E of the existing palace. It was later used as an audience chamber and ballroom by the Grand Dukes, and underwent many modifications. Evidence of these changes can still be seen on the N façade of the palace immediately to the L of the door leading into the Dogana. The three large round-headed windows at the top of this section of the façade were added when the roof was raised in the 1560s. Below them can be seen an assortment of filled window frames, including a beautifully dressed arch with a pointed profile and, above it, an oculus, remnants of Il Cronaca's original Sala del Maggior Consiglio.

In 1540, Duke Cosimo I and his family moved from the Medici Palace (Walk 8) into the Palazzo della Signoria. The seat of the ruler and the seat of government now became one, underlining the point that Cosimo *was* now the government, in case anyone was still in doubt! The palace was extended further to the E, along the flank of Via de' Gondi, and a positive army of artists and craftsmen moved in to transform Palazzo della Signoria into Palazzo Ducale. Later, the area to the S, between the palace and the Arno, was also cleared, but we'll come on to that later, when we walk round to that side. For the moment, let's stay put in 'Uberti Square' and consider briefly its other buildings and monuments.

The Palazzo Mercanzia (the Gucci Museum) and the Palazzo Uguccioni
On the E side of the piazza stands the Palazzo Mercanzia, now home to the Gucci Museum, a collection of creations by the famous design house – a few stunning dresses and many more handbags and suitcases. I seem to remember the air-conditioning here being extremely efficient – you may need to put on an extra layer. The 'Tribunale di Mercanzia' ('Merchants' Tribunal') was founded in 1309 to adjudicate guild matters, and established itself in this building in 1359. We'll learn more about the guilds when we visit Orsanmichele (Walk 3). On the façade of the palace are the coats-of-arms of the guilds (some of them very worn).

On the N side of the square lies Palazzo Uguccioni (nothing to do with Gucci despite the similarity of names). The building was commissioned by Giovanni Uguccioni, who had risen to prominence in the service of Cosimo I, in 1550. The façade of the palace, with its pairs of twinned Ionic and Corinthian half-columns, was set forward from the adjacent buildings and the neighbours objected vociferously, but Cosimo overruled all objections. The pride that the Uguccioni felt on basking in ducal favour was advertised by the bust of Francesco I (by Giovanni dell' Opera) above the portal.

The statue of Cosimo I and the Neptune Fountain

The bronze equestrian statue of Cosimo I was commissioned from Giambologna in 1587 by Ferdinando I. The reliefs on the base show important incidents in Cosimo's life. Cast in 1591 and placed here in 1595, the statue was the first permanent equestrian monument erected in Florence, though not the first mooted. In the 1540s the staunchly republican Michelangelo had offered to create and erect in the Piazza della Signoria, at his own expense, an equestrian statue of Francis I, the French king, if Francis would drive out the Medici and restore the Florentine republic.

Moving back into the main part of the piazza, let us next consider the Neptune Fountain. Large decorated public fountains were unknown in Florence before the time of Cosimo I. He intended Baccio Bandinelli to have the commission, which didn't please Benvenuto Cellini one little bit (there was no love at all lost between the two sculptors). Near the end of his highly entertaining autobiography, Cellini tells how he tried to talk Cosimo into holding a competition for the fountain, rather than simply giving the commission to Bandinelli. He was motivated, he says, not by envy, but by pity for the poor, unfortunate marble destined for the figure of Neptune. While the matter was still in the balance, Bandinelli died, and Bartolommeo Ammannati was then given the commission instead. In 1565 part of the 'ringhiera' platform was demolished and the fountain installed, the water for it being piped across the Ponte alle Grazie from a spring near the Torre S. Niccolò (Walk 14). In the bronze groups, Ammannati was assisted by Giambologna and his workshop.

Behind the fountain, on the W façade of the Palazzo Vecchio close to the corner, is a plaque bearing an inscription dated to July 1720, which reconfirms a decree issued in the 1640s by the 'Otto Signori di Guardia e Balia', a magistracy of eight officials who were in charge of law and order. We'll come across several of their decrees on other walks. This one expressly forbids any person, of whatever state, degree or condition, to do anything dirty within 20 braccia (*c.* 11m) of the fountain, under penalty of four ducats. In addition to the obvious, dirty acts that are specified include the washing of clothes, the rinsing out of inkpots, and the dumping of wood or other rubbish and filth. In front of the Neptune Fountain, a porphyry disc set into the pavement of the piazza marks the spot where, in May 1498, Savonarola and two of his colleagues were hanged and burned (see further Walk 8).

The sculptures along the W façade of the Palazzo Vecchio

Along the W façade of the Palazzo Vecchio are several sculptures. First come copies of Donatello's Marzocco lion (an emblem of the Republic; original in the Bargello (Walk 9)) and Judith and Holofernes (original inside the palace). The latter was moved to the Piazza della Signoria from the Medici Palace following the expulsion of the Medici in 1494, and became a symbol of the victory of republicanism over tyranny. Next, flanking the W door of the palace, come Michelangelo's David (this is a copy; the original is in the Accademia (Walk 8)) and Bandinelli's group of Hercules and Cacus.

Michelangelo's David

In the early 1460s, Agostino di Duccio (or Donatello according to some) was commissioned by the Operai del Duomo to carve a marble statue of David for the Cathedral. He went to Carrara and, in order to lighten the load for the homeward journey, partly blocked out the figure at the quarries, roughing out the torso and removing the stone between the legs. The blocked-out statue reached the headquarters of the Opera del Duomo safely, but the project foundered and the stone lay abandoned for years. In the spring of 1501, while he was in Rome, Michelangelo received news that it was to be offered as a commission once more. He returned to Florence, for he had long coveted this marble and his was not the only name in the hat. Other artists were being considered, Leonardo da Vinci, for example, and Andrea Sansovino. The latter had assured the Operai that, by adding on pieces of marble, he could produce a suitable statue. Perhaps Michelangelo won the commission by going one up on this, promising to produce a statue from the block as it was. It appears that Duccio's statue was to have been clothed. Perhaps the only way to find sufficient marble for a new figure in the partially worked block was to take David's clothes off.

Michelangelo began work in September 1501 in the courtyard of the Opera del Duomo (at the site of the present museum; Walk 1). As the work progressed, the original idea of placing the statue high up on the exterior of the Cathedral was dropped. This change of plan may have been linked to a change in the city's political life which occurred in autumn 1502, when it was decided that the Gonfaloniere should be elected for life and live in the Palazzo della Signoria, just like the Venetian Doge in his palace. On 25th January 1504 the Operai del Duomo convened a meeting to discuss and advise on a location for the statue. Those present included Giuliano da Sangallo, Filippino Lippi, Sandro Botticelli, Perugino and Leonardo da Vinci. Several proposals were put forward, including outside the main door of the Duomo, under the Loggia della Signoria (later Loggia de' Lanzi), and inside or outside the Palazzo della Signoria. No overall decision was reached, but the Duomo had clearly been ruled out, because in April Michelangelo was instructed to move his statue to the Piazza della Signoria.

The statue was suspended by ropes from a wooden framework which was eased along on a surface of greased wooden beams. More than forty men were needed to pull it, and part of the wall above the entrance to the Opera del Duomo had to be demolished to get it out. On 14th May, the David emerged into the streets of Florence, and four days later arrived in the piazza. He received a mixed response. Some youths even threw stones at him and were promptly imprisoned. The decision was eventually made to place him next to the entrance to the palace, but his nakedness was deemed too shocking and he was provided with some gilded leaves, which is how he remained for centuries. In 1527, during the anti-Medicean insurrection known as the 'Friday Rebellion', one of his arms was broken in two places. Vasari and a friend gathered up the fragments and saved them until the statue could be restored. In 1873, the David was moved to the Accademia and housed in a tribune specially designed for him by Emilio de Fabris.

Bandinelli's Hercules and Cacus

In 1525, a colossal block of marble was quarried at Carrara, intended for a statue of Hercules as a pendant to Michelangelo's David. Sketches reveal that Michelangelo was thinking of a group showing Hercules wrestling with Antaeus. However, another sculptor wanted this commission. Baccio Bandinelli was making models of Hercules fighting with Cacus. Bandinelli was a Medici loyalist and had managed to curry favour with Pope Clement VII. He got the commission, perhaps because Clement didn't, at that juncture, want Michelangelo distracted from his current projects in the Library and New Sacristy at S. Lorenzo (Walk 6).

On the final day of the journey from Carrara, while it was being transferred from barge to ox-cart, the marble fell into the Arno and sank into the sand, necessitating a salvage operation. When news broke that Bandinelli had been given the commission, there was general outrage, and one wag suggested that the marble had thrown itself into the river in despair. To mollify Michelangelo, Clement suggested that, instead, he should sculpt a statue for the corner of Piazza S. Lorenzo. The artist's none-too-happy response to this offer is given under Walk 6 in the section entitled 'Michelangelo's mighty temper'.

After the fall of the Medici regime in 1527, Bandinelli absented himself from Florence and the republican government offered the marble to Michelangelo, but he never worked seriously on it. Perhaps he was too busy building fortifications (see Walks 14 and 15). Three years later the Medici were reinstated and Bandinelli returned to reclaim his block. His Hercules and Cacus was installed, to general criticism, in 1534. Cellini claims in his autobiography that he told Bandinelli, in front of Cosimo I, that if Hercules' hair were shaved off, there'd not be enough space for his brains, that his shoulders looked like saddle pommels and his muscles like sacks of melons, and that it was impossible to tell which leg he was standing on.

Before moving on to the Loggia de' Lanzi and its sculptures, look behind the Hercules and Cacus group near the RH corner of the Palazzo Vecchio. Here, roughly 3-4ft above the top of the 'ringhiera' platform, you'll see a graffito of a head in profile scratched into the fabric of the palace façade. Who was responsible, and whom it represents, are unknown, though one legend says that it was a debtor of Michelangelo's, carved by the great man himself – I'm not sure that I believe this.

The Loggia de' Lanzi

As noted earlier, construction of the Loggia de' Lanzi (originally called the Loggia de' Priori and then the Loggia della Signoria) was approved in 1356,

though work didn't start until the 1380s. Much of the building's architecture, variously attributed to Orcagna, Benci di Cione and Simone Talenti, recalls that of the Duomo. The statues of the Virtues, set against blue backgrounds in the spandrels of the arches, were designed by Agnolo Gaddi. Originally a platform for civic ceremonies, the loggia was later used by the 'Lanzichenecchi', the ducal bodyguards; hence the name Loggia de' Lanzi. It was subsequently used as an outdoor sculpture gallery, a function that it retains to this day. The steps up to it are flanked by two lions, one of which is Roman (with later restorations), while the other

dates to the 16th century. As well as Roman statuary (all clearly labelled), here can be found two wonderful groups by Giambologna, the Rape of the Sabine Woman and Hercules and the Centaur (see page 45 for illustration). It is well worth going into the loggia and walking right round these two magnificent sculptures, designed to be seen from all angles. The pearl of the loggia, however, stands at the front, under the L arch – Cellini's Perseus.

Cellini's Perseus

When Cellini got the commission for the Perseus, Donatello's Judith and Holofernes (see page 87) stood under the R arch of the loggia, and the later bronze deliberately invited comparison with the earlier one. Both groups show divinely aided decapitations, and both protagonists stand with one arm raised above their vanquished enemies, who are each supported on a cushion atop an ornamental base. The bronze statuettes on the base of the Perseus are copies, the originals being housed in the Bargello (Walk 9). When Duchess Eleonora saw these wonderful figures of Zeus and Danae (Perseus' parents) and Athena and Mercury (his protectors), she wanted them for herself, but Cellini was having none of this and, without her knowledge, soldered them into position on the base, thus incurring her wrath. The Capricorn emblems on the base are a nice nod to Cosimo I, who became Duke under this zodiacal sign.

In his autobiography, Cellini gives a graphic account of the casting of the Perseus. First of all, the workshop caught fire. Then wind and rain contributed to cool the furnace down too much. Struggling against these difficulties, Cellini was struck down suddenly by a bout of fever and forced to take to his bed, leaving operations to his assistants. Things didn't go well, so he hauled himself up again and took charge once more. The metal had caked, so Cellini had hurriedly to procure some young oak and stuff it into the furnace. This produced a roaring blaze that quickly got out of control, so that men had to be sent up on to the roof to fight the fire. Then Cellini threw in a 60lb lump of pewter and piled on more fuel, so the metal again became molten. Suddenly, there was an explosion and a tremendous flash, caused by the cover of the furnace cracking. Realizing that the alloy must all have been consumed in the tremendous heat, Cellini frantically sent for all his household pewter, consisting of about 200 plates, bowls and salvers. Into the furnace they all went, and this, coupled with prayers, did the trick. The bronze flowed beautifully and filled up the mould.

Once Cellini's Perseus had been installed in the loggia, he had to work on finishing and polishing it. Having attended Mass one morning at the neighbouring church of S. Pier Scheraggio, he encountered another goldsmith, Bernardo, Purveyor to the Mint. Bernardo was hardly through the door of the church when, according to Cellini, he let out a series of four socially unacceptable noises so loud that they could have been heard from S. Miniato! An incensed Cellini railed at him (Cellini had a mighty temper) and subsequently punished him by composing a scurrilous verse and sticking it up in the corner of the church where members of the congregation went to relieve themselves – well, Masses were very long, and you weren't allowed to use the fountain!

S. Pier Scheraggio and the buildings of the Uffizi

The church of S. Pier Scheraggio was demolished in the 16th century when the area between the Palazzo Vecchio and the Arno was cleared to make way for the Uffizi. You can still see three of the nave columns on the S side of Via della Ninna, beneath the bridge that links the palace to the Uffizi buildings. Between the two nave columns closest to the Piazza della Signoria, a wall plaque tells us that S. Pier Scheraggio gave its name to one of the six 'sestieri' of the city and that, at a time when the church was used for government meetings, the voice of Dante could be heard ringing out from within its walls giving advice to the citizens.

Once Cosimo I had moved from the Medici Palace into the Palazzo della Signoria/Ducale in 1540, he decided to house all the administrative bureaucracy of the state under one roof – his roof. The entire area between the palace and the Arno was cleared to make way for his new 'Uffizi' ('Offices'). Giorgio Vasari was put in charge of the project and construction began in 1560. Work proceeded rapidly, and the Uffizi were largely complete by 1574, when both Cosimo and Vasari died. Under Francesco I, the project was brought to completion by Bernardo Buontalenti.

You have to hand it to Vasari, who came up with such an ingenious solution to the problems of both site and structure. The Uffizi had to be utilitarian and user-friendly, yet courtly as well. Sufficient accommodation and ease of access had to be provided for all the organs of government, but the space had to be imposing enough to act as a backdrop for civic and courtly ceremonies. The long, narrow, shady Piazza degli Uffizi is wrapped round on three sides by the office buildings, and Vasari used the perspectival vistas to full advantage. At the S end a view through to the hillside of the Oltrarno is framed by a lovely Serlian loggia, while  from this loggia the great tower of the Palazzo Vecchio is perfectly framed at the N end. The long, regular, unified façades have details well adapted to their shady setting picked out in pietra serena stone. Insistent horizontals at cornice level and between the storeys enhance the perspectival effects, but monotony is avoided by dint of breaking the façades up into 3-bay units articulated by piers. Vasari worshipped Michelangelo, and his detailing here owes much to the Laurentian Library (Walk 6). At the level of the piano nobile, the windows have balustrades and alternating triangular and segmental pediments. Below this, the mezzanine level has deep rectangular windows separated by consoles. Some of these mezzanine windows are blind, while others open into the barrel vault of the colonnade, forming an integral part of the coffered pattern and admitting light.

Walking along Piazza degli Uffizi from Piazza della Signoria towards the Arno, the entrance to the Uffizi Gallery lies on your L. The piers articulating the 3-bay units of Vasari's façades have niches containing 19th century statues of famous Florentines, all labelled. In case you're wondering what Farinata degli Uberti is doing here, when his family was held in such opprobrium in the 13th century, it's because following the Battle of Montaperti in 1260 when the Ghibelline commanders wanted to destroy Florence utterly Farinata managed to dissuade them. Dante refers to this (*Inferno* X.91-93), as does Giovanni Villani (*Chronicle* VI. 81).

Living statues

In the vicinity of the Uffizi, in addition to the statues of illustrious Florentines set in the niches along the façades of the building, you'll probably encounter other statues too, for this is a favourite haunt of people who, to supplement whatever other income they may or may not have, dress up and stand motionless on make-shift plinths for hours. This phenomenon has a longer history than you may think. By way of illustration, let me tell you of the triumphal entry into Florence of Giovanni de' Medici, who, in 1515, celebrated his first official visit to the city as Pope Leo X. His processional route was punctuated by specially constructed temporary works of fictive architecture, including triumphal arches, columns and obelisks, and all along the pope's path, performers were painted to look like statues and to declaim to the new pontiff as he passed by. The pageant included numerous floats, designed, carved and painted by, among others, del Sarto, Pontormo and Bandinelli. Vasari describes the float depicting the 'Age of Gold', represented by a naked child, gilded all over, rising from the 'corpse' of the 'Age of Iron', represented by a prostrate man clad in rusty armour. The authorities soon had another corpse on their hands, for, a few days afterwards, the poor child died from the effects of the gilding on his skin.

Halfway along Piazza degli Uffizi, on the R as you face the river, Via Lambertesca leads off to the R. Here, at no. 2 on the R, is Buontalenti's 'Porta delle Suppliche', designed as a depository for supplications and petitions to Francesco I. The Duke preferred to receive these supplications indirectly, and the slot for posting them can be seen to the R of the door. Of course, this indirect system encouraged people to pass on information anonymously, but what these snakes in the grass didn't know was that their comings and goings could be, and frequently were, secretly observed by Francesco himself. Herein

lies the explanation for the bizarre broken pediment over the door, which, besides framing a bust of Francesco (by Giovanni Bandini), conceals a peep-hole.

The multi-talented Buontalenti

Buontalenti's inventiveness was not confined to architecture. He came up with all sorts of ideas, among which was a design for a condom. It consisted of an appropriately shaped bag made from the finest silk, coated with wax and fastened at the top with a ribbon! An example survives in the archival collections of the Gondi family, about whom we'll learn more on Walk 9.

The Torre de' Pulci and back to Piazza della Signoria

Continue along Via Lambertesca. A few yards along on the L, at the corner with Via de' Georgofili, stands the Torre de' Pulci. Almost destroyed when a Mafia car bomb exploded here in 1993, the tower has been reconstructed (there is a commemorative plaque). A few yards further along Via Lambertesca turn R up the narrow Chiasso de' Baroncelli, which was the site of many of the minor guildhalls (we'll learn more about the guilds at the end of Walk 3). The chiasso leads back directly to the Piazza della Signoria.

Events in the piazza

Luca Landucci records in his *Diary* many of the incidents that took place in the Piazza della Signoria, so, before leaving the square, let's recall one or two of the more joyous spectacles. On 11th November 1487 certain animals arrived from the Turkish Sultan, and on 18th November his ambassadors presented them to the Signoria here in the piazza. They included a beautiful and graceful giraffe, whose picture could be seen painted in many parts of Florence, where she lived for several years. In November 1500 there was such heavy snow that boys made snow-lions in the square – forget snow-men! In June 1510 the festivities here for the feast of S. Giovanni included tightrope-walking, jousts and a bull hunt. A great number of raised seats had been constructed and, says Luca, the whole of Florence was there. The hunt in June 1514 was even more spectacular, with lions, bears, leopards, bulls, buffaloes, stags and horses. Contraptions resembling a tortoise and a porcupine had been made, inside of which were men who wheeled them all over the Piazza and kept thrusting at the animals with lances. The wooden platforms and enclosures were crowded, as were all the windows and roofs. A large fountain had been constructed in the middle of the square, which threw the water up in four jets, and round this fountain was a band of greenery, with dens for the animals to hide in. But, says Luca, somebody did an awful thing, putting a mare into an enclosure together with the horses, thereby offending decent people.

The interior of the Palazzo Vecchio

The ground floor – the Museo di Firenze Com' Era

The ticket office, information centre, cloakrooms, bookshop and café are all accessed from the 'Dogana' ('Customs Hall'), the entrance to which lies in the N façade of the palace. Right next to the ticket office are two small rooms in which are exhibited a few items from the collections of the erstwhile museum of 'Firenze Com' Era' ('Florence as it used to be'). The Bigallo Museum (Walk 1) had the distinction of being the smallest museum in Florence. Perhaps it still is, but it must be a close run thing now between it and this minimal display. I very much hope that the Florentine museum authorities will see fit, sooner rather than later, to rehouse the Museo di Firenze Com' Era in more extensive surroundings.

On the opposite side of the Dogana to the ticket office lies the monumental staircase giving access to the first floor (there is a lift for those who need it). Beyond the stairs lies the pretty Cortile di Michelozzo, which we'll see at the end of our visit. All the accessible rooms in the Palace have excellent and very full information boards in both Italian and English, so only minimal descriptions are given below.

The first floor

The Sala de' Cinquecento, Studiolo and Quarters of Pope Leo X

The monumental stairs lead up to the huge 'Sala de' Cinquecento' ('Room of the 500'). This hall, designed by Il Cronaca at the end of the 15th century to accommodate the new legislative body of the Great Council, was originally called the 'Sala del Maggior Consiglio' ('Room of the Great Council'). It was subsequently used by the Grand Dukes as an audience chamber and ballroom, and, of necessity, underwent many radical modifications. These modifications obliterated traces that may once have survived of a mural by Leonardo da Vinci on one of the long walls, showing the Florentine victory over Milan at the Battle of Anghiari. Michelangelo was asked to represent the victory over Pisa at the Battle of Cascina on the opposite wall, but he only got as far as completing the cartoons. The present decoration, by Vasari and others, shows episodes from Florentine history, victories in her several wars, allegories of the cities of Tuscany under Florentine dominion and, at the centre of the ceiling, the Apotheosis of Duke Cosimo I. Michelangelo's statue of Victory, presented to Cosimo by the artist's nephew, is here, along with works by Giambologna and Vincenzo de' Rossi. On the raised tribune or 'Udienza' are statues of distinguished members of the Medici family by Bandinelli, de' Rossi and Giovanni Caccini. Off one side of the Sala lies the exquisite little Studiolo of Francesco I, also by Vasari and his assistants. It is entirely decorated with paintings and bronzes celebrating Francesco's interest in alchemy and the natural sciences. Behind the lower paintings are cupboards where he kept his treasures. The four walls symbolize the Four Elements, Water (L wall), Air (far wall), Fire (R wall) and Earth (near wall).

You exit the Sala opposite the Studiolo and proceed through the so-called Quarters of Pope Leo X, a series of rooms decorated by Vasari and his assistants with murals illustrating the political history of the Medici family. There are rooms devoted to Cosimo Il Vecchio, Lorenzo Il Magnifico, Pope Leo X, Pope Clement VII, Giovanni delle Bande Nere (father of Cosimo I), and Duke Cosimo I himself, but not all of these are always open. There is also a tiny chapel (likewise not always open).

The second floor

The Quarters of the Elements and the Quarters of Eleonora di Toledo

Stairs decorated with grotteschi decorations lead out of the Sala di Leone X up to the so-called Quarters of the Elements, a series of rooms with decorations, again by Vasari and his assistants, showing allegories of the Elements and classical divinities. The decorative programme here was cleverly devised both to glorify the Medici and to link these rooms with those of the Quarters of Pope Leo X below – each classical divinity matches the Medici 'deity' directly beneath. The little Terrazzo di Giunone, once open on three sides and surrounded by a hanging garden, was enclosed in the 19th century. Here is displayed Verrocchio's Putto with a Dolphin, which graced the little fountain in the Cortile di Michelozzo. We'll see the copy of this in the courtyard later. From the Terrazzo di Saturno there is a fine view over the city.

From the Quarters of the Elements, a balcony runs across the end of the Sala de' Cinquecento to the Quarters of Eleonora di Toledo, wife of Duke Cosimo I. The chapel here was entirely decorated by Bronzino, and constitutes one of his most important works. The Sala di Ester has a charming frieze of putti intertwined in the letters of the name 'Eleonora', while in the Sala di Gualdrada is a series of paintings showing festivals in Florence. The paintings include views of Via Largo (now Cavour) with the Medici Palace (Walk 8), Piazza del Duomo (Walk 1), Piazza S. Spirito (Walk 12), showing the church minus its later façade, Piazza S. Maria Novella (Walk 7), Piazza della Signoria (Walk 2), Piazza S. Croce (Walk 5), again with the church minus its later façade, the old Ponte S. Trinità and the old Piazza di Mercato Vecchio (swept away in the 19th century to make way for the Piazza della Repubblica).

The Rooms of the Priors and the Sala delle Carte Geografiche

A passage from the Sala di Gualdrada leads through to the older rooms of the palace, called collectively the 'Rooms of the Priors'. First comes the chapel, decorated by Ridolfo del Ghirlandaio. One of the paintings here depicts the Annunciation and includes a view of the church of SS. Annunziata (Walk 10) before the addition of the portico.

The 'Sala delle Udienze' ('Audience Room') has a magnificent 15th century ceiling by Benedetto and Giuliano da Maiano. The mid-16th century mural paintings by Francesco Salviati illustrate stories from the life of the Roman hero Marcus Camillus. Over the door which leads through to the 'Sala de' Gigli' ('Room of the Lilies') is a statue of Justice by the da Maiano duo. The inlaid wooden doors, by the same duo plus Francione, have figures of Dante and Petrarch.

The Sala de' Gigli is named from the lilies which decorate the room. The fresco, by Domenico Ghirlandaio, shows S. Zenobius and saints, while the lunettes have ancient Roman heroes. Above the doorway is a statue of S. John the Baptist by the da Maiano duo again. The Sala de' Gigli houses Donatello's bronze group of Judith and Holofernes. A door in one corner of the room leads to the 'Cancelleria' ('Chancellery'), built in 1511 and used as an office by Niccolò Machiavelli. There is a portrait of him by Santi di Tito and a bust made from a cast of his death mask (*c.* 1575).

Next door to the Cancelleria lies the 'Sala delle Carte Geografiche' ('Room of the Geographical Maps'). Commissioned by Duke Cosimo I, the room was to be a 'virtual cosmos', a nice play on the Duke's name. Its walls were to be adorned with maps of all the lands of the known world, and its ceiling with constellations. The maps, by Egnazio Danti and Stefano Buonsignori, are astonishingly accurate. From a landing next to the Sala de' Gigli, stairs lead up to the Tower, with spectacular views of Florence, and down to the Mezzanine floor.

The Mezzanine floor and the Cortile di Michelozzo

The Mezzanine floor houses the collection of art left to the city in 1928 by Charles Loeser. The collection, well worth a visit, includes works by Tino di Camaino, Jacopo Sansovino, Rustici, Bronzino and many others. The stairs lead back down to ground floor level. At their base is the Cortile di Michelozzo, which we caught a glimpse of earlier. The courtyard was reconstructed by Michelozzo in the 1450s. It was elaborately decorated by Vasari in the 1560s for the marriage of Cosimo I's son, Francesco, to Joanna of Austria. The columns are covered with stucco, the ceilings have grotteschi decoration, and the walls bear charming views of Austrian cities. The central fountain bears a copy of Verrocchio's Putto with a Dolphin, the original of which we saw inside the palace. You can leave the courtyard on its E side to return to the Dogana, or exit via the W portal to emerge on the Piazza della Signoria. Before you go, let me draw your attention to three Dante plaques in the courtyard, all of them on the E wall to the R of the door leading back into the Dogana. Two of them bear quotations from *Paradiso*. Dante has met his ancestor, Cacciaguida, in paradise, and the latter, recalling the Uberti clan whose properties were demolished to make way for the original Piazza della

Signoria, has this to say:

'Oh those whom I saw who are now undone by their pride' (*Paradiso* XVI.109-110).

He goes on to recall the good old days:

'I saw Florence in such peace that there was nothing to cause her grief. With these people I saw her populace glorious and just, so that the lily was never reversed on the flag-pole, nor, through dissension, made red' (*Paradiso* XVI.149-54).

The white lily on the city's standard used to be turned upside-down in defeat. When the Guelfs wrested power back from the Ghibellines and established the Secondo Popolo (see historical summary), they substituted a red lily for the white one. The third plaque bears a quotation from the *Inferno*. Dante has met Farinata degli Uberti in hell, and the latter reminds the poet that, when the Ghibelline commanders wanted to raze Florence to the ground following their victory at the Battle of Montaperti, it was he alone who managed to save the city:

'But I was the only one there, when all were determined to make an end of Florence, who defended her openly' (*Inferno* X.91-3).

The Uffizi Gallery

It's hard to know where to begin with a gallery the size and prestige of which is legendary, and which houses works by, among others, Cimabue, Duccio, Giotto, Simone Martini and Lippo Memmi, Ambrogio and Pietro Lorenzetti, Bernardo Daddi, Nardo di Cione, Orcagna, Giovanni da Milano, Gentile da Fabriano, Fra Angelico, Lorenzo Monaco, Jacopo Bellini, Paolo Uccello, Masaccio and Masolino, Piero della Francesca, Filippo and Filippino Lippi, Baldovinetti, Piero and Antonio Pollaiuolo, Ghirlandaio, Botticelli, Perugino, Verrocchio, Leonardo da Vinci, Michelangelo, Bronzino, Raphael and Titian, to name just some of the artists. Perhaps the best place to start is at the beginning. Once you actually get inside and make it to the ticket booth, you still have to queue for a short while before you reach the turnstiles giving access to the stairs. Make sure, before you pass through, that you are equipped with a plan showing the lay-out of the rooms and what can be found where, and, perhaps, with a book giving the highlights of the collection, for there is no way that you can hope to see it all at one go; you will need to be very selective. There are lifts beyond the turnstiles, but they are small, and **strictly** reserved for those visitors who really need them, so be prepared to climb – there are an awful lot of steps! Once you've got your breath back at the top and have passed through another entry check, you'll find yourself in the corridor that runs around the entire top floor of the building, and it is a beautiful corridor. The ceiling is decorated with grotteschi and, along the sides, there are many sculptures. The rooms housing the paintings lie off the corridor on the L as you proceed clockwise. Once you make it to the end of the first part of the corridor, you will be rewarded with lovely views of the Arno. At the end of the second part of the corridor lies the café, and, weather and crowds permitting, you can take some refreshment on the terrace outside. You're actually sitting on the roof of the Loggia de' Lanzi here, with the tower of the Palazzo Vecchio looming over you.

From the café stairs lead down to the first floor, where you proceed through a series of rooms housing many more paintings – I wouldn't want you to think that you'd finished once you reached the café! You are now going anticlockwise, and you end up at the top of a flight of stairs which will bring you down to a series of gift shops on the ground floor. Having negotiated these, you exit the gallery via the back door on to Via de' Castellani. If you are, by this time, exhausted, never fear, for several enterprising café and restaurant owners have set up here, so you can take your ease, read the books you may just have purchased and write up your postcards.

Detail of the W façade of Palazzo Vecchio

Tower of the Palazzo Vecchio as seen from the hill of S. Miniato

Walks 3 and 4 – Mediaeval Florence

If you intend to do both these walks, I recommend that you do no. 3 first, followed by no. 4. If, owing to lack of time, you have to choose one or the other, I'd advise you to do Walk 3.

Walk 3

Begins at the Ponte Vecchio and ends at Orsanmichele.
Takes in: the Ponte Vecchio, SS. Apostoli, Palazzo Davanzati (housing the 'Museo della Casa Fiorentina Antica'), the Mercato Nuovo and Orsanmichele.
Duration: 1 hour 30 minutes, excluding time spent at any of the above. You should allow *c.* 1 hour each for Palazzo Davanzati and for Orsanmichele Church and Museum.
Tips: the Ponte Vecchio and Via Por S. Maria can become so crowded as to be well-nigh impassable, so start as early as is practicable.
The Ponte Vecchio to SS. Apostoli
Until 1218 the Ponte Vecchio was the only bridge over the Arno. It had already been destroyed by floodwaters in 1177, and in 1333 it was swept away again. By 1345 it had been reconstructed, probably to a design by Neri

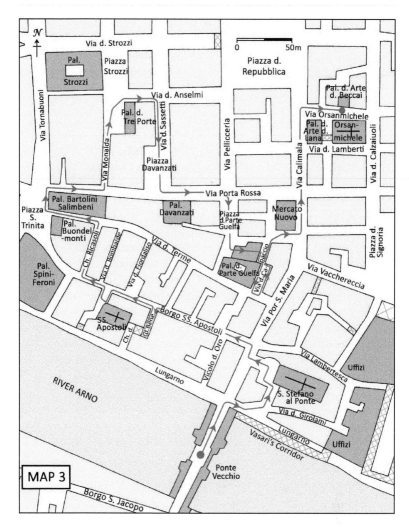

di Fioravante. The rebuilt bridge was three times as wide as its predecessor and had regular rows of shops running along each side. Rentals for these premises were levied with the aim of recouping the cost of rebuilding over a twenty year period. In 1495 the symmetry of Neri's design was destroyed when the shops were privatized and thereby allowed to expand irregularly both upwards and, by dint of cantilevered corbels, outwards over the water. Vasari's Corridor, erected in the 1560s, disrupted the symmetry even further. The original design of the bridge can best be appreciated at its centre, where four square stone turrets flank two terraces. On the downstream terrace

is a bust of Cellini, the most famous of Florentine goldsmiths, aptly set here in 1900 among the jewellers' shops. Don't miss the old sundial on the top of the turret at the RH end of this terrace. The addition of Vasari's Corridor converted the upstream terrace into a loggia, from which there are lovely views. On the S wall of the loggia is a Dante plaque quoting *Inferno* XIII.146, which refers to the Arno. Next to this is a plaque commemorating Gerhard Wolf and the role he played in saving the Ponte Vecchio from destruction during the Second World War. The story of Vasari's Corridor is recounted at the beginning of Walk 15, under the sections entitled 'the Ponte Vecchio to Piazza di S. Maria Sopr' Arno' and 'avoiding the *hoi polloi*'.

As you leave the Ponte Vecchio heading N (i.e. back towards the Duomo), note the Dante plaque on the façade of the shop at the end of the bridge on the R:

'But it was fitting that, in her last days of peace, Florence should offer a sacrificial victim to that worn stone which guards the bridge' (*Paradiso* XVI.145-7).

In mediaeval times a Roman statue of Mars stood near this spot, and in 1215 a murder was committed here. The victim was Buondelmonte de' Buondelmonti. He had contracted to marry a daughter of the Amidei family, but jilted her. The Amidei avenged this slur by assassinating Buondelmonte at the foot of the statue of Mars, thus precipitating a feud which, says Dino Compagni at the start of his *Chronicle*, led to the division of all the citizens into two factions who became enemies under new names, Guelf and Ghibelline – hence Dante's reference to the city's last days of peace.

Just across the Lungarno from the N end of the Ponte Vecchio, directly opposite the great arcade carrying Vasari's Corridor, lies the tiny triangular 'Piazza del Pesce' ('Fish Square'). This was once the home of the fish market, until it was relocated in the mid-16th century by ducal decree (more on that in Walk 15). From Piazza del Pesce, Via de' Girolami leads off at an angle under a series of arches. We are not going along here, but up the alley next to it, away from the Lungarno. This leads to a little piazza in front of the deconsecrated church of S. Stefano al Ponte. The church has a lovely decorated Romanesque doorway. Leave the piazza opposite the church to join Via Por S. Maria. On the other side of the road, slightly over to the L, lies the Torre degli Amidei, so the assassins of Buondelmonte didn't have far to run home! The Torre degli Amidei is the first of several mediaeval fortified tower-houses that we'll see on Walks 3 and 4. It too has a Dante plaque referring to the murder:

'The house from which your (i.e. Buondelmonte's) sorrow sprang, on account of the just disdain that brought death to you and made an end of your happy life, was honoured, it and its associates' (*Paradiso* XVI.136-9).

A few yards along from the tower to the R you'll see the entrance to Borgo SS. Apostoli, which is where we're heading. The Torre de' Baldovinetti lies on your R as you enter the borgo. After a few yards Vicolo dell' Oro opens out on the L. A few yards past this, also on the L, is a building which once belonged to the Buondelmonti family. Here is

another Dante plaque:

'O Buondelmonte, (how ill it was that you shunned their nuptials at another's behest:) many would be happy who are sad if God had consigned you to the river Ema the first time that you came to the city' (*Paradiso* XVI.140-44; the road to Florence from Montebuoni (the Buondelmonti seat) crossed the river Ema). On the L at no. 19 red/9 blue is the rear façade of the Palazzo Acciaiuoli, with the escutcheon of Cardinal Angelo Acciaiuoli (d. 1409) over the door.

The ownership of the palace remained in the family until the 18th century. In the mid-19th century it was converted into a hotel – Ruskin, Dickens, Swinburne, Longfellow and Henry James all stayed here. Directly opposite no. 9 blue lies the 12th century Torre de' Buondelmonti and, next to it, another Acciaiuoli palace. The Acciaiuoli were one of the wealthiest families in mediaeval Florence. Just to give you some idea of the scale of their operations, the 1353 inventory of company papers included 1,501 account books which were kept in twenty-five cities from London to Constantinople. Over the doorway to the palace (now the Hotel Torre Guelfa) can be seen the emblem of the Certosa del Galluzzo, built by the Acciaiuoli family.

Chiasso de' del Bene runs off to the L. On the flank of the building on the near corner of this chiasso is a small stone plaque bearing a damaged inscription referring to the 'Signori', those eight officials in charge of law and order whose decree concerning the Neptune Fountain we saw on Walk 2. If you want a view of the campanile and apse of the church of SS. Apostoli, pop down the chiasso and turn R. Otherwise, continue along Borgo SS. Apostoli. A few yards beyond Via del Fiordaliso on the R, an inscription over a small shop tells you that the chiasso here was blocked off in 1826.

Piazza del Limbo opens up on the L. The piazza takes its name from the cemetery that lay beside the church of SS. Apostoli, where were buried infants who had died prior to being baptized and whose souls were thus confined to limbo. To the L of the church of SS. Apostoli lies the Palazzo Rosselli del Turco, formerly Palazzo Borgherini. This 16th century palace, designed by Baccio d' Agnolo, has a relief of the Madonna by Benedetto da Maiano on the piazza façade. The Borgherini continued to live here until the mid-18th century, when the palace was bought by the Rosselli del Turco family, in whose hands it has been ever since.

The Borgherini bedroom

Baccio d' Agnolo not only designed the Palazzo Borgherini, but made the bedroom furniture for the marriage of Pierfrancesco Borgherini to Margherita Acciaiuoli in 1515. Fifteen years later, when Pierfrancesco was in exile, the Florentine government officials decided that they wanted to give this magnificent furniture, made of walnut and decorated by artists of the calibre of Pontormo, Granacci and Andrea del Sarto, as a gift to the French king. However, they had reckoned without an irate Mrs. Borgherini, who was having none of it. She told them, in no uncertain terms, that if they wanted to give the French king a gift, they could strip their own palaces to do so! If you visit the Bargello (Walk 9), you will see a magnificent fireplace from the palace, which, like the bedroom furniture, was made on the occasion of the marriage between Pierfrancesco and Margherita.

SS. Apostoli

The church of SS. Apostoli is one of the oldest in Florence. An inscription on the façade tells us that it was founded in 805 by Charlemagne, and Giovanni Villani says the same in his *Chronicle* (III.3). This is probably just a legend,

but the church is mentioned in 11th century documents as being already ancient. The present architecture dates to the mid-11th century, though the door is 16th century; adorned with the wolf rampant arms of the Altoviti (who had the patronage of the church), it is attributed to Benedetto da Rovezzano. Vasari says that Brunelleschi used SS. Apostoli as his model for S. Lorenzo and S. Spirito (Walks 6 and 12). The basilican interior has a painted timber roof and green marble columns with lovely capitals. The altarpiece of the Madonna and Child enthroned with saints is by Niccolò di Pietro Gerini and Jacopo di Cione (brother of Andrea Orcagna). At the end of the N aisle is the splendid della Robbian glazed terracotta Tabernacle of the Blessed Sacrament. Benedetto da Rovezzano was responsible for the nearby tomb of Oddo Altoviti. In the church were preserved pieces of flint from the Holy Sepulchre in Jerusalem, brought back by Pazzino de' Pazzi from the First Crusade and used to strike the holy fire at Easter.

A coveted sarcophagus

Before leaving SS. Apostoli, you may like to know of another tomb by Benedetto da Rovezzano, though you will have to travel to London to see it. Rovezzano came to England in 1524 to design a sarcophagus for Cardinal Wolsey. Following Wolsey's fall from grace Henry VIII coveted it, as did Charles I a century later. It was eventually used to house the body of Admiral Lord Nelson, and you can see it in the crypt of S. Paul's Cathedral.

SS. Apostoli to the Palazzo Davanzati

Continue along Borgo SS. Apostoli for a few more yards. Between Via delle Bombarde and Chiasso Ricasoli on the R lie the Palazzo and Torre Altoviti. Turn R up Chiasso Ricasoli to reach Via delle Terme, another lovely mediaeval street. Here we turn L. The rear entrance to the Hotel Porta Rossa lies on your R at no. 16 blue. Directly opposite this there is an arched doorway on the L bearing the Bartolini poppy emblem and the family motto 'per non dormire' ('so as not to sleep'). The stories attached to this emblem and motto are told under Walk 12. Just to the L of the door of no. 59 red is a wine hatch. You'll see wine hatches everywhere on our walks around the city. They were outlets where landed families who owned vineyards could sell off their surplus wine supplies direct to the public – a sort of Renaissance off-licence. The trade was strictly controlled by the authorities and there were regulations governing sales. One rule, for example, forbade the serving of salted bread with the wine to increase a customer's thirst – a bit like telling a pub not to serve crisps! Just before entering Piazza S. Trinità, a small stone plaque on the flank of Palazzo Buondelmonti on the L bears a directive from the eight Signori, those law and order officials whom we referred to earlier, prohibiting shameful acts. Opposite, on the flank of Palazzo Bartolini-Salimbeni, a wall plaque tells us that this was the old Hotel du Nord, where James Russell Lowell stayed in 1874.

The piazza and church of S. Trinità are described under Walk 12, so resist the temptation to linger here now and, hugging the façade of the Palazzo Bartolini-Salimbeni, bear round R and R again and head up Via Porta Rossa. High up on your R you can see the 'per non dormire' motto of the Bartolini family inscribed on the windows, and the corbels of the Hotel Porta Rossa are decorated with their poppy emblem. Directly opposite the Hotel Porta Rossa, turn L up Via Monalda to reach Piazza Strozzi. The huge Palazzo Strozzi, which lies at the far end of the piazza on the L, is described under Walk 13. Here we are only concerned with the lovely palace that lies in the near corner on the R. Called 'Palazzo delle Tre Porte' ('Palace of the Three Doors'), it was built in the mid-15th century for a minor branch of the Strozzi family, and is therefore sometimes referred to as 'dello Strozzino'. The ground floor is thought to have been designed by Michelozzo and the upper floors by Giuliano da Maiano. The abrupt change in the rustication near the top of the ground floor level clearly indicates

a change of plan/architect. The palace belonged to the 'Strozzini' until the mid-19th century. In the early 20th century, much of the building, including the lovely 15th century courtyard, was destroyed in order to build the Odeon cinema! The palace is currently used by the language school of the British Institute of Florence.

Leave Piazza Strozzi on Via degli Anselmi, which runs along the flank of the erstwhile Palazzo dello Strozzino past the offending cinema. At the crossroads with Via de' Sassetti turn R to reach Piazza Davanzati. On the corner with Via Porta Rossa on the R lies the Casa Torre Foresi, while ahead of you is the Palazzo Davanzati.

The Palazzo Davanzati

The Palazzo Davanzati, the best preserved 14th century residential palace in Florence, houses the 'Museo della Casa Fiorentina Antica' (the 'Ancient Florentine House Museum'). Built by the Davizzi family in *c.* 1330, the palace passed to the Davanzati in the 16th century. You enter via the ground floor loggia, used originally for business/commercial activities. As you pass through the great wooden doors, note the shafts in the ceiling above you. These were defensive features from which hot oil and molten lead could be poured on to attackers attempting to enter the premises. If this smacks of overkill, wait until you read the section on 'the big bad barons' at the end of Walk 4. In the ground floor loggia you'll find the ticket office. There are information boards in English throughout, so an overview only is given here.

The loggia gives access to an internal courtyard from which stairs lead to the upper floors. Each floor has a large room at the front, corresponding in size to the loggia below, and suites of smaller apartments arranged around the well of the courtyard. Many of the rooms are decorated with delightful frescoes, and some have fireplaces, a luxury in the mid-14th century, as indeed was window glass. The latter was even condemned by a particularly ardent friar as being one of the vanities that had called down God's wrath in the flood of 1333. In the rooms are displayed works from the museum's collections of statuary, bronzes, paintings, furniture, majolica-ware and tapestries. On the third floor is the kitchen, with views over the roofs of Florence. You'll notice graffiti on many of the walls, but these are not the result of modern vandalism. Some rooms in the palace were used by the tax departments of the Grand Ducal government, and people waiting to present their tax declarations passed the time scribbling.

Florentine taxation and tax evasion

The graffiti in Palazzo Davanzati provide me with the perfect excuse to tell you a bit about Florentine taxation and tax evasion. In the 14th century taxes were levied on the basis of assessments made by neighbourhood committees. This system, besides encouraging citizens to conceal the true extent of their assets, cannot always have led to the best of neighbourly relations, and was, moreover, open to bribery. In 1394, one Giovanni Morelli even moved neighbourhoods to try to get a better deal! In 1427 the government changed its strategy and introduced the 'catasto', whereby each head of household had to submit a detailed inventory of taxable assets – i.e. a tax return. The original returns for 1427 survive (close on 10,000 of them) and are generally considered to be reasonably accurate. The Florentines, however, quickly learned how to doctor their records, and subsequent returns contain attempts at evasion. In 1430 the authorities suspected that one Andrea Banchi was trying to conceal the real value of his estate, but, when they inspected his books, they found his accounts in such disarray that they eventually gave up and accepted his return, as they could not spare the time to clear up the mess! Eventually, realizing that the only valid tax base was land/property, they changed the system again, abandoning the 'catasto' in 1495 and introducing the 'decima' property tax.

Paying taxes on time was important if you wanted to hold political office, for anybody in arrears with their tax payments was considered ineligible. Gregorio Dati (1362-1435) did not immediately declare the dowry of his second wife (whom he married in 1393) in order to put off paying the tax on it. He was clearly a last-minuter when it came to paying up, for in May 1412 his name was drawn as standard-bearer for his district militia company and, as he tells us in his *Diary*, just fifteen minutes before it was drawn, he'd finished paying off his debts to the Commune. Buonaccorso Pitti (he of the singed legs; see under Walk 2 the section entitled 'pity poor Pitti') was not so lucky. In October 1417 his name was drawn as Gonfaloniere of Justice, but he was declared ineligible as he was found (unfairly according to him of course) to be listed in the book of tax delinquents! He did eventually get to be Gonfaloniere in July 1422.

The Palazzo Davanzati to the Mercato Nuovo

On exiting from the Palazzo Davanzati turn R along Via Porta Rossa until you reach the crossroads with Via Pellicceria. The name of Via Pellicceria recalls the furriers whose shops once occupied this area. Turn R here towards the little Piazza della Parte Guelfa. Ahead of you is a Gothic building with an attractive external staircase. This is the

Palazzo di Parte Guelfa. The Guelf Party was established in the 13th century as the political organization of the Guelfs in their struggles with the Ghibellines. With the triumph of the Guelfs it became an influential branch of government, but its authority declined towards the end of the 14th century, and in the 15th century it no longer played a significant role. On the L, between the palace and Vicolo della Seta, is the ex-church of S. Maria Sopra Porta, formerly S. Biagio. The church has had a chequered history. Deconsecrated in the 19th century, it was used as a fire station. It is now a public library and you can go in and admire the frescoes in the little Chapel of S. Bartolomeo (attributed to the school of Maso di Banco). The room beyond also has a fresco and a vaulted ceiling decorated with coats-of-arms and the lilies of Florence. This room was the hall of the Palazzo dell' Arte della Seta (the Silk Guild), which adjoined the church. You can exit via the door here on to Via di Capaccio. On the outside wall over the door is the coat-of-arms of the Silk Guild encircled by cherubs. If the library is closed, just leave Piazza della Parte Guelfa along the L flank of the church on Vicolo della Seta and you'll arrive at the same place.

You are now standing at the SW corner of the Mercato Nuovo, but resist the temptation to shop for a moment and head away from the market down Via di Capaccio.

Immediately in front of you is a small corner loggia at first floor level built by Vasari. Beyond this on the R is the fine 15th century extension to the Palazzo di Parte Guelfa by Brunelleschi, which he never completed – there is a good view of this from Via delle Terme. Via delle Terme takes its name from the Roman baths that once stood here, and the name of Via di Capaccio derives from a corruption of the latin *caput acquae*, the end of the Roman aqueduct that served the baths.

Retrace your steps back to the Mercato Nuovo, the site of a market since the 11th century. It was called the 'Mercato Nuovo' ('New Market') to distinguish it from the 'Mercato Vecchio' ('Old Market'), which was swept away in the 19th century to make way for Piazza della Repubblica. This was the area of the old city where the money-changers and bankers clustered.

Money-changers
Money-changers were a real necessity in a market awash with foreign coins – remember that towns of any size all had their own mints. As late as 1591, sixty-two types of coins were specified as being legal tender. In 1480 Bernardo Machiavelli, father of the famous Niccolò, sold some oil to a dealer who paid him in coins from Florence, Genoa, Rome and Bologna. He took these coins to a bank and exchanged them all for florins. It was only a small step from money-changing to banking – in fact, money-changers came to be called bankers from the counter ('banco' - usually covered with a decorative carpet) across which they did business.

The loggia of the Mercato Nuovo was erected in the 1540s for the sale of gold and silk. On the S side of the loggia (nearest to you as you emerge from Via di Capaccio) is a copy of Il Porcellino, a bronze boar copied by Pietro Tacca from an antique statue. The original Hellenistic marble was given to

Cosimo I by Pope Pius IV; it is now housed in the Uffizi. The bronze copy was probably commissioned by Cosimo II for the Pitti Palace. Don't miss the delightful depictions of reptiles, amphibians and other creatures on the base (see page 117 for illustrations). Ferdinando II decided to use Tacca's bronze for a fountain, which was already installed at the Mercato Nuovo by 1640. What you now see is a copy of Tacca's bronze; the original is in the Bardini Museum (Walk 14). Up to the L of the bronze is a plaque commemorating Hans Christian Andersen, who stayed many times in Florence and wrote a fairy story inspired by Il Porcellino called *The Bronze Hog*. Set into the pavement at the very centre of the loggia is a marble disc showing a six-spoked wheel. This is the 'carroccio stone'. The 'carroccio' was the wagon of the Republic

and Giovanni Villani tells us all about it in his *Chronicle* (VI.75). It was a four-wheeled chariot, painted red, upon which stood two tall masts to which the standard of the Commune was fastened. It was drawn by a great pair of oxen, caparisoned with red cloth and set apart solely for this purpose. The carroccio was used in triumphs and solemnities (see the section entitled 'the big bad barons' at the end of Walk 4 for one such occasion), and when the army was called to go forth to battle it was brought to the Mercato Nuovo by an escort of knights and committed to the keeping of the soldiers, the strongest and most virtuous of the citizens being chosen to guard it. It must have been a spectacular sight.

The Mercato Nuovo to Orsanmichele

Head to the NE corner of the loggia (diagonally opposite the point where we entered the square) and leave the Mercato on Via Calimala. On the R

immediately beyond the crossroads with Via de' Lamberti, you'll see some shops at nos. 16-20 red, which contain mediaeval frescoes. This is because they occupy part of the Palazzo dell' Arte della Lana (the Wool Guild), behind which we're standing. Turn R up Via Orsanmichele. A few yards along on the R you'll see the church of the same name. On the L lies the Palazzo dell' Arte de' Beccai, the erstwhile headquarters of the Butchers' Guild. The Butchers clearly knew how to entertain well. In 1605 their guild received a request from the Ducal Court asking to borrow

rugs and tableware for a family marriage! The palace eventually became the headquarters of the 'Accademia delle Arti del Disegno', founded in 1563 with Cosimo I and Michelangelo as honorary members. The façade of the building is still adorned by both the coat-of-arms of the Butchers' Guild (the goat) and the three interlocking wreaths of the Accademia (laurel, olive and oak, symbolizing painting, sculpture and architecture). The palace is occasionally opened by volunteers. Inside you'll find frescoes by Mariotto di Nardo and Pontormo, busts of Cosimo and Michelangelo, and portraits of all the presidents of the Accademia from 1563 to the present day. From the door of the palace you get a good view of the 14th century Palazzo dell' Arte della Lana (the Wool Guild), with a splendid tabernacle on the corner. The tabernacle, which was moved here from the nearby Mercato Vecchio when Piazza della Repubblica was created in the 19th century, houses paintings of the Madonna enthroned and the Coronation of the Virgin by Jacopo del Casentino and Niccolò di Pietro Gerini respectively. The high-level footbridge linking the palace to the upper storeys of Orsanmichele was added in the 16th century.

Walk 3 ends here, giving you the opportunity to visit Orsanmichele. If it happens to be lunchtime, you are very close to Paoli's restaurant, and Orsanmichele may appear even more beautiful after lunch. Continue along Via Orsanmichele, cross over Via de' Calzaiuoli into Via de' Tavolini, and Paoli's is on the L. Originally opened in the first half of the 19th century by the Paoli brothers, the restaurant is a confection of neo-mediaeval vaults, polygonal stone pillars, lunettes, wrought ironwork and ceramics, with painted decorations by, among others, Carlo Coppede, Galileo Chini, Luciano Guarnieri and Pietro Annigoni. For long the meeting place of the Italian intelligentsia, the visitors' book contains the autographs of many famous figures, including Leoncavallo and Puccini.

Details on the base of Il Porcellino

The Florentine Guilds

Passing mention has been made of the Florentine guilds on Walks 1-3, and it is now time to say something more about these institutions. The oldest guild was the 'Arte di Calimala', formed by Florentine wool merchants operating abroad to protect their interests, and first documented in the 1180s. The next two to appear were the Bankers' Guild and the Wool Guild, first documented in 1202 and 1212 respectively. The distinction between the Calimala and the Wool Guild was that members of the former imported ready-spun cloth for dyeing and finishing, while members of the latter imported the raw wool. Other guilds and trade associations appear during the 13th century, and documentary evidence points to the existence of more than seventy such groups. The fact that these numerous associations eventually coalesced into twenty-one recognized guilds was due entirely to political considerations.

During the 1260s the Guelfs, having finally got the better of the Ghibellines, set up the government known as the Secondo Popolo (see historical summary). Initially, things didn't work out too well and, eventually, draconian laws were introduced in an attempt to curb the power of the unruly and violent landed magnate class. These laws were the famous 'Ordinances of Justice', enacted in 1293, under which the nobles were barred from holding political office and the guilds were made the formal foundation of the republican constitution – Florence became a guild republic.

Power was initially concentrated in the hands of the seven major guilds of the time, which were the Calimala, the Bankers' Guild, the Wool Guild, the Judges' and Notaries' Guild, the Physicians' and Apothecaries' Guild, the Furriers' Guild and the Guild of the Por S. Maria, which consisted mainly of cloth retailers. This last guild eventually came to be dominated by silk merchants and was widely known as the Silk Guild. The large number of other small guilds and trade associations proved too unwieldy for political purposes, and a process of agglomeration began. Eventually, fourteen conglomerate minor guilds were brought into the constitutional structure. These were the guilds of the Butchers, Bakers, Oilmakers and Cheesemongers, Vintners, Shoemakers, Linenmakers and Second-hand Clothes Dealers, Innkeepers, Leatherworkers and Tanners, Harnessmakers, Armourers and Swordmakers, Smiths, Locksmiths, Carpenters and, finally, Construction Workers (called the 'Masters in Stone and Wood'). In 1320, legislation reaffirmed the exclusive status of the seven major and fourteen minor guilds. From thenceforth, any group aspiring to a role in political life had to find a place within one of these twenty-one guilds. Inevitably, this led to some surprising mergers. The Silk Guild, for example, accepted goldsmiths amongst its members, probably because many of them manufactured the metallic threads necessary for the production of luxury fabrics. The Physicians' and Apothecaries' Guild included painters, glassmakers and pigment vendors, the Innkeepers'

Guild admitted carriers, and the Construction Workers' Guild took in kilnmen, quarrymen, sand and gravel dealers, carters and cesspit diggers.

The guild umbrella did not shelter everybody. Certain of the labouring class groups, including the so-called 'Ciompi', fell outside the guild system and were thus excluded from involvement in political life. In 1342, Walter of Brienne, Duke of Athens, gave some of these groups guild status (see historical summary), but, following his expulsion from Florence in 1343, their newly won rights were quickly revoked. Festering resentment erupted into violence in 1378 with the famous 'Ciompi Revolt'. The revolt was savagely suppressed, and in 1382 an oligarchic government called the 'Popolo Grasso' was established. Under this regime there was a shift of political power away from the guilds towards more centralized government. The guilds remained the formal foundation of the republican constitution, but they ceased to be instruments of political power, which was concentrated more and more into the hands of the oligarchs. Reforms of the electoral system meant that, by the 15th century, the process of election to political office had become an instrument that could be controlled by the elite – or, rather, by whichever elite faction held the upper hand. The guilds were, in effect, now controlled by such factions, and guild officials were more responsive to their political masters than to the desires of their own memberships.

Because the guilds were now routes to political activity rather than active agents in the political process, men often found it advantageous to belong to more than one. Dual membership was, of course, often logical or necessary because of overlaps in professional activities. A woodworker, for example, might be enrolled in both the Carpenters' Guild and the Guild of Construction Workers, and a metalworker might be a member of both the Smiths' and Locksmiths' Guilds. However, skill was not a criterion for enrolment, and social status was in no way damaged by membership of a minor guild. For example, Antonio di Pucci was a mason/carpenter back in the 14th century. He was, in fact, one of the contractors responsible for the scaffolding during construction of the Loggia de' Priori (Walk 2). He was enrolled in the Guild of Construction Workers, and was elected as Guild Consul twelve times. His sons, Puccio and Saracino, moved out of construction into the banking and silk sectors, doing very nicely thank you. Saracino was a member of the Silk Guild and Puccio was enrolled in the Bankers' Guild. Puccio's son, Antonio, was a partner in a silk business with Luca Pitti and was worth a fortune. All this notwithstanding, the Pucci, whose family palace we'll pass on Walk 10, often named the Guild of Construction Workers as their official guild for purposes of communal political activity.

The lumping together of diverse groups of professions under one umbrella meant that conglomerate guilds could not respond to the needs of their members in the same way that their prototypes had done. With no internal compatibility of interests, social cohesion within each body was weakened, and the guilds gradually receded from the social and religious lives of their members. This, perhaps, helps to explain the rise of other religious confraternities. In the mid-14th century, for example, the painters, who'd been absorbed into the Physicians' and Apothecaries' Guild, established the Confraternity of S. Luca. Their chapel at SS. Annunziata was taken over in 1565 by the Accademia delle Arti del Disegno (whose headquarters we saw on Walk 3).

The fall of the republic in 1530 signalled major changes for the guilds. They represented the traditional foundation of the republican constitution, and Dukes Alessandro and Cosimo I quickly took measures to undermine this status. The fourteen minor guilds were consolidated into four larger conglomerates called 'università', which were eventually housed in the Uffizi under the direct supervision of ducal government officials. For example, the Guilds of Construction Workers, Carpenters, Smiths, Locksmiths and Armourers found themselves united in the 'Arte de' Fabbricanti', while the Butchers, Bakers, Oilmakers and Cheesemongers merged into the 'Arte di Por S. Piero'. In 1583 these two conglomerates were themselves merged. The final axe fell in 1770, when, with the introduction of new legislation, the guilds lost all their identity as corporate entities.

The history and exterior of Orsanmichele

The form of Orsanmichele is unique and its name unusual. To understand both, it is necessary to recount its history. In 750 AD a small church was built dedicated to S. Michael the Archangel. Because it was near land used for market gardening it was known as 'S. Michele in Orto' ('in the garden'), or 'Orsanmichele' for short. After the destruction of this church by fire in 1239, the site was used as a grain market, and in the 1280s Arnolfo di Cambio (who later went on to oversee the building of the Duomo and the Palazzo Vecchio) was commissioned to construct a loggia for the grain merchants. On one pillar of the loggia was an image of the Madonna to which numerous miracles were attributed. A confraternity known as the 'Laudesi' was founded in her honour and its officers were called 'Captains of Orsanmichele'. One of their principal roles was to distribute offerings made to this miraculous Madonna among the neediest citizens. In 1304 a fire (the result of quarrels between rival factions; see the section on 'the big bad barons' at the end of Walk 4) destroyed much of the city centre, including Arnolfo's loggia. In 1336 the Signoria decreed the construction of a new three-storey stone loggia to serve the dual purpose of providing secure storage space for grain on the upper floors and preserving a place of worship for the Madonna on this venerated spot. The government entrusted the patronage of the new grain loggia to the Silk Guild. The guilds played an important role in both the economic and the civic life of Florence, for the financing of many public works was entrusted to them. The Baptistery and the Duomo, for example, were under

the patronage of the Calimala and the Wool Guild respectively. This acted as a spur to the arts, for the guilds competed with each other in the upkeep and embellishment of the buildings under their patronage, spending vast sums of money and commissioning works from the leading artists of the day. The Silk Guild appointed Neri di Fioravante, Benci di Cione and Francesco Talenti as architects. Benci's input clearly left something to be desired, for eventually, in 1361, the guild took action against him and petitioned the Commune to appropriate and sell all of his property in compensation for his incompetence and defective workmanship on the job!

In 1343 there occurred the insurrection which resulted in the expulsion from Florence of the Duke of Athens, the success of which, on 26th July, was attributed both to the Madonna and to her mother, S. Anne, whose feast day that was. It was decided, therefore, that altars should be erected to both the Madonna and S. Anne within Orsanmichele. The original image of the Madonna was lost, presumably in the fire of 1304. A new painting, generally attributed to Bernardo Daddi, was commissioned in 1346, and in 1349 Andrea Orcagna was charged with constructing a tabernacle to house this image. Poor Bernardo never saw his painting in Andrea's stupendous setting, for he died during the plague epidemic of 1348. It was decided during the following decade to move the grain market elsewhere (it ended up behind the Palazzo Vecchio), so that mercantile activity need not take place near the tabernacle, though the upper floors of Orsanmichele continued to be used as granaries until the 16th century. By 1380, Simone Talenti, son of Francesco, had closed in the arcades of the loggia, thus turning it into the church that we see today.

The city guilds, who had been assigned niches and pillars outside and inside the new loggia on which to portray their patron saints, eventually set about the embellishment of these in true competitive spirit. The fourteen external faces of the pillars of the loggia were assigned to thirteen of the guilds and to the Guelf Party (see Walk 3), although the last-mentioned pillar subsequently passed to the Tribunale di Mercanzia, the tribunal court that adjudicated all guild matters (see Walk 2). These guilds commissioned sculptures of their patron saints and set them in tabernacles. High above the tabernacles, the coats-of-arms of the respective guilds were displayed in medallions, ten being frescoed and four being of glazed terracotta. The frescoed medallions have not fared well, but the four della Robbian terracottas are still there above the tabernacles of the Construction Workers, the Physicians and Apothecaries, the Silk Merchants, and the Tribunale di Mercanzia (see the illustration opposite for the last three of these). The Butchers' medallion was originally frescoed, but a terracotta coat-of-arms was installed in 1858, when all the medallions were restored.

Orsanmichele by night

Let's now walk around Orsanmichele to see the statuary and, at the corners of the building, charming little reliefs representing aspects of the agricultural year. The sculptures that you see in the tabernacles today are copies. The originals are, with one exception, displayed in the museum housed on the first floor of the building, above the church (the exception is the S. George by Donatello, made for the Armourers and Swordmakers, which you'll find in the Bargello; Walk 9). The statues are described street by street, beginning in Via Orsanmichele, where we ended Walk 3, and continuing around the church anti-clockwise.

The statues of S. Peter, S.Philip, the four crowned saints and S.George

Via Orsanmichele

S. Peter – the Butchers' Guild

This marble statue, which dates to the first quarter of the 15th century, has been variously attributed over the years to Ciuffagni, Nanni di Banco, Brunelleschi, Michelozzo and Donatello. Vasari gives it to Donatello, but I believe that Brunelleschi leads the field at the moment. The terracotta coat-of-arms high above was made and installed in 1858. To the L, on the corner of the building at about shoulder height (on the torus moulding immediately above the base socle), is a relief showing ears of corn.

S. Philip – the Shoemakers' Guild

Nanni di Banco did the tabernacle and the marble statue in *c.* 1410. Vasari says that Donatello was offered the commission first, but asked for too much money. When the work was finished, however, Nanni demanded more than the contract sum. The guild appealed to Donatello as an arbitrator, but Donatello got his own back in a clever way, saying that as Nanni wasn't in the same league as a sculptor, he'd had to put far more effort into the statue and that the guild should, therefore, pay him for all that extra time necessarily expended! Note the guild's coat-of-arms on the base of the tabernacle.

The four crowned saints – the Construction Workers' Guild

Nanni di Banco also did the tabernacle and marble group of the four crowned saints, sculptors/stonemasons who were martyred by Diocletian. The delightful relief below shows them at work. Note the terracotta coat-of-arms of the guild in the medallion high above.

S. George – the Armourers' and Swordmakers' Guild

Donatello's S. George is thought by many to have been a source for Michelangelo's statue of David (Walk 2). Donatello's original statue (housed in the Bargello) exhibits several drill holes that contained corroded metal, indicating that the saint probably once had a sword, scabbard and helmet, attributes that would have been highly appropriate for this guild. The relief at the base of the tabernacle shows the killing of the dragon. It uses a technique called 'stiacciato', in which, by adhering to rules of perspective, a scene can be shown as apparently receding far into the background within a depth of just a few millimetres.

Via dell' Arte della Lana
S. Matthew – the Bankers' Guild
This tabernacle, designed by Ghiberti, was originally assigned to the Bakers, but they lost the proprietary rights in 1416 because they hadn't got on fast enough with commissioning a statue to go in it. It passed instead to the Bankers, who commissioned Ghiberti to make this bronze. The first casting failed, and poor old Ghiberti had to undertake a second at his own expense. The coat-of-arms of the guild can be seen in the pediment surmounting the tabernacle. To the L, on the corner of the building, is a relief showing trees.

S. Stephen – the Wool Guild
Andrea Pisano had sculpted a statue for the Wool Guild in 1340 (now in the Museo dell' Opera del Duomo; Walk 1). By the 1420s this was looking out of date, so the guild, one of the most prestigious in the city, decided to replace it and commissioned Ghiberti to do a bronze for them too. Note the *Agnus Dei*, emblem of the guild, in the pediment surmounting the tabernacle.

S. Eligius – the Smiths' Guild
Nanni di Banco sculpted this marble between 1415 and 1421. Eligius became the patron saint of smiths and farriers on account of two miracles. In one, armed with red-hot pincers, he chased away a demon disguised as a woman, as a result of which he acquired the capacity to handle red-hot irons without burning himself. In the other, he re-attached a horse's hoof and fetlock that had been cut off. These miracles are represented in the reliefs at the base of the tabernacle, also by Nanni; the female demon appears behind the anvil. Note the pincers, emblem of the guild, decorating the tabernacle.

The statues of S. Matthew, S. Stephen and S. Eligius

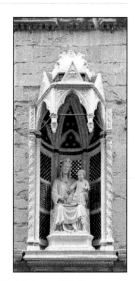

The statues of S. Mark, S. Jacob (James the Greater) and the Madonna of the Rose

Via de' Lamberti

S. Mark – the Linenmakers' and Second-hand Clothes Dealers' Guild

Donatello sculpted this marble statue between 1411 and 1413. Vasari tells an amusing anecdote concerning it. When the guild officials first saw it, before it had been hoisted up into its niche, they were not happy with its proportions. Donatello agreed to make any necessary adjustments once it was in position, and the officials consented to this. The sculptor then screened off the niche for fifteen days, pretending to work on the statue meanwhile, though in reality doing nothing. When he finally uncovered it, everyone was filled with admiration. The frescoed medallion high above the tabernacle is very faded. To the L, on the corner of the building, is a relief showing trees.

S. Jacob (James the Greater) – the Furriers' Guild

The coat-of-arms of this guild includes the *Agnus Dei* because the Furriers were, at one time, members of the Wool Guild. Niccolò di Pietro Lamberti sculpted this statue between 1410 and 1422, and also did the relief of the saint's decapitation. The frescoed medallion high above the tabernacle is very faded.

The Madonna of the Rose – the Physicians' and Apothecaries' Guild

The Madonna holds a bunch of dog-roses, the precise significance of which is uncertain. The statue (*c.* 1399) has been variously attributed. At the time of writing, Piero di Giovanni Tedesco was the front runner, with the niche attributed to Simone Talenti. Note the terracotta coat-of-arms in the medallion high above the tabernacle (see the illustration on page 123).

The statues of S. John the Evangelist, S. John the Baptist, the Incredulity of S. Thomas and S. Luke

S. John the Evangelist – the Silk Guild

This bronze by Baccio da Montelupo was installed in 1515, replacing a marble statue of *c.* 1380 by Simone Talenti which is now in the Ospedale degli Innocenti (Walk 10). Note the terracotta coat-of-arms in the medallion high above (see the illustration on page 123) showing the Por S. Maria, emblem of the guild, also sculpted in the pediment surmounting the tabernacle.

Via de' Calzaiuoli

S. John the Baptist – the Calimala Guild

Between 1412 and 1416, the Calimala Guild commissioned Ghiberti to make this statue. It was the first life-size Renaissance figure to be cast in bronze, and Ghiberti's notebooks reveal just how concerned he was about the enterprise. The frescoed medallion high above is very faded, but the coat-of-arms of the guild (the eagle clasping a bale of cloth) can be seen at the base of the tabernacle. To the L, the little agricultural relief that once adorned the corner of the building is completely worn away.

The Incredulity of S. Thomas – the Tribunale di Mercanzia

This niche originally held Donatello's S. Louis, now in the S. Croce Museum (Walk 5). When the niche passed from the Guelf Party to the Tribunale di Mercanzia, a new statue was required. Vasari again tells us that Donatello asked for too much money. The bronze group showing Thomas and Christ was commissioned from Andrea del Verrocchio in 1467 and installed in the 1480s. Note the terracotta medallion, showing the Lily of Florence, high above the tabernacle (see the illustration on page 123).

S. Luke – the Judges' and Notaries' Guild

This tabernacle was originally occupied by a marble statue carved at the beginning of the 15th century by Niccolò di Pietro Lamberti (now in the Bargello). 200 years later, the Judges and Notaries wanted something less old-fashioned, so they commissioned a bronze from Giambologna. This statue, the last to be installed in the niches of Orsanmichele, was put in place at the beginning of the 17th century. The frescoed medallion high above is very faded.

The interior of Orsanmichele and the Orsanmichele Museum

The entrance to the church lies in Via dell' Arte della Lana. The interior of Orsanmichele always takes my breath away. The walls, vaults, pillars and pilasters are almost entirely covered with 14th-16th century frescoes by a variety of hands. Patriarchs and prophets, each framed by a golden mandorla, gaze down from the rich ultramarine blue of the vaults, while close on forty patron saints of Florence and the city guilds adorn the pillars and pilasters. We begin our tour in the near L corner. In the huge corner pillar here is a door giving access to a staircase within the pillar leading up to the first floor. The architrave over the door has recesses for three shields which bore emblems of the Republic, while above the architrave is a relief of a 'staio', a grain measure, for Orsanmichele was once, remember, the city's grain market, and it continued in use as a granary until the 16th century. In the ceiling above you is an opening through which sacks of grain were hoisted up into the granary above. The pillar bears a depiction of S. Julian (patron of the Innkeepers' Guild).

Moving on to the next pilaster along the L wall, note the discharge chute at its base. Sacks were filled here, the grain cascading down inside the pilaster from the granary above. This pilaster has depictions of S. Bartholomew (patron of the Oilmakers and Cheesemongers), the four crowned saints (protectors of the Construction Workers) and S. Stephen (patron saint of the Wool Guild). At the base of the next pilaster along the wall there is a second discharge chute. On this pilaster can be seen S. Martin and S. Jacob, patron saints of the Vintners and the Furriers respectively.

At the E end of the N nave stands the altar of S. Anne, on whose feast day the Duke of Athens was expelled from Florence in 1343. In the vault above the altar is a fresco showing S. Anne holding a model of Florence (you can see the Baptistery clearly). The lovely marble group on the altar, showing the Christ Child with his mother and grandmother, is by Francesco da Sangallo (1522-26). The inscription on the base, a Latin phrase incised in Hebraic characters, reads *ego sum lux mundi* 'I am the light of the world'. The frescoes on the far corner pillar and behind the altar include images of S. Catherine with her wheel (protectress of all Millers), S. Dominic and S. Francis.

At the E end of the S nave stands the stunning mid-14th century tabernacle by Andrea Orcagna, housing the painting of the Madonna delle Grazie by Bernardo Daddi. Following the terrible plague epidemic of 1348, which killed Bernardo off, the Laudesi confraternity, formed in honour of the original miraculous image of the Madonna from the grain loggia (see above), found itself in possession of a huge number of legacies. They decided to splash out, and no expense was spared on the commission for a tabernacle to house the recently deceased Bernardo's new image. Andrea's work is Gothic run riot. The marbles, coloured glass, bronze and gilt inlays sparkle and dance in flickering candlelight, producing a truly sensational surround for the iconic devotional image. The marble carving is exquisite. Figures of angels top the barley-sugar columns at the corners of the surrounding balustrade, while the twelve apostles gaze down from the tops of the corner pillars of the tabernacle itself (three on each pillar). On the base of the shrine is a series of relief panels showing episodes from the Virgin's life. Depending on their position, these panels are difficult/impossible to see, as is the magnificent relief of the Death and Assumption of the Virgin on the rear of the tabernacle. However, all the reliefs are beautifully illustrated in the Orsanmichele guide.

The frescoes alongside the tabernacle are, like the panels of the Virgin's life, difficult/impossible to see. The pilaster to the R of the tabernacle has frescoes of S. John the Evangelist and S. Augustine, patron saints of the Silk Guild and the Leatherworkers and Tanners, while the next pilaster along has three depictions of S. Matthew, protector of the Bankers' Guild. The corner pillar bears representations of S. George (for the Armourers and Swordmakers), S. Julian again (for the Innkeepers) and S. Nicholas of Tolentino (a patron saint of Florence). The pillar between the doors has S. John the Baptist (patron saint of Florence and of the Calimala Guild), S. Michael Archangel (protector of corn weighers), S. Stephen again (for the Wool Guild) and S. Zenobius (another patron of the city).

The two pillars dividing the N and S naves include depictions of SS. Zenobius or Augustine, the Holy Trinity (the Harnessmakers), the Annunciation (the Carpenters) and S. Martin (the Vintners), S. Bartholomew (the Oilmakers and Cheesemongers), S. Lawrence (the Bakers) and S. Mary Magdalene. You can't see the eighth fresco, on the side nearest to the altars. It shows the good thief, and was commissioned by a repentant thief just prior to his death. The Latin inscription reads *magnam fidem habuisti quando Jesum cognovisti Deum miserum credidisti* 'you had great faith when you recognized Jesus and believed in a God of mercy'. There is an illustration in the Orsanmichele guide.

The stained glass windows of Orsanmichele glow with deep, rich colours. While some doubts subsist regarding the designers, they certainly included Niccolò di Pietro Gerini and Lorenzo Monaco. The subjects include angels, saints, scenes from the Virgin's life and miracles attributed to her intercession.

The first floor of Orsanmichele houses the original statues from the niches on the exterior. The only one missing is the S. George by Donatello, which is in the Bargello (Walk 9). The statues have already been described above. The top floor of Orsanmichele, accessed from the first floor via a modern spiral staircase, is often used for temporary exhibitions. There are good views from here across the city.

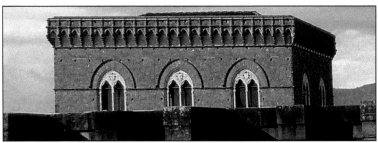

The top floor of Orsanmichele as seen from the roof of the Loggia de' Lanzi

Walk 4

Begins and ends in Piazza della Signoria.

Takes in: the Casa di Dante Museum, the Badia and the Oratory of S. Martino.

Duration: 1 hour 15 minutes, excluding time spent at any of the above. You should allow *c.* 1 hour for the Casa di Dante Museum and *c.* 30 minutes for the Badia. The Oratory of S. Martino will take only 10-15 minutes of your time.

Piazza della Signoria to Orsanmichele

Leave Piazza della Signoria midway along its N side on Via delle Farine. On the far R corner with Via della Condotta stands the huge mediaeval Palazzo Giugni. Turn L along Via della Condotta. On the R on the far corner of Via della Condotta with Vicolo de' Cerchi lies the 13ᵗʰ century Palazzo Cerchi, incorporating the Torre Alepri. The shop on the ground floor here has a decorated vaulted ceiling. Turn R down Vicolo de' Cerchi to reach Via de' Cimatori, with more mediaeval tower-houses. To the L can be seen Orsanmichele and to the R the tower of the Bargello, with the campanile of the Badia next to it (you have to crane your neck to see this).

Via de' Cimatori

The construction of Via de' Cimatori was one of many projects undertaken towards the end of the 13ᵗʰ century by the government of the Secondo Popolo in an attempt to curb the power of unruly magnate families. The street was intended to run from Orsanmichele all the way to the Bargello (see Map 4), cutting through the enclaves of several great families and facilitating the rapid movement of government troops to wherever they might be needed. The government had the power of compulsory purchase and demolition, but secular lost out to sacred here, for the abbot of the Badia was having none of it. He claimed violation of ecclesiastical liberty and eventually won his battle for restitution of the land seized. As a result, Via de' Cimatori had to be aborted behind the Badia.

Turn R along Via de' Cimatori. On the far R corner of the crossroads with Via de' Cerchi, just beneath the street signs, is an old stone marking the position of the erstwhile Loggia de' Cerchi. Turn L along Via de' Cerchi. The Torre Cerchi lies on your R. A few yards further on, Via de' Tavolini leads off to the L. We are going up

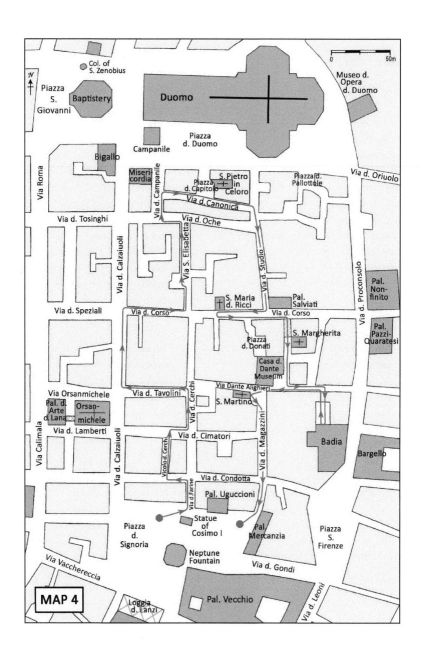

N

Piazza S. Giovanni

Col. of S. Zenobius

Baptistery

Duomo

Museo d. Opera d. Duomo

Campanile

Piazza d. Duomo

Bigallo

Via Roma

Via d. Tosinghi

Misericordia

Via d. Campanile

S. Pietro in Celoro

Piazza d. Capitolo

Piazza d. Pallottole

Via d. Oriuolo

Via d. Canonica

Via d. Oche

Via d. Speziali

Via d. Calzaiuoli

Via S. Elisabetta

Via d. Studio

Via d. Corso

S. Maria d. Ricci

Pal. Salviati

Via d. Corso

Pal. Nonfinito

Via d. Proconsolo

Pal. Pazzi-Quaratesi

S. Margherita

Piazza d. Donati

Casa d. Dante Museum

Via d. Tavolini

Via d. Cerchi

Via Dante Alighieri

S. Martino

Via Orsanmichele

Pal. d. Arte d. Lana

Orsanmichele

Via d. Lamberti

Via Calimala

Via d. Calzaiuoli

Vicolo d. Cerchi

Via d. Cimatori

Via d. Magazzini

Badia

Bargello

Via d. Condotta

Via d. Farine

Pal. Uguccioni

Piazza d. Signoria

Statue of Cosimo I

Neptune Fountain

Pal. Mercanzia

Piazza S. Firenze

Via Vaccchereccia

Via d. Gondi

Via d. Leoni

MAP 4

Loggia d. Lanzi

Pal. Vecchio

0   50m

here in a minute. Before we do, however, look at the buildings on each corner of Via de' Tavolini. That on the L is the Torre Galigai, and it bears a Dante plaque:

'and Galigaio already had in his house the gilded hilt and pommel' (*Paradiso* XVI.101-102).

Dino Compagni says in his *Chronicle* (I.12) that in 1293, when he, Dino, was Gonfalonier of Justice, he led government troops to destroy houses belonging to the magnate family of the Galigai in punishment for a crime against a member of the 'popolani' – a crime that flagrantly violated the newly formulated laws known as the Ordinances of Justice. We'll learn more about these important laws in the section entitled 'the big bad barons' at the end of this walk. The building on the R corner of Via de' Tavolini bears a Dante plaque referring to Giano della Bella:

'Everyone who bears the noble arms of the great baron (whose name and esteem are kept alive by the feast of Thomas), had from him knighthood and privilege, though he who today sides with the people surrounds it with a border' (*Paradiso* XVI.127-132). The 'great baron' was Ugo, Margrave of Tuscany, who died on S. Thomas' Day in 1001 and whose tomb you'll see if you visit the Badia. Ugo created many knights in Florence and they, for love of him, retained and bore his arms. The nobleman who surrounded his arms with a border was Giano della Bella, who, in 1293, helped promulgate the above-mentioned Ordinances of Justice, thereby giving more power to the people. Head up Via de' Tavolini. The della Bella tower lies on your R, as does Paoli's restaurant, mentioned at the end of Walk 3. Further along on the R, just before the junction with Via

de' Calzaiuoli, is a Dante plaque marking the site of the erstwhile home of the Abati family. Dante and Virgil have reached the circle of Hell where traitors are gathered, and when, inadvertently, Dante treads on one of them, the offended shade reacts:

'Weeping, he yelled at me "why are you trampling on me? If you haven't come

to add to the revenge for Montaperti, why are you molesting me?"'
(*Inferno* XXXII.79-81).

The shade then refuses to reveal his identity to Dante, who resorts to pulling his hair out and making him scream, thus prompting another shade to intervene:

'When another shouted "what's the matter, Bocca? Isn't it enough for your jaws to rattle (i.e. for your teeth to chatter), but you must bark? What devil is injuring you?"' (*Inferno* XXXII.106-108).

Dante then realizes that the shade is Bocca degli Abati, who fought in the battle of Montaperti in 1260 against the Ghibelline forces of King Manfred of Sicily, but who turned traitor and cut the Florentine cavalry standard from its bearer's hands, thus helping to precipitate the defeat of the Guelfs and the fall of the Primo Popolo.

Orsanmichele to Piazza del Capitolo

Via de' Tavolini brings you out opposite the corner of Orsanmichele. Turn R here along Via de' Calzaiuoli and then take the next R, Via del Corso. A few yards along on the L, over the door to no. 18 blue, a Dante plaque marks the site of one of the homes of the Adimari family, from whence sprang Filippo Argenti:

'All were shouting "at Filippo Argenti!" and that mad Florentine spirit turned upon himself with his teeth' (*Inferno* VIII.61-63).

Filippo is mentioned again at *Paradiso* XVI.5ff., where he is castigated for insolence, and stories of his arrogance and irascibility are numerous in the early

commentators (see for example Boccaccio, *Decameron* IX.8). A little further along on the L, on each corner of Via S. Elisabetta, are Donati tower-houses, two of several belonging to this family.

Turn down Via S. Elisabetta, passing Piazza S. Elisabetta with its round tower known as 'La Pagliazza'. The only round tower in the city, it is perhaps a survival from the Byzantine or Lombard fortifications. It was a prison in the 13th century and the name comes from the straw used as bedding. It now forms part of the Hotel Brunelleschi. More or less opposite the end of Via S. Elisabetta, where it meets Via dell' Oche, is the Torre de' Visdomini, which

bears a Dante plaque:
'So did the fathers of those who, whenever your church is vacant, make themselves prosperous sitting in consistory council' (*Paradiso* XVI.112-114).

The Visdomini controlled and allegedly exploited the revenues of the See of Florence during a vacancy of the bishop's seat. Turn L and then immediately R down Via del Campanile. Palazzo Visdomini lies on your R, with its mock stone façade and friezes with sails, rings and church names emblazoned thereon. On the L, on the flank of the Misericordia building opposite the end of Via della Canonica, is a tabernacle bearing a Latin inscription which translates 'for the sake of our happiness, pray for us'. This is linked to the story of Ginevra degli Almieri, which I referred to in Walk 1.

The story of Ginevra degli Almieri

At the end of the 14th century, the father of the lovely Ginevra degli Almieri decided to marry his daughter off to a business associate, Francesco Agolanti, despite the fact that the girl was in love with one Antonio Rondinelli, a love that was reciprocated. Once married, Ginevra pined away and her health deteriorated rapidly. One morning she was found apparently lifeless on her bed, so she was dressed in her white wedding gown and taken to the Cathedral cemetery for burial. Ensconced in the tomb, she came round during the night, forced her way out and tottered back to her husband's house. The terrified Francesco thought she was a ghost and barred his door to her. She then went to her father's dwelling, but the reaction there was the same. In desperation she staggered to Antonio's house. He, of course, let her in, comforted her and gradually restored her to health. On learning that Ginevra was alive and living in the Rondinelli household, Francesco got very hot under the collar and took the matter to the Ecclesiastical Court. The Court's decision, however, was unexpected. As the marriage had been dissolved by 'death', Ginevra was free to marry again. This she did, and Ginevra and Antonio lived happily ever after!

Turn down Via della Canonica to the Piazza del Capitolo. This area was where properties of the Chapter of the Canons of the Cathedral were situated. The Chapter still uses the ex-church of S. Pietro in Celoro in the piazza to house archives. The corbelled building on your R is the current office of the Opera di S. Maria del Fiore (i.e. the Opera del Duomo), whose headquarters used to stand on the site of the present museum (Walk 1). We shall see their workshop at the end of the street.

Piazza del Capitolo to the Casa di Dante

Continue along Via della Canonica. On the L at the end of the street is the 13th century Palazzo Tedaldini, the door to which lies just around the corner in Via dello Studio. Over the door is a bust of Antonino Pierozzi and a plaque commemorating this man who, during the course  of his career, was prior at the monastery of S. Marco and archbishop of Florence, and was later canonized. He received part of his education here, Via dello Studio being the area occupied by the University, founded in a bid to attract scholars to Florence after the terrible plague epidemic of 1348. On the opposite corner of Via della Canonica lies the workshop of the Opera del Duomo, where statuary and masonry from the Duomo are restored and replicated. Do take a peep inside, for this gives you an idea of what a sculptor's workshop must have looked like. Follow Via dello Studio away from the Duomo right back to the T-junction with Via del Corso. On the L here lies the huge Palazzo Salviati, now a bank. We'll return to this palace shortly, but for the moment we're going to turn R here and head up Via del Corso for a few yards to the church of S. Maria de' Ricci on the R. The church houses a painting of the Annunciation to which the tragic tale of Antonio Rinaldeschi is attached.

The tragic tale of Antonio Rinaldeschi

In July 1501 the young Antonio Rinaldeschi, staggering home in a drunken haze after having lost all his money and most of his garments at dice, scooped up a handful of horse dung and hurled it angrily at an image of the Virgin housed in a tabernacle in a little alley just off Via del Corso, uttering many blasphemies as he did so. Alas for Antonio, there were witnesses to this outrageous behaviour. They reported the incident to the authorities, and Antonio was arrested and put on trial. Deeply repentant for his drunken excesses he begged for mercy, but to no avail. He was hanged from a window of the Bargello. Luca Landucci tells us in his *Diary* that all of Florence came to see the image and that, when the bishop had removed the dirt, votive offerings were placed in front of it. In 1508 an oratory was built, which was afterwards enlarged and made into a parish church. The revered image is over the high altar, while in the last side chapel on the L is a copy of a painting showing the entire story in a series of panels (the original panels are in the Stibbert Museum, which is quite a way out of the centre of town).

More or less opposite the church of S. Maria de' Ricci, at nos. 47-49 red, is a narrow passage between the buildings. The story goes that this passage was originally opened up by the authorities at the end of the 13th century to separate properties belonging to the families of the Cerchi and Donati, both of which names we've encountered already on this walk. The Cerchi and the Donati, leaders of the White and Black Guelf factions respectively, hated one another's guts. We'll learn more about them in the section entitled 'the big bad barons' at the end of this walk.

Retrace your steps back along the Corso towards the afore-mentioned bank housed in the huge Palazzo Salviati. As you go, note, on your R, a Donati tower-house bearing a Dante plaque on the corner of the entrance to

Piazza de' Donati. Dante has just met Forese Donati in Purgatory. Forese was the brother of Corso Donati, leader of the Black faction, who was in part responsible for having Dante, a White Guelf, banished. Dante tells Forese that he has no great wish to live:

"'For the place where I was set to live (Florence), from day to day is stripped of goodness and seems destined to become a sad ruin." ("Now go," he (Forese) said,) "for the one who is most to blame (Corso) I see dragged at the tail of a beast towards the valley where there is no exculpation (hell)"'
(*Purgatorio* XXIV.79-84).

Opposite the bank housed in Palazzo Salviati is the arched opening to Via S. Margherita, where we're going shortly. Before we do, though, let me just tell you that the palace was built by the Portinari family in the 1470s, then bought and enlarged in the mid-16th century by Jacopo Salviati, whose aunt Maria was the mother of Grand Duke Cosimo I. Dante's Beatrice was a Portinari and the palace bears a Dante plaque referring to her:

'Encircled with olive over a lily-white veil, a lady appeared to me, clothed under her green mantle in the colour of living flame' (*Purgatorio* XXX.31-33). The colours of Beatrice's clothing represent the three theological virtues, faith (white),

hope (green) and love (red), while the olive crown symbolizes wisdom, for Beatrice is the divine light illuminating the virtues. Leave Via del Corso opposite the bank on Via S. Margherita (under the arch). On your L is the church of S. Margherita de' Cerchi, its porch bearing the arms of the Cerchi, Donati and Adimari families. Much (far too much) is now made of the Dante connection, that this is where he met Beatrice, that she is buried in the church, and that Dante eventually married Gemma Donati here, all of which statements are doubtful. Forget the Dante hype – just go in and see the wonderful altarpiece by Neri di Bicci.

Neri di Bicci's record book

Neri di Bicci ran one of the busiest workshops in the city, ranked as the wealthiest painter in the 1480 'catasto' (tax census), and managed to set his sons up in the silk business. His record book, kept from 1453 to 1475, provides fascinating insights into his dealings. One transaction provides a glorious example of the process known as 'off-setting'. In 1466 one of Neri's tenants, a silk weaver, wanted to pay off some of his rent, so he asked a spinner with whom he had credit to pay Neri. The spinner, in turn, asked a silk firm with whom he had credit to pay Neri. They informed Neri, and he, in his ledger, credited his tenant's account and debited the silk firm. He then used his credit with the firm to pay off one of his debts – and all the while no cash changed hands.

The Casa di Dante Museum, the Badia and the Oratory of S. Martino

A few yards further along Via S. Margherita on the R is the Casa di Dante Museum (there is a good view of the exterior from the little piazza at the end of Via S. Margherita). The museum contains much that is interesting

regarding mediaeval Florence, mainly in the form of models and information panels, but if you are expecting to lie on Dante's bed, sit in his chair, hold his quill, or even eat his porridge, you will be mightily disappointed. Fortunately, the shop can be accessed without the necessity of visiting the museum, so you can pop in, peruse the guidebook and then decide for yourself if you wish to spend time here.

The Casa di Dante Museum, but not the Casa di Dante

I'm afraid that I have to destroy any illusions you may have about the Casa di Dante Museum being Dante's house. 1865 was both the 600th anniversary of Dante's birth and the year in which the capital of the new kingdom of Italy was transferred from Turin to Florence. To mark the occasion a project was initiated to locate and reconstruct the great poet's house. A committee of experts scoured all available sources, including historical documents and tax rolls, and identified this site as the most likely one. Drawings and plans were produced, but shortly after this the capital of Italy was transferred to Rome, leaving poor Florence in such disastrous financial straits that many projects had to be set aside, Dante's house included. The idea was taken up again in the early 20th century and entrusted to the prominent architect Giuseppe Castellucci. He created the little piazza at the end of Via S. Margherita, and the house that borders it, incorporating a tower-house that had belonged to the Giuochi family into his design - Dante's family was the Alighieri, not the Giuochi. One of the sources used by the 19th century committee was a legal document dealing with a suit brought against the Alighieri by the priest of the church of S. Martino al Vescovo. He complained that the roots of their fig tree were damaging the wall of the garden belonging to the church. The church has gone, but the little Oratory of S. Martino survives.

If the restricted opening times of the Badia fit your schedule and you wish to visit, turn L at the end of Via S. Margherita down Via Dante Alighieri and you'll find the entrance a few yards along on the R. A Dante plaque on the wall to the R of the entrance refers to the tolling of the Badia bell, which

regulated life within the circle of the old city walls: 'Florence, within the ancient circle from whence she still takes tierce and nones, lived in peace, sober and modest' (*Paradiso* XV.97-99).

Inside the Badia you'll find, among other treasures, a painting by Filippino Lippi showing the Madonna appearing to S. Bernard, a tomb by Rossellino's workshop, and two tombs and an altarpiece by Mino da Fiesole. One of these last tombs is that of Ugo, Margrave of Tuscany, who died in 1001. He was originally buried in a recycled Roman sarcophagus, but in the mid-15th century the monks decided to give him this splendid new sepulchre. While at the Badia you may be lucky enough to gain access to the 'Chiostro degli Aranci' ('Cloister of the Oranges'), with its 15th century frescoes illustrating scenes from the life of S. Benedict.

If the opening times of the Badia don't fit your schedule, stay put in the piazza outside the Casa di Dante Museum. On the wall opposite the end

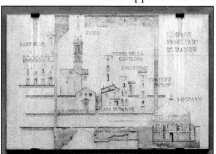

of Via S. Margherita there are two plaques, a big modern one showing the places in Florence that would have been familiar to Dante and, some way to the L of it, a very small old one bearing a directive from the eight Signori, the law and order officials whose decrees feature also in some of the other walks. Here, they prohibit the ball game of pallottole and all other uproar within 20 braccia (c. 11m) of the Badia under pain of rigorous penalty. To the R of the above-mentioned plaques lies the 13th century Torre della Castagna. It bears a third plaque telling us that it was the seat from which the priors governed Florence before the strength and glory of the Commune raised the

Palazzo della Signoria (i.e. the Palazzo Vecchio). Opposite this plaque can be seen a Dante plaque

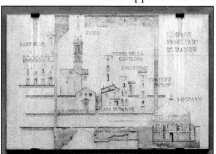

on the flank of the Casa di Dante Museum quoting *Inferno* XXIII.94-95, where Dante says that he was born and grew up on the lovely river Arno, in the great city of Florence. The entrance to the Torre della Castagna lies

just around the corner in Piazza S. Martino. Next to the door is a plaque quoting Dino Compagni, who, in his *Chronicle* (I.4), tells us that the priors stayed secluded here so that they did not have to fear the threats of the powerful.

The Torre della Castagna

The elders of the Guelf government of the Primo Popolo (1250-60) used to

meet in the Torre della Castagna, which didn't belong to any magnate family but was originally built to protect the Badia. When the Secondo Popolo was established towards the end of the 13th century, the priors again chose this tower as their official residence, thereby symbolically linking the Primo and Secondo Popoli. The choice of the tower made other political statements too. Not only did it offer defence against hostile and unruly magnates, but it also appropriated their customary type of dwelling and, being located in an area dominated by so many powerful elite families, invaded their space. To prevent intimidation and bribery, the priors, during their two-month period of office, would stay in the tower under lock and key, from whence comes our term 'conclave'. The name of the tower came from the procedure for voting. The priors used chestnuts ('castagne'), which, in Florentine dialect are called 'ballotte', from which comes the term 'ballot'. When the Popolo eventually built the Palazzo de' Priori (i.e. the Palazzo della Signoria/Palazzo Vecchio), the priors vacated the Torre della Castagna.

On the other side of Piazza S. Martino, directly opposite the entrance to the Torre della Castagna, lies the Oratory of S. Martino, which I urge you to visit. In the mid-15th century it became the seat of a charitable institution called the 'Buonuomini' ('Good Men'). This institution was founded by Antonino Pierozzi, whom we encountered earlier on this walk (we saw his bust over the door to Palazzo Tedaldini). It helped the 'shame-faced poor', people from good families who, perhaps through illness, death or political persecution (of which there was much) had fallen on hard times but were too proud to ask openly for charity. The interior of the Oratory is decorated with a delightful series of frescoes by the Ghirlandaio workshop illustrating scenes from the life of S. Martin and works of charity performed by the Buonuomini. These good works included, among other things, payment of bills, debts and dowries, provision of food and clothing, special help for widows and orphans, and payment of burial expenses. All assistance was provided with the utmost tact and discretion, so that those benefiting would not be humiliated. In the outside wall to the L of the door is a slot with the inscription 'per le istanze' ('for the requests'), where people could apply anonymously for assistance. To the R of the door is a slot for donations, with a lengthy inscription enumerating all the spiritual benefits (papal pardons, indulgences and the like) that would accrue to donors (see page 146 for illustration). When funds got low, the Buonuomini would place a lighted candle at the window, indicating that they needed a financial top-up. The institution still functions today and performs its charitable work. It has an archive going back to the date of its foundation, and it still protects the embarrassment of the 'shame-faced poor' by keeping the beneficiaries on its ledgers secret.

Piazza S. Martino to Piazza della Signoria

On exiting from the Oratory leave the piazza on Via de' Magazzini, which runs off to the R. On the wall directly opposite the end of Via de' Cimatori is a tiny plaque bearing the same directive from the eight Signori that we saw opposite the Casa di Dante Museum, so you couldn't use the excuse that you hadn't seen the first one! Via de' Cimatori was intended to run all the way to the Bargello, through land belonging to the Badia, but the abbot wouldn't allow it and the street had to be aborted here. Continue along Via de' Magazzini, crossing over Via della Condotta where, on the near L corner, stands the huge Torre Sacchetti. Via de' Magazzini leads back into Piazza della Signoria, where this walk ends. Time for a drink and, if you feel like it, a short history lesson (the section entitled 'the big bad barons') about some of the personalities we've encountered on Walks 3 and 4.

Palazzo Vecchio from Via de' Cerchi

The big bad barons

On Walk 3 we saw how the murder of Buondelmonte by the Amidei led to the emergence of the Guelf and Ghibelline factions in Florence. By the end of the 1260s the Guelfs were dominant and, eventually, the government of the Secondo Popolo was set up. However, the final decades of the 13th century were far from peaceful, for the Guelfs then started to quarrel among themselves.

While certain of the Guelfs wanted none of the Ghibellines, others were not opposed to some form of compromise. The 'Guelf/Ghibelline' bloc appealed to Pope Nicholas III and he sent Cardinal Latino to Florence to act as mediator. Villani tells us that the cardinal arrived with 300 horsemen on 8th October 1278 and that the carroccio was sent out to meet him, escorted by many jousters (*Chronicle* VII.56; see page 115 for the carroccio). A peace plan was drawn up and solemnized in the old piazza of S. Maria delle Vigne (Walk 11), but the anti-Ghibelline faction gradually contravened the treaty and discord erupted again. In an effort to remedy the situation some of the nobles turned to the popolo. Six officials were chosen, one from each sestiere (sixth) of the city. They were called priors and Dino Compagni was one of them. As we've seen on Walk 4, Dino tells us in his *Chronicle* that they stayed shut up in the tower of the Castagna so that they did not have to fear the threats of the powerful (I.4).

Still things didn't work out. Villani (*Chronicle* VIII.1) says that there was much unrest, and that many magnates used force and violence against those who were unable to resist them. Eventually, a group crystallized under the leadership of Giano della Bella, whom we encountered on Walk 4. This nobleman, who joined forces with the people, was elected as a prior and, together with his colleagues in office, took rapid steps to strengthen the popolo. New draconian laws called the Ordinances of Justice were enacted in 1293. These laws were intended to curb the power and arrogance of the magnates. Magnates were no longer eligible for government office and, in addition, became answerable for crimes committed by their families. Their properties could be destroyed as punishment. The guilds were brought more into government, with some authority being given to their consuls, and the new office of Gonfalonier (Standard-Bearer) of Justice was created. Militia groups were drawn up for each sestiere, which, says Villani, were to assemble on the summons of the Gonfalonier to do execution against the magnates. We saw on Walk 4 how, when Dino Compagni was Gonfalonier, this militia force went against the Galigai family. Unsurprisingly, the magnates were furious, and they missed no opportunity to try to derail the government and break down the new laws. The priors, no longer feeling safe in the Torre della Castagna, decreed the construction of the Palazzo de' Priori, begun in 1298.

There had long been bad feeling between the Donati and the Cerchi families. The Cerchi were powerful merchants, part of the *nouveaux riches* if Villani is to be believed (*Chronicle* VIII.39), while Corso Donati and his house were gentlemen.

Two Guelf factions crystallized, known as the Whites and the Blacks, with Vieri de' Cerchi and Corso Donati as their respective leaders, and there were constant brawls between them. In 1298 some Cerchi family members died in custody, ostensibly killed by eating poisoned black pudding, and Corso Donati was widely held to have been behind this. In 1300, during a fight at the Mayday celebrations in Piazza S. Trinità, Ricoverino de' Cerchi lost his nose. A furious priorate banished many Blacks, Corso Donati included.

The Whites were now in a dominant position. Pope Boniface VIII had already made several attempts to mediate, to no avail. Now the Blacks played up the possibility of a White/Ghibelline coalition and persuaded Boniface to intervene more forcefully. He did this by appointing Charles of Valois (brother of King Philip IV of France) as peacemaker in Tuscany. The Whites (ill-advisedly) agreed to this. Compagni (*Chronicle* II.7) tells us that the Signoria called a general council of the Guelf Party and asked each guild to submit a statement on whether they wanted Charles or not. All agreed that he should come except the bakers, who maintained that he was coming to destroy the city. The bakers were clearly savvy political thinkers. Charles arrived at the beginning of November 1301 and was granted overlordship of Florence. Many banished Blacks began to return, ostensibly to pay their respects to Charles, but as soon as they were strong enough they hastened to seize the city. Charles, far from doing anything to stop them, sat back and let it all happen. Corso Donati returned from exile and was acclaimed by his supporters. The priors resigned (Villani says that Corso terrified them into laying down the government) and new officials were elected; unsurprisingly, they were 100% Black. More than 600 Whites were exiled, Dante included. When Charles finally left Florence in April 1302 the city was firmly under the control of Corso Donati and his cronies.

Before long, discord broke out again. Corso, dissatisfied with his division of lordships and offices, formed a new faction, recruiting to it many Whites who'd remained in Florence. Villani (*Chronicle* VIII.68) says there was fighting throughout the city for many days, with engines to hurl missiles set in many of the towers and strongholds. Corso's faction was principally composed of magnates, while his rival, Rosso della Tosa, had aligned himself with the better-off popolani who controlled the government. During the hostilities, one Testa Tornaquinci wounded a popolano. Compagni says the militia went, armed with the banner of justice, to the Palazzo Tornaquinci and burnt it (*Chronicle* III.3).

The pope, by this time Benedict XI, again tried to intervene, sending Cardinal Niccolò of Prato as mediator. A peace plan was ratified on 26th April 1304, but those who didn't want peace fomented strife. Generally speaking, Rosso's faction, who already held control, opposed the cardinal, while Corso's lot, along with the Whites and the Ghibellines, supported him. In the end, the cardinal gave up and departed in furious mood. After his departure things became (literally) heated.

Compagni (*Chronicle* III.8) tells how the della Tosa and Medici came into the Old Market armed with crossbows, shooting towards the Corso degli Adimari and Via Calimala, and attacking a barricade in the Corso. The fighting eventually resulted in a fire that destroyed much of the city centre, including Orsanmichele, where many wax devotional images caught fire. All the houses around were burned, along with warehouses in Via Calimala, and all the shops around the Old Market, the New Market, Via Vacchereccia and Via Por S. Maria all the way to the Ponte Vecchio. Compagni says that more than nineteen hundred properties were destroyed, and that nothing could be done to stop the fire.

Aided and abetted by the Cardinal of Prato, still smarting from the failure of his peace plan, the Whites and the Ghibellines decided to take matters into their own hands and launch an attack on Florence, but they were repulsed (the story is told more fully in the section entitled 'a failed attack on Florence' at the end of Walk 11). Such external threats did not, however, quell the internal discord. Corso Donati had on his side a large part of the magnates, still smarting under the Ordinances of Justice, which Corso promised to annul. In 1308 things came to a head when it was discovered that Corso had made a pact with his father-in-law (who was a Ghibelline) and had sent to him for support. The priors condemned Corso as a traitor. Corso, expecting help from his father-in-law, barricaded himself inside his enclave near S. Pier Maggiore. The story is told at more length under Walk 5 in the section entitled 'the battle at Piazza S. Pier Maggiore'. Suffice it to say here that, being overcome and forced to flee, he was captured and injured near the abbey of S. Salvi, where he subsequently died.

In August 1312 Henry of Luxembourg was crowned as Holy Roman Emperor. He stirred the hopes of many a White and Ghibelline, Dante and Compagni included. The Black Florentines had openly revealed themselves as Henry's enemies and Henry prepared to attack the city. After a short while, however, he retreated, and then died in August 1313, much to the relief of the Blacks. As for Rosso della Tosa, who, after Corso's death, lorded it in Florence, Compagni (*Chronicle* III.38) says that he kept God waiting a long time, for he was more than seventy-five years old when he died. He fell over a dog that ran between his feet, broke his nose, which became infected, and died from the agony. Watch out for runaway dogs – you have been warned!

Inscription on the façade of the Oratory of S. Martino

The campanile of the Badia with Brunelleschi's lantern behind

Walk 5

Begins at Piazza del Duomo and ends at Piazza S. Croce.
Takes in: the Museum of Anthropology and Ethnology, the church of
S. Ambrogio, the Casa Buonarroti and S. Croce.
Duration: 2 hours for the full walk, excluding time spent at any of the above,
and 1 hour for the shorter version, omitting S. Ambrogio. You should allow
at least 1 hour each for the Museum of Anthropology and Ethnology and
the Casa Buonarroti. S. Croce is a large complex and there is a lot to see. It is
hard to judge how much time should be allowed for it, as this will depend on
how long you wish to gaze at frescoes. I would allow either side of 2 hours.
Tips: this walk is best begun in the morning. The church of S. Ambrogio
closes for the afternoon from 12 noon onwards, so if you're doing the full
version of the walk you'll need to take this into account. Small binoculars
may prove useful for looking at the frescoes in S. Croce.

Piazza del Duomo to the Museum of Anthropology and Ethnology
Leave the Piazza del Duomo at its SE corner on Via del Proconsolo and walk
along to Borgo degli Albizi (on the L). This was the site of the E gate of the
Roman city. On the near corner of the borgo is the Palazzo Nonfinito, begun
by Buontalenti in 1593. The palace houses the Museum of Anthropology
and Ethnology. The stunning collections are displayed in eighteen rooms on
an upper floor and contain objects from Siberia, Lapland, N America, Brazil,
Bolivia, Columbia, the Guyanas, Peru, Venezuela, the sub-Saharan cultures,
Ethiopia, Eritrea, Somalia, the Kalahari, the Andaman Islands, Indonesia,
Borneo, New Guinea, Japan, Polynesia, Australia and New Zealand – and
I've probably missed a few! To my mind the most stunning exhibits are
the ritual cloaks from the Tupinamba culture of Brazil made of scarlet ibis
feathers. At the time of writing the labelling was mainly only in Italian, but
there was a booklet available in English.

The Museum of Anthropology and Ethnology to Piazza S. Pier Maggiore

On the far corner of Borgo degli
Albizi lies Palazzo Pazzi-Quaratesi.
Jacopo de' Pazzi acquired the
necessary site in the usual manner
by buying up properties adjacent to
the family house in the 1460s. The
design of the palace is attributed to
Giuliano da Maiano, who, following
the famous Pazzi conspiracy of 1478,
applied to the courts for payment
of money owed to him on Jacopo's

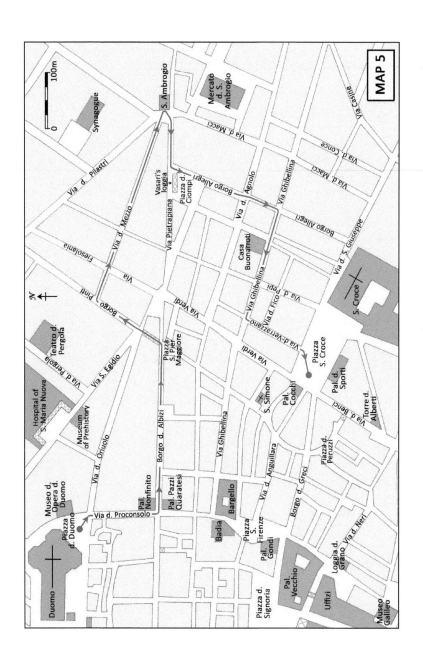

confiscated property. The ground floor is rusticated while the upper floors are faced with smooth stucco, throwing into relief the lovely bifore windows decorated with vines, wreaths and billowing sails. The coat-of-arms on the corner has the family dolphins (cf. also the Pazzi Chapel at S. Croce).

 The capitals of the columns round the courtyard use the dolphin motif together with flaming urns, the latter a reference to the pieces of flint brought back from the Holy Sepulchre in Jerusalem by the crusader Pazzino de' Pazzi and used to light the fireworks at Easter (see Walk 3 under SS. Apostoli). The story of the Pazzi conspiracy is recounted at the end of Walk 8. Following its failure, Jacopo fled but was caught and hanged. Francesco de' Pazzi hid in the palace but was found by the mob, hauled out and likewise hanged. So violent was the mob's rage that Jacopo's body was dragged through the streets, tied to the door-pull of this palace, symbolically flogged and then thrown into the Arno. Pazzi properties were confiscated, and the palace eventually passed to Lorenzo Il Magnifico's son-in-law, Francesco Cibo (illegitimate son of Pope Innocent VIII), and, later, to the Strozzi and Quaratesi families. On a happier note, Luca Landucci notes in his *Diary* that during the winter of 1510/11, when Florence lay under two feet of snow, many great snow statues by good masters were made here.

Food, fun and fireworks

When Lorenzo Il Magnifico's daughter Maddalena married Francesco Cibo, the erstwhile Pazzi Palace passed to the Cibo family and became their chief residence in Florence. The word 'cibo' means 'food', and was a gift for satirists and lampoonists. Francesco and Maddalena's eldest son, named Innocenzo after his grandfather Pope Innocent VIII, eventually became a cardinal. His ecclesiastical rank notwithstanding, he carried on a blatant affair with his sister-in-law Ricciarda Malaspina, his brother Lorenzo's wife, apparently with the blessing of Lorenzo himself. Ricciarda's sister Taddea, meanwhile, became the mistress of Duke Alessandro, who spent many an evening at the palace. This intimacy allowed a third Cibo brother, Giovanbattista, to plan Alessandro's assassination. The plan was to hide barrels of gunpowder in the palace and blow Alessandro sky-high. The plan was discovered, however, and Giovanbattista was tortured to extract from him the names of his accomplices. He escaped with his life, thanks no doubt to his family connections. Less than two months later, however, Cardinal Ippolito de' Medici, the instigator of the plot, who was jealous and wanted Florence for himself, died of poison while en route to Naples.

We now follow Borgo degli Albizi all the way along to Piazza S. Pier Maggiore. The street is lined with imposing palaces, many of them still bearing Pazzi or Albizi coats-of-arms. Unfortunately, because the borgo is so narrow, one can't really get far enough away from the handsome façades to admire them properly (this is a frequent frustration when trying to appreciate Florentine Renaissance architecture). On the L, at no. 28 blue, is the 16th century Palazzo Vitali (or 'Palazzo Pazzi della Colombaria') and next to it, at no. 26 blue, is Palazzo Ramirez di Montalvo. Following the Pazzi conspiracy the property at no. 28, which belonged to Francesco de' Pazzi's brother, was confiscated. About a century later a Pazzi from another branch

of the family bought it back and rebuilt the façade, which is attributed to Ammannati. Note the Pazzi emblems of the flaming urns and dolphins on the pediments. The palace was owned by the Pazzi family until the end of the 19th century.

The 'Accademia della Colombaria'

The palace at no. 28 blue is called the 'Palazzo Pazzi della Colombaria' because, in the 18th century, Giovanni Girolamo de' Pazzi started gatherings of his learned friends here and, as they used to meet in the library high up in the palace, they referred to themselves as the 'Accademia della Colombaria' ('Academy of the Dovecote'). Rather charmingly, the Academy members named themselves after different types of dove – Pazzi himself was the 'torraiuolo' (domestic pigeon).

The façade of the Palazzo Ramirez di Montalvo at no. 26 is also by Ammannati. Antonio Ramirez di Montalvo, who bought this property in 1558, was a Spaniard in the court of Eleonora di Toledo, wife of Cosimo I (you can see a portrait of him by Vasari in the Sala di Cosimo I in the Palazzo Vecchio). Antonio proudly displayed the Medici arms on his palace, and the sgraffito decorations, executed by Vasari's workshop, illustrate the virtues most becoming to a faithful courtier – modesty, temperance, prudence, fidelity, affection and fortitude on the ground floor, felicity, secrecy, obedience, vigilance, labour

and perseverance on the first floor. One of Cosimo I's insignia, the tortoise with sail, can still be seen in an octagonal surround above the first floor windows. The family owned the palace for 300 years, when the male line died out. One tenant in the 18th century was Baron Filippo de Stosch, whose devotion to learning provided a useful cloak for concealing his true purpose – to spy for the English government on the Young Pretender and his brother, who were then in Florence trying to rally support for their cause (see Walk 10 for the palace bought by the Young Pretender).

On the corner of Via de' Giraldi is a fine tabernacle with a 14th century painting of the Madonna enthroned with saints and angels. A few yards

further on, at no. 27 on the R, is the 16th century Palazzo Tanagli, while a house with mediaeval fragments survives at no. 22 on the L. Note the little blue and yellow tile with a Pazzi dolphin at the extreme LH edge of this façade. Next to no. 22 is the huge Palazzo Altoviti-Valori at no. 18. The original 15th century palace was enlarged in the 16th century, when marble portraits of famous Florentine citizens by Caccini were placed on the façade. A ducal bust graces the door, while under the L window there is a plaque commemorating a miracle performed by S. Zenobius, when he resurrected the son of a pilgrim. Directly opposite Palazzo Altoviti-Valori is another Palazzo Valori, which preserves its iron work for the window canopies.

The little Piazzetta Piero Calamandrei opens up on the R. Note the plaque on the far corner with the borgo informing you that in

1733 the city officials issued a decree prohibiting unseemly behaviour in this piazzetta under penalty of arrest and/or any other punishment which they deemed necessary. Facing the piazzetta at no. 14

is the 13th-14th century Torre degli Albizi, while next to it at no. 12 lies the Palazzo degli Albizi. Both buildings bear the Albizi arms. The shops housed on the ground floor of the palazzo have lovely frescoed decoration. The 14th century fabric of the palace survives only at the end nearest the piazzetta; the nine bays on the R of the façade were reconstructed later. The palace stayed in the Albizi family until 1877, with the death of Marchese Vittorio degli Albizi. A plaque above the entrance records Vittorio's many virtues, saying that he gave work to many and was an example to all patricians. His only daughter was the wife of Marchese Angiolo de' Frescobaldi, and so to the Frescobaldi family came the palace and the vineyards now famous for their wines.

Talking of wines, opposite the Albizi palace, the little palace at no. 17 has a wine hatch (see Walk 3 for the purpose of these) as a letter box, while the Palazzo degli Alessandri at no. 15, which is still owned by the Alessandri family, has much of its 14th century façade intact.

On the L at no. 10 the Palazzo da Filicaia has a bust of the poet Vincenzo Filicaia (1642-1707) over the door, while no. 11 on the R has a bust of Cosimo II (as well as another wine hatch). If you press yourself against the wall opposite no. 11 and look up, you'll see a mediaeval tower rising above it. This tower was one of several belonging to the Donati clan. Borgo degli Albizi ends at Piazza S. Pier Maggiore. Over to the R can be seen another Donati tower (see page 155 for illustration). The piazza takes its name from the church that once stood here, of which only the 17th century arch of the portico survives. The church housed the body of Michelangelo

Michelangelo's two funerals

Michelangelo had died and been interred at Rome, but Cosimo I, having tried unsuccessfully for years to persuade the great man to return to his native city, was determined to regain possession of the corpse and give it burial in Florence. Michelangelo's body was secretly disinterred and smuggled out of Rome concealed as merchandise. On arrival in Florence it was brought to the crypt of S. Pier Maggiore, where it lay overnight and all the next day. The funeral procession to S. Croce was planned for after dark so as to keep it as secret as possible. Word got around, however, and crowds gathered. Partly to please the crowds, the coffin was opened and it was found that, despite being more than three weeks old, the corpse showed no signs of decay. Vasari gives an account of the entire proceedings. A few months later elaborate obsequies, likewise described by Vasari, were held at the church of S. Lorenzo (Walk 6).

The battle at Piazza S. Pier Maggiore

If you have done Walk 4 and read the section at the end of it on 'the big bad barons', you'll already be familiar with Messer Corso Donati, who, along with others of his ilk, caused such trouble for the nascent Republic of Florence at the end of the 13th/beginning of the 14th century. In 1308, following the discovery that he'd sent to his (Ghibelline) father-in-law for armed support to overthrow the government, he was condemned as a rebel and a traitor. Villani (*Chronicle* VIII.96) tells us that the priors, the Podestà and the Capitano, along with their retainers, troops and standard-bearers of the companies, went to Corso's house at S. Pier Maggiore to carry out the sentence. Corso, expecting imminent help from his father-in-law outside the city, had barricaded himself and his supporters in, blocking all the entrances to the piazza. A battle ensued which lasted the greater part of the day. Father-in-law, meanwhile, hearing that Corso was besieged, turned back. Dino Compagni (*Chronicle* III.20) says that the government forces attacked the barricades with crossbows, stones, and fire. Corso's soldiers defended themselves vigorously, but eventually began to despair of reinforcements and to desert. Corso escaped and fled, but was captured near the abbey of S. Salvi, a few miles outside the city. His pleas to his captors fell on deaf ears, so he apparently fell deliberately from his horse, thereby provoking an attack in which he was mortally wounded. He was buried in the abbey. Compagni, despite being his adversary, gives an objective assessment of the man, saying that, although he lived dangerously and died reprehensibly, he was a knight of spirit and renown, noble in blood and handsome in appearance, a charming and elegant speaker accustomed to dealing familiarly with great men, and famous throughout all Italy (*Chronicle* III.21).

before his funeral at S. Croce. If you are pushed for time and would prefer to do the shorter version of this walk, skip to the section entitled 'the Casa Buonarroti' (page 158). To get to the Casa Buonarroti, head under the great 17 century portico arch of the former church of S. Pier Maggiore, turn R down Via Verdi, and then L at the crossroads with Via Ghibellina. You'll find the Casa Buonarroti three blocks along Via Ghibellina on the L.

Piazza S. Pier Maggiore to S. Ambrogio

Leave Piazza S. Pier Maggiore on the Volta di S. Pier Maggiore, an archway lined with shops and eateries (on the L of the piazza if you're facing the

portico arch of the erstwhile church). The building over the archway is very handsome and bears the Albizi arms. The LH end of it was clearly once a tower, now reduced in height. The volta brings you out opposite Borgo Pinti, which we follow for part of its course. The borgo, another attractive narrow mediaeval street lined with fine buildings, used to lead to one of the city gates. We shall traverse another stretch of it on Walk 10. Opposite the end of Via di Mezzo is a splendid palace at no. 13. Turn R down Via di Mezzo. At the end of the street can be seen the church of S. Ambrogio, which is

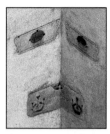

where we are heading. Note the marker on the L of the church façade showing the level of the 1966 flood. On the R corner of the façade are the 'Red City' markers. The lower one (15th century) shows a walled city with three towers; the upper one was added in 1577. On the opposite side of the street can be seen the 'Red City' glazed terracotta tabernacle, with the figure of the parish saint. The 'Red City' was one of several 'potenze' (associations of artisans and labourers) that existed in Florence.

The Florentine 'potenze' and the sorry tale of Donato Pennechini

The Florentine 'potenze' (associations of artisans and labourers) operated like little plebeian kingdoms. Often transgressing the accepted rules of social order and status (rather like the reign of the 'Lord of Misrule' in mediaeval England), they were harmless enough, and were, in the main, recognized by their local churches and tolerated by the authorities. But I must now relate the sorry tale of Donato Pennechini, a textile labourer who was crowned monarch of the 'Red City' in the church of S. Ambrogio in 1600. These were the days of the Counter Reformation, when, in the aftermath of the Council of Trent, zealous reformers were increasingly intolerant of any unorthodox ritual. Donato and those who took part in his coronation came up against some particularly zealous officials, who were outraged at what they regarded as a totally unacceptable mixture of sacred sacrament and lay festivity. The reaction was swift and harsh. The abbess of the convent attached to S. Ambrogio was deposed and the prior of the church was sacked, exiled from the diocese for a year and barred from performing the sacraments. The sacristan and other church officials were also sacked. Donato was initially jailed and then exiled from his neighbourhood for six months. You may be pleased to learn that the authorities later relented and cancelled his sentence.

The church of S. Ambrogio

The church of S. Ambrogio contains art works by and attributed to, among others, Niccolò Gerini, Orcagna, Lorenzo di Bicci, Raffaellino del Garbo, Agnolo Gaddi and Alesso Baldovinetti. The pearl of the church, however, is the Chapel of the Eucharistic Miracle, which lies to the L of the sanctuary. In 1230 the priest found drops of blood in the chalice. Thereafter, the miraculous vessel was regularly carried in procession and was credited with further miracles. The delightful 15ᵗʰ century fresco by Cosimo Rosselli shows such a procession in front of the church. It includes a self-portrait (on the L) and portraits of several of Rosselli's contemporaries. The exquisite tabernacle housing the chalice is by Mino da Fiesole (1481), who is buried at the entrance to the chapel. Francesco Granacci, Il Cronaca and Verrocchio are also buried in the church.

S. Ambrogio to the Casa Buonarroti

If you were to head down Via de' Macci (running off at a right-angle to the R of the church as you face the façade) and take the first turning to the L, you'd come to the Mercato di S. Ambrogio, a smaller version of the S. Lorenzo market (Walk 6). However, I'm going to take you along Via Pietrapiana (the next street round clockwise) to the Piazza de' Ciompi. Named after

those troublesome workers who got such a raw deal in the 14ᵗʰ century, this piazza is now home to Vasari's delightful little fish merchants' loggia (1568), moved here from the Mercato Vecchio when the latter was swept away in the 19ᵗʰ century to make way for Piazza della Repubblica. The loggia is decorated with charming terracotta roundels depicting marine life. On the E side of the piazza (to your L as you enter from S. Ambrogio) plaques at nos. 11 and 13 mark the sites of the house of Ghiberti and the workshop of Cimabue respectively. Continue along the E side of the piazza, leaving it at its SE corner on Borgo Allegri (there is a

good view of Brunelleschi's cupola from the corner). According to Vasari, this borgo was named for the festivities that accompanied the viewing of Cimabue's Maestà (now in the Uffizi) and the joyful procession when it left his workshop. Follow Borgo Allegri straight across the first crossroads and on down to Via Ghibellina. Turn R here to reach the Casa Buonarroti (one block along on the R), which houses a small museum dedicated to Michelangelo and his family.

The Casa Buonarroti

In the early 16th century Michelangelo Buonarroti bought several adjoining properties here. Much work was later undertaken by Michelangelo's nephew, Leonardo, and by Leonardo's son, Michelangelo Buonarroti the Younger (1568-1647). The latter, a famous figure in the cultural world of early 17th century Florence, was responsible for the restructuring of four monumental rooms on the first floor celebrating his family and, in particular, his famous great-uncle. The most spectacular is the 'Gallery', decorated between 1613 and 1635 by some of the most important artists then working in Florence, and celebrating the life and achievements of Michelangelo the Elder in a series of magnificent wall and ceiling paintings. The museum contains important works by Michelangelo, including the Madonna of the Steps, the Battle of the Centaurs, a model for the façade of S. Lorenzo (Walk 6) and a model for a statue of a river god, intended for the New Sacristy but never carved (again see Walk 6). There is also a large collection of drawings by the great man (displayed on a rotational basis), a collection of sculptural models, and other miscellaneous antiquities and works of art acquired over the generations by the family. Here too are the family archives, going back to a ledger kept by Michelangelo's grandfather.

The Casa Buonarroti to Piazza S. Croce

On leaving the Casa Buonarroti, turn R along Via Ghibellina and then take the second L, Via da Verrazzano. Giovanni da Verrazzano discovered the Hudson River (the Verrazzano Narrows Bridge in New York is named after him) and a plaque commemorating his achievement can be seen on the L as you enter the street.

Verrazzano's voyage to the New World

Giovanni da Verrazzano was a member of the French branch of the powerful and wealthy Rucellai company, who, wanting to open up new markets, advanced much of the capital necessary to undertake an expedition across the Atlantic. Appointed as 'Captain of the fleet to India' by the King of France, Verrazzano left Dieppe in 1523 with four ships. Two were lost before reaching Spain, and Spanish galleons did for a third, leaving Verrazzano's flagship to continue alone. Another major financial sponsor of the venture was Antonio Gondi, one of the leading

Italian bankers on the French scene. We shall learn more about the Florentine branch of the Gondi family on Walk 9. Antonio was married to a Frenchwoman named Marie-Catherine de Pierrevive, and Verrazzano, on reaching the Hudson River, named one of the islands there after this lady, calling it 'Pietra Viva'. It appears that Antonio, besides sinking large amounts of his own cash in the venture, had had a general whip round – the Gondi family cook, for example, contributed 30 scudi towards the expedition.

A little further along Via da Verrazzano on the L is Via del Fico, which used to form part of Via de' Pepi. On the flank of the building on the far corner of this street you'll see a small plaque set into the wall. This informs you that, by

a decree of 22nd January 1714, the respected eight Signori of the Guard and Balia of the city of Florence, whose decrees feature also in some of the other walks, prohibited all registered prostitutes from residing in Via de' Pepi, under pain of arrest and other penalties imposed in a law of 31st August 1688. Why just the Via de' Pepi one wonders? Continue along Via da Verrazzano and, on the L between the garages at nos. 2 and 4, you'll see another old plaque. Written in Latin, it commemorates the jubilee year in 1300 when thousands of pilgrims, including many from Florence, travelled to Rome to receive plenary indulgences/blessings from Pope Boniface VIII. The last sentence, written in Italian, reads:

'e andovi Ugoli-no cho la molgle' ('Ugolino went there with his wife'). It's nice to think that this little plaque has survived for c. 700 years. Via da Verrazzano leads into Piazza S. Croce, where there are several cafés and restaurants. I advise you to choose one and to have a sit down while you read about the piazza and the church.

Piazza S. Croce

The huge Piazza S. Croce is dominated by the church of the same name. In the early 13th century the Franciscans arrived in Florence and eventually selected this spot, then outside the city walls, for a monastery. The first churches built here were quickly rendered inadequate sizewise and in 1294 a new church was begun, the design of which has been attributed to Arnolfo di Cambio, architect also of the Duomo and the Palazzo Vecchio. The church was finished by 1385 except for the façade, but building work continued at the monastery throughout the 15th century. The old campanile was destroyed by lightning in 1512, and although a new one was begun it was never finished. Gaetano Baccani's neo-gothic structure was built in 1842. The neo-gothic façade was designed by Niccolò Matas and erected in the 1850s-60s. Matas asked the best local sculptors to participate in the project, of whom the most renowned was Giovanni Dupré. The statue of the Virgin in the aedicule over the main door is his work, as is the relief showing the Triumph of the Cross in the lunette. Dupré was not happy at the decision to place his Virgin in the aedicule, which he likened to a candle-snuffer! Despite the participation of the best artists of the day, the façade was not universally admired. E. M. Forster describes it as being of 'surpassing ugliness' in his novel *A Room With a View*.

On the side of the piazza opposite the Via da Verrazzano (where we entered the square) lies Palazzo degli Sporti (formerly Palazzo dell' Antella), with its painted façade. Nearly all the palaces along this S side of the piazza have retained their 'sporti' (corbels supporting the upper floors). Such corbels were

a common feature on all manner of buildings until Duke Alessandro decreed their abolition in the mid-16th century. In the early 17th century the Palazzo dell' Antella belonged to Niccolò dell' Antella, who was Vice-Principal of the

Accademia del Disegno and decided to get his fellow Academicians to paint his façade. More than a dozen of them were involved. Can you spot the copy of Caravaggio's Sleeping Cupid? This painting, which belonged to the family, is now in the Palatine Gallery at the Pitti Palace. At the end of the piazza opposite the church lies Palazzo Cocchi, built in the 1470s-80s on land formerly occupied by the second circuit of city walls (demolished in 1295). The palace has a very unusual façade, generally attributed to Giuliano da Sangallo.

Jousting in the Piazza S. Croce

Piazza S. Croce has long been used for public spectacles. Jousting tournaments were held here, in which the aristocratic young bloods of Florence made their debut into public life. Tournaments in the 1460s and 1470s were held in honour of Lorenzo Il Magnifico and his brother Giuliano respectively. Lorenzo's horse was a gift from the King of Naples, his armour a gift from the Duke of Milan and his second horse a gift from the Marquis of Mantua. His banner was painted with devices by Verrocchio, while the harness of another entrant was embellished with reliefs and enamels by Antonio Pollaiuolo. Giuliano had silver armour by Verrocchio and a standard painted by Botticelli. Benedetto Salutati, a rich banker, had armour and trappings made using 10kg of gold and 58kg of silver, worth *c.* 4,500 florins in total. After the event it was all melted down and converted back into money! Equestrian ballets were also held here. In 1616 two such events were staged. In both cases the music was provided by Jacopo Peri, whom we shall get to know much better on Walk 7.

The traditional football game (the 'calcio storico fiorentino') celebrating the feast of S. Giovanni has been held in Piazza S. Croce for centuries and you can still see the plaques marking the halfway line of the pitch. The one on the S side, dated February 1565, is set into the wall at no. 20 blue, while that on the N side (a small disc divided into red and white quadrants) is set high up on the façade of no. 7, just under the first floor windows. The huge statue of Dante by Enrico Pazzi (1865), which originally stood in the centre of the piazza, was eventually moved to its present position L of the church façade because it interfered with the arrangements for the football! Our walk ends here, giving you the opportunity to visit S. Croce if you wish.

The interior of S. Croce

The N aisle

At the time of writing entry to the church was via the loggia on the L flank of the building, so we'll start at this point of entry, at the E end of the N aisle. Set against the wall to the L as you enter is the tomb of Carlo Marsuppini (1398-1453) by Desiderio da Settignano, possibly with some input by Verrocchio and Leon Battista Alberti (a close friend). Marsuppini was Chancellor of the Republic, and the tomb takes its inspiration from that of Leonardo Bruni, Marsuppini's predecessor in this office, which we'll see later. Over the door by which we entered is the organ (1579) by Nofri da Cortona. The fresco of the Assumption of the Virgin to the L of this has been attributed to Agnolo Gaddi (late 14th century). The aisle walls were once covered with frescoes, but many of these were obliterated when the side altars were added during Vasari's remodelling of the interior in the 1560s in response to the concerns of the Council of Trent. The side altars have fine paintings by, amongst others, Naldini, Bronzino, Santi di Tito and Vasari himself.

S. Croce became the mausoleum *par excellence* of the city and many notable Florentines are buried or have cenotaphs here. For example, further along the N aisle, set in the pavement by the fourth pillar from the inner façade, is the tomb-slab of Lorenzo Ghiberti and his son, Vittorio, while beside (L of) the next altar along is the tomb of Eugenio Barsanti (d. 1864; inventor of the internal combustion engine). To the R of the next altar are memorials to Guglielmo Marconi (inventor of the radio) and Raphael, while to the L of it is a memorial to Leonardo da Vinci. Opposite the first pillar from the inner façade is the tomb of Galileo Galilei, designed by Foggini in 1642 but not completed until 1737, when Galileo's remains were at last allowed a Christian burial. The surrounding fresco fragments have been attributed to Mariotto di Nardo (early 15th century).

The nave

From the W end of the nave you get a view along the full length of the church thanks to Vasari, who removed the rood-screen. The view is closed by the windows of the sanctuary, which retain their 14th century glass. Much of the glass in S. Croce is original. That in the oculus window of the façade, for example, was designed by Ghiberti. The huge nave has a wooden roof and its floor is littered with tomb-slabs. Between the first pillars is the tomb of a second Galileo Galilei, a 15th century physician, and ancestor and namesake of the great scientist. This is the tomb-slab that Ruskin waxed so lyrical about in his *Mornings in Florence*. Forster, in *A Room with a View*, gives an amusing account of Lucy Honeychurch's visit to S. Croce. A small fellow pilgrim stumbles over one of the raised tomb-slabs, tangling his feet in the features of the recumbent image and falling heavily on to the upturned toes. Such hazards are now, in the main, roped off, but you have been warned – watch your step!

The S aisle

The S aisle, like the N, contains altars and funerary monuments. Against the first pillar is the Madonna del Latte by Antonio Rossellino. It marks the burial place of Francesco Nori, loyal to Lorenzo Il Magnifico and killed in the Pazzi conspiracy of 1478. On the wall opposite is the tomb of Michelangelo, designed by Vasari. Michelangelo died in Rome in 1564 and was buried there. How he came to be buried here as well is told under Walk 5 in the section entitled 'Michelangelo's two funerals'. On either side of the tomb there survive parts of the painted cornice which once connected all the side altars.

The next monument along the aisle is the cenotaph to Dante by Stefano Ricci (1829). Its neo-classical style aroused much criticism – many felt that Dante in classical garb just wasn't right. Next comes another neo-classical monument, that to the poet Alfieri by Canova (1810), erected at the expense of the Countess of Albany (see Walks 10 and 12 for more on her). Opposite, attached to the third pillar, is the wonderful pulpit (1472-6) by Benedetto da Maiano, decorated with the Virtues (below) and scenes from the life of S. Francis. Then comes the tomb of Machiavelli (d. 1527) by Innocenzo Spinazzi (1787), commissioned after the republication of the great statesman's works. Next to the door to the Cloisters is the gilded Cavalcanti tabernacle with its relief of the Annunciation by Donatello (c. 1435). On the far side of the door is the tomb of Leonardo Bruni (d. 1444) by Bernardo Rossellino, which formed the model for Marsuppini's tomb opposite (see above). Bruni, Chancellor of the Republic before Marsuppini, was an eminent humanist and scholar. He is shown crowned with laurel, while on his breast he clasps his monumental work, *The History of the Florentine People*, which had rested on his corpse during the funeral. The epitaph on the tomb, written by Marsuppini, says that after Bruni's death history was in mourning, eloquence dumb and the Muses overcome by tears. Next to Bruni's tomb, and clearly modelled on it, is the tomb of Rossini (1792-1868).

The S transept, sacristy, Leather School and Chapel of the Medici

Rounding the corner into the S transept we reach the Castellani Chapel on the R. Against the L wall of the chapel is a monument to the Countess of Albany, whom we encountered above. The chapel was frescoed in c. 1385 by Agnolo Gaddi and his workshop with scenes from the lives of S. Nicholas of Bari and John the Baptist on the R side, and John the Evangelist and S. Anthony Abbot on the L. The painted Crucifix is by Gerini and the 15th century tabernacle below it by Mino da Fiesole. The altar frontal, a relief of the Maries at the Sepulchre, is by one of Nicola Pisano's pupils (14th century) and the two white della Robbian statues represent S. Francis (R) and S. Bernardino of Siena (L – he preached here).

Next to the Castellani Chapel is the Baroncelli Chapel, frescoed between 1332 and 1338 by Taddeo Gaddi (father of Agnolo) with scenes from the life of the Virgin. These include (to the L of the altar) a night scene of the angels appearing to the shepherds – the sheep are pretty laid back about it, but the dog doesn't look too happy! The polyptych on the altar is by Taddeo's teacher, Giotto. On the far R wall of the chapel the 15th century fresco of the Madonna of the Girdle is by Sebastiano Mainardi. On your R while looking at the Mainardi fresco is a funerary monument of the Bandini-Baroncelli family by Giovanni di Balduccio (1315-49).

Next to the Baroncelli Chapel a door leads to a barrel-vaulted corridor by Michelozzo, off the L of which lies the 14th century sacristy. Here are frescoes of the Road to Calvary (attributed to Spinello Aretino), the Crucifixion (Taddeo Gaddi), and the Resurrection and Ascension (Gerini and pupils). Here too is a della Robbian bust of Christ and Cimabue's wonderful Crucifix, restored after it was damaged in the 1966 flood. The Rinuccini Chapel (closed by a grille) was frescoed in c. 1365 by Giovanni da Milano and an unknown artist called, unsurprisingly, the Master of the Rinuccini Chapel. The frescoes here depict scenes from the lives of Mary Magdalene (R wall) and the Virgin (L wall). The polyptych on the altar is by Giovanni del Biondo (1379).

Rooms off the sacristy contain paintings (all beautifully labelled) and a shop. From here there is access to the Leather School. Re-entering Michelozzo's corridor, the Medici Chapel, also by Michelozzo, lies to your L. The glazed terracotta altarpiece of c. 1480 is by Andrea and Giovanni della Robbia. The stained glass window above, by Alesso Baldovinetti, shows SS. Cosmas and Damian, patron saints of the Medici. Return along the corridor to the church.

The E end of the church and the N transept

At the E end of the church lie the sanctuary and ten smaller chapels, five to each side of it. Starting at the RH (S) end, the Velluti Chapel has damaged frescoes of the Victory of the Archangel Michael and the Apparition of the Bull on the Gargano by a follower of Cimabue. The 14th century altar polyptych is by Giovanni del Biondo and Neri di Bicci. The Calderini Chapel, refurbished in the 17th century, has frescoes by Giovanni da S. Giovanni and paintings by Biliverti and Passignano. The Giugni Chapel contains the 19th century tombs of Charlotte and Julie Clary Bonaparte.

Next come the Peruzzi and Bardi Chapels, both with frescoes by Giotto. Those in the Peruzzi Chapel (c. 1317-18) depict scenes from the lives of John the Baptist (L wall) and John the Evangelist (R wall). The Bardi Chapel, frescoed in *c.* 1325, has scenes from the life of S. Francis; the 13th century panel on the altar also shows scenes from his life. Giotto was the author of great innovations in the pictorial language of the time, imbuing his figures with a sense of monumentality and an intense humanity. Michelangelo later made a careful study of these frescoes. On the outer wall of the chapel, above the entrance, is a scene of S. Francis receiving the stigmata.

The sanctuary was frescoed in *c.* 1380 by Agnolo Gaddi. The frescoes depict the Legend of the True Cross. The Crucifix is by the Master of Figline, another of Giotto's pupils, and the 14th century polyptych on the altar is by various hands, including Giovanni del Biondo and Gerini.

The chapels to the L (N) of the sanctuary are usually inaccessible, as the N transept is generally closed off for private prayer. Above the first chapel is a fresco of the Assumption of the Virgin, attributed to the Master of Figline. The last two chapels on the L are, confusingly, also Bardi Chapels. The first was frescoed in *c.* 1330 by Bernardo Daddi (one of Giotto's assistants) with scenes of the Martyrdom of S. Lorenzo (R wall) and S. Stephen (L wall). The glazed terracotta altarpiece is by Giovanni della Robbia (late 15th century). The last chapel on the E wall is also called the Chapel of S. Sylvester, after the mid-14th century frescoes by Maso di Banco (another of Giotto's followers) showing scenes from the life of the saint. The two tombs in the chapel have frescoes of the Last Judgement (Maso di Banco) and the Deposition (probably Taddeo Gaddi), and the altar has a 14th century triptych.

In the extreme NE corner of the N transept lies the Niccolini Chapel, designed by Giovanni Dosio between 1575 and 1584 and topped by a 17th century dome. To the L of this is another Bardi Chapel. This houses the Crucifix by Donatello (*c.* 1425) which prompted Brunelleschi to carve one of his own to show Donatello how Christ should be portrayed. The story is told in the section on S. Maria Novella (Walk 7). On the L (W) side of the transept is the Salviati Chapel, containing Bartolini's mid-19th century tomb of Sofia Zamoyska (you can see a cast of this in the Accademia; Walk 8). Another example of Bartolini's work, his monument to Leon Battista Alberti, can be seen on the end pillar of the nave (there is a cast of this in the Accademia too).

The First Cloister and the Pazzi Chapel

A door near the E end of the S aisle leads to the First Cloister, where stands the Pazzi Chapel. Andrea de' Pazzi commissioned this building from Brunelleschi in 1429. Following Brunelleschi's death in 1446 many other artists were involved. The names of Giuliano da Maiano, Michelozzo, Leon Battista Alberti and Bernardo Rossellino have all been mentioned in connection with the design of the façade, left unfinished at the time of the Pazzi conspiracy in 1478. The columned portico has a barrel-vault with a mini-cupola decorated in glazed terracotta by Luca della Robbia, at the centre of which a garland of fruit surrounds the Pazzi emblem of two dolphins. The frieze of terracotta tondi with cherubs' heads has been variously attributed to Desiderio da Settignano and the Donatello and della Robbian workshops. The tondo with S. Andrew over the doors to the chapel is by Luca and Andrea della Robbia, and the doors themselves are by Giuliano and Benedetto da Maiano. The beautiful Brunelleschian interior is conceived as a cube extended laterally by barrel-vaulted zones and topped with a charming melon dome. The architectural elements are picked out in pietra serena against a plain stucco background. The blue and white glazed terracotta tondi of the twelve apostles are by Luca della Robbia, while the design of the polychrome tondi of the four evangelists in the pendentives is attributed by many to Brunelleschi himself. Note the Pazzi dolphins again at the bases of the pendentives. The altar recess has its own mini-cupola, with a fresco which, according to some scholars, depicts the night sky on 4th July 1442, the day of the arrival in Florence of Rene of Anjou, who, it was hoped, would lead a new crusade against the Turks. The stained glass window is attributed to Alesso Baldovinetti.

On the lawns in the First Cloister are statues of God the Father by Baccio Bandinelli and a Warrior by Henry Moore. Along the S flank of the church runs a 14th century arcade with undercroft which houses memorials from the old cemetery.

The Second Cloister and the Museum

The Brunelleschian Second Cloister was completed in 1453, probably by Bernardo Rossellino. In the passage between the cloisters lies the entrance to the small museum, containing frescoes, sinopie, statuary, relief sculpture, polychrome terracottas and stained glass. There is also a wonderful 14th century funerary monument to Gastone della Torre by Tino di Camaino. The Refectory has works by (among others) Taddeo Gaddi, Domenico Veneziano, Giovanni del Biondo and Orcagna. Here too is Donatello's gilded bronze statue of S. Louis, which originally occupied the Guelf Party niche at Orsanmichele. In the 1460s it was moved to the façade of S. Croce, where it stayed until the 19th century. Vasari thought that this was a bungled effort and by far the worst statue that Donatello ever produced. It was probably also one of the most dangerous, for it was fire-gilded – gold and mercury were applied to the statue which was then roasted over charcoal to bond the gold to the bronze.

You exit the complex via the First Cloister. Near the exit, don't miss the memorial to Florence Nightingale, who was named after the city of her birth.

Walk 6

Begins and ends in Piazza S. Giovanni.

Takes in: S. Lorenzo and the Laurentian Library, the Mercato Centrale, the Cappelle Medicee and the Casa Martelli.

Duration: 2 hours for the full walk, 1 hour 30 minutes for the shorter version, excluding visits to any of the above or time spent for lunch/coffee and shopping in the market. You should allow *c.* 90 minutes for a combined visit to S. Lorenzo and the Laurentian Library, and 1 hour for the Cappelle Medicee. At the time of writing there were guided tours of the Casa Martelli, in Italian only, every hour on the hour, the tour lasting approximately 1 hour.

Tips: this walk is best done on a weekday, starting as soon as the opening times for S. Lorenzo and the Laurentian Library permit. Bear in mind that the Mercato Centrale is only open until lunchtime.

Piazza S. Giovanni to Piazza S. Lorenzo

Leave Piazza S. Giovanni at its NW corner and head N up Borgo S. Lorenzo. Luca Landucci notes in his *Diary* that during the winter of 1510/11, when Florence lay under two feet of snow, many snow sculptures were made, including, here in Borgo S. Lorenzo, a model of a city with fortresses and many galleys. It must have looked wonderful – forget sand castles! The borgo leads to the piazza of the same name. Opposite you as you enter the square is the Palazzo della Stufa, topped with a lovely 15th century loggia.

Piazza S. Lorenzo is dominated by the rough brick façade of its church. A church has stood on this site since AD 393, and it served as the Cathedral before the bishop's seat was transferred to S. Reparata in the 7th century. The church of S. Lorenzo became closely associated with the Medici from the 15th century onwards, after they commissioned Brunelleschi to rebuild it. It subsequently became their mausoleum, and it houses the burials of all the principal members of the family from Giovanni di Bicci, who died in 1429, through to Grand Duke Cosimo III, who died in 1723. This is not immediately apparent to the tourist, for on a visit to the church you will see only the burial places of Giovanni di Bicci and his wife, their son Cosimo Il Vecchio, his son Piero the Gouty, and Piero's brother

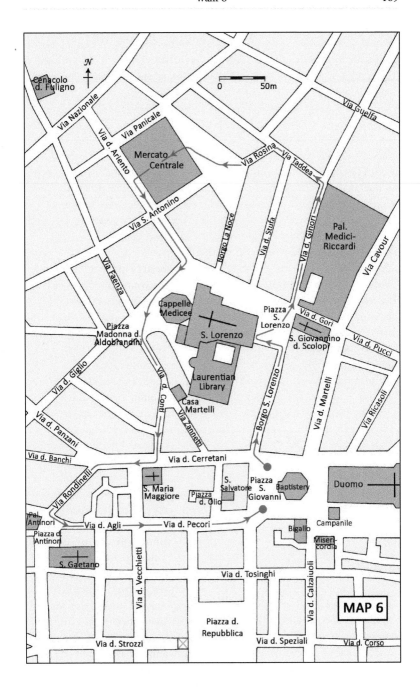

N

0   50m

Cenacolo
d. Fuligno

Via Nazionale

Via d. Ariento

Via Panicale

Via Rosina

Via Taddea

Via Guelfa

Mercato
Centrale

Via S. Antonino

Borgo La Noce

Via d. Stufa

Via d. Ginori

Pal.
Medici-
Riccardi

Via Cavour

Via Faenza

Cappelle
Medicee

S. Lorenzo

Piazza
S.
Lorenzo

Via d. Gori

S. Giovannino
d. Scolopi

Via d. Pucci

Piazza
Madonna d.
Aldobrandini

Via d. Giglio

Via d. Conti

Laurentian
Library

Casa
Martelli

Borgo S. Lorenzo

Via d. Martelli

Via d. Ricasoli

Via d. Panzani

Via Zannetti

Via d. Banchi

Via d. Cerretani

Via Rondinelli

S. Maria
Maggiore

S.
Salvatore

Piazza
d. Olio

Piazza S.
Giovanni

Baptistery

Duomo

Pal.
Antinori

Via d. Agli

Via d. Pecori

Bigallo

Campanile

Piazza d.
Antinori

S. Gaetano

Via Vecchietti

Miseri-
cordia

Via d. Tosinghi

Via d. Calzaiuoli

MAP 6

Piazza d.
Repubblica

Via d. Strozzi

Via d. Speziali

Via d. Corso

Giovanni. Medici burials from Lorenzo Il Magnifico onwards are housed
in the New Sacristy and the Chapel of the Princes, called collectively the
'Cappelle Medicee' ('Medici Chapels'), access to which is behind the rear of
the church in Piazza Madonna degli Aldobrandini. We'll visit the Cappelle
Medicee later on this walk. When inside the church, however, you should
remember that the New Sacristy lies in precisely the same relation to the
R transept as the Old Sacristy does to the L, and that the great octagonal
Chapel of the Princes is slap bang behind the main altar, the rear wall of the
church forming one of its eight sides.

The ticket office for the church and the Laurentian Library is situated
in the corner of the piazza to the L of the church façade, under the portal
leading through to the attractive 15th century cloister. The graceful ground
and first floor arcades surrounding the cloister have slender columns with
Ionic capitals, while in the centre is an orange tree.

The Laurentian Library, the crypt and the treasury
The Laurentian Library, which is accessed directly from the cloister, was
commissioned from Michelangelo by Pope Clement VII in 1523 to house
the private collection of books and manuscripts amassed over the years by
the Medici family. It consists of two elements, the vestibule and the reading
room. Because it was built over the W wing of the cloister and Clement
wanted minimal interference with the spaces below, the structure had to be
kept as light as possible.

The vestibule, a constricted and very tall space, is visually perverse,
nothing less than a façade on the inside of a building, architecture turned
literally inside out and upside down. The huge pietra serena columns that
mark the level of the reading room are set back in alcoves behind the wall
plane. They had to be positioned thus because they rest on the walls of the
conventual rooms below and are the principal supports that carry the weight
of the roof above, the walls between them being merely thin infill. The
volute consoles beneath the pillars have no structural function whatsoever.
Between the pillars are blind windows and tabernacles. The fluted pilasters
on the sides of the tabernacles taper downwards rather than upwards, and are
topped by capitals narrower than themselves. This topsy-turvy entrance hall
is almost filled by a free-standing staircase that cascades down from the door
giving access to the reading room like a lava flow.

The reading room could not be more different. Whereas in the vestibule
everything is topsy-turvy and irrational, here logic, rationality and intellect
reign. Pietra serena pilasters carry the weight of the roof. Between them, huge
windows both illuminate the reading desks below and minimize the weight
on the conventual walls beneath. The glass in the windows is decorated with
both Medici arms and papal motifs. The books were chained to the reading

desks, and the lists of volumes to be found on each desk can still be seen on the ends of the benches. To keep the structure as light as possible a wooden roof was decided on. The decorative patterns of the lovely coffered ceiling are mirrored in the terracotta floor, and here we find Medici motifs again. The tribune to the R was added in 1841 on a design by Pasquale Poccianti to house the collection of books and manuscripts that Angelo Maria d' Elci donated to the State in 1818.

Clement VII never saw his library, which was still incomplete at the time of his death in 1534, when Michelangelo left Florence for good. Cosimo I tried to persuade Michelangelo to return, but he would have none of it and the building was eventually completed to his design by Vasari and Ammannati. In 1558, following a request for information from Vasari, Michelangelo sent some instructions from Rome for the completion of the staircase, but had to confess that he couldn't really remember it clearly.

Entry to the crypt and treasury of S. Lorenzo is also from the cloister, near the base of the stairs leading up to the library. In the crypt can be seen the tombs of Cosimo Il Vecchio and Donatello.

The interior of S. Lorenzo

You have to return to the piazza in order to enter the church of S. Lorenzo. Designed by Brunelleschi, the beautiful interior, with its Corinthian columns and architectural details in pietra serena, is one of the most harmonious works of the Renaissance. Brunelleschi formulated an accurate system of linear perspective and applied this to his architecture. The interior of S. Lorenzo is a rational, unified space, all the parts of which conform to a consistent geometric system based on cubes. From the end of the nave there is a wonderful perspectival view towards the high altar. The little balcony for benedictions high up on the inner façade is by Michelangelo. The paintings over the side altars lining the aisles are all labelled. Near the far end of the L aisle the cantoria above a door leading to the cloister is attributed to Donatello.

At the end of the nave stand the last works of Donatello, two pulpits adorned with bronze reliefs including scenes from the Passion of Christ, the Crucifixion, Entombment and Resurrection. These stunning pulpits are a must-see. For me, the most amazing reliefs are those showing Christ's progress through Limbo. At the end of the R aisle don't miss the lovely tabernacle by Desiderio da Settignano. Desiderio has actually made a mistake with his barrel-vault here; classical norms would have placed a row of coffers at the apex, not a central rib. The R transept is usually closed off for private prayer. The tomb of Cosimo Il Vecchio, which you will have seen if you visited the crypt, is directly beneath the crossing under the dome, marked in the pavement here by a slab bearing the Medici arms, and visible through grilles in the floor. The high altar in pietre dure was designed by Niccolò Gaspare Maria Paoletti in the 18th century. If you like this type of work, don't miss out on a visit to the Museum of the Opificio delle Pietre Dure (Walk 8). The Crucifix is by Baccio da Montelupo. At one time the wall behind the altar was taken down, giving a view through to the Chapel of the Princes beyond.

At the end of the L aisle is a huge fresco by Bronzino showing the martyrdom of S. Lorenzo. Just round the corner in the L transept is the Martelli Chapel, which belonged to the family whose erstwhile home you may wish to visit later on this walk. In the chapel you'll find the marble sarcophagus of Niccolò and Fioretta Martelli, probably by Donatello and in the form of a wicker basket, and a painting of the Annunciation by Filippo Lippi, still in its original frame and in the place for which it was painted. The chapel also contains a 19th century monument to Donatello, who is buried near Cosimo Il Vecchio in the crypt below. The chapels opposite, to the L of the high altar, contain interesting paintings and sculptures, all labelled.

In the far corner of the L transept lies the entrance to the Old Sacristy, built for Cosimo Il Vecchio's father, Giovanni di Bicci de' Medici, and one of Brunelleschi's most perfect architectural creations. Giovanni and his wife are buried here, in the centre of the room beneath the charming little melon dome. The tondi in the pendentives and lunettes, showing the four Evangelists and scenes from the life of S. John the Evangelist, are by Donatello, as is the frieze of cherubs' heads and, perhaps, the bust of S. Lorenzo (attributed by some scholars to Desiderio da Settignano). The doors to either side of the altar have bronze panels showing apostles and martyrs, attributed by some scholars to Donatello and/or Michelozzo. The larger reliefs above the doors, showing SS. Cosmas and Damian and SS. Stephen and Lorenzo, have also been attributed to Donatello and/or Michelozzo. Brunelleschi apparently disapproved of Donatello's additions, saying that they disrupted the harmony of the architecture, and you might agree. As regards the fresco in the little dome over the altar, there is disagreement. Some scholars say that it shows the night sky on 4th July 1442, as does the fresco in the Pazzi Chapel at S. Croce (Walk 5), while others maintain that it represents the sky as it was on 6th July 1439, the date of the agreement at the Council of Florence (see Walk 8 under the Palazzo Medici-Riccardi for more information on this famous event). I'm afraid that I cannot resolve this issue for you. The altar was originally adorned by Brunelleschi's bronze relief of the Sacrifice of Isaac, made for the competition held in 1401 for the Baptistery doors and now housed in the Bargello (Walk 9) alongside Ghiberti's (winning) entry. Set into an arch through the wall on your R as you leave the sacristy is the great porphyry and bronze sarcophagus of Piero de' Medici (the Gouty) and his brother Giovanni, the sons of Cosimo Il Vecchio. This sarcophagus was commissioned from Verrocchio in 1472 by Lorenzo Il Magnifico and his brother Giuliano. The metal ropework is stunning – and don't miss the lovely little tortoises supporting the tomb.

Piazza S. Lorenzo to the Mercato Centrale

On exiting from the church, walk diagonally across the piazza to the statue of Giovanni delle Bande Nere by Baccio Bandinelli. The statue was commissioned in the middle of the 16th century by Giovanni's son, Duke Cosimo I, but didn't get put on its plinth until 1850. There had been plans to erect a statue by Michelangelo here earlier in the 16th century, but they all came to nothing following a bitter and sarcastic diatribe that the artist directed at his then patron, Pope Clement VII (see the section entitled 'Michelangelo's mighty temper').

Michelangelo's mighty temper

When Bandinelli got the commission for the statue of Hercules and Cacus outside the Palazzo della Signoria (Walk 2), Pope Clement VII, in an attempt to mollify Michelangelo, suggested that the latter should, instead, sculpt a statue for the corner of the Piazza S. Lorenzo nearest to the Medici Palace. A furious Michelangelo retorted that such a statue would look better in the opposite corner of the piazza and, since there was a barber's shop there, the figure should be shown seated and holding a cornucopia, with the said shop under its backside and the cornucopia acting as a chimney. Moreover, if the head were hollow it could be used as a pigeon loft. Better still, if he, Michelangelo, increased the size of the statue, he could transform it into a campanile for the church. One wonders if anybody before or since ever had the temerity to speak to a pope in this manner. Unsurprisingly, the idea was dropped.

At the corner of the piazza by the statue, between Via de' Gori and Via de' Ginori, can be seen the rear of Palazzo Medici-Riccardi (Walk 8). In 1434, when Cosimo Il Vecchio returned from exile, the city decreed the construction of a new piazza in front of S. Lorenzo in his honour, and Brunelleschi submitted a model for a palazzo to front this square. According to Vasari, Cosimo considered the scheme too grand and likely to arouse ill-feeling. The idea was abandoned, but some ill-feeling remained;

a disgruntled Brunelleschi smashed his model! Instead, Cosimo bought up more than twenty properties on the block just off the corner of the piazza, between Via de' Ginori and Via Cavour. Here he subsequently built his palace, with Michelozzo as architect. When, in 1512, the Medici returned from exile for a second time, another grandiose scheme was put forward, this time by Leonardo da Vinci. For this story, along with that of the brick frontage on the church, see the section entitled 'Leonardo's lavish scheme and the fiasco of the façade'.

Pluto and Proserpine in the piazza

In April 1533, Margaret of Austria, the illegitimate daughter of Charles V and future bride of Duke Alessandro de' Medici, passed through Florence on her way to Naples. During her week-long stay, many lavish spectacles were staged, and Piazza S. Lorenzo was the scene of a 'girandola'. A huge canopy, reaching from the church right across to the Medici Palace, was suspended some fifteen feet above the ground. Beneath it were constructed sets showing scenes of the Underworld and the story of Pluto and Proserpine. The whole space was filled with fireworks, smoking, flaming and fizzing so as to create a suitable 'inferno'. Fortunately, the entire spectacle apparently passed off without injury to anyone.

Leonardo's lavish scheme and the fiasco of the façade

In 1512 the Medici returned from exile courtesy of Pope Julius II and a Spanish army. Within six months of their return Julius died and Giovanni de' Medici became Pope Leo X. A scheme for a bigger, better Piazza S. Lorenzo was put forward by Leonardo da Vinci. It will help if you look at Map 6 at this point. Leonardo wanted to demolish not only the church of S. Giovannino degli Scolopi and the adjacent buildings lying on the opposite side of the piazza to S. Lorenzo, but also buildings beyond Via de' Martelli to the S of Via de' Pucci as far as Via Ricasoli. The flattened area he proposed to turn into a vast symmetrical piazza. On the corner of Via Cavour and Via de' Pucci would be a new palace, equal in size to Michelozzo's existing one. The two palaces and the church of S. Lorenzo would define the N and W sides of the new piazza respectively. This magnificent 'Piazza de' Medici' would thus lie on a direct line with Piazza del Duomo/Piazza S. Giovanni and form a counterpart to the N of the latter to balance Piazza della Signoria to the S.

Like many Florentine churches, S. Lorenzo had been left without a façade, and Pope Leo X now wanted one worthy of Leonardo's scheme. In the event the piazza never got off the ground – or rather never got on to it – but, in 1516, following the untimely death of his brother Giuliano, Duke of Nemours, Pope Leo X, together with his cousin Cardinal Giulio de' Medici, commissioned Michelangelo to work up a design for a church façade in collaboration with Baccio d' Agnolo. By the spring of 1517, Michelangelo, never one to collaborate, was demanding complete control of the project, suggesting a budget of 35,000 ducats (10,000 more than the original figure proposed) and estimating a completion date six years hence. These terms were accepted, though pope and cardinal were concerned that, to date, they had seen no model. Not until December did they see one – perhaps the one kept in the Casa Buonarroti (Walk 5). In January a contract was agreed. Michelangelo's design had clearly aggrandized. The price was now 40,000 ducats and the completion date eight years hence. The contract stated that the façade was to be made entirely of the finest marble from either the quarries at Carrara or those near Pietrasanta. The opening up of the latter was a project dear to the hearts of pope and cardinal, for Pietrasanta lay in Florentine territory, so it would not be necessary to pay taxes on the stone!

The proposal to construct the façade entirely of marble was a daunting one. The stone had to be quarried high in the mountains, manoeuvred down the slopes, transported to the sea, shipped to Pisa, floated on barges up the Arno and carted into Florence, a journey of close on 100 miles. In addition, Michelangelo's design called for twelve solid columns c. 20 feet high. Simply finding and quarrying unflawed blocks of this size would be difficult, let alone transporting them. For the next eighteen months or so Michelangelo moved constantly between Florence, Pisa and the quarries. Things did not go well. The Florentine masons employed at Pietrasanta were unfamiliar with, and inexpert at, quarrying marble, and the Carraresi, angered by the opening up of rival quarries, bribed many bargemen not to accept Michelangelo's stone. The first column quarried near Pietrasanta was successfully manoeuvred down the slopes, but cost one mason his life. The marble for the second turned out to be flawed, and the quarrying operation had to be repeated; the column subsequently broke. Owing to lack of rain, the level of water in the Arno fell and, bribery or no bribery, the marble which reached Pisa couldn't be transported upstream. In April 1519, while manoeuvring another column down the mountain, a ring on the tackle broke; the column fell and shattered.

Pope Leo's younger brother Giuliano, Duke of Nemours, had died in 1516, and in May 1519 the pope's nephew Lorenzo, Duke of Urbino, died aged only twenty-six. Shortly afterwards, loads of marble began arriving at Florence. Construction could at last begin. The death of Lorenzo, however, had dealt a blow to Medici hopes, for he was the last legitimate male heir. Michelangelo was ordered to proceed no further with the façade. He later reflected bitterly that he'd lost three years of his life on a project that came to nothing. The marble was reassigned to repave the Duomo, but some of it was later used in an unexpected manner (see Walk 14 under the section entitled 'the siege of Florence and Michelangelo as a wanted man'). Every cloud, however, has a silver lining. The premature deaths of Giuliano and Lorenzo may have turned the thoughts of Pope Leo X and Cardinal Giulio away from a façade for S. Lorenzo, but these thoughts were now channelled instead towards a mausoleum. Thus came about the idea for the New Sacristy.

We are now going to walk up the street that runs along the rear of Palazzo Medici-Riccardi, Via de' Ginori. On the L side of the street there are several notable palaces that deserve mention. First up is no. 7, the Palazzo Neroni. Dietisalvi Neroni joined ranks with Luca Pitti against Piero the Gouty, and had to flee fast in 1466. The property was subsequently acquired by the Gerini. At no. 9 is the Palazzo di Montauto, formerly Gerini, with 'inginocchiate' ('kneeling') windows attributed to Ammannati. This type of window, resting on protruding consoles, was first designed by Michelangelo for use on the Palazzo Medici-Riccardi; we will see Michelangelo's windows on Walk 8. Kneeling windows became a typical feature of 16th and 17th century Florentine architecture, as anyone who has tried to walk the narrow pavements of the city will know to their cost! The sgraffito work on the palace features the shell, emblem of the Neroni, while the coats-of-arms are those of the Gerini and di Montauto families (L and R respectively). At no. 11 lies the early 16th century Palazzo Ginori, perhaps designed by Baccio d' Agnolo, which, if for no other reason, would deserve a mention as the erstwhile home of Marchese L. Ginori Lisci, from whose magisterial survey of Florentine Palazzi I have drawn most of my information on these magnificent buildings. There are, however, plenty of other reasons for drawing attention to this palace (see the section entitled 'jiggery-pokery, Ginori, porcelain and pigeons'). In 1729, keen to extend their holdings, the Ginori acquired the house next door at no. 13. It belonged to the Bandinelli family and had once been home to the sculptor Baccio Bandinelli, whose statue of Giovanni delle Bande Nere we've just seen. The two families did a swap and, in return for this palace, the Ginori gave the Bandinelli their palace at no. 2 Piazza S. Lorenzo. Finally, Palazzo Taddei at no. 15 was designed by Baccio d' Agnolo. Taddeo di Francesco was a cultured and erudite man, and many artists frequented the palace, including Michelangelo and Raphael. Michelangelo gave Taddeo a marble tondo of the Madonna and Child with S. John, which you can see if you visit the Royal Academy in London, and Raphael, who was a guest here for a long time, painted the Madonna del Giardino (now in Vienna) for Taddeo. So why is the plaque commemorating Raphael and his connection with the Taddei family gracing the palace on the opposite corner of Via Taddea? Well, one theory is that for a short period in the 19th century no. 15 belonged to a Jewish gentleman who, not wanting a Christian devotional object on his façade, moved a tabernacle containing a painting of the Crucifixion by Giovanni Antonio Sogliani to the wall of the latter palace, where it can still be seen. This subsequently caused confusion, and the plaque commemorating Raphael's visit was erected on the wrong building! No such confusion attends the home of Luigi Pampaloni, the sculptor responsible for the statues of Arnolfo di Cambio and Brunelleschi which we saw on Walk 1. A plaque on the house opposite the end of Via Taddea tells us that he lived and died here in 1847.

Head down Via Taddea and take the second turning on the L, the short Via Rosina, which leads to a piazza behind the Mercato Centrale. The magnificent cast-iron market building by Giuseppe Mengoni dominates the square. It was erected in 1874 and restored in 1980. This is the principal food market of Florence, with a plethora of stalls offering tempting arrays of produce. It is well worth a visit and great fun. If you decide to take a break for refreshments before exploring, remember that the market is only open until lunchtime.

Jiggery-pokery, Ginori, porcelain and pigeons

The palace at no. 11 Via de' Ginori was built in the early 16th century for Carlo di Lionardo Ginori, and subsequently passed to Carlo's nephew, Lionardo, who was married to Caterina, daughter of Tommaso Soderini. Duke Alessandro de' Medici had designs upon the fair and chaste Caterina, and her nephew, Lorenzino, who was a very distant relative of the Duke, used this fact to entice Alessandro to his death. Expecting an assignation with Caterina, the Duke instead found himself confronted by assassins – and that was the end of him. A later Carlo Ginori started the famous Doccia porcelain works in the 1730s – we'll pass the company's magnificent showroom near the end of Walk 6. Moving on to the 19th century, another Marchese Carlo Ginori arranged the famous annual Palazzo Ginori conferences, which covered history, art and literature. For some years, this gentleman rented the island of Montecristo and, because he was a member of Parliament and could not be cut off from his political and business concerns, he started a carrier-pigeon service between the island and his Florentine palace. When a bird landed on its perch, it set off a bell in the porter's lodge! The palace is still owned by the Ginori, who have family archives going back to the time of Dante.

The Mercato Centrale to the Cappelle Medicee

From the piazza behind the Mercato, walk through the market (or along its flank if it is closed) to emerge at the other end on Via dell' Ariento. The name Ariento derives from 'argento' ('silver'), because here were concentrated the workshops of the silversmiths. Walking through the market stalls along Via dell' Ariento is a bit like walking through an oriental bazaar. As well as tourist trinkets, silk ties, aprons, scarves, shawls and the like, there's a bewildering array of leather goods. Turn L towards S. Lorenzo. Pope Clement VII's agents housed Michelangelo in the Via dell' Ariento while he was working on the New Sacristy in the 1520s, so he practically lived on site. As you near the bottom of the street, look up at the marble lantern topping the little hemispherical tiled dome of Michelangelo's New Sacristy. Lanterns were normally crowned with balls and crosses (witness the Duomo), but Michelangelo has gone one better here and, instead of a ball, we have a complex polyhedron. Its form alluded to the Medicean device of the diamond, and,

like that gem, it was intended to reflect the light. What you're looking at now is a copy; the original, made by a goldsmith named Giovanni di Baldassare, is (I hope) on display in the New Sacristy. At the bottom of Via dell' Ariento turn R. The Cappelle Medicee lie on your L – the entrance is just a few yards

further along. Michelangelo's New Sacristy is a must-see and the queue may well herald the fact! Later on this walk we'll pass the Casa Martelli, the guidebook to which was, at the time of writing, only available in Italian from the shop at the Cappelle Medicee. As said shop is beyond the ticket barrier, you may wish to enquire about the book now if you intend to visit.

The Cappelle Medicee

The so-called Medici Chapels comprise the Chapel of the Princes and the New Sacristy. Although the Chapel post-dates the New Sacristy, it comes first on the itinerary, so I shall describe it first.

The Chapel of the Princes

A new burial chapel for the Medici Grand Dukes was planned as early as the mid-16th century by Cosimo I and his architect Giorgio Vasari. It was to be like Michelangelo's New Sacristy but larger and more magnificent, all of marble, mosaic and 'pietre dure' ('hard stones'). However, this 'third sacristy' never got built, despite the enthusiasm of Cosimo's son, Francesco I, for the project and the fact that Francesco had got as far as searching out and gathering together rare and costly stones and minerals for its construction. When Francesco's brother Ferdinando became duke, he organized the craftsmen in pietre dure into a state workshop (the 'Opificio', originally housed in the Uffizi and now to be found on Via degli Alfani; Walk 8) and again considered design ideas for the new burial chapel. In 1602 designs by his half-brother, Don Giovanni de' Medici, a bastard son of Cosimo I by Eleonora degli Albizi, were approved. Construction began in 1604 and continued through until 1737.

The architecture of the Chapel of the Princes deliberately evokes the imagery of the Holy Sepulchre in Jerusalem, and a project was even conceived of 'rescuing' the Holy Sepulchre from the Turks, transporting it to Florence and re-erecting it in the new chapel. Originally, entry to this huge, lavish space was directly from the choir of the church, the rear wall of which was opened up to create a vista along the length of the nave. The choir was subsequently reconstructed and the vista closed off, but even without it the chapel is breathtaking, to say the least. The walls and floor exhibit a positive riot of inlays in marbles, porphyry, lapis lazuli and countless other semi-precious stones and gems. The workmanship on the coats-of-arms of the various Tuscan cities and on the high altar is magnificent. If you like what you see here, you'll enjoy the Museum of the Opificio (Walk 8). The tombs around the walls are cenotaphs, the actual burials being in a crypt below. In 1857 the bodies were exhumed and the corpses examined (the story is told under Walk 12 in the section entitled 'some convenient deaths'). From behind the high altar there is access to the Treasury, where are kept, among other things, Leo X's papal tiara and staff, and a processional banner which he presented to the church.

The New Sacristy

Following the deaths of the Duke of Nemours and the Duke of Urbino, the minds of Pope Leo X and Cardinal Giulio de' Medici turned towards the construction of a family mausoleum. Work began soon after the death of the Duke of Urbino in 1519 with Michelangelo as capomaestro. The plan was to build a mirror image of Brunelleschi's Old Sacristy on the opposite side of the church. This New Sacristy would contain the tombs not only of the two dukes but also of the pope's father, Lorenzo Il Magnifico, and the cardinal's father, Il Magnifico's younger brother Giuliano, assassinated in the Pazzi conspiracy. In 1521 Pope Leo X died and in 1523 Cardinal de' Medici became Pope Clement VII. Work began in earnest on the interior of the sacristy in 1524. Many of the (large) team of masons had nicknames – the Porcupine, Lefty, the Godfather, the Friar, the Chicken and Little Mouse. Michelangelo made drawings, models and templates; in the 1970s a series of working drawings was discovered on the walls of the altar chapel. The designs included not only the figures that we see today, but river gods reclining on the ground in front of the ducal tombs. A model for one of these can be seen in the Casa Buonarroti (Walk 5). In the event, the river gods were never sculpted, and neither was the architectural framework for the double tomb of Lorenzo Il Magnifico and his brother ever carved. History intervened and Michelangelo left Florence for good in 1534 leaving both the New Sacristy and the Laurentian Library projects unfinished.

The two dukes are depicted on their tombs as idealized Roman warriors. There is no attempt at portraiture, and Michelangelo apparently said that one thousand years on nobody would know that they were otherwise than the way he'd carved them. The theme of the tombs is the inexorable passage of time and the sweeping away of all earthly things. Dawn, Day, Dusk and Night succeed one another, and their course inevitably leads to death. The conceit here is that, deprived of the light of the Medici, the eyes of

Dawn, Day, Dusk and Night are sealed and can no longer shine upon the earth; they are all blind, with no incised irises or pupils. Dawn (female) and Dusk (male) grace the tomb of the Duke of Urbino, Night (female) and Day (male) that of the Duke of Nemours. Only the figure of Night has attributes, a tiara with moon and star, an owl, a bundle of poppies to induce oblivion and a mysterious mask, the precise significance of which is uncertain.

The Duke of Nemours and the Duke of Urbino are both shown with their heads turned towards the wall containing the (unfinished) tomb of Lorenzo Il Magnifico and his brother Giuliano. The simplicity of this tomb compared with the ducal tombs causes confusion to some visitors, because of the duplication of names. Duke Giuliano and Duke Lorenzo left little mark on the history of Florence owing to their premature deaths, whereas their eponymous forebears were much more famous. The Madonna and Child is by Michelangelo. The statues of SS. Cosmas and Damian, patron saints of the Medici, were carved by Giovanni Angelo Montorsoli and Raffaello da Montelupo after designs by the great man.

In the room to the R of the altar chapel is displayed (I hope) the crown of the lantern alluded to earlier on this walk.

A conscientious employee

The 'purveyor' of the building works at the New Sacristy was one Giovan Battista Figiovanni. He was a sort of business manager, whose responsibilities complemented those of the foreman and the architect. He arranged supplies, checked deliveries, administered finances, kept accounts, disbursed payments, and generally sorted the paperwork. Figiovanni was extremely proud at his involvement in such a high profile project and he threw himself at the job with zeal. His memoirs have survived and I cannot resist giving you extracts from the translation of them that appears in Prof. Richard Goldthwaite's book on *The Building of Renaissance Florence* (p. 162).

'Every morning at dawn I am there key in hand with everything open, awaiting the wallers and labourers to give them their orders .... Everything passes through my hands, and ... I want to see everything with my own eyes in order that the wallers do not use brick where they could use rubble..... I have never had a moment to myself and do not now. Everyone marvels that I can handle it and that I can give such an operation so much supervision .... without there ever being any confusion .... Michelangelo wanted me to take on an assistant and pay him three or four ducats a month; but I wanted to do everything myself so that what turns out to be good is mine, and likewise what turns out badly.'

The Cappelle Medicee to the Casa Martelli

On exiting from the Cappelle Medicee, spare a glance for the Palazzo Mannelli-Riccardi opposite, with a ducal bust over the door and traces of the mid-16th century painted façade. Turn L into the small, attractive Piazza Madonna degli Aldobrandini. The name here refers not to the Virgin but to La Signora Giovanna degli Aldobrandini, a venerable and venerated lady who died in 1395 at the (then) remarkable age of ninety. Bear L and leave the piazza on Via de' Conti. Where the road forks and Via Zannetti runs off to the L, the Casa Martelli lies on your L at no. 8. Remember that guided tours take place on the hour only. This palace, which until 1986 belonged to the Martelli family (famous as patrons of Donatello and whose chapel we saw earlier in S. Lorenzo), is now owned by the State and open as a museum and gallery. The Martelli family collection is housed on the first floor in a series of ten rooms with charming 18th century décor and furnishings. Among the many paintings you'll find masterpieces by Domenico Beccafumi, Salvator Rosa and Luca Giordano, a tondo of the Holy Family by Piero di Cosimo (a most eccentric character if Vasari's account of him is to be believed) and two works by Pieter Brueghel the Younger. On the ground floor is the delightful Winter Garden, the walls of which are completely covered with painted trellis-work and vines, home to a variety of birds and animals. In the vestibule to a second painted room can be seen a lovely tabernacle by Mino da Fiesole showing the Madonna and Child with S. John, which originally stood on the exterior of the palace.

The Casa Martelli to Piazza S. Giovanni

On exiting from the Casa Martelli, there is an either/or option. If you are opting for the shorter version of this walk, turn sharp L down Via Zannetti and L again along Via de' Cerretani to reach Piazza S. Giovanni. If, on the other hand, you like porcelain and textiles, and want to see where Dante's teacher is buried, turn L along Via de' Conti and follow me for a little longer.

At the bottom of Via de' Conti, on the other side of Via de' Cerretani, lies the church of S. Maria Maggiore, once the local church of the great Baronci family, mentioned both by Dante (*Paradiso* XVI.104) and Boccaccio (*Decameron* VI.5 and 6). The Baronci were renowned for their proverbial ugliness. They were also proven, by one Michele Scalza, to be the gentlemen of longest descent in Florence. If you want to know how he proved it, you must read Boccaccio! High up on the wall of the tower of S. Maria Maggiore can be seen a small stone head of a woman. This head has given rise to two stories. According to one, it is a memorial to a 13th century woman named Berta, a cabbage seller who left her money to pay for a church bell. The bell was rung each evening to warn market gardeners working on their allotments outside the city walls that the gates were about to be closed for the night. According to another story, the head represents a parish priest who, from his vantage point up in the bell tower, enraged a supposed sorcerer who was being led this way to execution in 1327. The condemned man cursed the priest, declaring that his head would never leave that spot – at which point the prelate's head turned to stone.

On the wall to the L of the church is a Dante plaque referring to Dante's teacher, Brunetto Latini, who is buried here. Despite placing him in hell among the sodomites, Dante was obviously exceptionally fond of his teacher

. . . . . . .IN LA MENTE M'E FITTA, E OR M'ACCORA
LA CARA E BVONA IMAGINE PATERNA
DI VOI, QVANDO NEL MONDO AD ORA AD ORA
M' INSEGNAVATE COME L'VOM S'ETERNA!

DANTE _ INF. _ XV _ 82-84.

and aware of how much he owed to him, as is clear from his words to Latini here:

' "For in my mind is fixed, and now it distresses me to the heart, the dear, kind paternal image of you when, in the world, time and again you taught me how man makes himself eternal" ' (*Inferno* XV.82-85).

Turn R along Via de' Cerretani away from Piazza S. Giovanni and take the second turning on the L, Via Rondinelli. On the R of Via Rondinelli, at no. 17 red, is another Palazzo Ginori, which houses the magnificent porcelain showroom of the Richard-Ginori company. I recommend that you take a peek in here, even if you don't intend to purchase anything. The palace façade bears a plaque commemorating Carlo Collodi, author of *Pinocchio*. His parents worked as a cook and a maid for the Ginori family, and his brother was employed in the famous porcelain factory. Carlo visited them frequently and wrote a large part of *Pinocchio* here.

Via Rondinelli brings us to Piazza degli Antinori, with the lovely 15th century Palazzo Antinori on the R. We'll learn more about the Antinori and their palace on Walk 7. Leave the piazza opposite the palace on Via degli Agli, which eventually becomes Via de' Pecori. Keep straight on across Via de' Vecchietti. Just before the tiny Piazza dell' Olio opens up on the L, those interested in textiles may like to note the Casa de' Tessuti at nos. 20-24 red, which, besides being a famous fabric emporium, houses a small museum devoted to the history of textiles. In Piazza dell' Olio can be seen the lovely little Romanesque façade of the church of S. Salvatore al Vescovo, incorporated into the huge Palazzo Arcivescoville. Via de' Pecori leads into Piazza S. Giovanni, where this walk ends.

Piazza S. Giovanni as seen from Via de' Pecori

Walk 7

Begins at Piazza della Repubblica and ends at Piazza S. Maria Novella.
Takes in: Ognissanti and the Cenacolo del Ghirlandaio, the Farmacia
di S. Maria Novella, the Museo Novecento and S. Maria Novella.
Duration: 1 hour 15 minutes, excluding time spent at any of the above. You
should allow a minimum of *c.* 45 minutes for Ognissanti and its Cenacolo,
c. 30-45 minutes for the Farmacia and *c.* 1 hour for the Museo Novecento.
S. Maria Novella is a large complex and there is a lot to see. It is hard to judge
how much time you will need, for this will depend on how long you wish to
gaze at frescoes. I would allow *c.* 1 hour 30 minutes.
Tips: the opening hours for the Cenacolo del Ghirlandaio are restricted,
so do check before you go all the way down there. Small binoculars/opera
glasses may prove useful for looking at the frescoes in S. Maria Novella.
Piazza della Repubblica to the Croce al Trebbio
The Piazza della Repubblica, formerly called the Piazza Vittorio Emanuele,
was created in the 19th century in the euphoria surrounding the expulsion of
the Austrians and the unification of Italy, when, for a short time, Florence
was the capital of the new state. Here stood the Roman Forum and, later, the
'Mercato Vecchio' ('Old Market') of the mediaeval city.

Leave Piazza della Repubblica in its NW corner on Via de' Brunelleschi
(on the R as you face the huge arch), then take the first turning on the
L and continue straight on along Via del Campidoglio and Via de' Corsi
until you reach the T-junction at Piazza degli Antinori. On the L at the
bottom of Via de' Corsi, opposite the flank of the church of S. Gaetano,
you'll see a plaque commemorating Jacopo Corsi and the gatherings of poets
and musicians organized by him. The plaque records the performance at one
of these gatherings of a drama entitled *Dafne* by Ottavio Rinuccini, with
music in part by Jacopo Peri. Besides being the birthplace of the Renaissance,
Florence also witnessed the birth of opera, and *Dafne* was the first example
of the genre. Peri's *Euridice*, the first opera to survive complete, was
performed in 1600 at the wedding festivities of Maria de' Medici and
Henry IV of France.

Jacopo Peri – Part I
Born in 1561, Jacopo Peri appeared on the musical scene in 1573 when he was
hired as a singer at SS. Annunziata. In 1579 he became organist at the Badia
and in 1586 was hired as a singer at the Baptistery. In 1588 he appears in his
own right on the list of court musicians. Apart from his multifarious musical
activities, Jacopo served in numerous government offices and worked on the staff
of two of the city's guilds. To give you just a few examples, during the course of

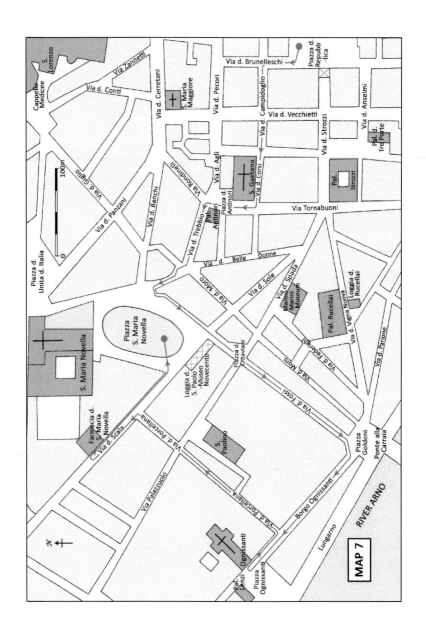

MAP 7

his life he was appointed as one of the Captains of Orsanmichele, served twice as one of the eight Signori, those law and order officials whose decrees feature in some of the walks, was employed three times as one of the officials in charge of the decima property tax, acted as one of the 'Maestri di Dogana' ('Customs Officials'), was appointed as one of the ten Captains of the Guelf Party, and was twice sent out of Florence to administer justice as Podestà at Pontassieve and at Sesto. He was also employed as 'Camerlengo' ('Comptroller') at the Physicians' and Apothecaries' Guild, and subsequently served as Consul there on five separate occasions. In 1618 he was appointed as Camerlengo Generale at the Wool Guild for life, at a monthly salary of 10 florins, and three years later, in 1621, he became a life member of the 'Consiglio de' Duecento' ('Council of 200'). As if all this wasn't enough, he was also a savvy investor in the financial, business and property markets, and amassed a substantial and varied portfolio.

Turn R into Piazza degli Antinori, with the lovely 15th century palace of the same name on the L. Built in the 1460s for the Boni family, the simple but imposing design of the building is attributed to Giuliano da Maiano. In 1475 the palace was acquired by the Martelli family, who sold it to Niccolò di Tommaso Antinori in 1506. The Antinori were involved in both the silk and wool industries, but they came eventually to concentrate on wine. Niccolò di Tommaso's direct descendants still own this palace, which has been beautifully restored, and the family continues to concentrate on the production of Antinori wines, which have for long held pride of place among the famous wines of Tuscany. You may sample some, if you wish, at the restaurant just inside the palace entrance, while in the courtyard you can see a so-called 'Crazy Cart' and read about how the wine was transported from the countryside into Florence.

Take the narrow street to the R of Palazzo Antinori, Via del Trebbio, noting the wine hatch on the flank of the palace as you go. Via del Trebbio leads into a tiny piazza with a granite column in the centre. On top of the column is a Gothic capital bearing the symbols of the Evangelists and, above this, a cross of the Pisan school. The column commemorates a massacre of heretics that took place here in the 13th century.

The Croce al Trebbio to Piazza Ognissanti

The name 'Trebbio' comes from the Latin *trivium*, a crossroads where three streets meet. The three streets in question here are Via del Trebbio, Via delle Belle Donne and Via del Moro. We entered on Via del Trebbio and we are going to leave on Via delle Belle Donne, the second street round going anticlockwise, which, after a few yards, leads into Piazza S. Maria Novella. We'll return here later, so resist the temptation to marvel at the façade of S. Maria Novella for the moment, turn L, walk along to the corner of the piazza, and then keep straight on through the tiny Piazza degli Ottaviani and down Via de' Fossi. On the corner of Piazza degli Ottaviani with Via de' Fossi lies the Palazzo Niccolini. The Marchese Carlo Niccolini (1844-1912) lived here with his English wife, Ginevra Colebrooke. She studied Florentine history and wrote a book (G. Niccolini di Camugliano, *The Chronicles of a Florentine Family (1200-1470)* (London, Jonathan Cape: 1933)). Jacopo Peri, our multi-talented opera composer, lived at no. 19 Via de' Fossi (on the R) from 1596 until his death in 1633. Next door but one to Jacopo's house, at no. 15, is a building which once belonged to the Silk Guild.

Jacopo Peri – Part II

Jacopo Peri was married three times, widowed twice, and fathered twenty-one children, many of whom died in infancy or childhood. Three marriages meant three dowries, which gave Jacopo a solid foundation for what became a substantial investment portfolio. During the course of his life he acquired several properties, some coming with the dowries and some purchased, including seven farms and two other houses in the city. The farms were run by tenant farmers and yielded a variety of saleable produce. One tenant was obliged to give the Peri family four capons, four dozen eggs and half a barrel of grapes annually, while another agreed to supply 300 eggs, twelve capons and ten chickens. Jacopo must have been mighty relieved when, on the birth of his twelfth surviving child in 1619, he requested and obtained a standard exemption from the decima property tax.

As well as real estate, Jacopo was involved in the wool and silk industries, investing, over time, more than 5,000 florins in four firms of wool manufacturers and two firms of silk merchants. He eventually set up his own wool partnership, sinking 2,000 florins into it, and he invested a further 400 florins as a partner in a firm of dyers. He was also active in the money markets, using several banking houses and all the financial instruments available to him, including government securities (rather like modern bonds), 'censi' (a type of annuity), and bills of exchange, which, as they defined interest not as a fixed rate but as the variable play of exchange rates, got around usury laws and restrictions.

Via de' Fossi is home to several antique shops. On the L a few yards beyond Jacopo's house, at no. 28 red, is the famous Frilli Gallery. The Frilli firm can make you a replica of just about anything you want, if your purse will stretch to it! Just beyond the Gallery, on the L at no. 12 red, note the doorway to an erstwhile church, with charming Romanesque reliefs showing the three kings before Herod and presenting their gifts to the Christ Child.

The foolish physician

Via de' Fossi means 'Street of the Ditches', of which there were several in this area. One of them features in Boccaccio's *Decameron* VIII.9, which tells the story of Simone, the foolish physician. Simone noticed that two poverty-stricken painters, Bruno and Buffalmacco, lived light-heartedly and contentedly, and he conceived the idea that they must, therefore, have a secret source of gain. Determined to uncover the truth he ingratiated himself with the men, who recognized him for the numb-skull that he was and spun him tales of a necromancer and a secret society. At society meetings, they said, there was feasting and entertainment on a lavish scale, and members had only to voice a desire for it to be granted immediately. Naturally, Simone wanted desperately to be enrolled, and to this end began to butter up Bruno and Buffalmacco, wining and dining them until he felt that he could ask the favour. They agreed to nominate him, and eventually brought him news of his election. On the night of the next banquet, he was to dress in his finest clothes and meet the society's messenger after dark in the Piazza S. Maria Novella. The messenger, he was told, would take the form of a black, horned beast. It would, initially, try to terrify him, but would then quieten down and carry him to the feast. At the appointed hour, Simone stood shivering outside S. Maria Novella. Buffalmacco showed up, duly disguised as a horned beastie, played his part with gusto, and bore Simone off to the nearest ditch, while Bruno must almost have ruptured himself laughing in the shadows. To find out what happened next, you must read Boccaccio!

At Piazza Goldoni turn R along Borgo Ognissanti, which contains several interesting buildings (all on the RH side). At no. 8 blue was the Hotel of the Black Eagle (now the Hotel Goldoni), where Mozart stayed in 1770 when he came to give a concert at Poggio Imperiale. At no. 12, the Palazzo Baldovinetti has a corbelled balcony and decorative balustrades. No. 20 was the site of the hospital of S. Giovanni di Dio, founded in the 14th century by Piero Vespucci (for which family see below). At no. 26 is a house in Art Nouveau style.

The church of Ognissanti and the Cenacolo del Ghirlandaio

As you enter Piazza Ognissanti, the church of Ognissanti is on your R. It was rebuilt in the 17th century, but the campanile is original (1258). Inside the church is an information board in English, and all the paintings are labelled. Here you'll find several frescoes by Domenico Ghirlandaio. In one of these, the Madonna is shown protecting members of the Vespucci family. Amerigo Vespucci (1451-1512) was the Medici agent in Seville. Following the route of Christopher Columbus, he made two voyages to America, one in 1499 and one in 1501, and subsequently gave his name to the continent. There's also a fresco of S. Jerome by Ghirlandaio. Jerome is surrounded by numerous implements, including a pair of eyeglasses, for which Florence was famous.

Florentine eyeglasses

Florentine eyeglasses were exported all over Europe, and the industry gained great fame abroad. Lenses could be ground for the far- and near-sighted, with gradations in power calculated according to five year intervals for people between the ages of thirty and seventy. At two soldi a pair, anyone could afford these lenses, but extra could be, and was, spent on frames and cases. For example, Cavalcanti, Bardi and Partners supplied silver-gilt frames and gold-gilt and silver-nielloed cases to two officials at the court of Henry VIII in England. The firm also did a nice line in textiles. They gained a license to import luxury cloths into England, and in 1519 Giovanni Cavalcanti accompanied Henry VIII to the Field of Cloth of Gold.

On the opposite side of the nave to S. Jerome is Botticelli's fresco of S. Augustine. Botticelli's family lived in this parish and he is buried in the S transept. In a chapel in the N transept is kept the habit worn by S. Francis when he received the stigmata. Also here is a magnificent Crucifix by Giotto.

Botticelli's belligerent neighbour

Vasari tells an amusing story about Botticelli and how he got the better of an unfriendly neighbour. A cloth weaver moved in next door to the artist and set up eight looms, which clattered away incessantly. The noise drove Botticelli to despair and the vibrations made him fear for the fabric of his property. When he raised his concerns with his neighbour he got nowhere, for the weaver retorted belligerently that he could and would do what he liked in his own house. This aroused Botticelli's ire, so, because his house was taller than that of the weaver, he obtained a large boulder, got it to the top of his property and placed it precariously on the edge of the dividing wall. Fearing that the vibrations from the looms would cause the boulder to crash through his roof, the weaver asked Botticelli to remove it. By way of reply he was told that Botticelli could and would do what he liked in his own house! I believe that some sort of compromise was subsequently reached.

The entrance to the convent lies to the L of the church as you face the façade. Over one door is a della Robbian terracotta with the coat-of-arms of Alessandro de' Medici. We enter by the next door along, at no. 42. The vestibule and the cloister have early 17th century frescoes of the life of Mary (by Ciocchi) and the life of S. Francis (mainly by Ligozzi) respectively. The latter series includes a remarkable snow-scene near the SW corner. Sir Joshua Reynolds came here to study and copy the frescoes in 1752.

In the NW corner of the cloister is the entrance to the 'Cenacolo' ('Refectory'), with its wonderful fresco of the Last Supper by Domenico Ghirlandaio (1480). It is a decorous depiction (note the glassware and the cherries on the table) with a superb stage setting. The garden behind contains fruit trees, and numerous birds fly to and fro, including goldfinches, ducks and a peacock (symbol of the Resurrection). Ghirlandaio gives us an illusionistic continuation of the space of the refectory, both as regards scale and fidelity of architectural detail. For example, light enters from the L, i.e. from the actual window here, and the pietra serena corbels at the base of the vaulting are used as part of the scene.

Piazza Ognissanti to the Farmacia di S. Maria Novella

On exiting from the convent, note the 15th century Palazzo Lenzi on the R side of the piazza. The sgraffiti decoration on the façade was restored in the 19th century. The palace now houses the French Consulate. We turn L

and retrace our steps back along Borgo Ognissanti for a few yards before turning L up Via del Porcellana. This leads up to the T-junction with Via della Scala, where we turn L. A few yards along on the R, at no. 16 blue, lies the Farmacia di S. Maria Novella, or, to give it its full name, the Officina Profumo-Farmaceutica di S. Maria Novella. No longer a practising pharmacy, but a perfumery, this is a delightful place, worth a visit even if you don't want to buy any of the deliciously perfumed products. As well as a series of lovely rooms (and smells!), the Farmacia houses the 14th century chapel of S. Niccolò, with frescoes attributed to Mariotto di Nardo (recently beautifully restored).

Piazza S. Maria Novella and the Museo Novecento

On leaving the Farmacia turn L along Via della Scala to reach Piazza S. Maria Novella, which is dominated by the church of the same name. Here are several cafés and restaurants, and I advise a sit down and some refreshment while you read about the piazza and before you visit the church and/or the Museo Novecento. From the time of Cosimo I onwards, chariot races were held here as part of the festivities on the Eve of S. John. The two obelisks (resting on charming bronze tortoises by Giambologna) were set up in 1608 as turning posts for the race. If you're thinking 'Ben Hur', think again! James Fenimore Cooper described the races in his *Gleanings in Europe* (1838). The chariots were large, clumsy four-wheeled vehicles, and in Cooper's opinion the race was reminiscent of drunken Irish cartmen on their way home of an evening in New York.

At the opposite end of the piazza to the church lies the charming Loggia di S. Paolo (1489-96) by Michelozzo, adorned with polychrome terracotta roundels by Andrea della Robbia and a terracotta lunette showing the meeting of S. Francis and S. Dominic. Here is the entrance to the

Museo Novecento, devoted to 20th century Italian art and incorporating the Alberto della Ragione collection. Here you will find works by, among others, Baccio Maria Bacci, Felice Casorati, Antonio Donghi, Giorgio Morandi, Giorgio de Chirico, Vinicio Berti, Franco Grignani and Carla Accardi.

On your L as you look towards the façade of the church, a plaque on the Grand Hotel Minerva commemorates Henry Wadsworth Longfellow and his translation of Dante. Longfellow was one of several foreign writers who made their temporary homes here on Piazza S. Maria Novella. In fact there were so many of them that, as the plaque tells us, the piazza was known as 'the Mecca of the foreigners'. Henry James, for example, began writing *Roderick Hudson* here in 1874.

The S. Maria Novella complex, one of the must-sees of Florence, is described at the end of this walk, but a few words about the church façade are apposite here. The lower part of the façade was faced with marble in the mid-14th century, but the rough masonry of the upper part was left unclad. In the mid-15th century, Giovanni di Paolo de' Rucellai, a wealthy businessman whom we will meet again on Walk 13 and who liked to spend his money to the honour of God, Florence and his own memory, decided to remedy this situation. His scheme, however, was blocked for many years by the Baldesi family, whose ancestors had paid for the embellishment of the lower façade. In the end a compromise was reached whereby it was agreed that the lower façade with its 'avelli' (arcaded tomb recesses) would be left intact. This presented a challenge for Giovanni's architect, Leon Battista Alberti, but it was a challenge to which he rose magnificently, combining old and new styles to form a harmonious whole. To the lower façade he added the classical central portal, the large columns and the terminal piers. Above this, the Rucellai emblem of a billowing sail decorates a frieze (the emblem appears too on the piers). The frieze over the central door is decorated with Piero the Gouty's motif of the diamond ring with ostrich feathers, and both Rucellai and Medici emblems surround the great mediaeval oculus window – Giovanni was clearly keen to flaunt his recent family connection with the Medici through the marriage of his son Bernardo to Nannina, daughter of Piero the Gouty and sister to Lorenzo Il Magnifico. Huge decorated volutes unite the nave and aisle roofs, and in the pediment is the motif of the sun, emblem of the Dominican convent and of this quarter of the city. The Latin inscription below the pediment proclaims Giovanni Rucellai's donation and the date of completion, 1470. The two astronomical instruments attached to the lower façade (an equinoctial armilla and a quadrant with sundials) were made by Egnazio Danti in the 1570s.

Leon Battista Alberti

Leon Battista Alberti was the model of the Renaissance 'universal man' – a poet, philosopher, artist, architect and theorist. He wrote a treatise on painting and dedicated it to Filippo Brunelleschi. It was first published in Latin (1435) and later translated as *Della Pittura* (1436). He also wrote a treatise on sculpture (*De Statua*) and one on architecture (*De Re Aedificatoria*; published posthumously in 1485). He was one of the first architects in the modern sense of the word, in that he submitted his designs for projects and then withdrew, leaving the actual construction to others. He recommended that an architect should choose his patrons with care, so as not to demean himself by work on mean constructions! He also advised that, when deciding on a façade, a wise man should use moderation so as not to arouse envy, and should adapt his house to those of his neighbours. I wonder how many modern architects have read his treatise?

Jacopo Peri – Part III

Let us return to Jacopo Peri, our multi-talented opera composer, and his family. Alas, the story does not have a happy ending. Jacopo died in 1633 and was buried in S. Maria Novella. He left a wife and ten surviving children, four daughters (all nuns) and six sons (none married). Dino, the eldest son, became head of the family. He'd studied at Bologna and taken a law doctorate at Pisa. At Pisa he developed an interest in mathematics, and subsequently became a student and a close personal friend of Galileo. Galileo's father, Vincenzo, was a fine musician who, in 1568, published a treatise on lute entablature (the 2nd edition, published in 1584, was dedicated to Jacopo Corsi) and who must have known Jacopo Peri. Four of Dino's brothers died between 1635 and 1637, and in 1640 Dino too died. The entire estate passed to the last surviving son, Alfonso, who, eighteen months later, married Maddalena Lioni. Five months after the marriage Alfonso stabbed his pregnant wife to death. He was condemned to hang but managed to flee. The official description of the murder, with the testimonies of witnesses, is in the archives of the eight Signori, those law and order officials with whom Jacopo had served twice. The entire estate was confiscated by the authorities, which, paradoxically, accounts for the survival of the documentation giving us our information on the family. Following a petition to Grand Duke Ferdinando II, Jacopo's widow was allowed to stay on in the family house at no. 19 Via de' Fossi until her death in March 1644. She was interred with her husband and their children, and the authorities sold the house a month later. So ends the story of this branch of the Peri family.

Florentine palazzi

We have already admired many palaces on Walks 1-7, and we'll encounter many more on Walks 8-15. At this point, roughly halfway through the itineraries, some remarks on the special nature of these magnificent buildings are apposite.

During the mediaeval period there was no such thing as an 'architect' in the modern sense of that word. Patrons left aspects of design and structure in the hands of master masons, men who had had no formal or theoretical training, but whose talents had been honed by direct experience 'on the job'. With the revival of interest in classical antiquity, however, humanist scholars had much to say regarding designs of buildings, and, in saying it, they opened up new horizons. Theoretical knowledge now became important and ideas concerning 'architecture' took on a life of their own, independent of the process of building. Now when patrons wanted a design they turned not to master masons but to men who had proved themselves as designers in other fields. Take the Campanile of the Duomo, for example. Andrea Pisano was a sculptor and Giotto a painter. Brunelleschi, whose work we've admired already on Walks 1 (the cupola), 5 (the Pazzi Chapel) and 6 (S. Lorenzo), was trained in a goldsmith's shop, as was Michelozzo, architect of the Medici Palace and of the library at the monastery of S. Marco (Walk 8). The list could be greatly extended, and the trend continued in the 16th century (one has only to think of Vasari and Ammannati), by which time construction and architectural practice had become distinct functions.

Architecture as a distinct discipline would (could) not have flourished without a demand for the product. The growing numbers of well-heeled bankers and merchants in Republican Florence had plenty of disposable wealth, and they elected to spend large proportions of it on private residences. Artists/designers aspiring to a role as 'architect' had no shortage of clients and, because an element of competition was in the air, they were stimulated and challenged to come up with original and inventive ideas.

The construction boom in Florence was helped by the fact that the city was blessed with an abundance of natural building materials. The hills around were rich in 'pietra forte' (a lovely golden limestone) and 'pietra serena' (a beautiful soft grey stone), and stone-working was an important local craft. The forests on the hillsides yielded timber, while sand and gravel came from the Arno. Tuscany was rich too in iron, used for the manufacture of lanterns, standard-holders, torch-holders and tethering rings. The only thing that Florence lacked was marble – and we've seen, on Walk 6, some of the problems that that deficiency could cause (see the section including 'the fiasco of the façade').

People often ponder the question of why the phenomenon that today we call the 'Renaissance' happened in Florence as opposed to anywhere else. The fact that, here, the arts flourished in an open market rather than within the confines of a courtly circle is a crucial point, so crucial, indeed, that its importance cannot be over-stressed. The city's guilds vied with each other in embellishing the civic buildings under their patronage, while personal disposable wealth resulted in private palaces and chapels which then had to be equipped and decorated. Their owners commissioned sculptures, paintings, bronzes and terracottas, furniture, carpets, tapestries and wall-hangings, silver and majolica tableware. Demand stimulated supply, and a competitive market guaranteed standards. Highly skilled artists and craftsmen proliferated, many becoming sufficiently well-off to become patrons in their own right, as wealth percolated down from the top echelons of society to the broader social spectrum beneath. This transformation of wealth into art was one of the prime forces that generated the Renaissance, and in this the private palaces of Florence played a key role.

As we've already seen, many of the Florentine palazzi are still owned and lived in by the descendants of the families who had them built. There are not many other cities that can claim a like degree of social continuity on such a scale.

The interior of S. Maria Novella

Shortly after the founding of their order in the early 13th century, the Dominicans arrived in Florence and were given the church of S. Maria delle Vigne, which stood on this site. This church, with its façade facing today's Piazza dell' Unità d' Italia (Walk 11), quickly proved too small and a scheme to enlarge it was begun in the mid-13th century. The axis was turned through 90 degrees and the present-day Piazza S. Maria Novella laid out in front of the new façade. The new church and convent were finished by the mid-14th century. The interior of the church was remodelled by Giorgio Vasari in the 1560s in response to the concerns of the Council of Trent.

The nave and aisles

The interior of S. Maria Novella is Gothic in style, not the exuberant Gothic of N Europe, but a Florentine Gothic, more simple and rational. On entering from the Old Cemetery, turn L and walk along to the inner façade. You'll pass my favourite tomb of the many in the church, that of the Blessed Villana delle Botti by Bernardo Rossellino (one of Leon Battista Alberti's master builders). On the inner façade, above the main entrance, is a Nativity scene by Botticelli, while to the R is a 14th century fresco of the Annunciation with scenes of the Nativity, Adoration of the Magi and Baptism of Christ below. The stained glass in the oculus window was designed and in part painted by Andrea di Bonaiuto (c. 1365). From here you get a view along the full length of the nave thanks to Vasari, who removed the rood-screen and added the side altars. Where the screen once was there now hangs a magnificent Crucifix by Giotto. The side altars have paintings by, amongst others, Naldini, Ligozzi, Allori, Santi di Tito and Vasari himself. Attached to the second pillar on the L is the pulpit, designed by Brunelleschi and decorated by his adopted son, Andrea Cavalcanti, with reliefs of the life of Mary. On the side wall just beyond this is Masaccio's famous Trinity (c. 1425-8). By means of a rigorous use of perspective, Masaccio creates a fictive classical chapel. However, he has made the same error with his barrel-vault as Desiderio da Settignano made on his tabernacle at S. Lorenzo (Walk 6); classical norms would have placed a row of coffers at the apex, not a central axis rib. The tomb on which the skeleton rests bears the inscription 'I was once what you are, and am what one day you will be' – a rather sobering thought!

The R transept

In the R transept there are numerous wall tombs, including that of the Patriarch of Constantinople, who came to Florence for the 1439 Council and died here. At the end of the transept is the Rucellai Chapel, decorated with 14th century frescoes. It houses a marble statue of the Madonna and

Child by Nino Pisano, and the bronze tomb-slab of Leonardo Dati by Ghiberti. In front of the chapel is the sarcophagus of Paolo de' Rucellai. Next to the Rucellai Chapel is the Bardi Chapel, decorated with ancient frescoes. This chapel once belonged to the Laudesi brotherhood and housed Duccio's Maestà, which was subsequently moved to the Rucellai Chapel and is now in the Uffizi. The chapel passed to the Bardi family in 1333; on the R pillar is a relief of Riccardo de' Bardi kneeling before S. Gregory.

The next chapel along to the L is the Strozzi Chapel. Behind the altar is the tomb of Filippo Strozzi by Benedetto da Maiano, who'd worked for Filippo on the Strozzi Palace (Walk 13). The chapel walls are decorated with unusual frescoes by Filippino Lippi, showing scenes from the lives of S. Philip (R wall) and S. John the Evangelist (L wall). The artist took the heirs of Filippo Strozzi to court, claiming that the cost of materials had risen so much that he couldn't continue work on the frescoes without an increase in his contracted fee. The Physicians' and Apothecaries' Guild agreed, and Lippi won his suit in 1497, when his fee was increased from 250 to 350 florins.

The main altar and the sanctuary

On the 19th century marble altar stands a Crucifix by Giambologna. Below the altar is buried S. John of Salerno, the 13th century founder of the convent. Behind the altar, the sanctuary is decorated with frescoes by Domenico Ghirlandaio and his workshop, which included the young Michelangelo. The R and L walls have scenes from the lives of John the Baptist and the Virgin respectively. In the vault can be seen the Evangelists, while on the end wall are the Miracle of S. Dominic, the death of S. Peter Martyr, and the donors, Giovanni Tornabuoni and his wife, Francesca Pitti. Giovanni was manager of the Medici bank in Rome. The same names keep cropping up – Medici, Bardi, Rucellai, Strozzi, Pitti, Tornabuoni etc. They all intermarried, forging kinship alliances and consolidating wealth and property. Giovanni's sister, Lucrezia, married Piero the Gouty and was the mother of Lorenzo Il Magnifico. Ghirlandaio's frescoes are set in 15th century Florence and include many portraits of his contemporaries. Tornabuoni ladies attend the births of S. John and the Virgin, and male family members are present in the scenes of the Angel appearing to Zacharius and the Expulsion of Joachim from the Temple. In the latter, the group on the R includes a self-portrait of the artist. He is dressed in blue and red, holds his R hand up to his chest and looks directly at us. In the scene of the Birth of the Virgin he has included his name on the intarsia panelling of the room. It is difficult to see, but hopefully you can make out 'Bighordi' at bottom L and 'Grillanda' at top R. His father, Tommaso Bighordi, made hair ornaments or 'grillandai' – hence the nickname 'Ghirlandai'.

The L transept

To the L of the sanctuary is the Gondi Chapel by Giuliano da Sangallo and Benedetto da Rovezzano. The chapel houses Brunelleschi's Crucifix. Immediately to the L of the Gondi Chapel lies the Gaddi Chapel by Giovanni Dosio, a pupil of Michelangelo. To Michelangelo are attributed the designs of the two wall tombs. At the end of the L transept is the Strozzi of Mantua Chapel. The mid-14th century frescoes are by Nardo di Cione and his brother Andrea (called Orcagna). Andrea also painted the altarpiece. The frescoes show the Last Judgement (altar wall), Paradise (L wall) and Purgatory and Hell (R wall), the last being a representation of Dante's *Inferno*. In a recess under the steps up to the chapel is a Strozzi sepulchre with frescoes by Agnolo Gaddi (1375-95). At the base of the steps is the door to the campanile, above which is a 14th century fresco showing the Coronation of the Virgin. Above this is a clock with verses beneath by Poliziano.

The story of Brunelleschi's Crucifix

According to Vasari, Brunelleschi's Crucifix was carved in order to show Donatello how Christ should be represented. The story runs as follows. Asked by Donatello for his opinion on that artist's Crucifix (housed in S. Croce), Brunelleschi commented that Christ looked more like a rustic than the Son of God. Donatello then challenged Brunelleschi to do better, a challenge that was taken up. When his Crucifix was finished, Brunelleschi invited Donatello to lunch. Having come by way of the market, Donatello arrived carrying some shopping. On seeing Brunelleschi's work, he was so overcome with admiration and emotion that he involuntarily dropped his purchases, which, alas, included eggs!

The opulent sacristy houses the shop. Note the lavabo with glazed terracotta decoration by Giovanni della Robbia to the R of the door on the inside as you enter. On the corner where the transept meets the nave aisle, the marble caryatid supporting a vase is attributed to Michelangelo. Turn R along the aisle to reach the entrance to the cloisters. Just before you get there, note a marble slab in the floor in front of the side altar. This marks the grave of Jacopo Peri, about whom we learnt so much on Walk 7.

The cloisters and museum

The door from the church leads directly to the Green Cloister. Its walls were frescoed with terraverde (from which the cloister gets its name) in the first half of the 15th century by Paolo Uccello and his workshop. The frescoes, illustrating Old Testament stories, are badly damaged but include charming details. The most famous scenes are on the E walk (alongside the church nave) and include the Creation of Adam and Eve, the Temptation in the Garden, the Flood and the Drunkenness of Noah.

Off the N walk of the Green Cloister lies the Cloister of the Dead, which has funerary chapels with remains of frescoed decoration, and the Chapel of the Annunciation with frescoes of the Nativity and the Crucifixion attributed to Andrea Orcagna. The Nativity scene has gorgeous sheep and, just as in Taddeo Gaddi's fresco in S. Croce, a very aggressive dog! The polychrome terracotta altarpiece of the *Noli me tangere* in the Cloister of the Dead is from the workshop of Giovanni della Robbia.

Further along the N walk of the Green Cloister lies the Chapter House, or Spanish Chapel, frescoed in 1365-7 by Andrea di Bonaiuto (also called Andrea da Firenze). The decoration was designed to instruct and inspire the Dominican defenders of the faith who met here. The R wall shows the Church Militant and Triumphant and the Way to Salvation. In front of the pink Duomo (recognizable as that of Florence but minus the drum under the dome) are the Pope, Emperor and church dignitaries. To the R are Dominic, Peter Martyr and Thomas Aquinas. Dominic sends out 'the hounds of the Lord' (*Domini canes*) to hunt down sin (shown as wolves) and protect the faithful (sheep). This is a pun on the name Dominican, and the hounds are black and white, just like the Dominican habit. Above, monks show the way to salvation, setting to one side the Vices, shown as seated figures on the R. The L wall depicts Christian learning and the Triumph of Catholic doctrine, with S. Thomas Aquinas (with vanquished heretics at his feet) accompanied by the Evangelists and other saints and prophets. The Liberal Arts and Theological Sciences are accompanied by their historical representatives. The end wall has the Road to Calvary, Crucifixion and Descent into Limbo, while the entrance wall (damaged) shows the preaching and death of S. Peter Martyr. In the vault are the Resurrection, Ascension, Navicella and Pentecost.

At the W end of the N walk is the entrance to the Great Cloister and the museum. The former is used by the police and is not generally accessible. Its walls were frescoed during the 16th century with scenes from the lives of Dominican saints. The museum lies to the L in the former Ubriachi Chapel and Refectory. It houses frescoes, sinopie and paintings from the church, together with reliquaries, silver and vestments.

The Rucellai emblem of a billowing sail on a pier on the façade of S. Maria Novella

Walk 8

Begins at Piazza S. Marco and ends at Piazza S. Giovanni.

Takes in: the Museo di S. Marco, the Botanical Gardens, the Geology and Palaeontology Museum, the Mineralogy and Lithology Museum, the Accademia, the Museum of the Opificio delle Pietre Dure, the Palazzo Medici-Riccardi and the Leonardo da Vinci Museum.

Duration: 1 hour, excluding visits to any of the above or breaks for refreshments. You should allow *c.* 2 hours each for S. Marco and the Accademia, and *c.* 1 hour for each of the other museums.

Tips: you cannot possibly hope to visit all of the above on one day. I would recommend that you begin the walk with a visit to the Museo di S. Marco and finish it by visiting the Palazzo Medici-Riccardi, perhaps sandwiching the Natural History Museums or the Museum of the Opificio delle Pietre Dure in between. The Accademia is a must-see, of course, but to visit both it and the Museo di S. Marco on the same itinerary is a tall order. As the queue for entry to the Accademia begins to form long before the place opens, you'd be well advised to make this a separate enterprise. A word of warning here; the queue can, and often does, stretch down the street and round the corner, and at the time of writing there was no shelter against the elements. The description of the Museo di S. Marco below is prefaced by a section on the history of the monastery, probably best read in the comfort of your hotel before setting out on the walk. One further tip. If you manage to make an early start and get to S. Marco as it opens, go upstairs and see the monks' cells first, before visiting the ground floor rooms. Each cell is roped off and the doors are quite narrow, so it is more difficult to view the frescoes here once the crowds arrive.

Fra Angelico and the history of the monastery of S. Marco

To understand the history of the monastery of S. Marco and what you are going to see there, you need to have a little knowledge of the reformed branch of the Dominican Order, known as the 'Observance'. Towards the end of the 14th century it was felt by some Dominicans that the original tenets of S. Dominic had been compromised and that reform was needed. A distinction came to be made between foundations that supported reform and those that felt no need for it. The former were called 'Observant' houses and the latter 'Conventual' houses. At Florence, S. Maria Novella remained a Conventual house and the monastery of S. Dominic at Fiesole was founded as an Observant one. The Dominican Order had always stressed the importance of learning as a necessary prerequisite for preaching. The reformers, however, prioritized prayer and preaching above study, and insisted on a return to individual and institutional poverty. This meant that Observant houses

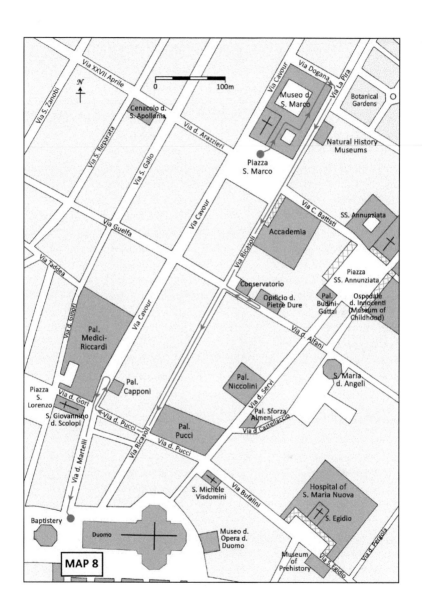

MAP 8

could neither tie themselves to any regular income nor own revenue-producing property. One result of this was that Observant recruits were encouraged to engage in trades in order to help fund their communities. Friars were also encouraged to develop personal, contemplative lives of prayer modelled on S. Dominic.

At the start of the 15th century Guido di Piero and his brother Benedetto were in Florence receiving training in a manuscript workshop, Benedetto as a scribe, Guido as a miniaturist. By *c.* 1420 both brothers had joined the Observant community of S. Dominic at Fiesole, Benedetto retaining his own name and Guido taking the name Giovanni. Soon after his death in 1455, Fra Giovanni was dubbed an angelic painter and has been called 'Angelico' ever since. Fra Angelico, as we shall henceforth call him, was encouraged to practise his craft, and all the income generated went to support his community.

From 1421 to 1424 the prior of S. Dominico was Fra Antonino. In 1424 he left Fiesole and took up a series of posts in Naples and Rome. In 1434 he returned. In the same year, Pope Eugenius IV was forced to flee from Rome when a group of dissident cardinals elected a rival pope; he fled to Florence and found refuge at S. Maria Novella. 1434 also saw the return of Cosimo de' Medici to Florence after a year in exile. So begins the story of the monastery of S. Marco.

The friars at Fiesole had begun to seek a city site for an Observant house as early as 1418. They instigated an inquiry into the Silvestrine monastery at S. Marco in the hope that the pope (then Martin V) would find in their favour and evict the Silvestrines, but this attempt came to naught. In 1435 they tried again (with Pope Eugenius), and this time the Silvestrines were ordered to go. They refused to leave, however, and put up a fight. A lengthy litigation process followed, during which the Dominicans settled instead at S. Giorgio alla Costa on the Oltrarno. The Silvestrines finally lost their battle in 1436, and were forced to obey a papal directive ordering them to swap churches with the Dominicans. When the latter arrived at S. Marco, they found that the Silvestrines had stripped the place and that the conventual buildings were in bad repair. Cosimo de' Medici stepped in and underwrote the costs of rebuilding and refurbishing the complex.

The establishment of the Observants at S. Marco caused much resentment. Old relationships within the parish were disrupted, patronal rights in the church were an issue, and agreements with confraternities using the conventual land and buildings had to be renegotiated. All this took two years, but by 1438 Cosimo had secured the patronal rights to the main chapel and had reached agreements with the confraternities regarding relocation. One of the confraternities was the 'Compagnia de' Magi' ('Company of the Magi'), with which we'll have more to do later on Walk 8.

Building work began in earnest, with Michelozzo as architect. Meanwhile, there had been a development. Niccolò Niccoli, a humanist scholar and bibliophile, had died in 1437, leaving his collection of books and manuscripts to pass into public use. Niccolò had died in debt to Cosimo, and in 1441 the executors agreed to turn the collection over to him. Cosimo decided to house the books at S. Marco and construction of Michelozzo's famous library began the following year. As already noted, in the Observance, prayer and preaching were prioritized above study. Unsurprisingly, therefore, not everyone was happy about the addition of the library, especially as Niccolò's collection was rich in texts of pagan, classical authors. Many felt that the integrity of S. Marco's as an Observant house was being compromised, and their concerns were compounded when Pope Eugenius consigned the office of parish priests to the friars. This guaranteed the monastery a regular income, in contradiction of the tenet of institutional poverty. It also took away this income from the parish clergy, which caused further resentment. Tensions ran high, and in 1445 the Observant houses of S. Marco and S. Dominico at Fiesole formally separated.

The new building complex of S. Marco was damaged by an earthquake early in the 1450s and had to be repaired. Later in that decade, however, Fra Lapaccini could write in his *Chronicle* that S. Marco was graced by its harmonious and commodious buildings, its painted decoration by Fra Angelico and, above all, by its magnificent library. He may have been a bit biased. A relation of Niccolò, he acted both as librarian and as Cosimo's agent, undertaking many trips to purchase new manuscripts.

The Museo di S. Marco

Walk 8 begins with a visit to the Museo di S. Marco, famous for its paintings and frescoes by Fra Angelico and his workshop. You'll also see Fra Girolamo Savonarola's cells, containing artefacts which belonged to him. A section devoted to Savonarola follows the description of the museum, the entrance to which lies on Piazza S. Marco, to the R of the church façade.

The Cloister of S. Antonino

The entrance from Piazza S. Marco leads through to the SW corner of the Cloister of S. Antonino, its graceful arcades supported on pietra serena columns with Ionic capitals. The lunettes of the arcade are decorated with 16th-17th century frescoes showing scenes from the life of S. Antonino, who became prior of S. Marco's in 1436, Archbishop of Florence in 1446, and was later canonized. At the NW corner of the cloister (straight ahead of you as you enter) is Fra Angelico's fresco of Christ on the Cross with S. Dominic kneeling below. The T-shaped marble frame was added in the 17th century. At the top can be seen part of the painted frame, which shows that the fresco was originally wider; Dominic may once have been accompanied by the Virgin and S. John. This image of S. Dominic encapsulates aspects of his personal prayer life as recorded in a 13th century treatise entitled *De modo orandi*. The knowledge was acquired by nosey friars who spied on Dominic when he believed himself to be alone. They record him as weeping, sighing and highly emotional when praying. We shall refer to the *De modo orandi* again when we visit the dormitory cells upstairs. To the L of the fresco is the door into the church. Over the door is a copy of Fra Angelico's fresco showing S. Peter Martyr enjoining silence. The original is displayed in the Chapter House, as are the originals of other of his lunette frescoes from the cloister. The reddish background was the preparation for blue pigment which has since flaked away.

If you intend to act on the tip given at the start of this walk and visit the monks' cells first in order to avoid overcrowding, continue past the frescoes just discussed, turn L into a vestibule and hop to the section below entitled 'The Annunciation'. Otherwise, retrace your steps back towards the entrance and turn L into the S walk of the cloister. On the R lies the erstwhile Pilgrims' Hospice, now a picture gallery. Over the door is another fresco by Fra Angelico, this one showing S. Thomas Aquinas.

The Pilgrims' Hospice
This room houses works by Fra Angelico and his school gathered from different locations. Here you will find, among other gems, the magnificent Deposition in its splendid ornate Gothic frame (the man in the black cap is thought by some to be a portrait of Michelozzo), the Last Judgement, the famous panels showing the life of Christ from the Silver Chest of SS. Annunziata (Walk 10), the huge Linenmakers' Tabernacle (with its angel musicians so familiar from Christmas cards) and several altarpieces in the new, single field rectangular format (which, in the mid-15th century replaced the polyptych). Some of the works are now displayed behind glass, which, alas, makes them quite difficult to see and appreciate properly. Leave the Pilgrims' Hospice by the door at the E end, over which there is another Fra Angelico fresco, this one showing two Dominican friars welcoming Christ as a pilgrim.

The Lavabo Room, Large Refectory, Fra Bartolomeo and Baldovinetti Rooms
At the opposite (N) end of the E walk of the cloister is the entrance to the Lavabo Room. Fra Angelico's lunette over this door shows the Man of Sorrows, a reminder to the friars that communal meals were to be related to the Last Supper and, via this, to the Eucharist. The Lavabo Room was where the friars washed their hands before entering the Refectory. Among other things, it contains a lovely terracotta by Andrea della Robbia of the Madonna adoring the Christ Child. In the Refectory are later works from the S. Marco complex (16th century onwards) and a large fresco by Sogliani depicting the miracle of S. Dominic feeding the brethren. On the opposite side of the Lavabo Room, the Fra Bartolomeo Room displays works by this artist (1475-1517), who, like Fra Angelico, was a friar at S. Marco. The

Baldovinetti Room has works by Alesso Baldovinetti (who belonged to Fra Angelico's circle) and other 15th century artists such as Benozzo Gozzoli, whose masterpiece we'll see later at the Palazzo Medici-Riccardi.

The Chapter House

Off the N walk of the cloister lies the Chapter House. This was once the meeting room of the Compagnia de' Magi and it retains its 14th century façade. Inside are the originals of the lunette frescoes that we have seen copies of in the cloister, together with the one that was formerly on the façade here, showing S. Dominic with the scourge. The scourge, also called the 'discipline', was a major feature of early Dominican life that was revived in the Observance, and the Chapter House was not only the place where meetings and ceremonies of a judicial, administrative and ritual nature took place, but also the scene of communal scourgings!

The room is dominated by Fra Angelico's fresco of the Crucifixion. This is not a narrative scene but a contemplative one. The only witnesses of the historical event were the Virgin, S. John and the two Maries. The other onlookers are all exemplars for meditation. To the L of the Virgin's group are (from R to L) SS. John the Baptist, Mark, Lawrence (Lorenzo), Cosmas and Damian. S. Mark was the titular saint of the monastery and S. John the Baptist one of the patron saints of Florence. The other three have more overt Medicean connections. S. Lawrence was the patron saint of Cosimo's brother Lorenzo (d. 1440) and titular saint of their parish church of S. Lorenzo (Walk 6). SS. Cosmas and Damian were the patron saints of the Medici in general, and Cosmas of Cosimo in particular. S. Cosmas is said to be a portrait of Fra Angelico's friend, the sculptor Nanni di Banco. To the R of the Cross is a group of eleven saints. From L to R kneeling are SS. Dominic, Jerome, Francis, Bernard of Clairvaux, Giovanni Gualberto and Peter Martyr. From L to R standing are SS. Augustine and Anthony Abbot (some authorities say Zenobius or Ambrose and Augustine), Benedict, Romuald and Thomas Aquinas. Fra Angelico used an expensive and luxurious palette – money was clearly no object with Cosimo as patron. The Virgin's cloak is pure ultramarine, the Maries are clothed in vermilion, gold and malachite green. Mark's cloak too is malachite, and Lawrence's dalmatic is vermilion and gold. All the saints have gilded haloes. The effect would have been even richer with the huge blue field behind the figures of Christ and the two thieves, which, alas, has not survived.

Around the border of the fresco are eleven hexagons, ten of which show figures holding scrolls. The first and last have non-biblical inscriptions taken from Pseudo-Dionysus the Areopagite and the Erythrean Sibyl (L and R respectively). These two texts define the opening and closing of the Passion cycle. The other eight inscriptions are from the patriarchs and prophets, and provide meditations on the Crucifixion. At the top, the central hexagon depicts the pelican of piety accompanied by a line from Psalm 101 ('I have become like a pelican in the wilderness'). Across the bottom of the scene runs a painted moulding of fictive pietra serena, beneath which are seventeen roundels showing famous Dominicans (S. Dominic is in the centre). Such depictions were a characteristic of the Order and evoked the concept of *traditio*, a concept that linked the present with the past in an unbroken continuum. The Dominicans believed that their authority to preach could be traced back via the luminaries of their Order to the Desert Fathers and holy men of the earliest church, and thence to the Apostles and Christ himself.

Also in the Chapter House is the 'Piagnona' Bell, which sounded when crowds besieged the monastery baying for Savonarola's blood (see the section on Fra Girolamo Savonarola). Because of these inauspicious associations the bell was later 'exiled' to S. Salvatore al Monte (Walk 14) and whipped along the way. An information board in the Chapter House gives full details.

The Annunciation

Turn R out of the Chapter House and R again into a vestibule. Through the door at the end you can see the Cloister of S. Dominic (no admission), decorated with 18th century frescoes. On the R side of the vestibule are the stairs leading up to the dormitories. As you turn the corner on the landing, you are in for a wonderful surprise, for ahead of you is Fra Angelico's stunning portrayal of the Annunciation. One of his best-known works, it was in fact designed to be viewed from the stairs. The dimensions of the door at the top of the staircase are actually projected forward perspectively on to the surface of the fresco. Fra Angelico also set the scene in a fictive pietra serena frame with an apparent ledge across the bottom, the profile of which imitates those of the stairs opposite. The present light levels are greater than they were in Fra Angelico's day (the large window to the L was introduced later). With flickering candlelight, the silica mixed into the intonaco under Gabriel's wings would have caused them to glitter. While the red inscription was added later, the one in black is original. It instructs the beholder to say an *Ave* when he comes before the Virgin's image; in other words, to do exactly as the angel Gabriel is doing.

The Madonna of the Shadows

At the top of the stairs turn L and then immediately R. Resist the temptation to peer into the monks' cells for a moment, for we shall return this way. About halfway along this E corridor, on the RH side between the doors to cells 25 and 26, is Fra Angelico's Virgin and Child enthroned with saints, also called the Madonna of the Shadows. According to a 13th century text called the *Vitae fratrum*, all Dominican dormitories had to have an image of the Virgin, in front of which matins was said before descending to the church. The Virgin and Child here are accompanied by (from L to R) SS. Dominic, Cosmas and Damian, Mark, John the Evangelist, Thomas Aquinas, Lawrence and Peter Martyr. S. Mark's book reveals the opening of his gospel. S. Dominic, who gazes directly at the viewer (i.e. at the friars, for only they saw this image), points to the text that he holds, which tells the friars to have charity and humility, and to possess poverty. God's curse is invoked on anyone introducing possessions into the Order. Wow! Who made the decision to include this, and does it reflect, perhaps, some of the tensions referred to in the section on the history of the monastery concerning the introduction of the library and/or the granting of the office of parish priests to the friars? We shall probably never know.

Savonarola's cells and the cells on the S corridor (see plan on page 213)
Continue to the end of the E corridor and turn R into the S corridor. At the far end lie cells 12-14, now called Savonarola's cells because they contain memorabilia pertaining to this famous firebrand of a preacher. The cells along the S corridor (nos. 15-21) were allocated to the novices, and the frescoes here all represent S. Dominic next to the Cross. The 13th century treatise entitled *De modo orandi*, which we referred to earlier, describes the various ways in which S. Dominic prayed, and the cells here depict seven of these modes of prayer. These frescoes are of inferior quality to those in the E and N corridors, and are almost certainly not by Fra Angelico's hand.

The cells on the E corridor (see plan on page 213)
The cells along the E corridor were those of the friars. The frescoes here vary in quality and reveal the presence of several hands, but they include some of Fra Angelico's masterpieces, marked in the lists below with an asterisk. It is important to remember that they were not intended as decorations or illustrations, but as a means of invoking a contemplative state of mind. In other words, they are iconic rather than narrative, and the cursory viewing to which they are now subjected is different to the use for which they were intended and designed. Most include a Dominican exemplar, either Dominic or Peter Martyr, whose gestures recall the modes of prayer described in *De modo orandi*. The lists below are set out numerically from 2-11 and from 22-30 (the E and W sides of the corridor respectively), though of course you'll be viewing nos. 2-11 in reverse order. Cell no. 1 is grouped with the cells of the N corridor, for reasons that will be explained below. Nos. 10-11 form a double cell which was probably allotted to the prior. Who made the decisions as to which subject was depicted in which cell is not known – possibilities include the prior, a monastic committee, the cell occupant or Fra Angelico and his workshop.

Cell no.	Scene
2	The Entombment
3*	The Annunciation
4	The Crucifixion
5	The Nativity
6*	The Transfiguration
7*	The Mocking of Christ
8	The Resurrection
9*	The Coronation of the Virgin
10*	The Presentation in the Temple
11	The Virgin and Child with two saints
22	The Virgin beside the Cross
23	The Virgin and S. Dominic beside the Cross
24	The Baptism of Christ
25	Christ on the Cross
26	The Man of Sorrows, with episodes of the Passion in brief
27	The Flagellation
28	Christ carrying his Cross
29	The Crucifixion
30	The Crucifixion

The cells on the N corridor (see plan on page 213)

The cells on the N corridor were those of the lay-brothers who saw to the domestic needs of the community – e.g. cooks, housekeepers, porters, sacristans. Here we move away from symbolic/iconic representations and find instead narrative scenes. Many lay-brothers came from the lower classes of society and were comparatively uneducated, so narrative scenes were more appropriate. Most of the frescoes here are almost certainly not by Fra Angelico's hand, but by the hands of Benozzo Gozzoli and others. Some scholars attribute the *Noli me tangere* in cell no. 1 to Gozzoli. With its narrative subject matter, lack of a Dominican exemplar, and naturalistic setting, it belongs in spirit more with the N corridor frescoes than with those of the E corridor, and this has led to the suggestion that cell no. 1 may have belonged to the friar who oversaw the duties of the laybrothers. Cells nos. 31-37 lie on the S side of the corridor, while nos. 38-44 are on the N side, as is the entrance to the library. Opposite the library entrance is a large window. This was constructed in the 17th century and its insertion resulted in the partial destruction of two cells here. The remnants of these two cells are now incorporated into cells 32 and 33. Cell 37 contains a fresco of the Crucifixion that is clearly derived from the scene in the Chapter House, and this has led some scholars to hypothesize that cell 37 may have been a

Chapter Room for the lay-brothers. Cells 38-39 were the private retreat of Cosimo Il Vecchio and are treated separately.

Cell no.	Scene
1	*Noli me tangere*
31	Christ in Limbo
32	The Sermon on the Mount
32a	The Temptation of Christ (not visible from the corridor)
33	The kiss of Judas
33a	The Entry into Jerusalem (not visible from the corridor)
34	The Agony in the Garden
35	The Institution of the Eucharist
36	Christ on the Cross
37	The Crucifixion
38-39	See further below
40-44	The Crucifixion

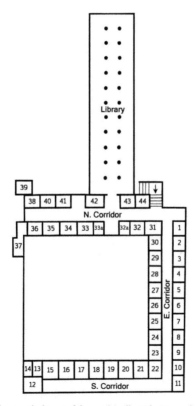

Plan showing the layout of the monks' cells at the Museo di S. Marco

Cells 38-39

These rooms were the private cells of Cosimo Il Vecchio. The lack of windows is due to alterations carried out in the 16th century. Originally there was access to an external terrace and thence to the library. The fresco in cell no. 38 shows Jesus consigning his mother to the care of S. John. SS. Cosmas and Peter Martyr are also present. The saints depicted are a nice allusion to three generations of the Medici, Cosimo, his father Giovanni, and his son Piero. The fresco in cell 39 shows the Adoration of the Magi and makes use of lavish pigments. The theme of the Magi was one that was particularly dear to the Medici, as we'll see when we visit the Chapel in the Palazzo Medici-Riccardi.

Michelozzo's library

The library at S. Marco's, one of Michelozzo's masterpieces, became the model for later Renaissance libraries in Italy. Placed on the first floor to help give protection against fire and flood, the form of the building was determined by its practical needs. It was long and narrow for optimal lighting, with reading desks placed at right angles to the walls under each window. Today it is used for temporary exhibitions.

The Small Refectory and the Guest Quarters

Descend the stairs to the ground floor. At the bottom of the stairs on the R is the Small Refectory, which now houses the shop. This was where guests took their meals. On the W wall is a wonderful fresco of the Last Supper by Domenico Ghirlandaio. On exiting from the Refectory, you pass through the erstwhile Guest Quarters, which now house architectural fragments from mediaeval Florence, including many from the Old Market, demolished in the 19th century to make way for Piazza della Repubblica. The exit from the S. Marco complex lies here and gives on to Via Dogana.

Fra Girolamo Savonarola

Fra Girolamo Savonarola (1452-1498) was invited to Florence by Lorenzo Il Magnifico and became prior at S. Marco's in 1491. Il Magnifico got more than he bargained for! This firebrand of a preacher denounced immorality loudly from his pulpit, attributing all the ills that befell Florence to the immoral lifestyles of her citizens. Pope Alexander VI also came in for a good deal of criticism. Following the death of Lorenzo in 1492 and the expulsion of the Medici from Florence in 1494, Savonarola found himself catapulted to prominence, and in a position to influence decision-making. In the spring of 1495, he declared that the Virgin Mary had revealed to him that, after going through much trouble, Florence would emerge as the richest, most powerful and glorious city that ever existed, that she would lead the purification of politics and religion, and that she would be both a new Jerusalem and a new Rome, an upholder of sobriety and godliness. Many chose to believe this, of course, and Savonarola's puritanical lead was followed fervently by thousands of citizens. Public festivals were suspended or converted into religious celebrations, sumptuary laws were enforced, and bands of youths patrolled the streets seeking out irreligious behaviour and curbing it, often in intimidating fashion.

In the summer of 1495 King Charles VIII of France was returning from S Italy with his huge army, and there was much fear and distrust in the air. Savonarola, who'd been one of the ambassadors sent to talk to Charles the previous year in the wake of Piero the Unfortunate's precipitate action (see the section entitled 'the French come to Florence' at the end of Walk 13), went to Poggibonsi to parley again with the king. It was said that this meeting was the cause of the French not advancing to Florence, and Savonarola's reputation was at an all-time high. Alas, Charles subsequently failed to live up to his promises to the Florentines, a fact that Savonarola's enemies were quick to latch on to. Feelings began to turn against the prior and the situation was exacerbated by a return of the plague. As well as disease there was famine. Savonarola's promises of riches, power and glory in return for a strictly moral lifestyle were beginning to sound hollow. In May 1497 he preached in the Duomo on Ascension Day, but, midway through his sermon, he was heckled and a fight ensued.

Feelings were running high and other ecclesiastics, unhappy at what they saw as Savonarola's undue influence, began to enter the fray. A friar at S. Spirito denounced him, declaring that he was no prophet. The government, having suppressed many public festivities on account of Savonarola's sermons, decided to heed his warnings no longer. Then, in June 1497, Pope Alexander excommunicated him and the excommunication was published in the major churches. When Carnival time came round the following February, Savonarola organized his famous 'Bonfire of the Vanities' in the Piazza della Signoria, and there was made 'a pile of vain things' estimated at thousands of florins. Ignoring the excommunication, he celebrated Mass at S. Marco's.

Councils were held to consider how best to act with regard to the troublesome prior, for, unless he were silenced, the pope threatened to put the entire city under an interdict. Merchants feared that their places of business in Rome would be sacked, and there was much disagreement and serious controversy. In desperation the Signoria sent a delegation to Savonarola, begging him to stay silent. He consented, but his friars continued to preach. One of them, Fra Domenico, invited a friar preaching at S. Croce against Savonarola to undergo a trial by fire. The challenge was accepted and arrangements were made. A great scaffold was erected in the Piazza della Signoria and on 7th April 1498 the friars from the two monasteries arrived with much ceremony. The assembled crowds awaited the great spectacle, which was constantly being delayed owing to some argument between the friars on a point of detail. Eventually the Franciscans left and the Dominicans followed suit.

The following day, 8th April, was Palm Sunday, and Savonarola's devotees had packed themselves into the church of S. Marco for Vespers. Incited by harangues from a number of Savonarola's enemies gathered for Vespers at the Duomo, a mob streamed up Via Ricasoli, gathered in Piazza S. Marco and demanded that Savonarola should come out. A proclamation came from the Signoria offering a reward for his capture and armed men arrived. The friars bolted the church doors and the entire congregation remained barricaded there for the rest of the day. When darkness fell many escaped through the garden behind the monastery. Luca Landucci was in the church and tells us in his *Diary* that if he had not managed to get out through the cloister, and go away towards the Porta di San Gallo, he might have been killed. Eventually the friars were left alone. By this time three catapults had been dragged into the piazza and the assault on the monastery began. The doors to the church and cloister were set on fire and volleys of rocks and stones rained down. About twenty people were killed and 100 wounded. Some of the mob managed to get into the rear cloisters and broke into the church via the sacristy at the same time as the main church doors gave way. One lay-brother grabbed a firearm from an intruder and began to fire at the crowd from the pulpit. The friars managed to retreat up their staircase to the library. Here Savonarola took his leave of them and, together with Fra Domenico and Fra Silvestro, surrendered himself up to the authorities.

Under torture Savonarola and his two companions confessed to false prophecy and treason. The confessions were read out at a Council in the Great Hall. Luca Landucci was again present and tells us how grieved he was to see such an edifice fall to the ground on account of having been founded on a lie. In May the pope sent an envoy and the General of the Dominican Order to try the friars. They were found guilty and sentenced to death. Luca describes the execution in the Piazza della Signoria in gruesome detail. Following it, the charred scaffold was hacked down and burnt on the ground so that all traces of the bodies were consumed. The ashes were then gathered up meticulously and dumped in the Arno in order that no remains should be found.

The Natural History Museums

Turn R along Via Dogana. Ahead of you, on the opposite side of Via La Pira, lie the Botanical Gardens, much of which can be seen through the railings. Here you will find collections of all sorts of specimens, including trees, palms, ferns, succulents, alpine plants, medicinal plants, aquatic plants, bromeliaceae, begonias and orchids. If you wish to visit, you should turn L at Via La Pira and then R along Via Micheli, where you'll find the entrance on the R. Otherwise, turn R down Via La Pira where, on the L at no. 4, lie two more institutions that form part of the University of Florence Natural History Museum, Geology and Palaeontology, and Mineralogy and Lithology. One ticket covers both museums. The Geology and Palaeontology Museum has a large collection of fossil invertebrates and a palaeobotany collection documenting the evolution of plants. Most popular with the public is the vertebrates collection, which illustrates the evolution of marine and terrestrial faunas. Here you'll find some spectacular skeletons, including flightless birds, equids, enormous mammoths and a *Hippopotamus antiquus*, as well as casts and models of dinosaurs. At the time of writing the labelling was, in the main, only in Italian, but there was a small booklet available in English. The small Mineralogy and Lithology Museum has a stunning collection of rocks, gems and crystals, beautifully displayed and labelled in state of the art showcases; this comes highly recommended. On exiting from the museums turn L and continue down Via La Pira back to Piazza S. Marco.

The Accademia and the Collezione del Conservatorio 'Luigi Cherubini'
Leave Piazza S. Marco at its SE corner on Via Ricasoli (which forms a continuation of Via La Pira, by which we entered the square). On your L lies a 14th century loggia that once belonged to the Ospedale di S. Matteo. Over three of the doors are della Robbian lunettes showing the Resurrection, the Madonna and Child, and (overleaf) the Madonna giving her belt to S. Thomas.

The entrance to the Accademia delle Belle Arti lies a little further along the street on your L. Most tourists visit the Accademia to see Michelangelo's David and his so-called Prisoners or Slaves (four unfinished statues intended for the tomb of Pope Julius II in Rome), and many do not have sufficient time to see what else this superb gallery has to offer. This is a shame, for the collections are stunning. You will find 13th-14th century works by Bernardo Daddi, Taddeo and Agnolo Gaddi, Gerini, Orcagna, Andrea di Bonaiuto, Giovanni da Milano, Lorenzo di Bicci, Giovanni del Biondo and Lorenzo Monaco. 15th-16th century works include masterpieces by Uccello, Bicci di Lorenzo, Neri di Bicci, Gozzoli, Baldovinetti, Perugino, Ghirlandaio, Botticelli, Filippino Lippi, Andrea del Sarto, Franciabigio, Pontormo, Bronzino and Allori. I could go on and on, but you get the picture (excuse the pun). Also here is a collection of 19th century plaster casts by Lorenzo Bartolini and Luigi Pampaloni. These include casts of the Arnolfo di Cambio and Brunelleschi statues in the Piazza del Duomo (Walk 1), and the Alberti monument and Sofia Zamoyska tomb in S. Croce (Walk 5). Everything is clearly labelled and the information panels, while succinct, provide interesting background material and help to set the works in context.

The Accademia also houses the Collezione del Conservatorio 'Luigi Cherubini', a collection of musical instruments dating from the 17th-19th centuries. There are strings, brass, wind and percussion instruments. There's a guitar, and an 18th century 'piano-guitar'. Here too are keyboard instruments made by Bartolomeo Cristofori, inventor of the piano (for the Accademia Bartolomeo Cristofori see Walk 13). These include a harpsichord, a piano and an oval spinet (the oldest of Cristofori's inventions known today, dating back to 1690). There's also an 18th century vertical piano, a pair of hurdy-gurdies, a 'tromba marina', a serpent and a salterio made of marble.

The Opificio delle Pietre Dure

On exiting from the Accademia turn L and continue down Via Ricasoli to the little Piazza delle Belle Arti, where lies the Music Conservatory whose collection is housed in the Accademia. If you wish to visit the Museum of the Opificio delle Pietre Dure, turn L here along Via degli Alfani and you'll find it a few yards along on the L at no. 78. The Opificio delle Pietre Dure (the workshop for the manufacture of artefacts in hard stones) was founded by Grand Duke Ferdinando I in 1588. The institute has for many decades now been the seat of a justly world-famous restoration and conservation laboratory. The small museum is, if you'll excuse the pun, an absolute gem. In Florence, the technique of crafting semi-precious stones reached levels unequalled elsewhere, to the extent that it is no exaggeration to speak of 'stone paintings', and here, housed in a series of nine small ground floor rooms, you will see mosaics and intarsia work that will take your breath away. A mezzanine floor houses a display of over 600 examples of the stones used, together with workshop furniture and equipment.

Pietre Dure picture, private collection (see also page 229)

The Opificio delle Pietre Dure to the Palazzo Medici-Riccardi

On leaving the Opificio turn R back to the Piazza delle Belle Arti and then turn L along Via Ricasoli. At the junction with Via de' Pucci turn R. If Leonardo da Vinci had had his way in 1512, there'd now be a second Medici Palace on your R and a huge Piazza de' Medici on your L (see Walk 6 under the section entitled 'Leonardo's lavish scheme'). Via de' Pucci brings you out on Via Camillo Cavour (formerly Via Larga) at the SE corner of Palazzo Medici-Riccardi.

Begun in the 1440s, the Palazzo Medici was built for Cosimo Il Vecchio to a design by Michelozzo. The largest private residence built in Florence up to that date, it became the prototype for all subsequent Renaissance palaces. The stone façade is carefully gradated, the rustication and articulation gradually diminishing from ground floor to top. Each storey is articulated by a denticulate string course, on which sit round-topped bifore windows embellished with roundels bearing Medici motifs (balls, diamond rings with feathers etc.). The façade is topped by a magnificent protruding cornice. On the corner nearest to us there was originally an open ground floor loggia. Such a loggia was a frequent feature of Florentine palaces, a place where ceremonies were held and business conducted. The Medici loggia was enclosed in 1517 and Michelangelo designed the windows that now fill the two arches in question. Resting on protruding consoles, these windows were known as 'inginocchiate' ('kneeling') windows.

Turn R up Via Cavour, keeping on the RH pavement, until you are opposite the entrance to the Palazzo Medici-Riccardi. The face of Michelozzo's original palace had a 10-bay façade. When, in the 17th century, the Riccardi family bought the palace from the Medici, they extended it northwards by seven bays, imitating the design of the original façade so perfectly that you can barely see the join. However, the sharp-eyed will notice that, on the 7-bay extension, the decoration of the bifore windows changes from Medici motifs to the Riccardi keys and initials.

Before crossing the road to visit the palace, try to imagine the scene here in 1471, when Duke Galeazzo Maria Sforza of Milan arrived to stay for nine days, bringing with him 2,000 horsemen, 500 infantry, 500 pairs of dogs and heaven knows how many hawks. This was not his first visit; he'd been before in 1459, a visit that we'll say more about shortly. Also, spare a moment to look at the palace behind you at no. 4, the Palazzo Capponi. If you look carefully at the door knockers you will see that they take the form of capons, and the bases of the window grilles are likewise decorated with capons' heads, a lovely allusion to the family name.

An irascible English tenant

At the beginning of the 19th century the Marchese Riccardi let part of his palace to an English poet, Walter Savage Landor, who lived here for five years. Landor, a very eccentric and irascible character who argued with everyone, was soon on bad terms with his landlord, whom he accused of having lured away his coachman. When the nobleman visited Landor to discuss this and failed to remove his hat on entering the Englishman's apartment, he had it struck from his head and was physically ejected. Landor then served notice, presumably before he was evicted. Eventually disowned by just about everyone, even his own family, he was 'rescued' by Robert and Elizabeth Barrett Browning, and ended up boarding with Elizabeth's maid close to Casa Guidi (Walk 12). Landor was a friend of Charles Dickens, who based the character of Boythorn in *Bleak House* on the eccentric Englishman's merrier side.

The Palazzo Medici-Riccardi

The courtyard

The ground floor of the Palazzo Medici-Riccardi consists of an arcaded courtyard, with a garden leading off it, and a series of rooms now used for temporary exhibitions. In the courtyard, the frieze running above the arches of the arcades is decorated with tondi and ribboned garlands. The tondi reliefs, by Donatello, use motifs from ancient gems and medals in the Medici collections. The courtyard was once also home to a work by another master, a work that is, alas, lost to posterity. Vasari tells us that here, one winter when a great deal of snow fell, Michelangelo made a snowman! In the courtyard were staged the grand events in the Medici family's life. Here, for example, was celebrated the marriage of Lorenzo Il Magnifico to Clarice Orsini and, many years later, in 1539, the marriage of Cosimo I to Eleonora di Toledo, the festivities for which were spread over several days.

The marriage of Cosimo I to Eleonora di Toledo

One night during the festivities accompanying the marriage of Cosimo I to Eleonora di Toledo, a comedy by Antonio Landi was performed, with seven musical 'intermedi' interspersed between the acts. The stage settings were by Niccolò 'Il Tribolo' and Bastiano di Sangallo. The nickname 'Tribolo' means 'tribulation' and was apparently earned by Niccolò early on in his life! Of the intermedi, I shall describe only two. The second intermedio showed a canal between the stage and the spectators, painted to resemble the Arno. In this canal three nude mermaids appeared, with tails of silver, green hair and head-dresses of shells and coral. Accompanying them were three sea nymphs and three sea monsters. The nymphs were dressed in green veiling, their long blonde hair adorned with pearls and shells. Each carried a lute hidden in a shell. The monsters had beards and long hair of moss, and were dressed in ferns, moss and algae. Each carried a flute disguised respectively as the backbone of a fish, a sea snail and a reed. These nine participants played and sang of the despair felt in Naples at the loss of Eleonora and of the joy on the banks of the Arno. The finale featured twenty Bacchantes, ten nymphs and ten satyrs. The satyrs were nude, with hairy legs and flanks, and goats' feet. The nymphs had short golden dresses. Their instruments too were disguised – e.g. a drum as a leather wine bottle and a cornetta as a goat's horn. Apparently this delighted the spectators so much that everyone went happily to bed!

The Medici Chapel

Stairs lead up from one corner of the courtyard to the Medici Chapel. If entering the vestibule of the Laurentian Library is like walking into a building turned inside-out (Walk 6), then entering the Medici Chapel is akin to opening a jewel-encrusted casket to find that the jewels are all on the inside. Before we even consider the frescoes, take just a few minutes to admire the inlaid stalls, the carved and gilded ceiling, and the beautiful marble and porphyry inlaid floor combining geometric and Medici motifs. Filippo Lippi's painting of the Adoration of the Christ Child once adorned the altar; it is now in Berlin, replaced here by a copy. The Chapel was originally regular in plan, but the corner where you entered was reshaped at the end of the 17th century to accommodate the new staircase introduced by the Riccardi, and the corresponding portions of fresco had to be repainted.

The frescoes were commissioned by Piero the Gouty from Benozzo Gozzoli, a pupil of Fra Angelico, and Gozzoli worked on them from 1459 to 1462. They show the procession of the Magi, and owe their inspiration to three separate events, the famous Council of Florence in 1439, the festivities organized for a state visit to the city in 1459 by Galeazzo Maria, son of Francesco Sforza, Duke of Milan, and Florentine celebrations connected with the Feast of the Epiphany, when a grand procession was staged by the Compagnia de' Magi. Let's deal with each of these in turn.

Cosimo Il Vecchio scored a political triumph when, in 1439, he persuaded Pope Eugenius IV to transfer the ecumenical council discussing the union of the Eastern and Western Churches from Ferrara to Florence. This brought to the city the Byzantine Emperor, John VIII Palaeologus, and Joseph, Patriarch of Constantinople, who died in Florence and is buried in S. Maria Novella. Melchior, the old Magus, is traditionally said to be a portrait of the Patriarch, though some scholars now believe that this is, in fact, Sigismund of Luxembourg, the Holy Roman Emperor who convoked the Council of Constance in 1414 and thus helped to end the Great Schism. Balthasar, the mature Magus, is a portrait of John VIII Palaeologus, while Caspar, the young Magus, is an idealized portrait of Lorenzo Il Magnifico, his head framed by a laurel bush in a pun on his name.

Behind Caspar's horse, an attendant splendidly attired in the Medici colours gazes back at the cavalcade following the Magi. Contemporaries would have recognized countless faces amongst this host. Today, scholarly debate rages in attempts at identifications. Let us stick to those that are reasonably certain. The cavalcade is led by Piero the Gouty on a white horse and Cosimo Il Vecchio on a mule. The man whose face appears between them may be Carlo, illegitimate son of Cosimo, or Piero's younger brother Giovanni. The young men riding the white horse and the brown horse in the foreground immediately to the L of Cosimo are Galeazzo Maria Sforza and Sigismondo Pandolfo Malatesta respectively. When Galeazzo visited Florence in 1459 (the year that Gozzoli began work on the frescoes) numerous other dignitaries came too, including Sigismondo and Pope Pius II. Pius was there to discuss with Cosimo the idea of a crusade against the Turks, who, by then, had taken Constantinople. Cosimo, who thought this a hare-brained scheme, was (perhaps diplomatically) indisposed with gout and never did see the pope. This irritated the pontiff, and he complained bitterly that money earmarked for his retinue had been diverted to entertain Galeazzo and his train. He may have had a point, for the celebrations staged in honour of Galeazzo included a joust in the Piazza S. Croce, a dance at the Mercato Nuovo, a hunt with wild animals in Piazza della Signoria, and a banquet at the Palazzo Medici followed by a *pas d' armes* outside on Via Larga. The last was led by the ten year old Lorenzo, wearing (apparently) the very outfit in which Gozzoli here depicted Caspar, the young Magus.

In the cavalcade behind Galeazzo and Sigismondo, Lorenzo appears as himself – he wears a red hat like that worn by Galeazzo. Lorenzo's brother Giuliano is shown slightly to the R, similarly clad and with his eyes cast down. Just above Lorenzo is a man wearing a red cap inscribed with the words *Opus Benotii*. This is a self-portrait of the artist, Benozzo Gozzoli. He portrayed himself more than once. Look on the opposite wall and you'll see a man holding up four fingers. To the L of this is a man wearing a blue and white turban – Gozzoli again. Let your gaze drift upwards diagonally to the L and you'll spot a chap wearing what looks like a black straw hat – Gozzoli again. And directly between the turban and the straw hat is a man dressed in maroon with his head turned towards us – Gozzoli again I believe. I like to think that the man holding up four fingers is telling us that Gozzoli appears four times, three times on this wall and once on the opposite one. However, I have read that, according to the system of finger calculation in use at the time, this gesture indicates the number 5,000. Perhaps, therefore, Gozzoli is telling us that the cavalcade consists of 5,000 people.

The Medici were closely associated with the magnificent Epiphany processions staged by the Compagnia de' Magi. The Compagnia met at S. Marco's, and Cosimo was a patron of both. The processions, which wended their way through the city, simulated the journey of the Magi to Bethlehem. Needless to say, members of the Medici family frequently played prominent roles in these festivities, and in 1459, the very year that Galeazzo made his state visit and that Gozzoli began work on the Medici Chapel, can you guess who took the part of the young Magus? No prizes for this one – Lorenzo, probably wearing the same apparel that he later wore for the *pas d' armes* and that is shown in the fresco.

The Salone Carlo VIII, the Sala Quattro Stagioni and the Sala Luca Giordano
You exit from the Medici Chapel past the Salone Carlo VIII, so called because it was in this room that Charles VIII of France attempted to force unacceptable terms on the Florentines following the expulsion of the Medici in 1494. The story connected with this, including the famous response made

to the king by Piero di Gino Capponi, is told in the section entitled 'the French come to Florence' at the end of Walk 13. Passing through a series of rooms of the Riccardi era, you eventually reach the wonderful painting of the Madonna and Child by Filippo Lippi. After this comes a vestibule, off which lies the Sala Quattro Stagioni, named after the tapestries depicting the four seasons and still used by the Commune for government meetings. The vestibule also gives access to the Sala Luca Giordano, a confection of stucco, gilt and mirrors, with a ceiling painting by Giordano showing the apotheosis of Cosimo III. You exit via the vestibule and stairs leading back down to the courtyard.

From the Palazzo Medici-Riccardi to Piazza S. Giovanni

On exiting from the palace you can, if you wish, turn L and head up Via Cavour to no. 21 on the L, where you'll find the Leonardo da Vinci Museum. This has interactive models, reconstructions, workshops and a bookshop (there is another such museum in Via de' Servi; Walk 10). If you don't wish to do this, turn R and head down Via Cavour and Via de' Martelli to Piazza S. Giovanni, where this walk ends. As you go, spare a thought for young Giuliano de' Medici, who, on 26th April 1478, unwittingly walked this way to his death. He'd just fathered an illegitimate son, who'd never see his dad but who'd eventually become Pope Clement VII. Once you're comfortably ensconced in a café, of which there are several in Piazza S. Giovanni, you can, if you wish, read the story of the famous Pazzi conspiracy and Giuliano's assassination, an account of which reads like a thriller.

Piazza S. Giovanni as seen from the Campanile

The Pazzi conspiracy

The Pazzi conspiracy of April 1478 was the most famous of the conspiracies against the Medici, partly owing to the fact that it involved many big-time players and partly because its failure left Lorenzo Il Magnifico in a stronger position than he could ever have hoped to achieve had it never happened. Lorenzo was well aware of anti-Medicean undercurrents in Florence. Sensing that the ambitious Pazzi clan might prove troublesome (despite a marriage alliance between the two families), he worked to block their political advance, thereby stirring up malice and resentment. He also blocked Pope Sixtus IV, whose expansionist ambitions in the Romagna he saw as bad for Florence. The Medici had long been the principal papal bankers, so when, at the end of 1473, Sixtus asked for a loan in order to secure the city of Imola for his nephew Girolamo, he was none too pleased when Lorenzo refused the request and urged other Florentine banks to do likewise. The Pazzi not only lent Sixtus the money, but told him that Lorenzo had cautioned them not to do so. An angry Sixtus changed his bankers. Lorenzo was furious, but Sixtus hadn't finished rubbing Medici noses in the dirt yet.

Filippo de' Medici, Archbishop of Pisa and a distant cousin of Lorenzo, died in 1474. Pisa belonged to Florence, so courtesy dictated that any new appointment should be floated past the Florentine government. Sixtus omitted to do this and, in October, appointed Francesco Salviati, who was related to the Pazzi, as archbishop. The Medici party was livid. Florence refused to accept the papal decision and denied Salviati entry to her subject city. A furious Sixtus threatened an interdict and excommunication, and Florence had, at last, to back down.

With relations at an all-time low, not much tinder was necessary to precipitate an all-out showdown. Francesco de' Pazzi (who was heading banking operations in Rome), Francesco Salviati (smarting in his new archbishopric) and Count Girolamo Riario of Imola (the pope's nephew) appear to have been the prime movers in the plot. Sixtus too was in on it, though he maintained that he only wanted a change of government in Florence, not the death of anyone. How he expected to achieve one without the other is unclear. By the end of 1477 Sixtus was pressing for quick action, for in September of that year papal forces had taken the castle of Montone from the anti-papal Fortebracci family, and the pope therefore had an army close to Florence and in a perfect position to back up an insurrection. By this time, others had been recruited to the cause, including the Count of Montesecco (a papal mercenary leader) and, in Florence, Jacopo de' Pazzi (Francesco's uncle), Bernardo Baroncelli and Jacopo Bracciolini. Whether the pope's seventeen year old great-nephew, the Cardinal of S. Giorgio, was also in on it is less clear. He may just have been a front, enabling the conspirators to get armed men into Florence without arousing suspicion.

In spring 1478 the young Cardinal of S. Giorgio, invested with the powers of a papal legate, was sent on an embassy to Florence. His retinue included Francesco

Salviati, Francesco de' Pazzi, and thirty mounted crossbowmen and fifty foot soldiers under the command of the Count of Montesecco. Protocol demanded that lavish hospitality be extended to the young churchman, and a special luncheon was arranged at Lorenzo's villa N of Florence on 19th April. Poison had been decided upon. The conspirators realized that both Lorenzo and his younger brother would have to be rubbed out simultaneously, so when Giuliano failed to show up for lunch, being indisposed, a plan B had to be hurriedly cooked up. Lorenzo was led to believe that the cardinal would love to see the famous Medici collections. Rising to the bait, he immediately invited everybody to lunch at the Medici Palace the following Sunday, 26th April, after High Mass in the Duomo.

On the appointed day, the cardinal and his train, having ridden into Florence from the Pazzi villa, went direct to the Medici Palace to change out of their riding habits. This unscheduled visit may have masked a recce or up-front preparations. Lorenzo was already at the church and had to dash home to greet his guests. The plotters now discovered that Giuliano would not be lunching. Plan C was hastily resorted to. By now fearing discovery (papal troops near the city were already on the move), the conspirators decided that the double assassination must take place at once, during Mass. Giuliano didn't return to the Duomo with the crowd, and Francesco de' Pazzi and Bernardo Baroncelli, on finding that he was missing, rushed post-haste back to the palace and cajoled him into attending Mass. Returning with him to the church, they feigned affection, embracing him to ascertain if he was wearing hidden armour – he wasn't!

The plot now ran into more problems, for at this point the Count of Montesecco, one of the designated assassins, had a fit of scruples and refused to spill blood on holy ground. Two priests with no such scruples immediately took on his role. At a pre-arranged moment the conspirators struck. Francesco de' Pazzi and Bernardo Baroncelli killed Giuliano, but the two priests botched it and Lorenzo managed to retreat into the N sacristy with a group of supporters.

Meanwhile, Jacopo de' Pazzi and Francesco Salviati had left the scene to pursue their allotted tasks. Vitally important for the success of the plot was the takeover of the Palazzo della Signoria. Archbishop Salviati arrived at the palace with an armed escort and, naturally, had no trouble gaining entry, for nobody there as yet suspected a thing. He went directly to meet Cesare Petrucci, the Gonfalonier of Justice, and spun a story about Pope Sixtus favouring Petrucci's son in Rome. Spinning his yarn out more and more, he waited for reinforcements, but these didn't arrive and he started to get agitated. Petrucci began to suspect that something was amiss, a suspicion that was confirmed when he encountered an armed Jacopo Bracciolini outside his door. Salviati's escort was overcome by the palace guards. The great bell rang out and citizens came running, some of them bringing news of Giuliano's murder.

Jacopo de' Pazzi now entered the piazza with a large troop of mercenaries, but found that Salviati had failed to take the palace. There was a stand-off as Jacopo awaited reinforcements, knowing that, by now, papal troops should be nearing the city. They didn't show up, however, perhaps having been informed that Lorenzo still lived, perhaps hearing the bells and realizing that things had gone awry. Losing hope, Jacopo was at last persuaded to flee.

Meanwhile, back at Piazza del Duomo, the Medici contingent had managed to leave the N sacristy and retreat to the Medici Palace. Guglielmo de' Pazzi saved himself by taking sanctuary there with them, while his wife Bianca, Lorenzo's sister, pleaded for his life. Nothing could save the rest of the Pazzi and their supporters. Salviati and Bracciolini were trapped in the Palazzo della Signoria. Francesco de' Pazzi was found hiding in the Pazzi Palace (Walk 5) and dragged to the same place. All three were hanged that very day from the palace windows. The soldiers in Salviati's escort were summarily killed, some thrown from the windows and battlements. The crowd below stripped them and hacked them to pieces. That day alone, more than sixty captives were executed. Jacopo de' Pazzi and his men were captured the next day and hanged along with Montesecco's soldiers. Jacopo's corpse was subjected to horrific treatment. Initially buried at S. Croce, it was exhumed and reburied in unconsecrated ground on 15th May when a furious mob threatened violence. Two days later, a mob dug it up, dragged it through the streets to the Pazzi Palace, tied it to the door and further defiled it, then dumped it into the Arno from the Ponte alle Grazie. Luca Landucci, who was a witness, says in his *Diary* that the stench was awful. On 3rd May the two priests who'd failed to kill Lorenzo were seized at the Badia, where they'd taken sanctuary. Their ears and noses were cut off and they too dangled from the windows of the Palazzo della Signoria. The Count of Montesecco was captured in flight and beheaded at the Bargello on 4th May. Bernardo Baroncelli got as far as Constantinople, but the Sultan extradited him and he too eventually swung in Florence. Leonardo da Vinci made a drawing showing him hanged. The young Cardinal of S. Giorgio didn't swing, though he was held hostage for over six weeks. Following Florentine custom, paintings of the chief traitors were publicly displayed. The artist was Sandro Botticelli, who received forty florins for the commission.

The death of the traitors was not enough. Pazzi assets were seized and sold off, and Pazzi symbols removed or covered over. Even florins bearing the Pazzi arms (a privilege accorded to families whose members had served as mint officials) were recalled and melted down. All surviving members of the family, including distant cousins, had, by a new law, to change their surname and coat-of-arms within six months. Another law decreed that any Florentine marrying one of his daughters to a Pazzi descended from Jacopo's father, or taking to himself a wife thus descended, would forever lose the right to hold public office. This draconian law was later relaxed. The eight Signori, those magistrates responsible for law and order whose decrees feature on some of these walks, cancelled every permit to carry arms, and citizens had to submit inventories of all the weapons in their households. Only Lorenzo was exempt. He was assigned an armed escort of about a dozen soldiers, many of whom had nicknames such as Garlic-Saver, Black Martin and Crooked Andrew.

Sixtus reacted furiously to the failure of the conspiracy. War was declared and the pope offered a plenary remission of sins to all who would take up arms against Florence. Papal and Neopolitan troops swept into Tuscany, and every effort was made to isolate Lorenzo. He offered to give himself up to spare the city the inevitable hardships and expenses of war, but his supporters would have none of it. Papal interdicts were declared illegal and were scorned, and the Bishop of Arezzo penned a blistering attack on Sixtus, which was printed and circulated.

As the war dragged on, anxiety spread and anti-Medicean murmurings grew louder. Plague broke out in 1478 and again in 1479, there were military losses in Tuscany, and in Florence there were food shortages and riots. Increasingly boxed into a corner, Lorenzo played a dangerous, but ultimately successful, diplomatic masterstroke. He left secretly for Naples to court King Ferrante personally. Amazingly, he succeeded. The King negotiated a peace deal, Sixtus agreeing to it reluctantly and angrily. In August 1480 the Turks stormed Otranto, and King Ferrante and Pope Sixtus suddenly found themselves facing another crisis. Four years later, Sixtus died and was succeeded by Pope Innocent VIII, whom Lorenzo went out of his way to court – but that's another story!

Following the death of Lorenzo Il Magnifico in 1492 the Medici were expelled from Florence in 1494. Just four days after Piero the Unfortunate's flight, descendants of the Pazzi were freed from exile, exonerated from blame, and again admitted to public office. A bill was passed, declaring that Jacopo and Francesco had acted out of zeal for the liberty of Florence. The Pazzi were authorized to take legal action to regain their assets, and Pazzi symbols could again be displayed.

Pietre Dure picture, private collection (see also page 219)

Walk 9

Begins at Piazza S. Croce and ends at the Bargello.

Takes in: the Museo Horne and the Casa Vasari, the Museo Galileo, the Bargello and the erstwhile Palace of the Guild of Judges and Notaries.

Duration: 1 hour 30 minutes, excluding visits to any of the above or breaks for refreshments. You should allow *c.* 1 hour for the Museo Horne, and up to 2 hours each for the Museo Galileo and the Bargello. The Guild Palace is now a restaurant, so how long you spend there will depend on circumstances and hunger!

Tips: attempting to see both the Museo Galileo and the Bargello on the same itinerary is a tall order, so I should choose one or the other, and return to visit the second on another occasion. The opening hours for the Bargello can be somewhat restricted, depending on season, so you should check this first.

Piazza S. Croce to the Museo Horne

Information on Piazza S. Croce is given under Walk 5. Leave the piazza near its NW corner on Via Torta. There are very few curved streets in Florence, but we are about to walk round three of them, Via Torta, Via de' Bentaccordi and Piazza de' Peruzzi, which follow the outline of the Roman amphitheatre. The amphitheatre, which could hold more than 15,000 spectators, was where S. Miniato was martyred (Walk 14). A few yards along Via Torta, Via dell' Isola delle Stinche leads off to the R. We're not going down here, but you may like to note that literally a stone's throw from the corner, on the L side of Via dell' Isola delle Stinche, lies Vivoli's ice-cream parlour, one of the most famous in Florence. Follow Via Torta round to the L and cross over Via dell' Anguillara into Via de' Bentaccordi. On the corner of these two streets, the house on the R bears a plaque recording that Michelangelo, born at Caprese in the Casentino, spent the years of his youth here.

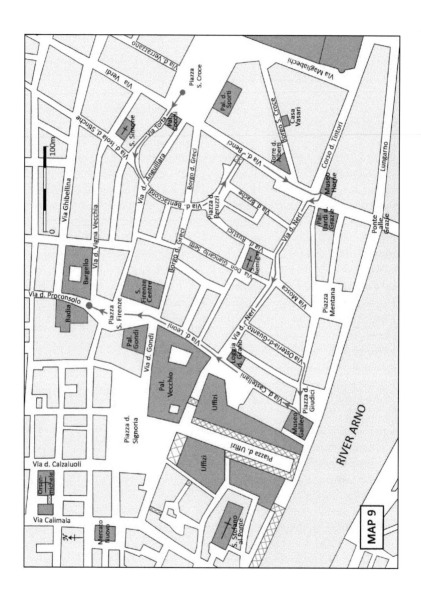

MAP 9

Via de' Bentaccordi crosses Borgo de' Greci and leads on into Piazza de' Peruzzi. You'll note that many buildings around this area still bear crests showing pears, the emblem of the Peruzzi. The Peruzzi were the famous bankers who got Giotto to fresco their chapel in S. Croce early in the 14th century and whose bank subsequently went bust in 1343 – not that the two events were related! Keep your wits about you at this point and spare a thought for poor Niccolò di Buono Busini, a wool manufacturer who, in 1407, had 300 florins nicked while he was having a nap on a bench outside one of the Peruzzi properties.

An arch leads out of the far end of Piazza de' Peruzzi into Via de' Benci, where you turn R. Via de' Benci follows the line of the second circuit of city walls, constructed at the beginning of the 13th century and demolished in 1295 (see historical summary). On the L at the corner of Via de' Benci and Borgo S. Croce is the 13th century Torre degli Alberti with a 15th century loggia. Just beyond this, on the far L corner of Via de' Benci with Corso dei Tintori, lies the Museo Horne.

The Museo Horne and the Casa Vasari

Museo Horne is housed in a 14th century palace. In the 15th century part of the building was rented out to the office of the eight Signori, those law and order officials whom we've come across on some of the walks, and in 1490 it was ceded by the Alberti family to the Corsi clan in order to cover a debt. Much remodelling was done at this time, most likely under the direction of Il Cronaca. During the 16th-18th centuries the palace was leased out, and in the 19th century it was sold to the Fossi family. At the beginning of the  20th century it was acquired by an Englishman named Herbert Percy Horne (1864-1916), who had trained as an architect and subsequently became an art historian and collector. Horne restored the palace as closely as possible to its Renaissance form. He intended to house his collections here, but died before he could do so. Two days before his death he bequeathed all that he had to the Italian State on condition that a foundation be established in his name.

You enter via a pretty courtyard. One of the ground floor rooms has a DVD presentation giving an introduction to the museum and its founder (the soundtrack is not all that easy to follow), and there is an interesting display of documents relating to Horne and the part played by the British in the 'Association for the Protection of Historic Florence', founded in 1898 to combat municipal plans to tear down even more of the historic centre than had already been lost to the Piazza della Repubblica. The Museum itself consists of three rooms on the first floor and three rooms on the second floor (there is no lift), and at the ticket office you can buy a very good little book in English that will guide you through the collections. The place has a lovely ambience and is well worth a visit, including as it does works by Giotto, Bernardo Daddi, Simone Martini and Lippo Memmi, and much else besides. The Giotto painting of S. Stephen was purchased in London in 1904 for less than £10!

If you happen to visit the Museo Horne on a day when such tours run, there are accompanied visits to the Casa Vasari, just around the corner in Borgo S. Croce at no. 8. On the first floor is a room frescoed by Vasari and his friends with allegories of the arts and portraits of the artists. A DVD presentation shows the recent restoration works.

The Museo Horne to the Museo Galileo

On leaving the Museo Horne, you will see a plaque directly opposite you on the wall of Palazzo Bardi delle Grazie. It commemorates Giovanni, Count of Vernio and his many achievements, military, scientific, literary and musical, and the fact that here, in Palazzo Bardi, were held the meetings of the Camerata famous in the history of music for developing the art of recitative towards the end of the 16th century.

Take the next street but one to the R of Palazzo Bardi, Via de' Neri, named after the confraternity who accompanied and comforted criminals on their way to the scaffold. Via de' Neri curves very slightly, following the line of the Roman port, and, at the Canto dei Soldani, Via Mosca leads off to the L. On the far corner of Via Mosca lies the Palazzo Soldani, a former 14th century tower-house. Opposite, on the corner of Via Don Giancarlo Setti (formerly Via di S. Remigio), are two inscriptions marking the levels of two floods. The lower one records the level reached by the waters of the Arno on 4th November 1333. The upper one indicates the height reached by the floodwaters on 4th November 1966. Best not to be in Florence on 4th November! Continue along Via

de' Neri and take the next turning on the L, Via Osteria del Guanto. As you turn, note the tabernacle set into the flank of the building on your R, with a charming relief of the Madonna and Child.

At the end of Via Osteria del Guanto turn R into Piazza de' Giudici. Here, housed in the Palazzo Castellani, is the stunning Museo Galileo. Outside it stands a superb modern meridian, with a tall bronze gnomon set into a wind rose, and the signs of the zodiac laid out along a 15m calibrated copper standard running between the gnomon and the museum entrance. Don't miss the little sub-meridian gnomon in the form of a lizard. Even if you are not interested in science, I strongly urge you to visit the Galileo Museum. Before you do, however, cross over to the parapet wall running along the Lungarno. Here, quite apart from the lovely views, you'll find a marble plaque set into the wall, which commemorates the horse of Carlo Capello, the Venetian ambassador. During the siege of Florence in 1530, when Capello was riding to the Palazzo della Signoria, a mortar fired by the imperial troops exploded here right under the belly of his horse. The poor animal was ripped to pieces, but Capello survived, protected by the bulk of the horse's body. The grateful ambassador gave his horse a public burial. The Latin inscription, with its allusion to Virgil (*Aeneid* XI.600), may be translated:

'The bones of the horse of Carlo Capello, Venetian ambassador. The grateful master of the memorable noisy-footed (creature) gave to you this grave in view of your merits. In the besieged town, 1530, three days before the Ides of March.'

The Museo Galileo

If I say that the Museo Galileo, named in honour of the famous Florentine scientist, comprises the Medici and Lorraine collections of scientific apparatus and instruments, many people may read no further. This would be a pity, because accurate though the statement is it in no way prepares one for the experience in store. One of the most important collections of its kind in the world, the museum contains, among other things, scales, compasses, calculators, sun-dials, nocturnals, clocks, globes, planispheres, polyhedral dials, quadrants, armillary spheres, astrolabes, jovilabes, telescopes, microscopes, spectroscopes, thermometers, barometers, pyrometers, hydrometers and odometers. These stunning artefacts range in date from the 10th to the 19th centuries AD. If you are ignorant as to the function and purpose of many of them, no matter – their sheer beauty and the craftsmanship involved in their manufacture cannot fail to impress. Those of you who are pressed for time may wish to restrict yourselves to the Medici collections, housed in nine rooms on the first floor. Included here are artefacts which belonged to Galileo, to his pupil Vincenzo Viviani (see Walk 11) and to Sir Robert Dudley, Duke of Northumberland (see Walk 13). The Lorraine collections are housed in nine rooms on the second floor. The rooms have themes (e.g. astronomy and time, representations of the world, navigation, warfare, etc.), the labelling throughout is in both Italian and English, and there are concise but instructive information boards in each room. There is also an English guidebook to the treasures of the collection available at the bookshop, which you can access prior to visiting the museum if you want to do any homework beforehand.

The Museo Galileo to the Bargello

On exiting from the Museo Galileo turn L along Via de' Castellani, which leads up past the exit of the Uffizi Gallery on the L. Opposite the Uffizi exit is the end of Via de' Neri, where we were earlier. On the near corner of Via de' Neri stands the early 17th century Loggia del Grano by Giulio Parigi and his son Alfonso. Via de' Castellani now becomes Via de' Leoni, because here, behind the Palazzo Vecchio, were kept caged lions (the lion being one symbol of the Florentine Republic). Follow Via de' Leoni along to Piazza S. Firenze. On the E side of the piazza (to your R) is S. Firenze, now an exhibition centre, with Borgo de' Greci leading back to Piazza S. Croce. Near the corner of Borgo de' Greci, on the R, is a Dante plaque referring to the gate known as the 'Pera' ('Pear') Gate in the old city walls, so named for the Peruzzi crest, referred to earlier on this walk:

'One used to enter the inner circle (of walls) by a gate that was named after those of the Pear (crest)' (*Paradiso* XVI.125-6).

On the W side of Piazza S. Firenze lies the lovely 15th century Palazzo Gondi, designed by Giuliano da Sangallo for Giuliano Gondi, a rich silk merchant. It has a complex building history and, although looking at it you may not believe it, the S end of the palace dates to the 19th century.

Palazzo Gondi

In the mid-15th century Giuliano Gondi, having made a fortune in the silk trade, bought the old Giugni palace that stood opposite the flank of the Palazzo Vecchio, on the corner of Piazza S. Firenze and a narrow mediaeval street called Via delle Prestanze. Giuliano's plans to extend the property were delayed because he fell foul of the political regime and was exiled. He retired to Naples and, being well in with King Ferrante, ended up playing a pivotal role in the negotiations between that monarch and Lorenzo Il Magnifico in the aftermath of the Pazzi conspiracy (described at the end of Walk 8). With his sentence of exile revoked, he returned to Florence, bought up more properties adjoining the Giugni dwelling to the N, and set about putting his plans for a new palazzo into action. He commissioned Giuliano da Sangallo to design the new building, which was begun in 1489-90.

Sangallo's façade is characterized by refined gradated rustication, lovely stepped voussoirs, denticulate string courses and an elegant cornice. But what length was it eventually meant to be? Assuming that the middle doorway was intended to be central, the options are a 5-, 7-, 9- or 11-bay façade. Four bays of the old Giugni property still occupied the S end of the site and parts of the building were occupied by tenants, one of whom was a notary named Piero da Vinci, who had a son called Leonardo. By dint of demolishing one of the Giugni bays, Sangallo gave himself room for a 5-bay façade (and the da Vincis had to move!). That there was an intention to go further is shown by the fact that Gondi was negotiating for the purchase of another property immediately to the N. This was inhabited by the elderly Mariotto Asini, who refused to sell. Mariotto's nephew, Bernardo, who was co-owner, wanted to sell, and the matter went to arbitration. In 1491 the arbiters decided in Bernardo's favour – and Sangallo extended the façade accordingly, inserting a second doorway here. A corresponding extension at the S (L) end would have resulted in a 7-bay façade, but this was never achieved by Sangallo. Furthermore, as can still be seen, the rustication at the N (R) end was left incomplete, surely an indication that, future purchases permitting, Gondi intended his palace to run to at least one or two more bays here. If so, then corresponding extensions at the S end would have resulted in a 9- or 11-bay façade, the latter running right to the corner of the narrow mediaeval Via delle Prestanze.

Gondi died in 1501 with his project unfinished. Over the years, as branches of the family died out, the property passed to the nearest collateral line, eventually ending up in the hands of Marchese Eugenio Gondi (1840-1924). His dream was to complete the palace begun by his ancestor, and he entrusted the project to the architect Giuseppe Poggi. During these years Florence was chosen as the capital of the new unified Italy, and the authorities badly wanted to widen the narrow mediaeval Via delle Prestanze to allow more light into the rooms of the Palazzo Vecchio, where several government offices were located. A deal was done, whereby the remaining remnants of the old 14th century Giugni palace were demolished to allow for the widening of the street. As part compensation for the loss of land here, Eugenio Gondi was given the stone for the necessary extension to Sangallo's façade on Piazza S. Firenze and for its continuation round the corner for five bays along the new widened street, appropriately renamed Via de' Gondi. Poggi did a good job, and the only indication that the southernmost bay of the façade is a 19th century addition is a slight difference in colour of the stone. An inscription was put up just inside the new Via de' Gondi entrance commemorating Leonardo da Vinci and his connection with the site. If you go round to this entrance, as well as seeing the inscription, you'll get a view through to the palace courtyard with its lovely fountain and staircase. Many of the delightful step-ends on Sangallo's staircase depict incidents from Aesop's fables (you'll probably need binoculars to see them). The 17th century fountain bears an inscription recording the donation of water made by Grand Duke Ferdinando II to Giuliano Gondi the Younger in 1647. It would have been connected to the aqueduct which flowed from the Boboli Gardens into the city to supply the Neptune Fountain in Piazza della Signoria and fountains in the Palazzo Vecchio (Walk 2).

In 2005 the palace passed to Marchese Bernardo Gondi. He and his wife had it restored inside and out, creating a beautiful venue for cultural events. The family retain apartments here, and, in continuance of a centuries-old tradition, still produce olive oil and Chianti wines on their estates outside the city.

At the N end of Piazza S. Firenze lies the Bargello. In 1250 the Guelfs established the Primo Popolo and created the post of Capitano del Popolo, an official responsible for military matters (see historical summary). He needed a palace, and construction was begun in 1255. Built in pietra forte, a local limestone, his palace incorporated a pre-existing tower known as 'La Volognana' (see also overleaf for illustration) after a Ghibelline family imprisoned here. One of the first acts of the Primo Popolo had been to reduce all private towers to a height of 50 braccia (c. 28m), but La Volognana

was left at c. 100 braccia, sending out a political message. The civic pride of the Primo Popolo is expressed in a Latin inscription on the façade of the building near the corner of Via del Proconsolo with Via della Vigna Vecchia. Among other things, this informs us that Florence was full of wealth, that she defeated her enemies, enjoyed fortune's favour, had a strong population, reigned over sea, land and the whole world, and that under her leadership all Tuscany enjoyed happiness. In 1261 the palace was renamed the Palazzo del Podestà. The building was extended to the rear round an impressive courtyard, and a great belfry was added to the tower. The palace was damaged by fire in 1332. The upper floors were then reconstructed by Neri di Fioravante. He created the vast 'Sala del Consiglio Generale'

('Room of the General Council'), with its great bifore window on the S side. This necessitated increasing the height of the façades and reconstructing the battlements; you can see the change in the stonework from the original finely-dressed ashlars to the later coarser masonry above. Under the Grand Dukes the palace became a prison and the residence of the chief of police, or 'Bargello'. In the mid-19th century it became the Museo Nazionale.

A rogues' gallery

Following Cosimo Il Vecchio's return from exile in 1434, his political enemies found themselves exiled in turn. When these Albizi party exiles tried to return by force, they were sentenced to death *in absentia* and, in accordance with custom, their names were inscribed on the walls of the Bargello and their portraits painted there by Andrea del Castagno, nicknamed 'degli Impiccati' ('of the hanged men'). We've seen already in the section on the Pazzi conspiracy at the end of Walk 8 how, later in the century, Sandro Botticelli received a lucrative commission to paint the chief traitors involved in that plot. On a happier note, Luca Landucci records in his *Diary* that, when Pope Leo X made his triumphal entry into Florence in November 1515, a huge piece of fictive architecture was constructed outside the Bargello, comprising twenty-four gilded columns, with great cornices all round, many figures and much ornamentation.

The Museo Nazionale of the Bargello

The Museo Nazionale, dedicated to Florentine sculpture and the decorative arts, occupies three floors of the Bargello. On the ground floor is a large hall containing, among many other things, Ammannati's Leda and the Swan, Giambologna's Mercury, Cellini's restoration of an antique statue showing Ganymede and the Eagle (I want this!), the same artist's bronzes of Danae, Mercury, Minerva and Jove from the base of the Perseus in the Loggia de' Lanzi, and Jacopo Sansovino's Bacchus. There is a tragi-comic story associated with the last. The model used went mad, and was often found stark naked holding the pose of various sculptures. Several works by Michelangelo are also displayed in this ground floor hall, including his Bacchus, a tondo of the Madonna and Child with S. John, and the bust of Brutus, carved in Rome in a fit of Republican ardour following the murder in 1537 of Duke Alessandro de' Medici, and later acquired and brought to Florence (somewhat ironically) by Grand Duke Francesco I. From the splendid Gothic courtyard, adorned with more sculptures, there is access to the upper floors. On the first floor is the huge Sala del Consiglio Generale, where are displayed works by Donatello, including his S. George from Orsanmichele (Walk 3), a bronze David and a marble David. Here too are

works by Michelozzo, Desiderio da Settignano, Agostino di Duccio, Luca
and Andrea della Robbia and Giovanni di Bertoldo. The Sala also houses
the trial relief panels showing the Sacrifice of Isaac made by Ghiberti and
Brunelleschi for the 1401 competition for the Baptistery doors. Also on
the first floor are rooms devoted to the decorative arts. The Cappella del
Podestà has damaged 14th century frescoes (the scene on the altar wall
includes a portrait of Dante, dressed in maroon on the R). On the loggia
can be seen a charming group of bronze birds, variously attributed. The
second floor rooms house della Robbian terracottas, collections of medals
and small bronzes, and a stunning series of portrait busts by masters
such as Verrocchio, Mino da Fiesole, Benedetto da Maiano, Desiderio da
Settignano and Antonio Rossellino.

The Palace of the Guild of Judges and Notaries

Walk 9 ends here and, if you are feeling weary, there are several eateries
on Piazza S. Firenze. If, however, you continue up Via del Proconsolo
for a few yards, you will find, on your R, the erstwhile Palace of the
Guild of Judges and Notaries, now the 'Alle Murate' restaurant. This
establishment has been through a couple of incarnations even during
the writing of this book. Last time I visited it was a fish restaurant, and a
very good one. The ground floor room was originally the Guild Audience
Chamber, and a restoration of the secular frescoes here was completed
in 2004. What survives dates back to *c*. 1360-1410, and includes, on
the walls, the personifications of Rhetoric, Logic and Grammar, together
with the oldest known portraits of Dante and Boccaccio. The frescoes
of the vault are by Jacopo di Cione. They show Florence as a circular,
perfect new Jerusalem, adorned with the arms of the lily of the city, the
eagle of the Guelfs, the red and white shield of the joint commune of
Florence and Fiesole, and the red cross of the people. Between these are
the arms of the four quarters of S. Giovanni, S. Maria Novella, S. Croce
and S. Spirito, along with the banners of the sixteen gonfalons. The badly
damaged quatrefoil panels surrounding these contained the symbols of
the twenty-one guilds – the gold star of the Judges and Notaries can
still be made out, as can the red chalice of the Vintners and the black
and white stripes of the Shoemakers. The next circle outwards probably
showed the patron saints of the guilds, the whole being surrounded
by a circle of walls complete with eight turrets and four gates. Around
this image of Florence are the four Cardinal Virtues, Justice, Fortitude,
Prudence and Temperance, along with two winged allegorical figures (the
bearded figure holding a scroll is perhaps the personification of Law). So,
enjoy your fish and chips, or whatever else 'Alle Murate' is serving up at
the time!

The Bargello - La Volognana at dawn

Walk 10

Begins and ends in Piazza del Duomo behind the Cathedral.

Takes in: Leonardo da Vinci Museum Activities, the Ospedale degli Innocenti with the Museum of Childhood, SS. Annunziata, the Archaeological Museum, the English Cemetery, the Synagogue and Jewish Museum, the Liceo Michelangelo with Perugino's fresco of the Crucifixion, the Museum of Prehistory and the Hospital of S. Maria Nuova.

Duration: 2 hours for the full walk, excluding time spent at any of the above, and 1 hour for the shorter version, omitting the English Cemetery, Synagogue and Jewish Museum. You should allow 1 hour for the Leonardo da Vinci Museum, 2 hours for the Ospedale degli Innocenti and Museum of Childhood, *c.* 45 minutes for SS. Annunziata, and *c.* 1 hour for each section of the Archaeological Museum (Ancient Egyptian, Etruscan and Classical). Allow *c.* 30-45 minutes for the English Cemetery, *c.* 1 hour for the Synagogue and Jewish Museum, and *c.* 10-15 minutes for Perugino's fresco. The Museum of Prehistory will, I think, attract only a few. The Hospital of S. Maria Nuova with its church of S. Egidio can be seen in *c.* 30 minutes.

Tips: you cannot expect to visit all the above venues on one walk. If this is your first visit to Florence I would recommend that you do the shorter version of the itinerary, taking in the Ospedale degli Innocenti with the Museum of Childhood, the church of SS. Annunziata, perhaps one section of the Archaeological Museum (Ancient Egyptian, Etruscan or Classical), and Perugino's Crucifixion. The longer version of the walk involves a considerable amount of foot-slogging, unavoidable if one is to get to the English Cemetery and back. The opening times for Perugino's fresco are restricted, so double-check them before you set off. As the walk is a circular one, you could, if you so wished, visit some of the venues on Piazza SS. Annunziata at the end – indeed, the restricted opening hours for the church may mean that you have to do this. If you leave the Museum of Childhood until the end of the walk, you can then indulge yourself with a more extended visit to the terrace café there, with its wonderful views.

Piazza del Duomo to Piazza SS. Annunziata

Leave Piazza del Duomo on Via de' Servi (behind the Cathedral) and you'll shortly come to the tiny Piazzetta di S. Michele Visdomini, with the church on your R. The original church was demolished in 1363 to make way for the E end of the Duomo, and rebuilt here a few years later. A plaque on the façade records that Filippino Lippi is buried here; it was put up by the Commune of Florence to mark the 500th anniversary of his death. The church contains fragments of 14th-15th century frescoes, and 16th century works by, among others, Pontormo. Over to the L, on the far side of the

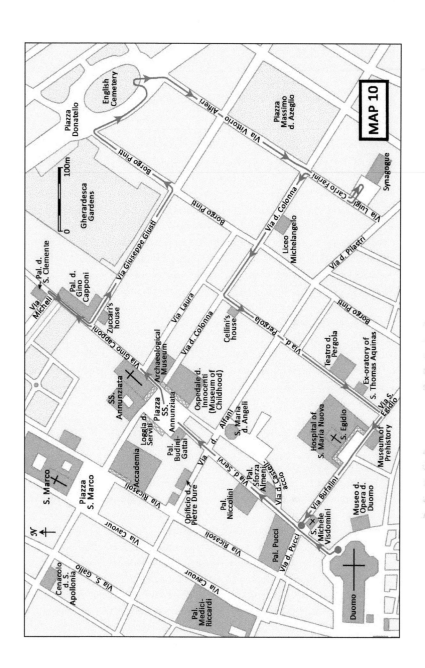

MAP 10

junction with Via de' Pucci, lies the Palazzo Pucci. Most of the palace still belongs to the family, and the central part, further along Via de' Pucci, has been cleverly transformed to incorporate a tasteful shopping mall.

The mystery of the blocked window

One of the ground floor windows of the Palazzo Pucci near the corner with

Via de' Servi is blocked up. In 1560 Pandolfo de' Pucci plotted against Cosimo I, hiring assassins and, so the story goes, telling them to keep watch for the Duke (who frequently passed this way en route to SS. Annunziata) from this window. The plot was discovered, all those implicated were hanged, and Cosimo apparently ordered that the window be blocked up. However, legend does not tally with history here. At the date in question, the palace garden lay on the corner. The palace façade was only extended this far much later, so why the window is blocked up I cannot tell you. In 1575 Pandolfo's son, Orazio, wishing to avenge his father's death, prepared a plot against Francesco I, but this too was discovered, and he was also hanged.

Continue along Via de' Servi until you reach the point where Via del Castellaccio branches off to the R. The building on the near corner of this junction bears a plaque saying that this was the site of the workshop of the sculptor Benedetto da Maiano. On the far corner of the junction, the Palazzo Sforza Almeni at no. 12 blue Via de' Servi bears a Medici-Toledo crest (this is a copy, the original being inside).

Palazzo Sforza Almeni changes hands

Palazzo Sforza Almeni, built in the early 16th century for the Taddei family, was confiscated in 1537 after Vincenzo Taddei fought against Cosimo I at the Battle of Montemurlo. It was given first to Giovanbattista Ricasoli, Bishop of Cortona and one of Cosimo's most devoted followers, and then it passed to Sforza di Vincenzo Almeni, another ducal favourite. Almeni, when he got possession of the palace, proudly erected the Medici-Toledo crest and had the façade painted with sgraffiti designed by Vasari. This decoration has not survived. Vasari tells us that it was severely damaged by a heavy storm not long after completion, the hail being so bad that, in some places, the wall was stripped of plaster. Almeni appears not to have been a very tactful or judicious person (later documents refer to his rashness and lack of discretion), for in 1566, Cosimo I, angered at impertinent accusations made by his courtier, killed him in a fit of temper.

Over the door to no. 14 blue Via de' Servi (on the R) can be seen the arms of the Wool Guild (the *Agnus Dei*). More or less opposite this, at no. 15, is the 16th century Palazzo Niccolini, with a 19th century painted façade and a rooftop loggia. It now houses the Ministry of Public Works. Back on the RH side

of the street, no. 20 blue (66/68 red) houses the Leonardo da Vinci Museum Activities, if you wish to discover more about that great man (there is another such museum at no. 21 Via Cavour; see Walk 8). Here you'll find models of many of his inventions, including an odometer, parachute, bicycle, hydraulic saw, diving suit, tank, and flying machines. On the LH side of the street opposite no. 24 blue is a plaque put up by the Lions Club to commemorate the 600th anniversary of the birth of Masaccio, who rented rooms here.

A painter's nickname

As with the names by which we know so many artists, Masaccio was a nickname. The painter's real name was Tommaso. Vasari tells us that he was good and kind, but so absent-minded and erratic, and so neglectful of himself and all worldly cares and possessions, that, instead of calling him by his proper name, everyone referred to him as (Tom)masaccio, or Masaccio for short, -accio being a suffix of a rather derogatory nature.

At no. 30 blue (80 red) on the R can be found the lovely old Pharmacy of SS. Annunziata, founded in 1561. The 17th century glass-fronted cabinets survive, as does a collection of pharmacy jars by the Ginori company, whose showroom we passed near the end of Walk 6. No. 30 blue also bears the arms of the Calimala Guild (the eagle with the bale of cloth). The Wool Guild arms on no. 14 and the Calimala arms on no. 30 mark the boundaries of the old 'tiratoio' that once stood here beside the meadows. The 'tiratoi' were large,

open buildings used for drying and stretching cloth, and they were found all over the city. The one in Via de' Servi was called 'il tiratoio dell' aquila' ('of the eagle'). At the beginning of the 16th century, the wool trade having diminished, some of these buildings were taken down and houses erected on the sites. Luca Landucci records that the houses in Via de' Servi were begun on 15th June 1510. The original form of these handsome houses can still be glimpsed at no. 22, which also happens to bear a Medici crest.

A plague of caterpillars
In the 15th century Via de' Servi was lined with meadows, and during the summer of 1498 there was a plague of caterpillars here. On 10th June Luca Landucci recorded in his *Diary* that the caterpillars devoured everything, so that the sloe-bushes became white and peeled. There was another such plague the following year; on 12th June 1499, Luca tells us that a multitude of hairy little caterpillars appeared, that they came into the houses and bit people, and that the bites became painful and swollen.

Via degli Alfani crosses Via de' Servi. If you were to turn R here you'd come, after a few yards, to the octagonal S. Maria degli Angeli, begun by Brunelleschi, completed by others and now used by the University. If you were to turn L at Via degli Alfani you'd shortly reach the Opificio delle Pietre Dure on the R at no. 78 (Walk 8). We are going to continue

straight on to Piazza SS. Annunziata. At the L corner of Via de' Servi where it joins the piazza stands the Palazzo Budini-Gattai (formerly Grifoni). Begun in the 1560s to a design by Bartolommeo Ammannati, it is practically unique in Florence in having façades of patterned brickwork. Over the door in Via de' Servi is a panel with allegorical bas-reliefs, including a tortoise beneath a billowing sail (an insignia of Cosimo I; cf. Palazzo Ramirez di Montalvo in Walk 5). An escutcheon at first floor level bears the Grifoni arms. In the 19th century the palace was purchased by Leopoldo Gattai, a building contractor, and his son-in-law/partner Francesco Budini. They eventually gave up building and invested their huge capital in numerous farms. The palace still belongs to the Budini-Gattai heirs.

Piazza SS. Annunziata

Piazza SS. Annunziata must be counted one of the loveliest squares in
the world. Over to your R lies the famous Ospedale degli Innocenti. The
Silk Guild purchased the site in 1419 and commissioned a design from
Brunelleschi. Other architects subsequently contributed to the completion
of the project, but the façade and internal courtyards are Brunelleschi's.
Virtually the complete set of contracts for the first phase of construction
(1419-1432) survives – supply contracts for wood, bricks, lime, sand, gravel
and decorative stonework, and labour contracts for foundations, masonry
and roofing. The original colonnaded portico of nine arches is a masterpiece
of Renaissance architecture. The façade was later extended by Brunelleschi's
successor, Francesco della Luna, and Andrea della Robbia's medallions
showing infants in swaddling clothes (see also page 43 for illustration) were

put in place in 1487 (two of these are now housed in the Museum of Childhood, having been replaced on the façade by copies – can you spot which two they are?). The façade was extended again in the 19th century. The bays of Brunelleschi's portico have hemispherical domes rather than vaults; the central dome was frescoed by Bernardino Poccetti in 1610. At the L end of the portico can be seen the 17th century Foundlings' Wheel (walled up in 1875), through which abandoned babies were swivelled into the orphanage.

Brunelleschi's design was so admired and so compelling that, between 1516 and 1525, it was duplicated on the opposite side of the piazza by Antonio da Sangallo and Baccio d' Agnolo for their Loggia de' Serviti (the religious order in charge of the church of SS. Annunziata). In 1600, Giovanni Battista Caccini repeated Brunelleschi's design again for his portico fronting the church, and so was created this beautiful, unified urban space.

In the middle of the piazza stands a bronze equestrian statue of Grand Duke Ferdinando I (see overleaf for illustration). This is the statue referred to in Robert Browning's poem *The Statue and the Bust* - the bust, alas, has disappeared. According to the poem, Ferdinando ordered the statue to be placed here so that he could gaze for eternity at the della Robbian bust of a woman whom he'd loved, a nice poetic conceit. The bronze for the statue came

from captured Turkish cannon. Commissioned from Giambologna, the statue was finished by his pupil, Pietro Tacca, in 1608. On the base, below the horse's tail, is a bronze panel depicting a queen bee surrounded by her swarm. The queen bee represents Ferdinando, presiding over the orderly, industrious and productive 'hive' of Tuscany. It is said that if you can count the bees correctly without touching them you will have good luck. Well, good luck! The two bronze fountains in the piazza, with their delightful marine monsters, are also by Tacca (see page 259).

The Ospedale degli Innocenti and the Museum of Childhood

The Museum of Childhood, housed in the buildings of the Ospedale degli Innocenti, is entered from the RH end of the portico. The basement rooms house an exhibition devoted to the history of the institution. The labelling is good and clear, and there are excellent information panels. The exhibition culminates in a room where are displayed many of the literally thousands of 'signs' that the Ospedale still holds in its archives. These signs, comprising small objects such as medals, coins, rings, crosses, buttons, or rosary and glass beads, were tucked into the swaddling bands of abandoned babies in the hope that they would aid identification in cases where parents might later be in a position to reclaim their children. It is a very moving and poignant display.

From the basement, you wend your way up to the ground floor to admire the architecture of the 'Cortile delle Donne' ('Women's Courtyard') and the 'Cortile degli Uomini' ('Men's Courtyard'), glimpses of which appear in Franco Zeffirelli's beautiful film *Tea with Mussolini*. From the Cortile delle Donne, stairs lead up past Simone Talenti's statue of S. John the Evangelist (originally at Orsanmichele; Walk 3) to the third floor, where is housed the collection of art amassed over the years by the Ospedale, together with a display of tabernacles with dressed sculptures (devotional objects linked to the religious activities of the many women who lived at the institution). Two of Andrea della Robbia's medallions from the façade are kept up here as well, as they were found, during restoration, to be in too precarious a condition to be remounted outside. The art collection includes works by, among others, Giottino, Giovanni del Biondo, Luca della Robbia, Botticelli, Buglioni, Jacopino del Conte (restored with the aid of a contribution from Zeffirelli), Neri di Bicci and Piero di Cosimo. It culminates with Domenico Ghirlandaio's magnificent Adoration of the Magi. The contract for this painting stipulated that Ghirlandaio was to be paid in instalments for the work, and the hospital archives contain a note saying that, on 28th June 1487, three florins were handed over to a young apprentice whom the artist had sent along for this purpose – his name was Michelangelo Buonarroti. On the fourth floor is the terrace café, which is well worth a visit for the views alone.

The church of SS. Annunziata

If the church of SS. Annunziata is closed, remember that Walk 10 is a circular one and that you can return to the piazza later if you so wish. The door under Caccini's portico leads directly into the Chiostrino de' Voti, an atrium decorated with a series of frescoes showing scenes from the life of the Virgin and dating in the main from the early 16th century (there is a full information board here). The artists include Alesso Baldovinetti, Andrea del Sarto, Pontormo, Rosso Fiorentino and Franciabigio. There is a story attached to Franciabigio's depiction of the Marriage of the Virgin, according to which the artist, continually pestered in his work by meddlesome friars, deliberately damaged the Virgin's face in a fit of anger (another version says it was because he was never paid the agreed fee). The chap standing behind Joseph is in the act of giving Christ's step-father a hefty punch, which, says Vasari, was part of the marriage ceremony at the time in Florence!

From the Chiostrino de' Voti a door leads into the church. Founded by the Servite Order in the mid-13th century, it was rebuilt (along with the chiostrino) in the mid-15th century by Michelozzo and others. Michelozzo's design, with a circular tribune at one end of the nave and a preceding atrium at the other end, was one that had been used for many Early Christian pilgrimage churches in the Holy Land, including the church of the Holy Sepulchre in Jerusalem. That shrine had long been held in reverence by the Florentines. During the First Crusade one Pazzino de' Pazzi had brought back pieces of flint from the Holy Sepulchre, which were kept in SS. Apostoli (Walk 3) and used to light the fireworks at Easter. The association of SS. Annunziata with the Holy Sepulchre was further strengthened by the fact that the foundation stone was laid in 1444 by the Patriarch of Jerusalem.

The major patron at SS. Annunziata in the mid-15th century was Piero the Gouty, son of Cosimo Il Vecchio. It was at Piero's expense that Michelozzo designed the marble baldachin for the shrine containing the miraculous painting of the Annunciation. This shrine, situated in the near L corner of the nave as you enter the church, was one of the most celebrated in Italy. Tradition says that the painting, which is still highly venerated, was begun in the mid-13th century by a monk who, on going to finish the task, found that the image had been completed by divine intervention. If you have already done Walk 8 and visited the Museo di S. Marco, you may recall seeing, in the Pilgrims' Hospice there, the famous panels showing scenes from the life of Christ from the Silver Chest of SS. Annunziata. The chest was intended for votive offerings in precious metals presented to the miraculous image of the Virgin Annunciate, and the panels were commissioned from Fra Angelico and his workshop by Piero the Gouty.

A Madame Tussaud's Gallery at SS. Annunziata

On 2nd October 1512 Luca Landucci recorded in his *Diary* that the Medici, recently restored to Florence by combined Spanish/papal forces (see historical summary), removed the image of Piero Soderini, the erstwhile Gonfaloniere, from SS. Annunziata. It was common custom for VIPs, both Florentine and foreign, to present to the miraculous image of the Virgin Annunciate life-size effigies of themselves in wax. It was also common for effigies of political enemies to be removed, which is what occurred on this occasion. Now try to imagine a rather bizarre scene. The wax figures were mounted on special platforms, which, of course, eventually became overcrowded. When this happened, those effigies which had to be displaced were hung with ropes from the ceiling. If one fell it presaged bad luck for that person and/or his family (not to mention anyone standing underneath). It is mind-boggling to picture a veritable Madame Tussaud's Gallery dangling from the rafters of SS. Annunziata.

Reverence for the church of the Holy Sepulchre notwithstanding, Michelozzo's design for SS. Annunziata did not find favour with all Florentines. After Gian Francesco Gonzaga of Mantua left a legacy towards the construction of the tribune, his son, Ludovico, was determined to complete the work as a memorial to his father. Florence and the Medici lost interest in the plan, and it became a Gonzaga project with a new architect, none other than Leon Battista Alberti (whom we've met already on Walk 7 and whom we'll encounter again on Walk 13). Since Michelozzo's and Alberti's time the church has been altered and embellished well-nigh beyond recognition. As you stand and gaze along the nave towards the great circular tribune, you have to summon up mighty powers of imagination to restore it in your mind's eye to its original state of white stucco articulated with lovely grey pietra serena.

The church contains many fine works, including frescoes and paintings by, among others, Alessandro Allori, Perugino, Bronzino, Andrea del Sarto and Andrea del Castagno, and sculptural works by Bandinelli and Giambologna, who are both buried here (as is Andrea del Sarto). The splendid early 16th century organ, by Domenico di Lorenzo da Lucca and Matteo da Prato, is the oldest in Florence. From the L transept a door leads to the great Chiostro de' Morti. Above the door on the cloister side is Andrea del Sarto's fresco of the Madonna del Sacco; the other frescoes in the cloister are 17th century. Further along the N walk lies the Cappella de' Pittori, also called the Cappella di S. Luca. In the mid-14th century, painters asserted their identity within the somewhat amorphous conglomerate Physicians' and Apothecaries' Guild by establishing the Confraternity of S. Luca. The chapel has belonged to the Accademia delle Arti del Disegno since 1565 (see the final section of Walk 3 for more information on this Academy). Here can be found works by Vasari, Pontormo, Allori, Santi di Tito and Luca Giordano. In the vault below are buried Cellini, Pontormo, Franciabigio and many other artists.

The Archaeological Museum

The Archaeological Museum stands on the corner of Piazza SS. Annunziata between the church and the Ospedale degli Innocenti. It houses outstanding collections of Ancient Egyptian, Etruscan and Classical artefacts. The Egyptian collection is second in Italy only to that of Turin. Don't miss the chariot, found almost intact in an 18th Dynasty Theban tomb and clearly used by its owner during his lifetime. The Etruscan sections include stone and terracotta statuary and sculpture, wonderfully carved cinerary urns and sarcophagi, and the most important collection of Etruscan bronzes in Italy. In the final Etruscan room is a cinerary urn bearing the motif of a doorway which looks just like the arms of the Silk Guild – was this their inspiration I wonder? Don't miss the spectacular bronze Chimera, discovered at Arezzo in 1553 and immediately transferred to Florence on the orders of Cosimo I. The Graeco-Roman sections on the second floor encompass bronzes, including the magnificent 4th century BC horse's head that belonged to Lorenzo Il Magnifico, statuary, including a 6th century BC marble Greek *kouros*, and a stunning collection of black- and red-figured vases.

Piazza SS. Annunziata to the Liceo Michelangelo

If you are doing the shorter version of Walk 10, omitting the English Cemetery, Synagogue and Jewish Museum, you should take in this paragraph and then omit the next two sections, skipping to the one entitled 'the Liceo Michelangelo to the Museum of Prehistory' (page 257). If you are doing the full walk, omit this paragraph and go on to the next section. Leave Piazza SS. Annunziata on Via della Colonna, under the arch between the Ospedale degli Innocenti and the Archaeological Museum. Via della Colonna is a busy road with very narrow pavements. Do take extra care. You'll pass the garden of the Archaeological Museum on your L, where are reconstructed several Etruscan tombs. Just a few yards beyond the crossroads with Borgo Pinti, you'll find the Liceo Michelangelo, where Perugino's wonderful fresco of the Crucifixion is housed, on the RH side at no. 9.

Piazza SS. Annunziata to the English Cemetery

Leave Piazza SS. Annunziata on Via Gino Capponi (to the R of the church). A few yards beyond Via Laura on the R is the ex-oratory of S. Pierino, home of La Dante in Florence, where you can attend Italian language courses if you have a mind to (www.firenze.ladante.it; e-mail: info@firenze.ladante.it). The oratory belonged to the 16th century Confraternity of S. Pietro Maggiore. Above the entrance a glazed terracotta lunette by Santi di Michele Buglioni

(1494-1576) has the Annunciation between two hooded brethren. The delightful cloister and vestibule beyond have late 16th century frescoes by Bernardino Poccetti and others, and a glazed terracotta triptych by Giovanni della Robbia.

At no. 22 blue Via Gino Capponi, on the near corner with Via Giuseppe Giusti, a plaque tells us that 'the painter without error', Andrea del Sarto, built and lived in this house on his return from France, and died here in 1530. The window frames are inscribed with the date 1578 and the name of the artist Federico Zuccari, who helped Vasari paint the cupola of the Duomo. Zuccari bought both this house and one round the corner, which we'll see shortly.

Continue along Via Gino Capponi. On the R just beyond Via Giuseppe Giusti lies the huge early 18th century Palazzo di Gino Capponi. A few yards further on, Via Pier Antonio Micheli runs off to the L. On the far corner of the junction, at no. 2 blue, lies the Palazzo di S. Clemente, built for the Guadagni family and attributed to Gherardo Silvani. In 1777 the palace was sold to Charles Edward Stuart, the Young Pretender, son of James Edward, the Old Pretender, and grandson of King James II of England. He used the title Count of Albany and, from his rooftop, flew a pennant with the monogram CRIII. One of the first guests at the palace was the poet

Vittorio Alfieri, whose monument by Canova you may already have seen in S. Croce. Alfieri fell madly in love with the Young Pretender's wife, the beautiful Princess Louisa of Stolberg, Countess of Albany. In the 19th century the Russian aristocrat Niccolò Demidoff lived here. The palace now belongs to the University.

Retrace your steps back along Via Gino Capponi, turn L along Via Giuseppe Giusti and look for no. 43 on the R. This is Federico Zuccari's other house. The bizarre façade is mannerist in the extreme and reflects the vogue then raging for grottoes. The external benches thrust themselves forward from great unworked blocks. Above them, the finished elements of the façade (pilasters, door-frame etc.) seem to be struggling to break free of this rocky outcrop. Three reliefs show implements used in architecture, sculpture and painting and, where stone gives way to brick, these three arts are given due space, architecture in the windows with their broken pediments, niches for sculptures, and a great central panel for a fresco. The apparently random and capricious mix of forms and textures is, in fact, a carefully considered design illustrating art emerging out of nature.

Continue along Via Giuseppe Giusti, past the Fondazione Scienza e Tecnica on the R, which houses laboratories, a science museum and a planetarium. Those wishing to visit need to book in advance (www.planetario.fi.it). Turn L up Borgo Pinti, where, on your L, you'll find the Four Seasons Hotel. The courtyard, with magnificent stucco bas-reliefs, is all that remains of the original 15th century palace. The Gherardesca family owned the property for close on 300 years, and in the 19th century the extensive grounds were made into a romantic garden, which has been beautifully restored and modified by the hotel. Borgo Pinti ends at the busy ringroad. Here once stood one of the city gates, the Porta de' Pinti. Slightly over to the R, across the ringroad in

the middle of Piazza Donatello, lies the English Cemetery. Here are buried numerous luminaries, including Walter Savage Landor (see Walk 8 under the section entitled 'an irascible English tenant'), Theodosia and Fanny Trollope (see Walk 11 under the section on 'Villino Trollope'), and Fanny Holman Hunt and Elizabeth Barrett Browning (Walk 12). Elizabeth's tomb was designed by Robert Browning and sculpted by Lord Leighton. To reach the entrance to the cemetery, turn R along the ringroad to the top of Via Vittorio Alfieri and cross using the pelican crossings. A map of the cemetery is available at the gatehouse.

The English Cemetery, the Synagogue, and the Liceo Michelangelo

On leaving the English Cemetery recross the pelican crossings and head down Via Vittorio Alfieri. The Piazza Massimo d' Azeglio opens up on your L (d' Azeglio, who was prime minister of Piedmont from 1849 to 1852, will be familiar to students of the Risorgimento). Keep going straight on. Beyond the piazza, Via Alfieri becomes Via Luigi Carlo Farini, and you'll find the 19th century Synagogue a few yards along here on the L. The small Jewish Museum is housed above the Synagogue. There is a lift, and the labelling is in both Italian and English.

The museum, as well as housing treasures from the Synagogue, presents a brief account of the Jews in Florence, with maps and archival photographs. There is also a memorial room with a film showing archival footage of World War II and interviews with survivors (soundtrack in Italian only at the time of writing). On exiting from the Synagogue turn R, retracing your steps along Via Luigi Carlo Farini to the corner of Piazza Massimo d' Azeglio. Turn L here into Via della Colonna. The entrance to the Liceo Michelangelo is on the L at no. 9, a few yards before the crossroads with Borgo Pinti. Here is the wonderful Crucifixion by Perugino, one of his masterpieces.

The Liceo Michelangelo to the Museum of Prehistory

On exiting from the Liceo Michelangelo turn L and, keeping on Via della Colonna, cross Borgo Pinti. Many artists, including Perugino himself, lived in this area. Take the next turning on the L, Via della Pergola. A few yards along on the R, at no. 59, a plaque marks the house of Benvenuto Cellini. Here he cast the bronze statue of Perseus, losing all his household pewter in the process and coming perilously close to setting fire to the neighbourhood (see Walk 2). The plaque tells us that he died in February 1570/71. Don't worry, he didn't die twice. The double date is due to the fact that, in Cellini's time, the Florentine calendar began on 25th March, the Feast of the Annunciation, so what we now call February 1571 was, for them, February 1570. We shall encounter another double date when we visit the church of S. Trinità on Walk 12.

Further down Via della Pergola, the Teatro della Pergola lies on the L. Founded in the 1650s, this was one of the first theatres to be built in the Italian style with a horseshoe arrangement of boxes rising through several levels. Such theatres began life as private venues, functioning as exclusive clubs for the nobility. I am told that, at the Pergola, the eldest surviving descendants of any of the founder members still have free access to the box at the lowest level nearest to the stage on the R (Prof. R. Goldthwaite, personal communication). Immediately beyond the Teatro della Pergola is the little ex-oratory of S. Thomas Aquinas, which once belonged to the Congregazione de' Contemplati. In 1568 Santi di Tito became a member of this confraternity, designed the oratory for them and painted its altarpiece. At the end of Via della Pergola turn R on to Via S. Egidio. The Museum of Prehistory lies on your L. This small museum will, I think, attract only a few. The labelling is nearly all in Italian only and when I visited in 2014 there was no guidebook in English.

The Hospital of S. Maria Nuova and the church of S. Egidio

Practically opposite the Museum of Prehistory lies the Hospital of S. Maria Nuova. Founded in 1286 by Folco Portinari, father of Dante's Beatrice, it is still one of the main hospitals of the city. Beneath the handsome 16th century portico by Buontalenti lies the church of S. Egidio (full information board in English inside). Of ancient foundation, the church was restored several times between the 16th and 18th centuries, resulting in the loss of 15th century frescoes by Alesso Baldovinetti, Andrea del Castagno, Domenico Veneziano and Piero della Francesca. Folco Portinari's tomb-slab lies in front of the altar rail, while on the L wall just beyond the steps up to the altar is a charming little 15th century tabernacle by Bernardo Rossellino, with a bronze door by Ghiberti (now replaced by a copy). The high altar was once adorned by a splendid triptych by Hugo Van der Goes, commissioned by Tommaso Portinari, the Medici agent in Bruges, and now in the Uffizi Gallery.

To the L of the church façade a passage leads to a courtyard housing a neo-classical monument to the benefactor Count Galli Tassi. Mounted on the R wall of the passage as you enter is the tomb-slab of Monna Tessa, Folco Portinari's servant and Beatrice's nurse, who persuaded her master to found the hospital and who herself founded the Oblates, a religious order of nurses. To the R of the church façade lies the entrance to the hospital. At the end of the entrance lobby is a reproduction of a fresco by Bicci di Lorenzo (1420) showing Pope Martin V consecrating the church of S. Egidio. There are plans to open a museum here to house the original fresco and other treasures pertaining to the church and the hospital.

The Hospital of S. Maria Nuova to Piazza del Duomo
On leaving the hospital turn R along Via Bufalini (be careful, this is a busy road). Just beyond the hospital forecourt, on the L at no. 1, a plaque marks Ghiberti's workshop. Here the Baptistery doors were cast. At the crossroads with Via de' Servi you have a choice. You can turn L to reach Piazza del Duomo, or turn R back up to Piazza SS. Annunziata. There were 91 bees by the way (but I've forgotten whether that includes the queen or not).

Details of the fountains by Pietro Tacca in Piazza SS. Annunziata

Walk 11

Begins at Piazza S. Giovanni and ends at Piazza S. Marco.
Takes in: the Cenacolo del Fuligno, the Cenacolo di S. Apollonia and the
Chiostro dello Scalzo.
Duration: 1 hour 45 minutes, excluding time spent at the three venues
mentioned above, for which you should allow 30-45 minutes each.
Tips: the opening times for the venues on this walk are very restricted.
At the time of writing the only opportunity for visiting all three on the
same itinerary was on a Thursday morning or a Saturday morning on the
1st, 3rd and 5th Saturdays in the month. I would only undertake this walk
if you have plenty of time at your disposal. Otherwise, just head directly
for those venues which appeal to you most.

Piazza S. Giovanni to Piazza dell' Unità d' Italia

Leave Piazza S. Giovanni at its NW corner on Via de' Cerretani. Keep
to the RH pavement. As the road bends round slightly to the R it
becomes Via de' Panzani. Here, in November 1515, a huge piece of fictive
architecture was erected for the entry into Florence of Pope Leo X. Luca

Landucci describes it in his *Diary*. It
took the form of a great triumphal
arch, complete with four columns,
six pilasters, cornices, ornaments and
numerous figures. A few yards along
Via de' Panzani, Via del Giglio leads off
to the R. Here, at no. 2 red on the R,
is a splendid wine hatch that belonged
to the Cantina Bartolini-Salimbeni Vivai. It takes the form of a portal set
in a rusticated façade, with the inscription 'Vendita di Vino'. A plaque

up on the wall to the R gives the opening times
of the cantina. Continue along Via de' Panzani
to reach Piazza dell' Unità d' Italia. The flank of
the S. Maria Novella complex can be seen over
to the L. The earlier church on this site, called
S. Maria delle Vigne, faced this piazza. S. Peter
Martyr preached here in the mid-13th century
and drew huge crowds. Both church and piazza
proved too small, and when, later in the century,
the church was enlarged, its axis was turned
through ninety degrees and the present Piazza
S. Maria Novella was laid out in front of the
new façade (Walk 7).

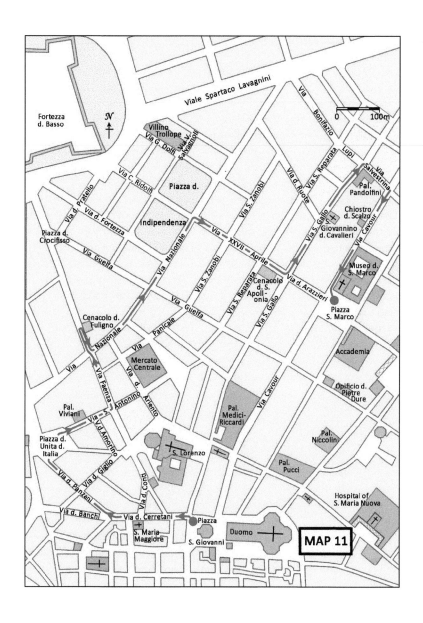

Cardinal Frate Latino visits Florence

The first stone of the new church of S. Maria Novella was blessed by Cardinal Frate Latino, the papal legate of Pope Nicholas III, when he came to Florence in 1278 to try to heal rifts between the various Guelf factions in the city. Giovanni Villani tells the story in his *Chronicle* (VII.56) – see under the section entitled 'the big bad barons' at the end of Walk 4. The cardinal managed to conclude a treaty, which was solemnized on the piazza fronting the old church of S. Maria delle Vigne (the present day Piazza dell' Unità d' Italia). Villani says that the piazza was covered with cloths and with great wooden scaffolds, on which were seated the cardinal, many bishops, prelates, clergy and monks, and the Podestà, Capitano and all the counsellors of Florence.

Piazza dell' Unità d' Italia to the Cenacolo del Fuligno

Leave Piazza dell' Unità d' Italia in the far diagonal corner, on Via S. Antonino. On the L as you enter the latter is a tabernacle containing a terracotta Madonna and Child by Andrea della Robbia. A few yards along Via S. Antonino, on the L at no. 11, lies the Palazzo Viviani. Vincenzo Viviani was a famous 17th century mathematician and a pupil of Galileo. He placed three inscriptions on the front of his palace, with Latin texts by himself, celebrating Galileo's many achievements, including the discovery of sunspots and of the so-called 'Medici planets', and the formulation of a putative method for calculating longitude at sea. The bust of Galileo above the door is by Foggini and the bas-reliefs to either side of it illustrate some of the discoveries and inventions mentioned in the texts. On his death Viviani left

some of his teacher's and his own scientific instruments to the Accademia del Cimento (see historical summary), and you can see these if you visit the Galileo Museum (Walk 9). A second della Robbian terracotta tabernacle can be seen on the corner of Via S. Antonino and Via dell' Amorino. At the crossroads with Via Faenza, we are going to turn L. Before we do so, however, don't miss the tabernacle at the far R corner of the crossroads. It has a 14th century painting (attributed by some to the school of Taddeo Gaddi) framed by 18th century stucco work.

As you head up Via Faenza you'll see, on the L next door to no. 43 blue, the attractive porch of the church of S. Jacopo in Campo Corbolini, which originally belonged to the Knights Templar and then to the Knights of S. John. Cross over Via Nazionale. A few yards further along on the R, at Via Faenza no. 40, lies the entrance to the Cenacolo del Fuligno. The Cenacolo (the refectory of the convent that once stood here) houses the wonderful fresco of the Last Supper by Perugino (discovered in 1843) and a small collection of paintings by artists influenced by the great man. There are comprehensive information boards in English. A room off to the L at the far end of the refectory contains a few 16th century frescoes along with some display cases containing Ancient Egyptian and Etruscan artefacts on loan from the Archaeological Museum (Walk 10). The refectory once housed the Egyptian and Etruscan collections, and an information board here gives the museum history of the place.

The Cenacolo del Fuligno to the Cenacolo di S. Apollonia

On exiting from the Cenacolo turn L back to the crossroads with Via Nazionale, where you turn L again. On your L, opposite the end of Via dell' Ariento, is a large glazed terracotta tabernacle by Giovanni della Robbia. If you've done Walk 5, seen the 'Red City' markers on the façade of the church of S. Ambrogio, and read the section that includes 'the sorry tale of Donato Pennechini', you'll already know of the Florentine 'potenze', associations of artisans and labourers. The 'Red City' was one such potenza; the 'Biliemme' was another. An inscription on this magnificent tabernacle tells us that the men of the Biliemme had it made and erected here in 1522, close to the tavern that was their headquarters. The Madonna and Child are flanked by SS. Lorenzo and James the Great and SS. Catherine and Barbara, while at the base of the frame stand SS. Sebastian and Roch,

protectors against the plague. Continue along Via Nazionale until you reach the S corner of Piazza dell' Indipendenza, a large pleasant square with a park and benches. Although it's probably not worth walking over to, you may just like to know that, at the N corner of the piazza, on the junction between Via Giuseppe Dolfi and Via Vincenzo Salvagnoli, lies Villino Trollope, which, for nearly two decades, was the home of the Trollope family.

Villino Trollope

Most people will have heard of Anthony Trollope, even if they haven't read his novels. Fewer people will know of his elder brother, Thomas Adolphus, and of their mother, Fanny. This indomitable lady bore her hopeless husband seven children in all, left him penniless in England while she sailed for America to try and increase the family fortune by setting up a bazaar in Cincinnati, became stranded there without a penny, turned instead (with resounding success) to writing, returned home, was impelled to retreat to Bruges in the face of more debts, lost a son and a daughter to consumption, was (mercifully perhaps) widowed, trotted around Europe writing, watched three more children die, and ended up in Florence with Thomas (Anthony having decided to stay in England). Fanny Trollope produced well over 100 volumes (mostly forgotten now) and Thomas over fifty. In Florence Thomas met Theodosia Garrow. Her grandfather, a British army officer, had married an Indian lady, and their son, Joseph Garrow, had married a rich Jewish widow twenty-three years his senior! At the age of fifty-nine (or so history relates) this lady gave birth to Theodosia, a poetic prodigy with a gift for languages. Thomas Trollope was smitten by this frail beauty and they were married in 1848. Soon afterwards, Theodosia lost both her mother and a step-sister. Her inheritance, coupled with funds from Fanny Trollope and Joseph Garrow (who came to live with his daughter), enabled the Trollopes to purchase Villino Trollope, which became famous as a liberal intellectual salon. A visitor to the villa reported that the interior was graced by marble pillars, suits of armour, carved furniture, Florentine bridal-chests, rare illuminated and engraved books, majolica-ware, a terracotta of the Virgin and Child by Orcagna, and many other Cinquecento objects. The pillared marble terrace was adorned with terracottas, bas-reliefs, inscriptions and coats-of-arms. It opened on to a garden stretching all the way to the ancient walls of the city, where grew lemon trees in huge pots, from whose fruit was made iced lemon squash. Here Anthony Trollope stayed when he visited Florence, here was born Theodosia's daughter, Beatrice, and here Theodosia died in 1865. Over the entrance to Villino Trollope, at no. 1 Via Vincenzo Salvagnoli, can be seen a commemorative stone erected to her memory, which reads: 'On 13th April 1865 there died in this house Theodosia Garrow Trollope, who wrote in English, with an Italian soul, of the struggles and triumph of Liberty.'

Continue on along Via Nazionale and turn R to leave the Piazza dell' Indipendenza on Via XXVII Aprile. On the far R corner of the crossroads with Via S. Reparata is the Cenacolo di S. Apollonia (entrance on Via XXVII Aprile at no. 1). The Cenacolo houses the astonishing fresco of the Last Supper by Andrea del Castagno (1447), a visually disturbing work, harsh and intense, with an intriguing system of perspective. The meal is depicted as taking place in a room lined with stone panels. The ceiling has black and white inlay, and the floor red and white tiles. Walk from one side of the refectory to the other and you will find that the angle of the room depicted in the fresco appears to shift with you. Above are frescoes of the Crucifixion, Deposition and Resurrection (all damaged, alas); the sinopie are on the opposite wall. Other frescoes and sinopie are also displayed here, while the vestibule has a small collection of paintings, including works by Neri di Bicci.

The Cenacolo di S. Apollonia to the Chiostro dello Scalzo
On exiting from the Cenacolo turn R along Via XXVII Aprile and then take the next L, Via S. Gallo. Up here on the R is the Loggia dei Tessitori (*c.* 1500), once part of the Silk Weavers' Guildhouse. On the L at the corner of Via delle Ruote is a tabernacle with a fresco by Andrea Bonaiuto (who decorated the Chapter House at S. Maria Novella; Walk 7), while a few yards further along on the R is the church of S. Giovannino de' Cavalieri, with the cross of the Knights of Malta on the façade. The church contains works by Bicci di Lorenzo and Neri di Bicci, and a magnificent 19th century Ginori terracotta of the Madonna and Child in the della Robbian style. The crucifix was apparently made from the wood of the elm that burst into leaf when touched by the bier of S. Zenobius (see Walk 1).

On the R immediately before the crossroads with Via Bonifazio Lupi (to the L) and Via Salvestrina (to the R) lies the Palazzo Pandolfini (see overleaf for illustration), the only building designed by Raphael to grace Florence. It was built on the outskirts of the city in the early 16th century for Bishop Giannozzo Pandolfini, who is recorded in the classical inscription

running beneath the cornice. Giannozzo was the son of Lorenzo Il Magnifico's legate to King Ferdinand of Naples and a close friend of both the Medici popes, Leo X and Clement VII, whose patronage is also recorded in the inscription. The main block of the building has four bays of two storeys, but the ground floor extends to nine bays, suggesting that the original plan was for a symmetrical façade on Via S. Gallo. Raphael combined Roman and Florentine architectural styles, and the façade mixes rusticated stonework with plain stucco. The windows have alternating triangular and segmental pediments carried on Doric pilasters (ground floor) and Ionic half-columns (first floor). The first floor windows alternate with inset panels, beneath which a dado is punctuated by balustrades, and a balustrade continues above the ground floor extension. The palace still belongs to the Pandolfini family.

Turn R down Via Salvestrina and continue along for just one block to Via Cavour, where you turn R again. On your R at no. 69 is the Chiostro dello Scalzo, a charming little cloister with wonderful grisaille frescoes by Andrea del Sarto and Franciabigio (1510-26). This 'Cloister of the Barefooted' belonged to a confraternity of S. John the Baptist, whose members (including del Sarto himself) walked barefoot carrying the Cross in processions re-enacting the Passion of Christ. Two members of the confraternity are shown flanking the Baptist in the della Robbian lunette above the door on Via Cavour. In the vestibule is an 18th century stucco of the Crucifixion with mourners. The cloister was modified in the 18th century, when the vaulting

was added and the resulting lunettes above the frescoes decorated. The frescoes depict the Virtues and scenes from the life of the Baptist. Working anti-clockwise from the entrance we have the figure of Faith (traditionally considered to be a portrait of del Sarto's wife, Lucrezia del Fede, whose name means 'of the faith'), the annunciation to Zacharias, the Visitation, and the birth and naming of John. Next come two scenes by Franciabigio, Zacharias blessing John prior to his leaving for the desert, and Christ and John meeting in the desert. Then comes the baptism of Christ, the figures of Charity and Justice, John preaching to the multitude, and John baptizing the multitude. The series ends with the capture of John, the dance of Salome, the beheading of John, the presentation of John's head to Herod, and the figure of Hope (perhaps a portrait of del Sarto's daughter Maria). Note the terracotta bust of del Sarto by Alessandro Geri (18th century) above the entrance door and, at the opposite end of the cloister, a bust of Antonino Pierozzi (one time prior at S. Marco; Walk 8) and a 15th century terracotta statue of S. John from the workshop of Benedetto da Maiano.

The Chiostro dello Scalzo to Piazza S. Marco

On leaving the Chiostro dello Scalzo turn R and continue along Via Cavour. A few yards along on the R, at no. 57, was the Cappella del Casino Mediceo di S. Marco. In 1568, Francesco I bought the land on which he built the Casino, which rapidly became a centre for scientific research. Work here led to such achievements as the tempering of steel for tools capable of carving porphyry, the melting of rock crystal to blow as glass, and the production of soft-paste porcelain. Piazza S. Marco opens up on the L, and Walk 11 ends here.

A failed attack on Florence

In the section entitled 'the big bad barons' at the end of Walk 4, mention was made of the attack launched on Florence by the White Guelfs and Ghibellines at the beginning of the 14th century. Cardinal Niccolò of Prato had been sent to Florence by Pope Benedict XI in 1304 to mediate between warring factions within the Black Guelf Party. His peace plan failed and he departed the city in a furious temper to report back to the pope, who demanded that the leaders of the factions appear before him. Off they all went, accompanied by splendid retinues of followers. Knowing that so many Blacks had left Florence, the vindictive cardinal sent secretly to the White Guelfs and Ghibellines in Tuscany telling them to go in arms to the city on a named day, and saying that this was by the pope's will. Off they trotted and Compagni tells us in his *Chronicle* (III.10) that twelve hundred horse and more troops on foot arrived and encamped a few miles from Florence. The attackers, however, had no unified plan, and by acting separately lost their opportunity. Some pressed forward prematurely and entered the suburbs, assembling just N of Piazza S. Marco. A few penetrated as far as the Baptistery, but there they were repulsed. Villani, who was present, tells the story in his *Chronicle* (VIII.72). As rumours spread that the coup had been unsuccessful, the forces waiting outside the city withdrew. The forward attackers were left to their fate. Many died and some prisoners were hanged from trees along the road. In Villani's opinion, if they had all held firm they would undoubtedly have gained the city.

Walk 12

Begins at Piazza S. Trinità and ends at Piazza Pitti.

Takes in: S. Trinità, the Salvatore Ferragamo Museum, S. Mark's English Church, S. Spirito, the Fondazione Salvatore Romano, S. Felice, the Casa Guidi, 'La Specola' Museum and the Pitti Palace.

Duration: 1 hour 30 minutes, excluding time spent at any of the above. You should allow up to 1 hour each for S. Trinità and S. Spirito, c. 30-45 minutes each for the Fondazione Salvatore Romano and the Casa Guidi, c. 20 minutes each for S. Mark's and S. Felice, and up to 2 hours each for 'La Specola' and the Pitti Palace. How long you spend at the Ferragamo Museum will depend on how interested you are in shoes and on the exhibition currently on display.

Tips: this walk should be done in the morning if possible, for that is when the natural light is best in the churches of S. Trinità and S. Spirito. At the time of writing you needed small change to operate the lights in the crypt and some of the chapels at S. Trinità. Binoculars may prove useful for fresco gazing. The church of S. Spirito closes in the afternoons, so you need to take this into account when deciding on a start time. The either/or options on tickets for the Pitti Palace/Boboli Gardens are explained at the end of the walk. You cannot hope to visit all of the above on one itinerary. If this is your first visit to Florence, I recommend that you begin the walk with a visit to the church of S. Trinità and end it by visiting one of the museums in the Pitti Palace, taking in the church of S. Spirito en route.

S. Trinità

Walk 12 begins with a visit to the church of S. Trinità. The façade, by Buontalenti, dates to the 1590s, but the church is of ancient foundation and its treasures make it a must-see. A church of the Vallombrosan Order stood here in the 11th century, but the present Gothic form of the building dates from the 14th century and is attributed to Neri di Fioravante. Only the inner façade and the crypt of the Romanesque structure survives. The church interior is dark, but the chapels have either coin-operated lights or time switches placed inconspicuously by their entrance piers. Above the entrances to many of the chapels there are the remains of 14th and 15th century frescoes, so don't forget to gaze heavenwards. The following account of the highlights of the church proceeds round the interior anti-clockwise. The art works are well labelled and there is an information board near the inner façade.

The third chapel along the R aisle contains damaged frescoes by Spinello Aretino and an altarpiece by Neri di Bicci. The fourth chapel was frescoed by Lorenzo Monaco in the 1420s with scenes from the life of the Virgin. The altarpiece of the Annunciation is also by him. Note the tomb-slab of

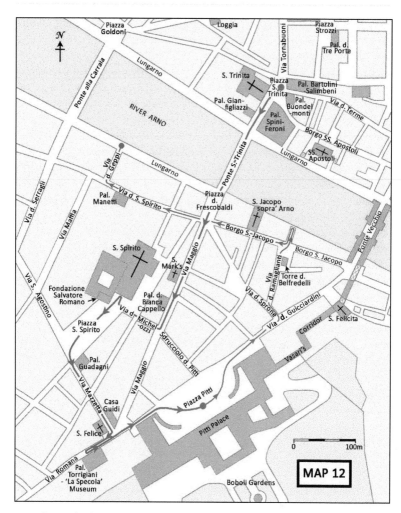

Bartolini-Salimbeni – it bears the family motto 'per non dormire' ('so as not to sleep'), of which more anon. Off the R transept are the side porch, which contains 'avelli' (arcaded tomb recesses), and the sacristy. The latter was formerly a Strozzi Chapel and was completed by Palla Strozzi, a rival of Cosimo Il Vecchio. The famous painting of the Adoration of the Magi by Gentile da Fabriano (now in the Uffizi Gallery) was commissioned by Palla for this chapel.

Next to the door to the sacristy lies the Sassetti Chapel, decorated during the 1480s by Domenico Ghirlandaio with frescoes showing scenes from the life of S. Francis. The altarpiece, showing the Adoration of

the Shepherds, is also by Ghirlandaio. Francesco Sassetti was the manager
of the Medici Bank in Florence and an influential figure in the city, but
even he had insufficient clout to pull off his 'plan A', which was to turn the
sanctuary at S. Maria Novella into a family chapel complete with fresco cycle
dedicated to his name saint, Francis – an idea not enthusiastically received
by the Dominican brethren at that establishment! Francesco had to content
himself instead with this chapel, but Ghirlandaio did him proud. Some of
the scenes are set in Florence. In the lunette above the altar, for example,
S. Francis receives the Rule of his Order from Pope Honorius against a
backdrop of the Piazza della Signoria; you can see the Palazzo Vecchio prior
to the building of the Uffizi behind it, and next door is a statue-free
Loggia de' Lanzi. In the foreground on the extreme R stand four figures who
represent (from L to R) Antonio Pucci, Lorenzo Il Magnifico, Francesco
Sassetti and his son Federico. Up the stairs comes Agnolo Poliziano, tutor
to Lorenzo's children, with his three young charges behind him, Giuliano
(later Duke of Nemours), Piero the Unfortunate and Giovanni (later Pope
Leo X). In the fresco depicting the restoration to life of a young child of the
Spini family, the Palazzo Spini-Feroni appears on the L, complete with said
sprog falling out of a window; the Romanesque façade of S. Trinità can be
seen on the R, with the old Ponte S. Trinità in the background. The figure
on the extreme R edge of the fresco is a self-portrait of Ghirlandaio, dressed
in blue tunic, red cloak and red hat. The altarpiece of the Adoration of the
Shepherds shows the donors, Francesco Sassetti and his wife, Nera Corsi,
kneeling. Their tombs, with black porphyry sarcophagi, are attributed to
Giuliano da Sangallo.

The chapel next to the Sassetti Chapel contains a miraculous Crucifix
(originally housed at S. Miniato; Walk 14) which is said to have bowed in
approval to S. John Gualberto, founder of the Vallombrosan Order, when he
pardoned his brother's assassin. The sanctuary has a 15th century altarpiece
and remains of frescoes by Alesso Baldovinetti. In the second chapel to the
L of the sanctuary are fresco fragments and the tomb of Benozzo Federighi,
Bishop of Fiesole (d. 1450), by Luca della Robbia. The lovely marble effigy
is surrounded by an exquisite glazed terracotta and gilded border. Hopefully
the quality of the finished product placated the bishop's nephew, who,
in 1458, took Luca to court for being three years behind on meeting the
deadline for the completion of the tomb agreed in the contract.

Moving on to the L aisle you come to the stunning wooden statue of
Mary Magdalene by Desiderio da Settignano. The fresco of a bishop/saint
is attributed to Baldovinetti. The next chapel has a fresco showing S. John
Gualberto with Vallombrosan saints, and a painting of the Annunciation
by Neri di Bicci. On the R wall of the chapel is a 19th century plaque

commemorating Dino Compagni, whose *Chronicle* features so prominently in some of the walks and who is buried here along with other family members. You can see his tomb-slab, bearing the date 1323, at the base of the L wall. The plaque on the R wall tells us that the vaults of this church, which resounded to Compagni's magnanimous words, have formed a fitting sanctuary for his bones since 26th February 1324. The discrepancy in the dates is due to the fact that, in Compagni's time, the Florentine calendar year began on 25th March, the Feast of the Annunciation, so what we now call February 1324 was, for them, February 1323. The 'magnanimous words' to which the plaque refers were uttered by Compagni at a meeting held by the Black Guelfs at the start of the 14th century here in S. Trinità. They were plotting the downfall of the White faction, and Compagni was at the meeting in the role of peace-maker, trying to dissuade the militants from violent action. His magnanimous words are quoted by him in his *Chronicle* (I.24):

'Against whom do you want to fight? Your brothers? What victory would you gain? Nothing except mourning.'

The third chapel in the L aisle contains another Neri di Bicci painting, while the altarpiece of the Coronation of the Virgin is by Bicci di Lorenzo. Here too is the recently restored Madonna and Child by Donatello, and a Davanzati family tomb (1444) attributed to Bernardo Rossellino and adapted from an early Christian sarcophagus. The next chapel has works by Ridolfo del Ghirlandaio. The crypt is entered directly from the nave.

Piazza S. Trinità and the Salvatore Ferragamo Museum

On exiting from the church, you'll see Via Tornabuoni running off to the L. On the R side of the street once stood the famous Doney's café, frequented by foreign visitors and residents. On the opposite side of the piazza to the church you'll see two palaces, which, although very different, are both attributed to Baccio d' Agnolo. The one on the R is the Palazzo Buondelmonti (*c.* 1530). The Palazzo Bartolini-Salimbeni lies on the L, between Via Porta Rossa and Via delle Terme. This palace was designed for the wealthy banker and merchant Giovanni Bartolini, and the building accounts survive complete. Giovanni's brother, Lorenzo, was Archbishop of Florence and Chamberlain to the Medici Pope Leo X, so the family had plenty of powerful connections, both Florentine and Roman. A taste for things Roman is evident in this palace, with its tabernacle windows surmounted by segmental and triangular pediments, and its niches and recessed panels set between the windows on the first and second floors. The strings of poppies decorating the friezes (damaged alas) allude to an incident in the family's history, when the Bartolini got the better of some business competitors by dint of drugging them with opium! The family motto 'per non dormire' ('so as not to sleep'), inscribed on the heavy mullions of the windows, alludes to the same incident, while the Latin inscription over the door, *carpere promptius quam imitari* 'it is easier to criticize than to imitate', refers more probably to the design of the palace. The first façade in the city centre to be built in Roman High Renaissance style, it came in for a lot of criticism.

The granite column in the centre of the piazza comes from the Caracalla Baths in Rome. It was presented to Cosimo I by Pope Pius IV and set up

here to commemorate Cosimo's victory in 1537 over the exiled Florentine republican die-hards at Montemurlo (see historical summary). The column marked part of Cosimo's so-called 'processional route' from Piazza di S. Felice (which we'll see later) to the Palazzo Vecchio and the Duomo. The figure of Justice on the top was added in 1581 and there is a nice story attached to it. Towards the end of the 16th century several jewellers on the Ponte Vecchio reported the theft of small gems, but the thief was never found. Several years later, during routine cleaning of the statue of Justice, the jewels were discovered in a magpie's nest in one of the dishes of the scales. It was not only for Cosimo I that Piazza S. Trinità formed part of a processional route. Pope Leo X came this way too on his triumphal entry into Florence in 1515. On that occasion the piazza was transformed into a circular arena, with twenty-two pillars surmounted by an inscribed frieze and a cornice.

A fight, a public row, and a street party

Piazza S. Trinità has witnessed many dramas over the years. In the year 1300, for example, it was the scene of a fight between the Black and White Guelf factions, during which Ricoverino de' Cerchi had his nose cut off. It was also the scene of a public row between Michelangelo and Leonardo da Vinci. A group of gentlemen who were debating a point in Dante called Leonardo over and asked him for his opinion. Michelangelo came along at that moment and, perhaps a touch maliciously, Leonardo suggested that they should ask him instead. Michelangelo's temper flared and he snarled back a response alluding to Leonardo's ill-fated bronze equestrian monument for the Duke of Milan, implying that it had never come to fruition because Leonardo was unable to cast it. He then walked off, leaving Leonardo red-faced and speechless. On a happier note, the piazza was the scene of many a street party thrown by the monks of the monastery here. They dispensed hospitality on a lavish scale, despite the rules of the Vallombrosan Order, which stressed isolation and silence. The register for 1360 survives and tells us that, on the feast of the Trinity (May 31st), the convent provided an open-air banquet for the entire neighbourhood at a cost of 30 florins. There were eggs, salads, fruit, bread, wine and 200lbs of spit-roasted beef, not to mention hired musicians and a tumbler.

The S side of Piazza S. Trinità is dominated by the huge crenellated Palazzo Spini-Feroni. The largest private mediaeval palace in Florence, it

was built for Geri degli Spini in 1289, possibly by Lapo Tedesco, the master of Arnolfo di Cambio. When a child of the Spini family fell from one of the upper floor windows, S. Francis appeared and restored the sprog to life. If you have just visited the church of S. Trinità, you will have seen this miracle illustrated in one of the frescoes by Ghirlandaio decorating the Sassetti Chapel. The Palazzo Spini-Feroni now houses the Salvatore Ferragamo Museum, devoted to the famous Florentine shoemaker. Exhibitions are staged here on a rotational basis, but you can be sure that there'll always be some shoes on display. Don't worry, the museum is in the basement, so you won't be needing the intervention of S. Francis. On the opposite side of Via Tornabuoni to the Palazzo Spini-Feroni is the 13th–14th century Palazzo Gianfigliazzi.

Chichibio the cook

Boccaccio tells a wonderful story about one Chichibio, cook to Currado Gianfigliazzi (*Decameron* VI.4). Currado went hunting one day and came back with a plump crane, which he gave to Chichibio to prepare for supper. Chichibio's sweetheart coaxed her lover into giving her one of the bird's thighs, so the crane was set before Currado and his guests that evening minus a leg. Currado demanded to know what had become of the missing thigh, and when Chichibio maintained that cranes have only one leg, his furious master decided to teach him a lesson. Accordingly, at daybreak the next morning, Chichibio was ordered to accompany Currado to the hunting grounds. Here many cranes were standing in the water, each one on one leg only, as is their wont when they are asleep. A relieved Chichibio pointed out the truth of his assertion, but Currado, drawing nearer to the cranes, let out a loud shout, which caused the birds to lower their second legs and take flight. The master then turned on his terrified cook, who, beside himself with fear, gave such a wonderful answer that all of Currado's wrath turned to laughter, and Chichibio was saved. To find out what he said you must read Boccaccio.

Piazza S. Trinità to Piazza S. Spirito
Leave Piazza S. Trinità with the Palazzo Spini-Feroni on your L and the Palazzo Gianfigliazzi on your R, and head for the Arno. At the RH corner where Via Tornabuoni meets the Lungarno there is a Dante plaque referring to the Gianfigliazzi arms:
'As I was going amongst them, looking around, on a yellow purse I saw an azure that had the face and bearing of a lion' (*Inferno* XVII.58-60).
Cross the river Arno on the Ponte S. Trinità, taking time to pause on the bridge for a view downstream to the Ponte alla Carraia (see page 289 for illustration) and a wonderful

view upstream to the Ponte Vecchio (see Walks 3 and 15). If you look back the way we've just come, you'll see the huge Palazzo Spini-Feroni to the R of Via Tornabuoni and the Palazzo Masetti three palaces along to the L. Here, in the early 19th century, the Countess of Albany (widow of the Young Pretender; see Walk 10) maintained a salon frequented by literary figures.

A hard-frozen sorbet and a delirious lover

Among the guests at the Countess of Albany's salon on one occasion was Massimo d' Azeglio, and this unfortunate gentleman, arriving late, attracted her criticism. Overcome by embarrassment he headed for the buffet to get a sorbet, which was, alas, so hard-frozen that it shot from under his spoon, hit the Sardinian minister and ricocheted across the floor to the august lady's feet. The young man fled and never returned. One of the Countess of Albany's lovers, the Italian poet and dramatist Alfieri, whose tomb you may already have seen in S. Croce, died in the Palazzo Masetti in 1803. Just before he expired, he apparently recited one hundred verses of Hesiod perfectly while in delirium!

The original Ponte S. Trinità was built in the 13th century. The flood in 1557 which destroyed the structure is referred to under Walk 13, as are the facts connected with the rebuilding of the bridge as part of Cosimo I's processional route and its subsequent restoration following bomb damage in

World War II. At the end of the bridge lies Piazza de' Frescobaldi, where the family of that name had its residences. For Pope Leo X's entry into Florence in 1515 a triumphal arch was erected here, as wide as the bridge.

A fracas at a Frescobaldi funeral

At the end of the 13th century Piazza de' Frescobaldi was the scene of a fracas between the Black and White Guelf factions. The occasion was the funeral of a lady of the Frescobaldi family. Compagni, whose tomb you may have seen in the church of S. Trinità, tells us in his *Chronicle* (I.20) that members of the opposing factions were seated on the ground facing each other. One of them stood up, perhaps to straighten his clothes or for some other reason. His adversaries, full of suspicion, also stood up, and set hand to sword. The others did the same and a fight began, but other men who were there came between them and stopped the violence.

We are now going to walk along part of Cosimo I's processional route, away from the Ponte S. Trinità and the river up Via Maggio, which name comes from 'maggiore', for this was, and still is, the principal thoroughfare of the Oltrarno. This handsome street, which became fashionable after the court moved to the Pitti Palace in the mid-16th century, is lined with elegant palaces. There are several high quality antique shops around here too, if your purse will stretch that far. On the L at no. 7 lies the Palazzo Ricasoli Firidolfi. The Ricasoli family consisted of several branches, of which the Firidolfi was one. Subsequent marriages united the Firidolfi with other branches and resulted, in the 19th century, in a surname of record-breaking length;   Ricasoli-Firidolfi-Zanchini-Marsuppini-Salviati-Acciaiuoli.   You'd have had to have had envelopes specially made! The palace still belongs to the Baroni-Ricasoli.

On the RH side of Via Maggio, at nos. 16-18, lies Palazzo Machiavelli, which once belonged to a branch of the famous statesman's family. Part of the ground floor of this palace now houses S. Mark's English Church. A sculpture of S. Mark by Jason Arkles (resident sculptor at the time of writing) graces a niche on the external façade. The church was created in the 1870s by John Roddam Stanhope Spencer. The Pre-Raphaelite decoration survives practically intact, though the 1966 flood took its toll – the brown watermark on the font shows the height reached by the flood-waters. Services are held here regularly (see www.stmarksitaly.com or tel. 055 294 764), and there's also a resident opera company (see www.concertoclassico.info or tel. 340 811 9192). One treasure that the church possesses is a chalice incorporating the engagement ring of Holman Hunt's widow (Spencer was a disciple of Holman Hunt).

On the LH side of the street at nos. 13-15 lived Marchese Cosimo Ridolfi (1794-1865), a politician, financier and philanthropist. There is a plaque commemorating him on no. 15. The Ridolfi family, who have owned the palace since the 15th century, still live here. Opposite nos. 13-15, at no. 26 on the R, is Palazzo di Bianca Cappello. The property, which had been bought in 1567 by Bianca's husband, Piero di Zanobi Buonaventuri, was restored and embellished by Grand Duke Francesco I for the beautiful Bianca, who became his mistress and, eventually, his wife. Bernardo Buontalenti designed the kneeling windows and placed the Cappello coat-of-arms over the door, while the sgraffiti decorations of *c.* 1579 were done by Bernardino Poccetti. The swans within the oval panels are a reference to Bianca's name. The scrolls surmounting the ovals bear the motto *non minus candore quam cantu et vaticinio sacer* 'not less sacred in candour than in song and prophecy'. The candour of the swan was considered by Theocritus to be a particularly feminine characteristic.

Some convenient deaths

There may have been dastardly deeds committed in connection with the open and infamous liaison between Grand Duke Francesco I and the beautiful Venetian Bianca Cappello. Bianca was married to a bank clerk, Piero Buonaventuri, but he (conveniently) got killed in a street fight. Francesco then (kindly) took Bianca under his wing and his sheets. In 1576 she bore him an illegitimate son, Don Antonio de' Medici. In 1578 Francesco's wife, Joanna of Austria, died, and just two months later Bianca became the new Duchess. Francesco legitimized Don Antonio and his succession, but then, while Cardinal Ferdinando de' Medici was visiting his brother the Grand Duke at Poggio a Caiano in 1587, both Francesco and his Grand Duchess died suddenly within hours of each other, ostensibly of malaria. Francesco's body was returned to Florence for a state burial, but Bianca's corpse was consigned to obscurity. She was not mourned by the Florentines, who had considered her to be a witch, and rumours were rife that she had faked her pregnancy and the birth of Antonio, rumours which Ferdinando took no pains to refute. Ferdinando overruled Antonio's claim to the throne, chucked away his cardinal's hat, and took over as Grand Duke, though he treated his nephew kindly and accorded him some honours later in life. William Wetmore Story, an American sculptor resident in Florence in the 19th century, has left an account of the exhumation, in 1857, of the bodies buried in the Chapel of the Princes at S. Lorenzo (Walk 6). Forty-nine corpses were examined, and it was found that some had been robbed and some attacked by vermin. The smell was apparently so dreadful that one of the people involved in opening the coffins died. Those corpses that had not been violated still had their jewelled and gold-embroidered clothes, their armour and their jewellery. Some were in a fair state of preservation, others in awful states of putrefaction. The two bodies which were best preserved were those of Joanna of Austria, wife of Francesco I, and their daughter Anna. They looked, says Story, as if they had only just died, and so, he adds, the rumour that ran through Florence at the time of their deaths was corroborated – that they had been poisoned and that the arsenic had preserved their bodies.

Take the next turning on the R, Via de' Michelozzi, which leads to Piazza S. Spirito, one of the most attractive squares in Florence and the scene of a small market. There are cafés and restaurants here, if you fancy a break. The church of S. Spirito lies on your R as you enter the piazza (remember that it closes between 12 noon and 4pm).

The church of S. Spirito

The Augustinians had a monastery on this site from the mid-13th century onwards, which was renowned as a great centre of learning. Boccaccio bequeathed his library to the monastery on his death in 1375, and Petrarch's education was strongly influenced by his contacts with the Augustinians here. Towards the end of the 14th century, the monks decided that they'd like a new church and, in 1397, the Commune allocated a sum of money for this purpose. To help with finances, the monks sacrificed one meal a day! Despite funds being allocated, however, it was thirty years before a works committee was appointed in 1428. The commission for the design of the new church went to Brunelleschi. His 'plan A' was for a building facing N on to a huge piazza extending to the Arno. Unsurprisingly, he encountered opposition, not least from citizens whose properties would have to be demolished to make way for this. In the end he had to settle for 'plan B', a S-facing church at right-angles to the old one. This design was accepted in 1434 and the foundations of the choir were laid in 1436, but work was then delayed until 1444.

Brunelleschi died in 1446, but his intentions were carried through (more or less) by a succession of architects and master-builders. Construction proceeded slowly for a quarter of a century, with the new church gradually taking shape alongside the old one, which was still in use. In March 1471, during the performance of a passion play, a fire broke out in the old church (which contained works by, among others, Cimabue, Giottino, Agnolo and Taddeo Gaddi and Simone Martini), causing irreparable damage. Tragic as this was, it did at least act as a catalyst for work on the new church. In 1479 Salvi d' Andrea's design for the dome was approved, and in 1487 the inner façade was completed, again to a design by d' Andrea. In both cases he departed from Brunelleschi's original conception, as we shall see when we visit the interior. In 1489 Giuliano da Sangallo gained the commission for the sacristy, and in 1491 the barrel-vaulted vestibule linking church and sacristy was started in collaboration with Il Cronaca. The dome of the sacristy was constructed in 1496 on a design by Antonio del Pollaiuolo. It collapsed first time round and had to be reconstructed in 1497. In 1503 work began on a new campanile to a design by Baccio d' Agnolo. Work on the monastery continued through the 16th and into the 17th century under Bartolommeo Ammannati, Alfonso Parigi, Alfonso's son Giulio, and Giulio's son Alfonso. The lantern and ball over the church dome were set in place in 1602, and the external façade of the church was constructed in 1792. It originally had painted decoration, but this was destroyed during a 20th century 'restoration'. From foundations to façade, the church had taken 356 years to build. I'll leave you to work out how many strokes of the works clock that added up to. The clock was struck every half-hour during the working day, and the man who tended it and kept the employment record got a bonus of one florin every six months.

S. Spirito is built on a Latin cross plan. The aisles on each side of the nave are part of a continuous arcade, carried on thirty-one columns and the four pillars of the dome, that runs right round the transepts and the choir. As each column was erected the stone-cutters were permitted to pass the booze round, and when the last column was in place they were treated to bread, sausages and four flasks of wine! Brunelleschi had wanted the arcade to run unbroken across the inner façade, and his plans provided for four entrance doors here to give access to the four bays that would have resulted from this. However, such a departure from tradition gave rise to heated arguments once construction had progressed this far, with Giuliano da Sangallo and Paolo Toscanelli (a famous geometrician who'd been a friend of Brunelleschi) advocating four doors, and Giuliano da Maiano and Salvi d' Andrea preferring three. The matter was put to the vote and tradition won the day. Sangallo, who was out of Florence on the day of the vote, was mortified and wrote to Lorenzo Il Magnifico, imploring him to intervene and prevent such an outrageous departure from the master's original plan. His letter had no effect and the façade was completed to Salvi d' Andrea's design in 1487. The design of the stained glass in the oculus window, depicting the descent of the Holy Spirit, is by Perugino.

The interior of S. Spirito is characterized by a geometric rigour and clarity which results in the most marvellous perspectival vistas. The use of pietra serena to articulate the architectural details against the white plastered walls heightens the effect. The columns of the colonnade and the corresponding half-columns set against the outer walls divide the arcade into forty bays, each bay having a dome and a semi-circular recess on the outer edge. These recesses house family chapels. According to Brunelleschi's design, the semi-circular walls of the chapels should have been visible from the outside, but at some stage during the construction process a decision was taken to enclose the entire fabric of the building within rectilinear walls. This doesn't affect the design of the interior, but, compounded with the change from four to three doors in the façade, it does mean that the exterior of the church looks nothing like Brunelleschi intended it to be.

Salvi d' Andrea's melon dome departs from Brunelleschi's design insofar as it is raised on a drum. Beneath the dome is Giovanni Battista Caccini's elaborate Baroque altar, complete with ciborium and baldacchino, installed in 1608. A confection of coloured marbles and semi-precious stones, it is a fine work in its own right, but it sits badly in this Brunelleschian church and disrupts the harmony of the architecture. The altar which it replaced was the one for which Michelangelo made his wooden Crucifix in 1494. This work, now housed in the sacristy, was carved as a gift for the prior. He had secretly provided bodies from the monastery's infirmary for Michelangelo to dissect, and had made available a room in which to prosecute this, highly illegal, activity.

The altarpieces and sculptures gracing the chapels around the arcade of S. Spirito constitute a veritable art gallery. The works are all labelled, so to give a complete list here would be otiose. Two, however, merit special attention. The Nerli Chapel in the R transept houses Filippino Lippi's Nerli altarpiece (c. 1495). The donors were Tanai Nerli and his wife Nanna, and the painting records an event in their lives. On 5th November 1494, Tanai was sent by the Signoria, along with four other ambassadors, to negotiate with Charles VIII of France. He returned on 11th November, the feast of S. Martin of Tours (shown on the L), and an accord between Charles and Florence was signed on 25th November, the feast of S. Catherine (shown on the R). In the background, Tanai, just returned from his mission, greets his family outside his home. The Porta S. Frediano (Walk 13), through which he would just have ridden, is shown behind. Nanna Nerli was aunt to the famous Piero di Gino Capponi, who responded to Charles VIII in such proverbial terms. The story of the threat posed by Charles, and of Capponi's response, is told under the section entitled 'the French come to Florence' at the end of Walk 13. In one of the chapels on the wall behind the high altar, note the depiction of the original 7-bay façade of the Pitti Palace in the predella of an altarpiece by Alessandro Allori.

From the L aisle, a door leads under the organ to the vestibule and sacristy by Giuliano da Sangallo and Il Cronaca. The barrel-vault of the vestibule is of a type derived by Sangallo from his studies of ancient vaulting, whereby concrete was poured over the moulded panels to form a bonded monolithic whole. Sangallo had used this system too in Lorenzo Il Magnifico's villa at Poggio a Caiano, having wisely tested it first in his own house. The door at the S end of the vestibule leads to the 17th century Chiostro de' Morti, by Giulio Parigi and his son Alfonso. Sangallo's sacristy (with dome by Antonio del Pollaiuolo) houses, among other works, the wooden Crucifix by Michelangelo referred to above.

The Fondazione Salvatore Romano

The only part of the old Gothic Augustinian monastery to survive is the 14th century refectory, which lies beside the church at no. 29 (on the L as you look at the façade). The refectory now houses the Fondazione Salvatore Romano. Left to the city of Florence by Romano in 1946, this eclectic collection of close on fifty pieces comprises statuary and reliefs ranging in date from Pre-Romanesque to Mannerist. Just to give you a flavour, my favourites are the 11th century Lombard architectural fragments showing human figures, a 13th century marble head of a lion, a 14th century little stone bear on a capital, a marble caryatid by Tino di Camaino (1270s-1330s) and a late 16th century pietra serena statue of a dog. Also in the refectory is a fresco of the Crucifixion by Andrea Orcagna and Nardo di Cione.

Piazza S. Spirito to S. Felice, the Casa Guidi and 'La Specola' Museum

Halfway along the NW side of Piazza S. Spirito (on the R if the church is behind you) is a plaque bearing a directive from the eight Signori, those law and order officials whose decrees feature in some of the other walks. Here they prohibit the ball game of pallottole in the piazza – they really were rotten old kill-joys.

On the corner of the piazza at the opposite end from the church (on the L if the church is behind you) stands Palazzo Guadagni, built for Rinieri Dei at the beginning of the 16th century. Rinieri served as a diplomat in Naples and the Near East, and made a fortune from the silk trade. Between 1502 and 1505 he bought up a series of properties on this corner, and his architect, most probably Il Cronaca, encased them in a unified façade. The ground floor is of dressed ashlar, and the first and second floors of stucco (originally

adorned with sgraffiti decoration by Andrea del Sarto). Note the magnificent wooden doors carved with rows of roses, the emblem of the Dei, and the superb wrought-iron lamp at the corner, attributed to Caparra. The masonry of the lovely ogival frames and voussoirs is carefully graded, becoming finer as it rises. The whole is topped by a loggia under a great overhanging roof. With the extinction of the Dei family in the 17th century the palace passed to the Guadagni. The last of the Dei family line left his estate to the Buonuomini di S. Martino, and the palace was sold at auction after lunch on Thursday 29th July 1683, 'to the sound of trumpets' according to a document in the Buonuomini archives, in front of the door of the Oratory of S. Martino (Walk 4). The highest bidder was the Marchese Donato Maria Guadagni, who paid 7,001 ducats for the property. The Guadagni family and their heirs have owned the palace ever since.

Leave Piazza S. Spirito on Via Mazzetta, which runs alongside the Palazzo Guadagni, and continue up to Piazza di S. Felice. On your R just before you enter the piazza is the flank of the church of S. Felice, and on your L, at first floor level and supported on corbels, is the balcony of Casa Guidi and the windows of Robert Browning's study. Casa Guidi was the home of Robert Browning and Elizabeth Barrett Browning from 1847 until Elizabeth's death in 1861, and they were visited here by numerous literary figures. The apartment has been furnished as closely as possible to the original and evokes beautifully the spirit of its famous occupants. It is worth a visit if you are a Browning enthusiast, but the opening times are somewhat restricted. The entry is at no. 8 Piazza di S. Felice.

The church of S. Felice has a façade by Michelozzo (1457). The church houses a Crucifix attributed to Giotto and his workshop, as well as several other interesting works of art (there is an information board in English inside). Just off the piazza in Via Romana (which runs off to the R as you exit from the church), in the Palazzo Torrigiani at no. 17 blue on the L, is the museum known as 'La Specola' from the astronomical observatory founded here in the 18th century by Grand Duke Pietro Leopoldo. On the second floor is the Tribuna di Galileo, erected by Leopoldo II in 1841 in honour of the great scientist. On the fourth floor is the Zoological Museum (there is a lift). If stuffed creatures aren't your thing, you'll probably want to give this a miss, but that would be a shame because the collections here are really splendid, with exhibits ranging from tapeworms to tigers, protozoa to pangolins, rats to rhinos and molluscs to man – don't worry, the taxidermist hasn't got hold of man yet! The huge collection of birds includes one resembling a dodo called a 'Becco a Scarpa'. There's also a collection of anatomical models – not for the squeamish.

Felicitous festivities at S. Felice

In April 1533, when Margaret of Austria, the future bride of Duke Alessandro de' Medici, passed through Florence on her way to Naples, many lavish spectacles were staged in her honour (see Walk 6 for the 'girandola' in the Piazza S. Lorenzo). One was a religious presentation, a 'sacra rappresentazione' of the Annunciation to the Virgin Mary, at the church of S. Felice. An elaborate stage machinery was erected across the transepts, with the Virgin in her chamber shown on one side. An angel appeared and called on numerous prophets and sibyls to come forth and recite their prophecies regarding the birth of Christ. After these recitals, the 'sky' opened to reveal the Angel Gabriel amid a heavenly host. Lights and lilies appeared around the chamber, and Gabriel announced to the Virgin the news that she was to bear the Son of God - a felicitous theme for a future bride.

Piazza di S. Felice and Piazza Pitti

On exiting from 'La Specola' turn R back into Piazza di S. Felice. The marble column now in the centre of the piazza was first set up by Cosimo I in 1572 to commemorate his victory over Siena and to mark part of his processional route. It was removed to the Boboli Gardens by Leopoldo II in 1838 and

returned here in 1992. Continue straight on to Piazza Pitti. On your L at no. 7 blue, you'll see a marker over the door bearing the number 1,702. This is not a year date, but an old house number. There used to be a single system for the entire city, only reformed in 1865, with numbers reaching into the 8,000s. Who'd have been a 19th century postman!

The huge Pitti Palace lies over to your R. If you visited S. Spirito earlier, you may have seen, in the predella of the altarpiece in the Pitti Chapel there, a depiction of the original palace with its 7-bay façade. Built for Luca Pitti in the 15th century, it remained incomplete on his death in 1472 and fell into disrepair. In the mid-16th century it was bought by Eleonora di Toledo, wife of Cosimo I, and Bartolommeo Ammannati was commissioned to enlarge and upgrade it into a residence suitable for the ducal family. He left the

original 7-bay façade virtually intact and added lateral wings, finished in stucco, running back towards the gardens. In the early 17th century Giulio Parigi and his son, Alfonso, extended the façade even further. The lateral wings sweeping forwards around Piazza Pitti were added later, in the 18th and 19th centuries. The palace was the seat of the ruling families of Tuscany from the 16th century through to 1919, when Vittorio Emanuele III presented it to the state and it was organized as a museum/gallery. Views on the design of the building vary. George Eliot considered the palace a wonderful union of Cyclopean massiveness with stately regularity. Arnold Bennett, on the other hand, thought it looked like a barracks.

Badly behaved guests
During the 18th and 19th centuries, balls were held regularly at the Pitti Palace. In 1740 Horace Walpole commented on how the ladies present would stuff comfits into their pockets and every other available space. Roughly a century later things hadn't changed. Thomas Trollope relates how the English guests would empty plates of bonbons into their handkerchiefs or pockets. Italian guests went even further, bundling up large portions of fish, ham and poultry in newspapers or napkins, and even wrapping up jellies! The Americans, apparently, behaved better.

On the opposite side of the piazza to the palace, high up on the L corner of the narrow street called Sdrucciolo de' Pitti, a smaller dwelling bears the Pitti coat-of-arms, a reminder, if one were needed, that pride often comes before a fall. Our walk ends here, giving you the opportunity to visit some of the museums housed in the Pitti Palace should you wish to do so. These are described below, after the coda to Walk 12, and include the Palatine Gallery, the Gallery of Modern Art and the Argenti Museum. The Carriage

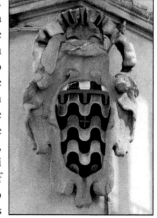

Museum has been closed for several years. The Porcelain and Costume Museums, which are accessed from the Boboli Gardens, are described under Walk 15, which brings you down through the gardens and which also ends here. I mention this because, at the time of writing, a dual ticket system was in operation. One ticket was needed for the Bardini and Boboli Gardens, and a separate one was required for the Palatine Gallery, the Gallery of Modern Art and the Argenti Museum. If this system still prevails, and if you intend to do Walk 15, you may prefer to concentrate your attention on the art galleries now rather than on the gardens. The tour of the gardens in Walk 15 begins at their upper entrance, but if you want to visit them now, all you have to do on entering from the lower entrance is, once you're at the rear of the palace, mount the axis rising up through the Amphitheatre to the statue of Plenty, and join the itinerary there (see page 327 onwards and the plan on page 329). If you don't wish to visit any museums at the moment, you can still gain entry to the palace courtyard, where you'll find a café, shop and toilets. Don't miss the charming memorial on the wall at the end of the colonnade outside the shop. It commemorates one of the mules who toiled here when building works were in progress. A delightful relief shows her at work, and the Latin inscription tells us that she carried, conveyed, dragged and bore litters/pallets, stones, marbles, timber and columns.

On exiting from the Pitti Palace, you can turn R and follow the road down to the Ponte Vecchio. Alternatively, if you have any energy left, you can take the following 30 minute stroll, a coda to Walk 12, which takes you through attractive streets, past mediaeval towers and handsome palaces, and brings you out on the Lungarno.

Coda to Walk 12

On exiting from the Pitti Palace turn R. Opposite the end of the lateral wing of the palace, a plaque on the building at no. 18 records the house of Toscanelli (1397-1482), the greatest geographer of his day. At no. 22, a plaque marks the house where Dostoyevsky stayed while writing *The Idiot* in 1868. Turn L down Via dello Sprone and then R down Via de' Ramaglianti. This leads to Borgo S. Jacopo, which retains many of its mediaeval towers. The magnificent Torre de' Belfredelli is on your R. A cul-de-sac opposite leads to a terrace overlooking the Arno, with views of the Ponte Vecchio to the R (see the illustration on page 102) and the Ponte S. Trinità to the L. The campanile of SS. Apostoli (Walk 3) can be seen opposite. On returning to Borgo S. Jacopo turn R, noting the Barbadori towers on your R at the corner. On the L side of the borgo,

between Via Toscanella and Via de' Sapiti, is the Torre de' Marsili (see the illustration on page 24), with a della Robbian terracotta of the Annunciation over the door. Just beyond Via de' Sapiti, the church of S. Jacopo sopra' Arno lies on the R. Next to the church is the ex-oratory of the Compagnia di S. Jacopo.

Borgo S. Jacopo leads to Piazza de' Frescobaldi, where we were earlier. Note the attractive fountain on the corner on the L. Continue straight on into Via di S. Spirito, a lovely street lined with handsome palaces. On the L immediately beyond Via de' Coverelli lie properties belonging to the Frescobaldi family. Over the arch to no. 11 can be seen a copy of Giambologna's 'little bronze devil', of which more in Walk 13. Inside the palace, a portrait of Dianora Salviati, wife of Bartolomeo de' Frescobaldi, apparently bears an inscription telling us that this lady had a total of fifty-two children, and never less than three at a time! On the L at no. 23 is Palazzo Manetti, home of Sir Horace Mann in the 18th century, when he was English envoy at the Court. Note the wine hatches here to either side of the door (see Walk 3 for their purpose). Immediately past Palazzo Manetti, on the near corner of Via de' Geppi on the R, is Torre Lanfredini.

Turn R down Via de' Geppi to Piazza Scarlatti on the Lungarno. Across the river is the huge 17th century Palazzo Corsini, home to one of the greatest private art collections in the city. Near the R end of its façade you may be

CHE QUI EBBERO I COMPAGNI LE CASE
DEMOLITE ALLA FINE DEL SECOLO XVII
PER DARE LUOGO AL PALAZIO DEI CORSINI
DEGNO E SI RICORDI
PERCHE IN ESSE
DINO COMPAGNI
TERZO GONFALONIERE DELLA REPUBBLICA
CON CUORE DI CITTADINO
E MENTE D' ISTORICO
DESCRISSE DAL VERO
I TEMPI SUOI E DI DANTE

able to see a small plaque, though I defy you to read it at this distance. It tells you that on this site was the home of our old friend Dino Compagni, demolished to make way for the palazzo. To the R lies the Ponte S. Trinità, the most direct route back if you wish to return to the area of Piazza della Repubblica/Piazza del Duomo. To the L is the Ponte alla Carraia, which provides the quickest route back to the area around S. Maria Novella.

The Museums of the Pitti Palace complex

<u>The Palatine Gallery</u>

The Palatine Gallery occupies twenty-eight rooms on the first floor of the Pitti Palace. Here you'll find a treasure-trove of pieces, including paintings by Filippo and Filippino Lippi, Botticelli, Perugino, Luca Signorelli, Andrea del Sarto, Pontormo, Rosso Fiorentino, Giorgione, Fra Bartolomeo, Ridolfo del Ghirlandaio, Raphael, Titian, Veronese, Tintoretto, Alessandro Allori, Caravaggio, Rubens, Anthony Van Dyck, Murillo and many more. You proceed directly from the Gallery to the rooms that constituted the Royal Apartments. From the 17th century onwards, these rooms were the residence of the Medici, Lorraine and Savoy ruling houses. Here are more art works, plus gilt, stucco, mirrors, chandeliers, damask wall coverings, fabulous carpets and elaborate furnishings. One caveat - E. V. Lucas, in his early 20th century guidebook *A Wanderer in Florence*, noted that the walls of the Palatine Gallery were very congested and many of the pictures difficult to see – a century later, not much has changed.

The Gallery of Modern Art

Do not be deceived by the name of this Gallery, housed in thirty rooms on the second floor of the Pitti Palace (with very good views). Everything is relative, and 'Modern' in this context means anything from 1750 through to the 20th century. As well as paintings, there are sculptures by Antonio Canova, Lorenzo Bartolini, Giovanni Dupré and others. There are some superb works here, so suck it and see – I don't believe that you'll regret the experience.

The Argenti Museum

Housed in a series of spectacularly decorated rooms accessed directly from one corner of the Pitti Palace courtyard, this museum exhibits an array of treasures amassed by the Medici and Lorraine ruling houses. Here you'll see precious and semi-precious stone vases that once belonged to Piero the Gouty and Lorenzo Il Magnifico, many of them incised with 'Laur. Med.'. It always thrills me to think that Piero and Lorenzo actually handled and admired these pieces. There are works of rock crystal and lapis lazuli that were owned by Duke Francesco I. There are reliquaries, jewels, stunning pieces of inlaid furniture, amazing examples of carved amber, objects of silver, gold, mother-of-pearl and shell, and a collection of Chinese and Japanese porcelain, while the collections of ivories and cameos include pieces that defy description.

View from the Ponte S. Trinità downstream to the Ponte alla Carraia

Walk 13

Begins and ends at Piazza della Repubblica.

Takes in: the Brancacci Chapel at the church of S. Maria del Carmine and the Marino Marini Museum with the Cappella del S. Sepolcro.

Duration: 2 hours for the full walk and 1 hour 30 minutes for the shorter version, excluding time spent at the above. The shorter walk misses out the Porta S. Frediano and the Ponte Amerigo Vespucci. If you have pre-booked tickets for the Brancacci Chapel, you should allow *c.* 50 minutes from Piazza della Repubblica to the Carmine complex. Allow *c.* 1 hour each for the Carmine complex and the Marino Marini Museum.

Tips: you do not always need to pre-book tickets for the Brancacci Chapel, depending on the time of day and the season that you visit, so do not be put off doing this walk simply because you haven't booked in advance.

Piazza della Repubblica to Piazza Strozzi

Leave Piazza della Repubblica under the huge arch on its W side and head along Via degli Strozzi. On the near R corner of the first crossroads lies

Palazzo Vecchietti. Just above head height on the corner of the palazzo is a cast of Giambologna's 'little bronze devil' (the original is in the Bardini Museum; Walk 14). The 'devil' is actually a satyr, originally one of a pair of standard-holders made for Bernardo Vecchietti. It came to be identified as the devil because legend has it that this was the spot where the black horse who disrupted S. Peter Martyr's preaching disappeared (see Walk 1). Continue along to Piazza Strozzi, from the corner of which there's a fine view of the huge palace begun in the late 1480s for Filippo Strozzi, who, alas, died in 1491, so never saw his dream home!

The accounts for the building of the Strozzi Palace, the largest private residence built in Florence to that date, survive complete, and the names of Benedetto da Maiano, Giuliano da Sangallo and Il Cronaca are all connected with the project. Sangallo's model survives and corresponds more or less with the appearance of the façades as eventually executed. However, Il Cronaca heightened the elevations to allow for internal vaulting, and designed the huge cornice (never finished). The three storeys (the upper two with bifore windows) are all rusticated, the articulation gradually diminishing from ground floor to top. The arrangement of the rustication was carefully

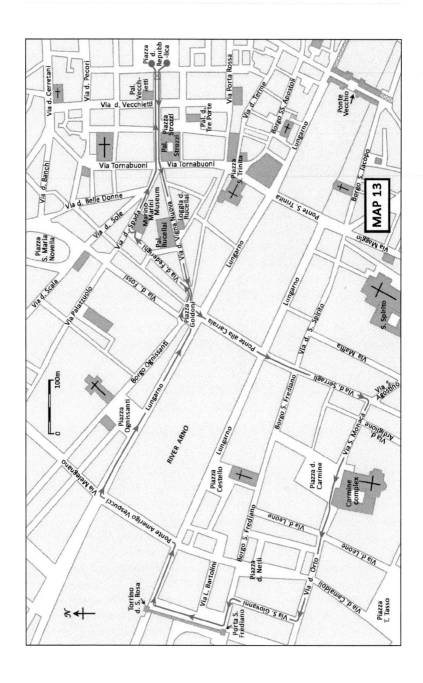

MAP 13

predetermined for maximum aesthetic effect. The huge rounded portals, one placed centrally on each side, lead through to one of the most magnificent courtyards in Florence. Luca Landucci tells us in his *Diary* that on 18th July 1495 the first row of windows was finished. On 29th October the same year Luca records that the crane which drew up the stones fell towards S. Trinità, one of the ropes having broken, but nobody was hurt. On 16th November 1500 the four great lanterns, forged by Niccolò Grosso Caparra, were placed at the corners of the building, each one costing 100 gold florins. Alas, on 3rd September 1512 the palace was struck by lightning and Mariotto da Balatro, a master-builder who was on the roof checking out a leak, was killed. Work on the palace ceased in the 1530s when political events brought the Strozzi into conflict with the Medici. The palace is now owned by the State and is used for exhibitions.

Problems of urban development

It is, perhaps, worth emphasizing that the construction of edifices on the scale of many of the private palaces of Florence often changed the character of a neighbourhood and led to problems of relocation for those displaced. Legislation was introduced on occasions to try to address the issue. In 1474, for example, and again in 1489 and 1494, tax relief was offered for every dwelling constructed on previously unbuilt land. Building works could also be highly disruptive. Luca Landucci, whose *Diary* we have referred to on several of the walks, had his apothecary's shop just opposite the Palazzo Strozzi on the erstwhile Piazza de' Tornaquinci, which was largely swallowed up by the new building. He records the foundations of the palace being dug in the summer of 1489 and tells us that, due to the necessary demolition works, the streets all around were filled with heaps of stones and rubbish, and with mules and donkeys who were carrying the debris away and bringing gravel in. The local shopkeepers were, apparently, continually annoyed by the dust and by the crowds of people who collected to look on.

Before leaving Palazzo Strozzi, note the plaque set into the rusticated stonework of the ground floor at the RH end of the façade facing the piazza. It informs you that in October 1762 the city officials in charge of such matters prohibited all manner of tradesmen, including second-hand clothes merchants, scrap-metal dealers, and sellers of water melons, melons and other fruits, from hawking their wares in Piazza Strozzi. Anyone caught transgressing this law would be fined 5 lire for each and every violation. All trading, unloading and bargaining was, from this date forward, to be confined to Piazza S. Maria Novella. I'm not sure if the law has ever been revoked, but perhaps we should warn the book-seller who regularly plies his trade at a stall here.

Piazza Strozzi to Piazzetta Rucellai

Continue along Via degli Strozzi to the junction with Via Tornabuoni. This was the site of the W gate of the Roman town. Cross over Via Tornabuoni to the forked junction between Via della Spada (on the R) and Via della Vigna Nuova (on the L). The palace on the irregular site between these two streets was, from 1614, the home of Sir Robert Dudley, Duke of Northumberland, who, on fleeing England, became a naval engineer and took charge of the Arsenal at Livorno for Grand Dukes Cosimo II and Ferdinando II. There's a plaque to this effect on Via della Vigna Nuova. Several of Dudley's instruments can be seen in the Galileo Museum (Walk 9). The house at the corner on the other side of Via della Vigna Nuova marks the site of the erstwhile Pension Suisse, where George Eliot was staying in 1860 when the idea came to her for her novel *Romola*. She said of the Pension Suisse that it was the quietest hotel in Florence, chosen to get clear of the stream of English and Americans who made the city seem like 'a perpetual noisy picnic.' Perhaps we'd better move along!

Follow Via della Vigna Nuova until you reach a small triangular piazzetta where, on your L, you'll see the arched Loggia de' Rucellai (now occupied by shops). The Palazzo Rucellai is on your R. Giovanni di Paolo de' Rucellai (1403-81) was a highly respected statesman and intellectual, and one of the wealthiest businessmen in Europe. The design of both the loggia and the palace are attributed to Leon Battista Alberti. In 1466 Giovanni's son, Bernardo de' Rucellai, was married to Piero the Gouty's daughter Nannina, a match that was something of a political coup for Giovanni. The loggia acted as the backdrop to the wedding. It is decorated with a frieze combining Giovanni's emblem of the billowing sail with Piero de' Medici's emblem of a diamond ring with feathers. The wedding feast lasted three days and nights, during which time 260 capons, 500 geese, 260 ducks and 1,500 chickens were consumed, along with 120 barrels of wine.

The façade of the Palazzo Rucellai is of pietra forte, the rustication being incised into the stonework for aesthetic purposes alone, independent of the actual joints. Alberti utilized classical architectural orders, with pilasters, friezes, and portals with architraves in the Roman manner. The friezes articulating the storeys again bear Giovanni's emblem of the billowing sail (upper frieze) and Piero's emblem of the rings (lower frieze). Interlocking rings also embellish the arched bifore windows. There is a colonnaded rooftop loggia, but it's set back so as not to disturb the proportions of the façade. Note that the rustication is unfinished at the RH end of the façade, so Giovanni clearly hoped to extend!

Piazzetta Rucellai to Piazza del Carmine

Continue along Via della Vigna Nuova to Piazza Goldoni, and cross over the Ponte alla Carraia, from which there is a fine view upstream of Ponte S. Trinità, with the Ponte Vecchio behind. Ponte S. Trinità was destroyed in 1557 by a flood and Cosimo I commissioned Bartolommeo Ammannati to rebuild it. The bridge formed part of Cosimo's processional route commemorating his victories over Siena and at the Battle of Montemurlo, so it was of particular concern to him. He had Vasari discuss the designs for the bridge with Michelangelo in Rome before its construction by Ammannati in 1567-70. The three graceful elliptical arches are an ingenious solution to a practical problem. The number of piers is reduced and the centre of each arch is as high as possible above the river, both factors lessening the risk of a

 repeat of flood damage. Note the 'Capricorn' keystone at the apex of the central arch; similar stones can be seen in the courtyard of the Pitti Palace. This is a nice nod to Cosimo, who became Duke under this zodiacal sign. Many say that Ponte S. Trinità is the most beautiful bridge in the world. Its importance to the Florentines can be gauged from the fact that after World War II it was carefully restored to exactly how it had been before, using original drawings, types of tools and methods of construction, and as many of the original stones as could be salvaged, with others replaced from the same quarries. Funding for the project came from popular subscription.

As for the bridge we're standing on, it too has its history. Giovanni Villani tells us in his *Chronicle* (VII.34) of the great flood of 1st October 1269, when a great part of Florence became a lake because wood brought down by the river got caught and lay across the foot of the Ponte S. Trinità. Eventually, the force was so great that the bridge collapsed, and the ensuing rush of water and timber struck and destroyed the Ponte alla Carraia. Disaster struck again in 1304, when a huge crowd was gathered on the bridge to watch a

mystery play entitled 'Inferno' being enacted on the river below. The Arno
was crammed with boats and rafts carrying performers dressed as demons
and their victims. Alas, the bridge collapsed under the weight of the crowd
and many people were killed, reaching their Inferno somewhat sooner than
expected. Perhaps we should get a move on!

At the end of Ponte alla Carraia continue
straight on along the attractive Via de' Serragli.
On the near RH side of the crossroads with Via
S. Agostino and Via S. Monaca is a tabernacle
containing a Madonna and Child with saints by
Lorenzo di Bicci (1427). This corner was called
'Canto alla Cuculia' ('Corner of the Cuckoo')
and Lorenzo has depicted the Christ Child
holding a cuckoo. Turn R at the crossroads down
Via S. Monaca. A few yards along on the L is
Via dell' Ardiglione. If you fancy a short detour
here, just beyond the arch over the street stands
the house where Filippo Lippi was born in 1406
(marked with a plaque). Otherwise continue
along Via S. Monaca to Piazza del Carmine.

Carryings on in the cloisters

Filippo Lippi was orphaned at an early age and subsequently reared by an aunt who put him into the monastery at the Carmine when he was eight years old. There he learnt to paint, and his fresco showing the Rule of the Order survives at the Carmine complex. However, a monkish life didn't suit Filippo. He left the Order about a decade later and subsequently ran off with a nun. In all fairness to Filippo and his nun, it should be stressed that convents were often the lot of many a young woman with little or no devotional calling. In an age when dowries had to be given with daughters in marriage, it was cheaper to place female offspring inside conventual walls – and the criminal records of the city reveal that such walls were a tempting target for many a high-spirited youth. For example, in 1421 three young men scaled the walls of the convent of S. Silvestro and, for two hours, ran amok through the rooms, searching for a girl named Dorotea, terrorizing the other nuns and threatening the abbess. Unsuccessful, they finally quitted the convent and fled the city to avoid paying the 1,600 lire fine. The danger, however, sometimes came from within, as anyone who has read Boccaccio will know (*Decameron* III.1 and IX.2). So bad was the problem that a special magistracy was set up with authority to inspect nunneries, ensure their proper governance and punish offenders. To qualify for office in this magistracy, a man had to be married and over fifty years of age!

The Carmine complex – the Brancacci Chapel

As you enter Piazza del Carmine, the great church of S. Maria del Carmine with its famous Brancacci Chapel stands on your L. In 1690 the chapel escaped demolition thanks to the efforts of Grand Duke Cosimo III's mum and the Accademia del Disegno – we have much to thank them for. There was another near disaster in 1771, when the 13th-14th century church was almost completely destroyed by fire - only the sacristy and two chapels (one being the Brancacci) survived. You enter the Carmine complex to the R of the church façade via the cloister, where there are toilets and a shop. Only the Brancacci Chapel, with its wonderful frescoes of the life of S. Peter, is described here, though other rooms are sometimes open. At busy periods entry to the chapel is restricted and you are only allowed to remain there for a set time, so you may prefer to read the following paragraphs before entering in order to use that time fully for fresco gazing.

Felice Brancacci, a statesman and silk merchant, commissioned the frescoes in the 1420s. Masolino and Masaccio worked on them together, but in 1428 Masolino left Florence, followed by Masaccio in 1429. The fresco cycle was not completed until the 1480s, when Filippino Lippi (none other than the son of Filippo and his nun; see the section entitled 'carryings on in the cloisters') took over, carefully integrating his style with that of Masaccio.

There are only two scenes in the chapel that are not taken from the life of S. Peter. These are the Temptation of Adam and Eve by Masolino and the Expulsion from Paradise by Masaccio, and they face one another on the upper registers of the entrance piers. The other scenes are as follows:

Masolino - S. Peter preaching (upper register; L of the altar); S. Peter healing a cripple and raising Tabitha (upper register; R wall).

Masaccio - S. Peter baptizing (upper register; R of the altar); S. Peter distributing alms (lower register; R of the altar); S. Peter healing with his shadow (lower register; L of the altar); The Tribute Money (upper register; L wall); S. Peter enthroned and raising the son of Theophilus - completed by Lippi (lower register; L wall).

Lippi - SS. Peter and Paul before Simon Magus and the Crucifixion of Peter (lower register; R wall); S. Peter liberated from prison (lower register; R entrance pier); S. Paul visiting S. Peter in prison (lower register; L entrance pier).

Masaccio's figures are very sculptural, so it comes as no surprise, perhaps, to learn that Michelangelo practised his drawing here as well as in front of the Giottos at S. Croce (Walk 5). He was not the only one. Many students came to study and copy the frescoes, including Pietro Torrigiano. On one occasion, angered by Michelangelo's teasing, Torrigiano punched him so hard in the face that he broke his nose. Torrigiano subsequently went to England and, among other things, made the effigies for the tomb of Henry VII and Elizabeth of York in Westminster Abbey.

If you are doing the shorter version of this walk, you should omit the next section and retrace your steps back to Piazza Goldoni via the Ponte alla Carraia.

Piazza del Carmine to Piazza Goldoni via the Porta S. Frediano

On exiting from the Carmine turn L and leave Piazza del Carmine on Via dell' Orto. Off to the L runs Via di Camaldoli. We are not going up here, but you may like to know that a few yards along on the L, at no. 7 red, lies the Accademia Bartolomeo Cristofori. Here you'll find a pianoforte museum, restoration workshop, library, and auditorium where are held master-classes and chamber music concerts (www.accademiacristofori.it or tel. 055 221646 for more information). Take the next turning to the R off Via dell' Orto, Via S. Giovanni. On the L at the far end of the street is a tabernacle with a 15th century Madonna and Child with

angels. Opposite the end of Via S. Giovanni, at no. 70 Borgo S. Frediano, is the Galleria Romanelli, the studio and gallery of a dynasty of sculptors. During the first half of the 19th century this was the studio of Lorenzo Bartolini, some of whose works you may have seen in S. Croce (Walk 5). After Bartolini's death the studio was taken over by his pupil, Pasquale Romanelli. This is a magical place, an Aladdin's cave of sculptural pieces, and I strongly urge you to take a look inside; you will receive a warm welcome.

On exiting from the Galleria Romanelli turn R along Borgo S. Frediano. Ahead of you towers the great Porta S. Frediano, with its wooden doors, ironwork and old locks. This towered gateway, built in 1324, guarded the road to Pisa. Through it would have passed countless stonemasons and sculptors, Michelangelo included, on their way to Carrara to seek out marble. Through it too passed the embassy sent to negotiate with King Charles VIII of France in 1494, and through it they returned, as illustrated in Filippino Lippi's Nerli altarpiece in S. Spirito (Walk 12).

Do not go through the Porta S. Frediano, but turn R immediately before it, following the line of the old city walls. The first turning on the R along here is Via L. Bartolini, named after the sculptor mentioned above. If you are interested in the process of silk manufacture you may wish to visit the Antico Setificio Fiorentino, which can be found down here on the L at no. 4 and which continues to operate using 18th century looms, machines and

techniques. Otherwise keep straight on, following the city walls along to the
Torrino di S. Rosa. Here you turn R along the Lungarno to the modern Ponte
Amerigo Vespucci, named after the Medici agent in Seville who, following
the route of Christopher Columbus, made two voyages to America, one in
1499 and one in 1501, and subsequently gave his name to the continent.
Turn L over the bridge. This is a good spot for ornithologists, with a variety
of water-birds to be seen. On the weir you may see a heron fishing. I've been
lucky enough to spot kingfishers too. At the end of the bridge turn R and
follow the Lungarno along past Piazza Ognissanti to Piazza Goldoni, where
we were earlier.

Piazza Goldoni to the Marino Marini Museum and Cappella del S. Sepolcro
Leave Piazza Goldoni on Via de' Federighi (the next street round anti-
clockwise from Via della Vigna Nuova, by which we entered the piazza
before). Continue up to Piazza S. Pancrazio, where, on your R, you'll see the
deconsecrated church of S. Pancrazio, its porch designed by Leon Battista
Alberti. The church now houses the Marino Marini Museum, with works
by the sculptor (1901-1980) that he left to the city of Florence. This was
Giovanni de' Rucellai's parish church and he wanted to be buried here, so
he commissioned Alberti to design a burial chapel. Even if you don't wish
to look at Marino Marini's sculptures, you should go into the museum to
see this. The barrel-vaulted chapel, with pilasters, entablature and arches in
pietra serena, houses Giovanni's exquisite inlaid marble tomb. He intended
it to be an exact replica of the Sanctuary of the Holy Sepulchre in Jerusalem,

and, being one of the wealthiest businessmen in Europe, actually sent agents there to obtain the necessary information and measurements. The tomb is like a marble-encrusted reliquary, a gem not to be missed. The inscription over the door into the tomb records a papal bull of indulgence granted by Pope Paul II in 1471 in recognition of this re-creation of a holy Christian shrine.

Piazza S. Pancrazio to Piazza della Repubblica

On exiting from the Marino Marini Museum turn R and R again up Via della Spada. A few yards up here, where Via delle Belle Donne joins Via della Spada on the L, note the wine hatch on the far corner of the two streets (see Walk 3 for the purpose of these features). An inscription above the hatch gives the opening times for sales. Continue along Via della Spada, cross Via Tornabuoni and take Via degli Strozzi back to Piazza della Repubblica, where this walk ends.

A bear, a brazier and a fire

Luca Landucci records in his *Diary* some of the incidents that took place by his apothecary's shop near the old Piazza de' Tornaquinci, a piazza that was largely swallowed up by the building of the Strozzi Palace at the end of the 15th century. On 9th May 1486 a huge bear, bred in the city, was being tormented by children. It seized a six year old girl by the throat, but she was freed and (miraculously) survived. On 12th November 1487 a lad who accompanied the lion tamer into the lions' cage was not so lucky. On 26th February 1501 (1500 in the old Florentine system of dating; see Walk 12 under S. Trinità) the brazier broke on the executioner's cart, so the officer in charge sent the executioner for more charcoal and a kettle from a nearby bakery in order to make a new improvised brazier, the better to torture with red hot pincers the criminals en route to execution! On 2nd August 1507 Luca's house next to his shop burnt down and he had to buy all household goods and clothes anew. His son's bed caught fire while he was asleep. The lad managed to escape stark naked, and had to run and borrow a shirt from a neighbour. As I don't wish to leave Luca on such a sad note, let's go back in time to 26th May 1471. On this day, a (clearly) very excited Luca recorded that he had bought some of the first sugar that came from Madeira. His excitement is understandable when you realize that over forty years later, in October 1513, sugar was still regarded as such a luxury item as to warrant the King of Portugal presenting Pope Leo X with life-size figures of the pontiff and twelve cardinals made of the stuff.

The French come to Florence

In the autumn of 1494 King Charles VIII of France crossed the Alps with a huge
army in pursuance of his historic Angevin claims to the crown of Naples. Piero
the Unfortunate (son of Lorenzo Il Magnifico) had come down on the side of
Naples and thus found himself in an awkward position when the French headed
for Tuscany. He rushed to meet Charles and, without signorial approval, agreed
to certain concessions, which included the handing over of key fortresses and
ports, Pisa among them. The Florentine government was furious and refused to
confirm these concessions. On 5th November five ambassadors were chosen by the
Signoria to go and negotiate with the king. They were Fra Girolamo Savonarola,
Pandolfo Rucellai, Giovanni Cavalcanti, Piero Soderini and Tanai de' Nerli.
Tanai commemorated this embassy in the altarpiece which you may have seen
if you visited the church of S. Spirito on Walk 12. Meanwhile the vanguard of
the French army began to arrive and went about the city marking up houses for
billets. They let it be understood that they would pay, but, says Luca Landucci
in his *Diary*, if and when they did, 'they paid for the horns and ate the ox' (an
old Tuscan saw). On 8th November Piero returned to Florence and, the next day,
foolishly showed up at the Palazzo della Signoria with an armed guard, thereby
provoking an uprising. Piero fled, but factional violence continued for several
days. In the midst of all this the French continued to arrive, thousands of them,
causing confusion, alarm and suspicion. By 16th November things had calmed
down and Florence had begun to decorate herself for Charles' state arrival the next
day. The arms of France could be seen emblazoned everywhere, and the Signoria
had ordered that, on the king's arrival, all citizens should go towards the Porta
S. Frediano in as fine array as they could muster to do him honour. No expense
was spared, for Florence hoped fervently that Charles would guarantee peace. The
king arrived in the evening and processed to the Palazzo Medici. The mood of
the citizens was tense and jittery. Luca Landucci says in his *Diary* that everybody
suspected that Charles had promised his troops that Florence should be sacked,
so people were hiding their valuables in 'safe' places. The king wanted the return
of Piero de' Medici, but this Florence wouldn't grant. At last Charles backed
down, but asked instead for 120,000 florins and other regular loans for his wars,
in addition to the forts that Piero had conceded to him and that the Signorial
ambassadors had failed to retrieve. The French too were jittery and took up arms,
seizing the Porta S. Frediano and the bridges, presumably so as to be able to escape
the city if necessary. It was presumably at this juncture that Charles threatened
to give his army free rein and was given the famous answer by Piero di Gino
Capponi: 'If you sound your trumpets we shall ring our bells.' At the sound of the
bells the citizens would have mustered, and the French, being scattered at billets
all over the city, would have had a hard job to repel such an attack. An agreement
was finally signed on 25th November. Charles left Florence three days later and

headed S towards Naples with his army. He returned N the following year, and Savonarola went to parley again with the king (see the section on Savonarola in Walk 8). Charles left the city unmolested, but subsequently failed to live up to any of the promises that he made regarding the handing back of Pisa and other places to Florentine control.

Detail of the ironwork on the Palazzo Strozzi

Walk 14

Begins and ends at the Ponte alle Grazie.

Takes in: the Casa Rodolfo Siviero, the church of S. Miniato al Monte, Piazzale Michelangelo, the Rose Garden and Japanese Garden, and the Museo Bardini.

Duration: allow half a day for this walk (*c.* 3-4 hours), including time spent at the above venues.

Tips: choose, if you can, a fine, clear day for this walk, as the views from the hill of S. Miniato and from Piazzale Michelangelo are magnificent. Most of Florence is built on flat ground. To reach S. Miniato, however, it's necessary to climb, and quite steeply. If you have any doubts about your ability to make it on foot, either take the hop on/hop off bus as far as Piazzale Michelangelo (though see the caveat regarding this in the Introduction) or jump in a taxi. If you take the bus, skip to the second paragraph of the section of the walk entitled 'the Porta S. Miniato to the church of S. Miniato' (top of page 309) and join the itinerary on Viale Galileo. If you take a taxi, ask the driver to take you to the entrance to the Porte Sante cemetery and skip to the penultimate paragraph of that section (bottom of page 309). If you want to walk all the way, but are pushed for time, then I advise you to omit the Casa Rodolfo Siviero, and to go direct from the Ponte alle Grazie to the Porta S. Miniato by dint of continuing straight on at the end of the bridge, turning L at the far end of Piazza de' Mozzi, and following Via di S. Niccolò along until you see the arch of the Porta S. Miniato set into the old city walls on your R. In this case, omit the first two sections of the walk and skip to the section entitled 'the Porta S. Miniato to the church of S. Miniato' (page 308).

The Ponte alle Grazie to the Casa Rodolfo Siviero

From the Ponte alle Grazie there is a good view downstream of the Ponte Vecchio, topped by Vasari's Corridor. Upstream can be seen the Tuscan hills and, over to the SE, the Torre S. Niccolò, with the church of S. Miniato

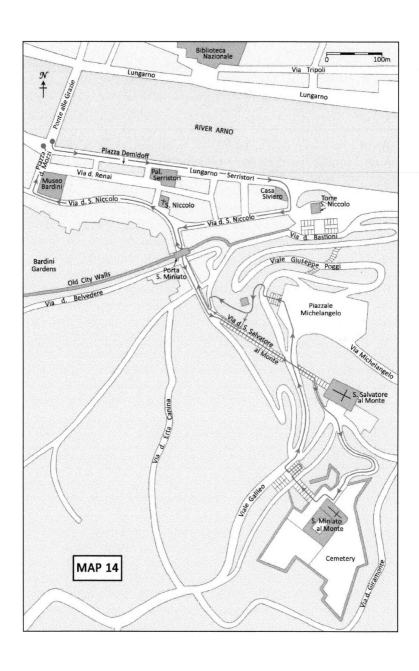

N

Walk 14

Biblioteca Nazionale

Via Tripoli

0   100m

Lungarno

Ponte alle Grazie

Lungarno

RIVER ARNO

Piazza Demidoff

Piazza d. Mozzi

Lungarno — Serristori

Via d. Renai

Pal. Serristori

Museo Bardini

Casa Siviero

Via d. S. Niccolo

S. Niccolo

Torre S. Niccolo

Via d. S. Niccolo

Via d. Bastioni

Bardini Gardens

Old City Walls

Porta S. Miniato

Viale Giuseppe Poggi

Via d. Belvedere

Piazzale Michelangelo

Via d. S. Salvatore al Monte

Via Michelangelo

Via d. Erta Canina

S. Salvatore al Monte

Viale Galileo

S. Miniato al Monte

Via d. Giramonte

Cemetery

MAP 14

perched up on the hill to the R. This is where we are heading. It's where S. Miniato headed too in AD 250. He wasn't exactly headless at the time, but his head wasn't in the right place. He'd just been decapitated in the Roman amphitheatre up the road near S. Croce (Walk 9). Instead of dying on the spot, he got to his feet, walked out of the amphitheatre and hastened up the said hill. Having got to the top, he expired. A shrine was erected on the spot, but it fell into neglect. Then, in the early 11th century, Bishop Hildebrand of Florence decided to do something about it. I'll tell you the story when we get up there.

At the end of the Ponte alle Grazie turn L along the Lungarno Serristori, named for the palace that stands on the opposite side of the road at the far end of Piazza Demidoff. There's a double-lane cycle path on the outside edge of the pavement here – watch your step and hug the wall near the river! The ground between you and the Arno is home to a variety of waterbirds, and, as you approach the Torre S. Niccolò, there's even a lido.

The 'Serristori Walk'

The Lungarno Serristori was opened up as part of a process of urban 'renewal' in the 1860s-70s, when Florence became, for a short time only as it happened, the capital of the new united Italy. Prior to this a mill-race serving two large mills ran parallel to the river from a weir behind the Torre S. Niccolò to the Ponte alle Grazie. At the beginning of the 19th century the land along the race was transformed by the Serristori family into a garden, and inventories in the family archives give details of this famous 'Serristori Walk'. There were paths, fountains, belvederes, a Kaffeehaus above one of the breakwaters of the Ponte alle Grazie, and boats on the mill-pond, and the garden was illuminated by eighty-four lamps raised on green columns. It must have looked absolutely wonderful, and one can only regret that it's not still here.

The Guelfs give Gregory the hump

The sandy area between the Arno and the Lungarno Serristori was the scene of pomp and ceremony in 1273, when Pope Gregory X and a host of cardinals came to Florence en route to a general council at Lyons. Giovanni Villani (*Chronicle* VII.42) says that the pope wanted to restore peace between the Guelfs and the Ghibellines, so, on 2nd July, a great assemblage was called here, huge scaffolds and stands of wood having been erected for the purpose. The pope caused representatives from each party to kiss each other and to give sureties, threatening excommunication for any who disobeyed his decree. It didn't work. Off-stage, the Guelfs told the Ghibellines that, unless they left Florence fast, they'd be hacked to pieces – so they left fast. Gregory was so mad that he too left, placing the city under an interdict. However, on his way back from Lyons two years later, flooding forced him to re-enter Florence in order to cross the Arno on the Ponte Rubiconte, now called the Ponte alle Grazie. While he was doing this, he took the interdict off the city and went on his way blessing all the people. As soon as he was clear of Florence, however, he slapped the interdict back on.

Cross over the road at the pelican crossing opposite the lido (watch out for bikes!) and you'll find yourself outside the Casa Siviero. This was the home of Rodolfo Siviero, who for many years was president of the Accademia delle Arti del Disegno, and who became famous for his efforts to ensure the restitution to Italy of numerous works of art stolen by the Nazis during the Second World War. The house contains the eclectic private collection that Siviero built up during his lifetime. Here you'll find antique Italian furniture, Roman sculpture, Romanesque capitals, a Giottesque predella, a diptych from the school of Bicci di Lorenzo, and works from the schools of Antonio Rossellino, Luca della Robbia, Andrea Sansovino, Agnolo Bronzino and Pietro Tacca. You'll also find paintings and drawings by Giorgio de Chirico and Pietro Annigoni, and much else besides. The study/library exhibits some of the medals awarded to Siviero for his work, and there is a photograph album of his life. The house has a wonderful ambience, and you feel that you may bump into Siviero himself at any moment.

The Torre S. Niccolò to the Porta S. Miniato

On exiting from the Casa Siviero turn R and immediately R again, and you'll find yourself opposite the huge 14th century Torre S. Niccolò. This gate retains its massive tower intact. With the appearance of cannon during the 16th century, the other gates of the city were lowered to make them less vulnerable to artillery attack. Torre S. Niccolò, being protected by the surrounding hills, didn't warrant such a reduction in height. Next to the gate, a ramped double stairway leads up towards Piazzale Michelangelo. You can go up this way if you wish and meet me again on the far side of the piazzale at the church of S. Salvatore al Monte. I prefer to go by a different route. Bear round to the R again and take

the attractive Via di S. Niccolò, leaving the Torre S. Niccolò behind you. As you head down the street, look back for a great view of the gate framed by the buildings on either side. Take the first turning L off Via di S. Niccolò. Ahead of you is the Porta S. Miniato – no towered structure here, just a fine 14th century arch in the wall.

The Porta S. Miniato to the church of S. Miniato

Just beyond the Porta S. Miniato, you get a fine view to the R of the 14th century city walls climbing up the hill to the Porta S. Giorgio (Walk 15). The Bardini Gardens lie just behind the walls. Over to the L on the far side of the crossroads is a tabernacle containing an early 16th century Madonna and Child of the Florentine school. Continue straight on – this is where the pull uphill begins. A few yards past the next crossroads, you'll see a ramped stairway forking off to the L. This is Via di S. Salvatore al Monte, at the base of which on the L there is a Dante plaque on the wall (it may well be smothered in foliage):

'In order to climb the hill where sits the church that dominates the well-guided city, above the Rubiconte the steep rise of the hill is broken by the steps that were made in an age when records and measures were safe' (*Purgatorio* XII.100-105).

The church referred to is S. Miniato, and the Rubiconte bridge is now the Ponte alle Grazie, where we began this walk. Dante has just met an angel who has promised him a safe journey up to the next level of purgatory. The route he has to take is compared to the stairs up to S. Miniato. We don't have an angel to help us, but up we must go. Halfway up, the ramps give way to steps. On the L here is an entrance to the Rose Garden, through which we'll walk on our way down later. On the R is the cats' home, with little moggie mansions set between the shrubs. Be careful as you proceed up the steps. At the time of writing several of the treads were in bad repair and there was no rail.

The stepped Via di S. Salvatore al Monte brings you out on the busy Viale Galileo. Cross the road here – be aware that the traffic moves very fast and that many motorists don't see any need to stop for pedestrians on the crossing! At this point you have a choice. You can turn R and follow Viale Galileo along past some public toilets to the base of a grand double staircase on the L, ascend the stairs, cross over the road at the top, and mount the steps opposite that lead directly up to the church of S. Miniato.

These steps too, at the time of writing, were in bad repair in places and lacking rails. Alternatively, you can mount the steps by the crossing that lead directly up to the church of S. Salvatore al Monte. Designed by Il Cronaca, Michelangelo called this church 'la bella villanella' ('the pretty country lass'). Skirt round the R flank of the church and continue up through the park to the entrance of the cemetery (follow signs for Parco della Rimembranza/delle Porte Sante).

If you walked up the steps directly in front of S. Miniato, head through the arch to the L of the church façade. Here you'll find those of us who either came up by taxi or walked up past S. Salvatore, and have just entered under the arch beneath the huge bastion wall. There are toilets here, should you need them. Enclosed by the walls of the great fortified bastion of S. Miniato is the cemetery – there is a board beside the entrance giving information about the place. The cemetery was laid out in the mid-19th century and contains, among others, the tomb of Collodi, author of *Pinocchio* (see Walk 6). After a meander among the neo-Gothic monuments, and a pause to consider the campanile that Michelangelo expended so much effort on (see the section

entitled 'the siege of Florence and Michelangelo as a wanted man'), let's leave the dead in peace and head for the terrace in front of the church. Exit from the cemetery by the same gate as you entered and turn L.

The view from the terrace in front of the church of S. Miniato is magnificent. The Duomo and Campanile dominate the scene. In front of the Duomo can be seen the tower of the Bargello and, to the L of it, the campanile of the Badia. The pale, pointed roof of the Baptistery and the great red-tiled dome of the Cappelle Medicee lie to the L. Further over to the L is the Palazzo Vecchio, with its massive tower and belfry, and the campanile of S. Maria Novella. On the far L is the Belvedere, while on the far R can be seen the campanile and flank of the church of S. Croce. Immediately below the terrace are tombs and family vaults, one belonging to 'Fam. Franco Zeffirelli'. I wonder if he could squeeze me in when the time comes? I can think of no lovelier place to be buried.

The siege of Florence and Michelangelo as a wanted man

Let me tell you how the bastion of S. Miniato began its existence. At the start of the 16th century, Italy was dominated by the armies of France and Spain. Pope Julius II and Pope Leo X managed to steer a course through the swirling currents of these times by dint of adroit manoeuvring. In 1519, however, on the death of his grandfather Maximilian, King Charles V of Spain became, in addition, Holy Roman Emperor, with control over the Low Countries, much of Germany, and Austria. He was, in effect, now head of a European superpower, and his position was strengthened further by a victory over the French near Milan in 1525.

Clement VII, the illegitimate son of Giuliano de' Medici and cousin to Leo X, was elected pope in 1523 with Charles' backing. Subsequently, however, he unwisely formed an anti-imperial alliance known as the League of Cognac. Charles was not pleased. In 1526 imperial troops entered Rome and Clement was obliged to agree terms of surrender. He then, foolishly, reneged on these. Imperial forces massed near Ferrara and, in March 1527, moved S towards the Papal States and Rome. Florence, the pope's home city, was a tempting target en route. Clement had appointed Cardinal Passerini to rule Florence on behalf of the under-age and illegitimate Alessandro and Ippolito de' Medici, a regime that was highly unpopular with the Florentines. On 16th April 1527 Charles' army entered Florentine territory, but troops loyal to the League of Cognac arrived, and the imperial forces moved off southwards. When they reached Rome, they sacked the city with savage brutality. It was at this point that the embassy arrived from England to discuss with Pope Clement the divorce of King Henry VIII from Catherine of Aragon. As Catherine was Charlie's aunt it was not a good moment! News of the sack of Rome reached Florence on 11th May. Anti-Medicean feeling finally erupted in force, Cardinal Passerini's regime fell and the republic was restored.

Clement survived the sack of Rome and at last came to realize that he could only hold on to power as Charles' ally. He signed a treaty with the emperor and the League of Cognac fell apart. This spelt disaster for Florence, for one of the terms of the treaty was the reinstatement of the Medici, who would, henceforward, rule the city as loyal subjects of Charles. The wisdom of strengthening the fortifications, a project that Florence's new republican government had put in train immediately, was proved. The Governor and Procurator General of the fortifications was none other than Michelangelo. A series of his designs for the fortifications survives and is kept at the Casa Buonarroti (Walk 5). The introduction of cannon into the equation had changed everything. The tall towers and curtain walls of Florence's mediaeval fortifications were no defence against this new form of artillery. One important stronghold was the hill of S. Miniato. Michelangelo covered it with an emergency system of bastions and walls made of brick linings packed with earth to absorb the cannon fire. We'll stand on another of his bastions on Walk 15.

In Autumn 1529 the imperial forces entered Florentine territory, and the bombardment began. Substantial fire was directed against the hill of S. Miniato. To protect the stump of the campanile, on which he'd mounted cannon of his own, Michelangelo encased it with 1,800 bales of wool and a large number of mattresses, so that the enemy's cannon-balls, when they struck, did no harm – hardly rocket science but an extremely effective solution. Many of the Florentine cannon-balls were made from the marble quarried for the projects of Pope Leo X and Pope Clement VII at S. Lorenzo (see Walk 6 under the section entitled 'Leonardo's lavish scheme' etc.).

Failing to breach the fortifications (testimony to Michelangelo's designs), the commanders of the imperial forces decided on a blockade to starve the city into submission. Florence held out for ten months, the surrender finally being signed on 12th August 1530. The republican leaders were arrested and executed or imprisoned. Michelangelo's name was on the list of traitors, but he managed to hide with the prior of S. Lorenzo, who probably realized that Clement would not want his foremost artist killed. And so it proved. Once the transfer of power back to the Medici was complete, Clement sent orders that Michelangelo should be found and protected, and that he should return to work immediately on the New Sacristy and the Laurentian Library (Walk 6).

Clement may have been willing to forgive Michelangelo's republican leanings, but Duke Alessandro's feelings were less cordial. Michelangelo was in no doubt that Alessandro would have got rid of him had it not been for Clement's protection. Increasingly ill at ease, he finally decided to leave Florence for Rome in mid-September 1534, leaving both the Laurentian Library and the New Sacristy unfinished. It was not a moment too soon. Just two days after his arrival in Rome, his protector died. Michelangelo never set foot in Florence again. Later in the 16th century, Duke Cosimo I converted S. Miniato into the imposing fortress the walls of which we see today. He tried to persuade Michelangelo to return, but to no avail. Following the great man's death, however, the Duke was determined that the corpse should lie in Florence, so he arranged for it to be stolen from Rome and brought back (see the section in Walk 5 entitled 'Michelangelo's two funerals').

The church of S. Miniato

Earlier on this walk I promised to tell you the story of Bishop Hildebrand's decision to build a monastery here. In AD 978 Willa, the pious mother of Margrave Ugo of Tuscany, founded the Badia (Walk 4). At the end of the century Ugo endowed his mother's foundation with so much property that, on his death in 1001, the monks gave him the honour of burial within their church. Not to be outdone, Hildebrand, who was Bishop of Florence from 1008 to 1024, decided that he too would found and endow a monastery. His decision may have been influenced in part by a desire to save his soul, for his rule smacked more of the secular than the sacred. His lavish ecclesiastical court was presided over both by himself and his mistress, the formidable Alberga, mother of his numerous children. What better spot for Hildebrand's new monastery than the hill of S. Miniato? The shrine to the saint had fallen into neglect, but Hildebrand unearthed the relics and proceeded to build his new abbey. Little was accomplished during his lifetime. The main work on the church was probably begun c. 1070 and continued through the 12th and into the 13th century.

The bichrome lower façade of S. Miniato recalls the Baptistery, with which it is roughly contemporary. In the five round-topped bays between the columns, three doors alternate with two inlaid panels of equal size. Above this, two bays embellished with roundels and more panels frame a central bay housing a window and a mosaic showing Christ between the Virgin and S. Miniato. The reticulated decoration around the central window recurs at the sides, over the ends of the aisles. The whole is topped by a pediment supported by two little caryatid figures. Here a 9-bay arcade, echoing the design of the lower façade, is surmounted by a frieze of intricate bichrome panels that give a foretaste of the stunning inlays to be found inside. An inlaid cross and a projecting cornice complete the design. The façade is crowned by an eagle clasping a bale of cloth, emblem of the Calimala Guild, who had the patronage of the building.

The church is built on a basilican plan, with nave and aisles but no transepts. The beautiful Romanesque interior is enough to induce religiosity in even the most hardened atheist. Here is balm for the soul and spirit. On the aisle walls can be seen frescoes ranging in date from the 13th to the

15th centuries. At the end of the church, above the 11th century crypt, is a raised choir. This is a typical Romanesque feature, as are the diaphragm arches on engaged columns in the nave – note the eagle with the bale again in the spandrels of the central arch. Some of the columns in both nave and crypt have antique capitals. The nave pavement has inlaid marble panels decorated with intricate animal motifs and the signs of the zodiac. At the end of the nave, in front of the crypt, is a free-standing tabernacle. Commissioned by Piero the Gouty in the 1440s to hold the miraculous Crucifix that bowed its head to S. John Gualberto (later transferred to the church of S. Trinità; Walk 12), this tabernacle was designed by Michelozzo specifically to fit its setting here. The columns that support the open barrel-vaulted aedicule have different capitals, and the marble frieze bears Piero's motif of the ring and feathers. The barrel-vault is decorated with glazed terracotta coffers by Luca della Robbia, who was also responsible for the brightly coloured tiles on the roof (best seen from the raised choir). Behind the forest of lovely slender columns in the crypt is an altar with the relics of S. Miniato.

Mount the steps on the R up to the raised choir and continue straight on. On your R is the sacristy, with late 14th century frescoes by Spinello Aretino showing scenes from the life of S. Benedict. Here too are two della Robbian statuettes and a bust of S. Miniato attributed to Nanni di Bartolo. Just outside the sacristy is a mid-14th century altarpiece by Jacopo del Casentino showing S. Miniato and scenes from his life. Make your way round to the front of the choir. The wonderful early 13th century choir-screen is decorated with inlaid and carved marble panels – don't miss the little imp-like figures to either side of the central entrance. The magnificent pulpit has a lectern incorporating the emblems of three of the four Evangelists, the lion of S. Mark, the angel of S. Matthew and the eagle of S. John. The apse of the choir has a blind arcade with opaque marble windows, above which is a huge 13th century mosaic showing Christ between the Virgin and S. Miniato. The carved and inlaid choir-stalls date to the 15th century.

Descend the steps at the opposite side of the choir. On your R, halfway along the aisle, lies the Chapel of the Cardinal of Portugal, added to the church in the 1460s. The cardinal, a member of the Portuguese royal house, had died in Florence in 1459 aged only twenty-five. He had expressed a wish to be buried in S. Miniato, and all the stops were pulled out for his funerary monument. The executors of his estate were the directors of the Cambini bank, who had long had strong business connections with Lisbon, and the bank's surviving accounts document all the expenses for the building of this beautiful chapel. Antonio Manetti, Brunelleschi's pupil, designed the architecture, and Luca della Robbia did the decoration of the vault, with tiles and five roundels showing the four cardinal virtues and the dove of the Holy

Spirit. The design of the tiles, with illusory cubes in black, green and yellow, can be found on an Etruscan cinerary urn in the Archaeological Museum (Walk 10), so perhaps this was Luca's inspiration! The cardinal's tomb (on the R wall) was the work of Antonio Rossellino. Set into an arched niche, it has stone curtains drawn back to reveal all the elements of the tomb like a tableau. The fresco decoration in the chapel was done by Alesso Baldovinetti and the Pollaiuolo brothers, Antonio and Piero, who were also responsible for the altarpiece (now in the Uffizi and replaced here by a copy).

S. Miniato to Piazza de' Mozzi

Following your visit to S. Miniato, you can reach Piazzale Michelangelo by going down the steps opposite the church façade, crossing the road at the bottom, descending the monumental staircase to Viale Galileo, turning R and following the road along. Alternatively, you can leave the hill via the bastion arch near the cemetery entrance and wend your way down past the church of S. Salvatore. If you walked up one way, you may like to return by the other route. If you came up by taxi, and/or are a bit unsteady on your pegs, I advise the S. Salvatore option, for the steps opposite S. Miniato are steep and there is no rail.

In the centre of Piazzale Michelangelo is a monument to the great man, erected in 1875, with copies of the David and the statues on the Medici tombs in the New Sacristy. From the piazzale there is a wonderful view of Florence, sweeping round from Piazza Piave and the Torre Zecca on the R to the Belvedere on the L, and encompassing all the features mentioned above in the description of the view from the terrace outside S. Miniato. There is a good view too of the Ponte Vecchio, surmounted by Vasari's Corridor. The huge green dome over on the R beyond S. Croce belongs to the synagogue (Walk 10). The building with the squat twin towers and rotunda between S. Croce and the river is the Biblioteca Nazionale.

Leave the piazzale by the stairs at its W end (nearest the Ponte Vecchio). If you are here at a time when the Rose Garden is closed, you will have to descend via the stepped/ramped Via di S. Salvatore al Monte, to reach which you turn L at the bottom of the stairs and walk along until you reach the top of the Via on the R. As noted earlier, take care, because, at the time of writing, the steps on the Via were in bad repair and there was no rail. If you wish to descend the hill via the Rose Garden, turn R at the bottom of the stairs and follow the road down for a few yards to the corner, where, on your L, you'll see the entrance gate. The gardens on this hillside include the Iris Garden (only open in May), the Rose Garden and the Japanese Garden. What we are now aiming to do is to wend our way down through the Rose Garden – watch your step as the paths are a little uneven and there are no rails in places – and exit either through the gate halfway down the ramped Via di S. Salvatore al Monte or through a narrow arched gateway in the wall near the bottom of that street. If you want to see the little Japanese Garden, which is at the bottom of the slope, you'll have to do the latter. Once safely at

the bottom of Via di S. Salvatore, carry on down the hill to the 14th century Porta S. Miniato. The great doors of the Porta S. Miniato were reinstalled in the 1990s, having been ripped from their hinges by the flood-waters of the Arno in 1966!

There are several restaurants and cafés in the vicinity of the Porta S. Miniato, should you wish to take a break. Otherwise, once through the gate, turn L and follow the Via di S. Niccolò along to Piazza de' Mozzi, where Walk 14 ends. If you've any energy left, you are standing next to the Museo Stefano Bardini, the entrance to which lies just round to the R in Via de' Renai.

The Museo Stefano Bardini

Stefano Bardini (1836-1922), whom we shall encounter again on Walk 15, was a dealer in antiquities who was nothing if not opportunistic. During the 1860s-70s, when so much of the centre of Florence was being reconstructed and much demolition was going on, Bardini bought eight draught-horses and carts and offered to remove rubble free of charge. Many discarded architectural elements and other objects thus found their way into his collections. In 1880 he decided to build his own exhibition gallery in 16th century style on the site of the erstwhile convent of S. Gregorio here in Piazza de' Mozzi. The décor of the rooms was carefully planned so as to create exactly the right atmosphere for the display of Bardini's stock to his clients. In the Sala della Carità on the ground floor, for example, Bardini himself modified a 16th century wooden ceiling to let light in from above, and walls throughout the palace were painted in striking shades of blue so as to set off works of art hung or placed against them. After years of success on the international antiquities market, Bardini eventually closed down his business and devoted himself to building up a private collection. Two days before his death he bequeathed his palace and his artworks to the city of Florence. The museum has now been restored to mirror the décor planned by Bardini himself for the display of his collections. These collections are wide-ranging and contain some spectacular pieces. Here, for example, you will find sculpture from the Roman and Romanesque periods, as well as works by Arnolfo di Cambio, Nicola Pisano, Tino di Camaino and Tullio Lombardo. Here are reliefs by and from the schools of Nanni di Bartolo, Desiderio da Settignano, Luca della Robbia, Donatello, Michelozzo and Benedetto da Maiano. There are marriage chests ('cassoni') and other items of furniture, picture frames, bronzes, carpets, weaponry and armour. The paintings include a magnificent Crucifix by Bernardo Daddi. The museum also houses Giambologna's 'little bronze devil' (see Walk 13 and the coda to Walk 12) and Pietro Tacca's Il Porcellino (Walk 3).

Walk 15

Begins and ends at the Ponte Vecchio.

Takes in: the Ponte Vecchio, the Bardini Gardens (with the Villa Bardini housing the Roberto Capucci Foundation and the Pietro Annigoni Museum), the Belvedere, and the Boboli Gardens (with the Porcelain and Costume Museums).

Duration: allow 3 hours at a leisurely pace for the shorter version of this walk, omitting the Boboli Gardens/Pitti Palace, and 6 hours for the full version.

Tips: choose, if you can, a clear day for this walk, as the views are stunning. While most of Florence is built on flat ground, visits to the Bardini Gardens, Belvedere and Boboli Gardens involve quite steep gradients. If you have doubts about your ability to make it on foot, take a taxi up to the Villa Bardini, from whence you can access the Gardens at the top and enjoy the views without the climb. In this case, omit the first two sections of the walk and skip to page 324, near the end of the section entitled 'the Bardini Gardens and the Villa Bardini'. From the Villa Bardini you can walk to the Boboli Gardens via a more or less level route, omitting the Belvedere if you wish (see further below). As you will be entering the Boboli Gardens at their upper entrance, it's more or less downhill all the way from here. On hot days a sunhat would be sensible, as would a small bottle of water and/or some sweets (on my last visit, there were no refreshment facilities inside the Belvedere or the Boboli Gardens). Binoculars might be useful for the views.

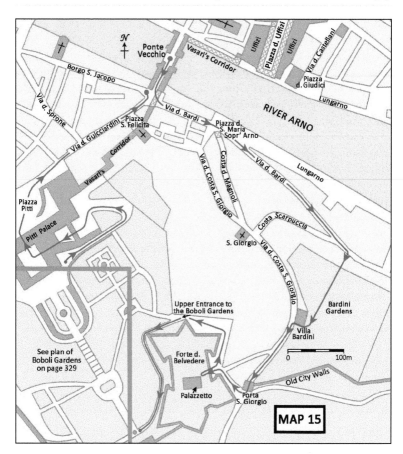

The Ponte Vecchio to Piazza di S. Maria Sopr' Arno

The history of the Ponte Vecchio up to the mid-16th century is recounted at the beginning of Walk 3. Here we take up the story in the 1560s, when Giorgio Vasari was commissioned to construct his Corridor linking the Palazzo Vecchio and the Uffizi with the Pitti Palace, new home of the ducal family. Vasari's Corridor, which you can visit on a special guided tour if you wish to, at great expense, crosses over the Lungarno from the Uffizi buildings and runs along to the Ponte Vecchio on a raised arcade. It then turns and passes over the shops on the E (upstream) side of the bridge, its uniform profile and line of regularly spaced windows standing in marked contrast to what lies below. At the middle of the bridge it runs above three arches, thus forming a small loggia from which there is a lovely view. Opposite the loggia, on the W (downstream) side of the bridge, is an open terrace from which there is a good view of the Ponte S. Trinità. The bust of Cellini (see page 104 for illustration), placed on the terrace in 1900, presides over the surrounding jewellers' shops, many of which had to be restored following the 1966 flood. The three large windows that overlook the terrace from Vasari's Corridor were inserted on the orders of Mussolini, so that Hitler could have a nice view when he visited in 1939. There's no arguing with a dictator, be he Mussolini or Medici. Though the Ponte Vecchio was the only Florentine bridge spared from destruction by the retreating German army in 1944 (see the plaque to Gerhard Wolf on the S side of the loggia), the areas at both ends of it were blown up to render it impassable.

Avoiding the *hoi polloi*

Vasari's Corridor, close on 1km in length, was rushed to completion in 1565 in time for the marriage of Cosimo I's son, Francesco, to Joanna of Austria. The project was executed in just five months by dint of using as many pre-existing structures as possible. Reserved for the exclusive use of the ducal court, it meant that guests attending the wedding could move from the Palazzo Vecchio to the Pitti Palace without getting their feet dirty or having to rub shoulders with commoners. They didn't even have to walk – they could, if they wished, be transported along the corridor in hand-drawn carriages. Neither did they have the unpleasantness of raucous voices and noxious smells rising from below. The fish market in Piazza del Pesce (at the N end of the bridge) was moved to the Old Market (now the area occupied by Piazza della Repubblica) and given a spanking new loggia under which to sell its produce. When the Old Market was demolished in the 19th century, this loggia, also by Vasari, was moved to Piazza de' Ciompi, where it can still be admired (Walk 5). Not content with the removal of all things fishy, at the end of the 16th century Grand Duke Ferdinando I evicted the grocers, butchers and blacksmiths from the bridge too, and replaced them with goldsmiths – quieter and much more genteel.

At the S end of the Ponte Vecchio turn L under Vasari's Corridor, which, supported on elegant corbelled brackets, does a jiggle here around the Torre de' Mannelli before crossing over Via de' Bardi and disappearing behind the buildings beyond. We'll see it again at the end of this walk. The Torre de' Mannelli was the only survivor of four mediaeval towers which once defended the bridge, and public sentiment dictated that it should be retained. Cosimo I wisely bowed to public pressure and ordered Vasari to go round rather than through it. Damaged in 1944, it was restored after the war. Follow Via de' Bardi along to Piazza di S. Maria Sopr' Arno.

Piazza di S. Maria Sopr' Arno to the Bardini Gardens

From Piazza di S. Maria Sopr' Arno there are good views over the river of the Uffizi (directly opposite) and of Vasari's Corridor, running first along the Lungarno on its raised arcade and then across the Ponte Vecchio. In the centre of the piazza is a statue of S. John the Baptist by Giuliano Vangi. We are going to leave the piazza at its E end, forking off to the R away from the Lungarno and continuing along Via de' Bardi, a lovely street lined with handsome buildings.

The Bardi bounce back from the brink

The Bardi, who owned several palaces in the vicinity of Via de' Bardi, were one of the wealthiest families in mediaeval Florence, but they suffered a setback in the 1340s when the Bardi bank collapsed, along with many others. One cause of the collapse was that King Edward III of England, who'd borrowed vast sums of money for his wars with France, defaulted on his debts. The Bardi soon bounced back, however, opening a new London branch in 1357 and dominating the Royal Mint for the rest of the century. King Richard II eventually made a final settlement with them in the 1390s.

On the L, at no. 36 Via de' Bardi, is the Palazzo Capponi delle Rovinate. Originally built for Niccolò da Uzzano in the early 15th century, it passed by marriage to the Capponi, and still belongs to the family. It was called 'delle Rovinate' ('of the ruins') because on several occasions part of the steep slope above it collapsed. Eventually, Cosimo I issued an edict prohibiting further building here.

A Raphael is rescued from the ruins

The steep hillside of S. Giorgio was the scene of several landslides during the 14th-16th centuries. In the 1540s, one such collapse destroyed the house of Lorenzo Nasi. He was one of Raphael's friends, for whom the artist had earlier painted a picture as a wedding gift. Vasari tells us that Lorenzo's son, Battista, found the painting among the debris. Today you can see this lovely painting, the Madonna del Cardellino, in the Uffizi Gallery.

At no. 28 Via de' Bardi, a plaque on the Palazzo Canigiani commemorates Sir John Pope-Hennessy (1913-94), who lived and died here. At no. 24, the church of S. Lucia de' Magnoli has a glazed terracotta lunette by Benedetto Buglioni over the door, though you may get killed trying to see it, given the speed at which traffic hurtles up the street. A plaque on the R side of the church façade bears a decree of the eight Signori, those law and order officials whose decrees feature also in several of the other walks. This one bans the playing of games within 100 braccia of the church (so no kicking of footballs or hitting of tennis balls against the wall opposite!). On the R side of the street, a small plaque set into the wall tells us that S. Francis of Assisi arrived here for the first time in Florence in 1211. The attractive Costa Scarpuccia climbs steeply uphill on the R. Continue along Via de' Bardi to the lower entrance of the Bardini Gardens, on the R at no. 1 red. At the time of writing, one ticket covered both the Bardini and Boboli Gardens. Make sure that you get a map of the gardens with your ticket.

The Bardini Gardens and the Villa Bardini

The hillside now occupied by the Bardini Gardens (see also page 19 for illustration) was once owned by the Mozzi family, who had gardens, orchards and agricultural land here. The W portion of the plot was eventually purchased by the Manadori family. In the 17th century they got Gherardo Silvani to design and build them a villa, which quickly earned the name of Villa di Belvedere. The Manadori eventually sold their villa and its garden to the Cambiagi, and they in turn sold the property to Luigi Le Blanc. In 1839 Pier Giannozzo Mozzi bought out Le Blanc, thus bringing the entire hillside back under single ownership. However, the Mozzi family ran into financial difficulties, and the property was seized in the 1880s. Villa and garden were purchased first by Princess Wanda von Carolath Beuthen of Silesia and then, in 1913, by Stefano Bardini, whom we met at the end of Walk 14. He immediately began a process of renovation and modernization, building new paths and carriageways and introducing several other features. In 1922 Stefano died, and his son, Ugo, inherited the villa and garden. Following Ugo's death in 1965, the property finally passed, after much entanglement with red tape, to the city of Florence, and work commenced on restoration in 2000.

We are going to walk up through the Bardini Gardens, passing several features including the 18th century Mozzi family crest, the statues of Vertumnus and Pomona (patrons of orchards and gardens), the small grotto, the flower garden, the Baroque stairway and the outdoor theatre. When you arrive at the 18th century niche of the caryatids, take the path up through the fruit orchard to the Belvedere circle, then double back via the pergola of wisteria and the hydrangea collection to reach the Belvedere terrace. From the terrace you get wonderful views across the city. The two 18th century Kaffeehaus buildings were linked by Stefano Bardini with a loggia, which now houses a café and toilets. Behind the loggia, under the old city walls, are the olive grove and rose garden, the camellia garden and the viburnum collection. At the W end of the loggia is a small grotto. From here, you can wend your way along inside the city walls to the lemon-house and greenhouse, and then meander down to the dragon canal, the azalea lawn, and the lawn in front of the villa, with its (partly 16th century) fountain of Venus. More views are to be had from the terrace next to the villa, where you'll also find the small temple and waterfall. The Villa Bardini, besides hosting temporary exhibitions, is home to the Roberto Capucci Foundation and the Pietro Annigoni Museum. The Capucci Foundation has a collection of the famous *haute couture* designer's creations, while the Annigoni Museum has landscapes, portraits and self-portraits by the artist. One of the great portrait painters of the 20th century, Annigoni's sitters included Queen Elizabeth II.

The Bardini Gardens to the Forte di Belvedere

Whether you decide to visit the museums and exhibitions in the Villa Bardini now or not, you exit through the villa on to Via della Costa S. Giorgio (there is no pavement so watch out for traffic). If you visited the Boboli Gardens on Walk 12 and don't wish to go on to the Belvedere, you can cut and run here, turning R down Via della Costa S. Giorgio. In this case, skip to the section entitled 'the Forte di Belvedere to Piazza S. Felicità' (page 326), and then skip again to the last paragraph of the final section of the walk (page 336). Otherwise, turn L up Via della Costa S. Giorgio, where you'll shortly come to a fork in the road. Keep L here to reach the 13th century Porta S. Giorgio, adorned with a fresco by Bicci di Lorenzo on its inner face and a stone relief of S. George on its outer face. Once through the gate turn R. The entrance to the Forte di Belvedere lies a few yards along on the L. If you wish to omit this, simply follow the road on round (hugging the base of the Belvedere walls) to reach the upper entrance of the Boboli Gardens, and skip to the section entitled 'the Forte di Belvedere to the Boboli Gardens' (page 327).

The Forte di Belvedere

Exhibitions are frequently held in the Palazzetto of the Forte di Belvedere. The views from the ramparts of the fort are truly spectacular and defy description. You can wander about admiring the vistas, which stretch round from S. Miniato to the hill of Bellosguardo, with the Tuscan hills behind.

The Palazzetto of the Belvedere was built in the 1560s on a design by Ammannati and/or Buontalenti as a private retreat for Francesco I. In keeping with Tuscan rural traditions (for this was regarded as a rural villa), the Palazzetto was given stuccoed walls, with flat stone quoins and a deep overhanging roof. In the 1590s Ferdinando I ordered the construction of the fortress surrounding the Palazzetto. Designed in the shape of a 6-pointed star by Buontalenti and Don Giovanni de' Medici (illegitimate son of Cosimo I), it formed a southern counterpart to the huge Fortezza da Basso on the N side of the city. Ostensibly built for the defence of Florence, the guns of both fortresses could also have been turned on the citizens, should any of them have been foolish enough to attempt a resurrection of republican ideals. A strong-room was built into the bowels of the fort to protect all the ducal treasures should need ever arise. Like the tombs of some Chinese emperors, the room was booby-trapped to kill anyone not privy to the secrets of its entry system.

You now have another choice. If you are omitting the Boboli Gardens and the Pitti Palace, continue on to the next section, and then skip to the last paragraph of the final section of the walk (page 336). If you are doing the full walk, omit the following section and jump to the one entitled 'the Forte di Belvedere to the Boboli Gardens' (page 327).

The Forte di Belvedere to Piazza S. Felicità

Return to Via della Costa S. Giorgio either via the Porta S. Giorgio or via the gated road directly opposite the exit of the Belvedere. Continue down Via della Costa S. Giorgio past the entrance to the Villa Bardini. A few yards further down on the L are properties associated with Galileo Galilei. The plaque on no. 11 blue commemorates Galileo's perfecting the use of the telescope, his astronomical observations and the discovery of the so-called 'Medici planets' (see also the description of the Palazzo Viviani in Walk 11). Nos. 17-21 have a painted façade with a portrait of Galileo in a central

medallion. The inscription tells us that Galileo lived here, and records Grand Duke Ferdinando II's admiration of the great scientist's genius. Just beyond the pretty Costa Scarpuccia on the R, the church of S. Giorgio lies on the L. This was the church to which the Silvestrines were banished when the Dominicans finally got their hands on the monastery of S. Marco (see the section on Fra Angelico and the history of the monastery at the beginning of Walk 8). Immediately past the church, take the L fork, which leads you down to Piazza S. Felicità.

The Forte di Belvedere to the Boboli Gardens

Exit from the Belvedere and follow the walls of the fortress round anti-clockwise to reach the upper entrance of the Boboli Gardens. The gardens contain uneven, sloping paths, and there are numerous ramps and stairs with no handrails. Watch your step! There are no café facilities in the gardens, though there are toilets. Once inside the grounds we're going to bear round to the L, hugging the huge walls of the Forte di Belvedere, to arrive at the top of one of the two main axes of the gardens, where stands the statue of Plenty, begun by Giambologna in 1608 and completed by Pietro Tacca and Sebastiano Salvini.

History of the Boboli Gardens

The earliest part of the garden is that along the axis directly behind the Pitti Palace (see plan on page 329). This area was bounded on the SW (to your L if you're looking down at the palace) by ramparts built by Cosimo I during his wars with Siena. The first task was to transform the orchards that stood here into a garden worthy of a ducal residence. This project was supervised by a series of architects, including Niccolò Pericolo (known as 'Il Tribolo'), Davide Fortini, Giorgio Vasari, Bartolommeo Ammannati and Bernardo Buontalenti. The area was laid out as a compartmental grid, with olives, vines and espaliers, known as 'ragnaie' from the nets for trapping birds that were hung there. At the bottom of the hill there were stone quarries, still being worked at the beginning of the 16th century. These quarries were transformed into the area that eventually became the Amphitheatre.

Under Cosimo II (1609-1621) the gardens were extended beyond Cosimo I's ramparts right down to the Porta Romana, the work being overseen by Gherardo

Mechini and Giulio Parigi. The axis of this new extension was the Cypress Lane. Cosimo II also had the idea of transforming the Amphitheatre into a masonry structure, though work on this didn't start until 1630 under Ferdinando II. Thereafter, elaborate court spectacles were held in the Amphitheatre, including the celebrations accompanying the marriage of Ferdinando II's son, the future Cosimo III, to Marguerite Louise of Orleans in 1661. Under the Lorraine-Hapsburg dynasty in the 18th century, further modifications were undertaken and several new buildings added, including the Kaffeehaus, Lemon House and Meridian Building.

Over the course of the centuries, numerous sculptures were brought in to adorn the gardens. Some were antique pieces, others were made specially or acquired from elsewhere. Many have now been replaced by casts in an on-going programme of conservation and restoration. They form a study in themselves and, like the plantings in the gardens, lie beyond the scope of this book.

A tour of the Boboli Gardens (with the Porcelain and Costume Museums)
Looking down from the statue of Plenty towards the Pitti Palace, you can see the Forcone Basin and, beyond it at the bottom of the slope, the U-shaped Amphitheatre. We'll go down to the basin shortly, but for now keep on the high ground and follow the walls round for a few more yards. You'll come to a double flight of steps on the L leading up to the Knight's Garden. Built on a bastion designed by Michelangelo in 1529, just prior to the siege of Florence, the Knight's Garden offers wonderful views. On the other side of the valley can be seen S. Miniato, site of another of Michelangelo's bastions. At one end of the garden lies the Casino, which now houses the Porcelain

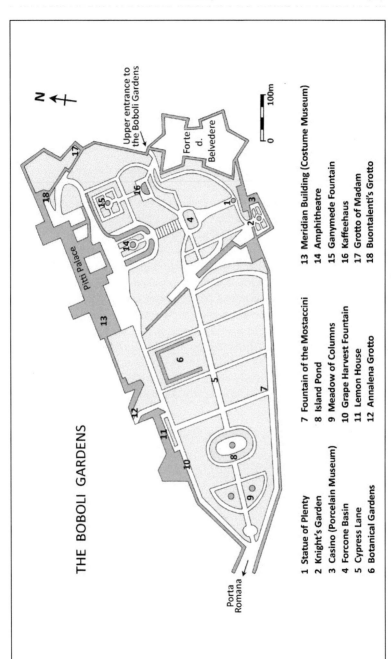

THE BOBOLI GARDENS

N

0   100m

Upper entrance to
the Boboli Gardens

Forte
d.
Belvedere

Pitti Palace

Porta
Romana

1 Statue of Plenty
2 Knight's Garden
3 Casino (Porcelain Museum)
4 Forcone Basin
5 Cypress Lane
6 Botanical Gardens

7 Fountain of the Mostaccini
8 Island Pond
9 Meadow of Columns
10 Grape Harvest Fountain
11 Lemon House
12 Annalena Grotto

13 Meridian Building (Costume Museum)
14 Amphitheatre
15 Ganymede Fountain
16 Kaffeehaus
17 Grotto of Madam
18 Buontalenti's Grotto

Museum (there are toilets here). From
the opposite end, the city walls can be
seen descending the hill. In the middle
of the garden is a fountain with bronze
monkeys by Pietro Tacca. The Porcelain
Museum houses the collections that
belonged to the Medici, Lorraine and
Savoy families. Here you will find
Italian, French, English and Viennese
porcelain. There are pieces from the
famous Doccia factory (founded by
Carlo Ginori in the 1730s), some of
them painted with views of Florence,
and examples of Worcester, Sevres and
Meissen wares.

On leaving the Knight's Garden, head for the Forcone Basin, either by
taking the path straight ahead and then turning R, or by retracing your
steps to the statue of Plenty and descending to the L. The basin collected
water from the aqueduct of Arcetri. The Fountain of Neptune is by Soldo
Lorenzi (1571). The basin is a good point to pause and consider some aspects
of Ammannati's additions to the Pitti Palace. The lateral wings which he

added to the original building were directed back towards the garden and
designed to correspond to the U-shaped Amphitheatre, which thus extended
their lines on into the landscape and unified the axis of palace and grounds.
Between the wings Ammannati created an imposing courtyard, but, because
the ground behind the palace is raised, this cannot be seen from the gardens.

From the rear, therefore, the palace appears as a two-storey structure, i.e. as a country villa, and from their apartments on the *piano nobile* the ducal family could look out directly on to the gardens.

With the Forcone Basin behind you and the palace in front of you, head off at an angle up to the L to reach the top of the Cypress Lane, the axis of Cosimo II's extension to the gardens. The planting of the cypresses began in 1612. To the S of the lane (L as you're looking down it), three large labyrinths were planted, but these were destroyed in the 1830s when, following the fashion of the time, curving paths were introduced. The lane is flanked by numerous sculptures, many of them classical. As you walk down you'll pass citrus groves, arboured walkways and, off to the R, the 19th century Botanical

Gardens with their aquatic plant pools. About two-thirds of the way down, at a crossroads adorned with four statues, turn L along to the 17th century Fountain of the Mostaccini, a long water trough decorated with sixteen gargoyle-like masks. This was a drinking trough for birds, for here were 'ragnaie', nets used for trapping.

Retrace your steps back to the Cypress Lane and turn L to reach the Island Pond (see also page 17 for illustration), with its statues, fountains and close on two hundred potted citrus trees. The tall espalier hedge surrounding the pond has niches containing 17th century statues with bucolic themes. In the centre of the island is Giambologna's Ocean Fountain (1576), moved here from the Amphitheatre in 1636. The original figure of Ocean is in the Bargello (Walk 9). The basin of the fountain is made from a single block of granite, brought from the island of Elba in the mid-16th century.

Continuing along the line of the main axis of the garden, leave the Island Pond on the opposite side to reach the semicircular Meadow of Columns. Here stand two red porphyry columns, erected in the 18th century. Around the meadow is a series of classical busts. The path continues on to the exit by the Porta Romana. At the time of writing, you could exit the gardens and re-enter on the same ticket for the course of that day. If this system still applies, you may like to go out and get a good look at the Porta Romana. If you can't exit and re-enter, don't despair, for you can get an oblique view of it through a perimeter gate a bit further round. The Porta Romana was built in 1328 on a design by Andrea Orcagna. The keystone of the arch on the inside face is adorned with a marble lily, emblem of Florence, sculpted by Giovanni

Pisano in 1331. The lunette has a 14th century fresco of the Madonna and Child with saints. For the triumphal entry of Pope Leo X into Florence in 1515, Luca Landucci tells us in his *Diary* that the wall of the outer gate was broken down and the portcullis laid on the ground, the outside of the gate being ornamented with four enormous pillars, 16 braccia in height and silvered all over.

We're now going to follow the path along the N side of the Boboli Gardens. On the L, opposite a path leading back to the Island Pond, is an early 17th century fountain showing the Grape Harvest. The 18th century rococo Lemon House, designed by Zanobi del Rosso, was built in the 1770s as a substitute for the former menagerie of wild and exotic animals, dismantled by order of Pietro Leopoldo of Lorraine. One visitor to this zoo, Richard Lassels, records how the animals were repenned after a prowl in their courtyard. A large wooden contraption like a great green dragon was wheeled into the court, while a man inside it held two lighted torches out of the 'eyes', which frightened the creatures back into their cages. A path leads down to the L to the 19th century Annalena Grotto. A few yards further along on the L lies the 18th-19th century Meridian Building, which now houses the Costume Museum. Its collections comprise more than six thousand pieces, and include theatrical costumes, decorative accessories and the funeral clothing used for Cosimo I, Eleonora di Toledo, and their son Don Garzia. The items are kept in storage and displayed on a rotational basis.

On leaving the Meridian Building turn L to reach the Amphitheatre, from which the axis of the earlier part of the gardens runs up to the Forcone Basin and the statue of Plenty, where we started our tour. The magnificent Amphitheatre is surrounded by tiered stands and a balustrade with aedicules housing urns and statues. In the centre stands an Egyptian obelisk of Ramesses II, brought from the Villa Medici in Rome and set here in 1790 – don't miss the lovely little tortoises supporting it. The huge ancient granite basin, placed here in 1840, came from the Caracalla Baths.

From the terrace behind the palace there are good views over the city. Take the broad sloping carriageway that leads on past the palace. This carriageway was introduced in the 18th century to link the Amphitheatre with the gate down near Buontalenti's Grotto. On your R is a huge retaining wall. Take the path off to the R at the end of this wall and wend your way up to the 16th century Ganymede Fountain, from where there is a good view of the Kaffeehaus, built, like the Lemon House, in the 1770s on a design by Zanobi del Rosso.

Retrace your steps, rejoin the sloping carriageway and turn R along it. Off to the R lies the Grotto of Madam, built in the 1550s for Eleonora di Toledo and with sculptures by Baccio Bandinelli and Giovanni di Paolo

Fancelli. Further along on the R lies Buontalenti's Grotto, the largest in the gardens. It was originally a plant nursery, built in the 1550s by Giorgio Vasari, but in the 1580s Buontalenti transformed it into a grotto. The statues of Apollo and Ceres in the niches flanking the entrance are by Bandinelli. In 1585 Buontalenti placed Michelangelo's so-called Prisoners or Slaves inside the grotto, and here they remained until the early 20th century, when they were taken to the Accademia (Walk 8) and replaced by casts. The circular opening in the vault (with frescoes by Poccetti) once housed a hollow crystal ball with fish swimming in it, and water gushed from hidden pipes around the walls to create spectacular effects.

I said earlier that we'd see Vasari's Corridor again at the end of this walk, and here it is. From outside Buontalenti's Grotto there's a splendid view of the Corridor, which here retains some sgraffito decoration, arriving at

the Pitti Palace. In the shadow of the Corridor is the little statue known as Bacchus, by Valerio Cioli, though it's actually the dwarf Morgante astride a turtle. Here too are the so-called Daci Prisoners, porphyry Roman statues dating to the 2nd century AD. The white marble heads were probably added in the 16th century, and the marble bases were probably taken from a 3rd century Roman triumphal arch.

Piazza Pitti to the Ponte Vecchio

Leave the Boboli Gardens by the exit here. On exiting from the Pitti Palace turn R and head down Via de' Guicciardini. Opposite the end of the lateral wing of the palace, plaques on the buildings at nos. 18 and 22 respectively mark the home of the great geographer Paolo Toscanelli (1397-1482; see page 286 for illustration) and the house where Dostoyevsky wrote *The Idiot* in 1868. On the R at no. 15 lies Palazzo Guicciardini. On this site was the house of Luigi Guicciardini, Gonfalonier of Justice, which was burnt down in 1378 during the Ciompi uprising and subsequently rebuilt. Francesco Guicciardini (1483-1540), author of the famous *History of Italy*, was born here (there is a plaque commemorating him). Many of his original manuscripts and letters are preserved in the archives of the family, who still live here. One of Francesco's memories concerns his wedding. It was, he says, a quiet affair, not by design, but owing to a terrible thunderstorm which dissuaded all right-thinking men from merry-making! Machiavelli lived nearby (house now destroyed), and the two men were friends. The present palace was built in the 1620s to a design by Gherardo Silvani (of Villa Bardini fame), though much work was also done in the 19th and 20th centuries, the latter necessitated by the terrible damage done by German mines in 1944 (there is a plaque commemorating this too).

A few yards further on, Piazza S. Felicità opens up on the R. The first church here was built in the 4th century. The present structure, by Ferdinando Ruggieri, dates to the mid-18th century and incorporates Vasari's Corridor, which runs over the porch and gives access to a private balcony from where the ducal family could attend Mass without having to mix with the populace at large. The church houses many treasures, including the superb frescoes by Pontormo in the Capponi Chapel. In the centre of Piazza S. Felicità stands a column, which according to some sources marks the site of an Early Christian cemetery and according to others a massacre of heretics that took place here. Continue down to the Ponte Vecchio, noting the fountain on the near corner of Borgo S. Jacopo, with a bronze Bacchus by Giambologna.

A prior gets his sums wrong

In the section on the history of the Boboli Gardens, mention was made of the stone quarries at the base of the hill there, on the site of the later Amphitheatre.

One of these quarries belonged to the convent of S. Felicità. In the 1480s, when work began on the huge Strozzi Palace (Walk 13), Filippo Strozzi had a contract with this quarry, drawn up with the prior. The prior promised to supply hewn stone blocks loaded on to carts ready for delivery, and Filippo agreed to take a minimum number of loads at a set price per load. The prior, however, had clearly underestimated the costs involved, for Filippo was continually having to advance sums above and beyond those agreed. Unsurprisingly, once he'd taken the minimum number of cartloads stipulated in the agreement, he did not renew the contract. Agreements were subsequently made with the owners of four other quarries, two at the Boboli and two beyond the Porta Romana. The contracts allowed the Strozzi unrestricted access to the quarries and full liberty in the working and removing of the stone. As before, there was a set price per cartload – thirteen soldi for the two Boboli quarries, but only eight soldi for the others owing to higher transport costs and the necessity of paying gate tax on the stone.

General index